DSAT Math

Test Prep. Workbook

JM EDU

PREFACE

Welcome to the DSAT Math Workbook, a comprehensive resource designed to help you excel in the DSAT Math test. My name is Joseph Pak, and I have spent over a decade teaching mathematics to students in Seoul, South Korea. Through this experience, I have recognized the critical need for high−quality educational materials that cater to the specific demands of the DSAT exam.

After analyzing the latest trends and changes in the DSAT test, I have meticulously developed this workbook to address the evolving requirements and challenges students face. With 991 carefully curated problems, this workbook offers extensive practice and thorough preparation, ensuring that you are well−equipped to tackle the DSAT Math test with confidence.

This workbook includes:

1. 5-Step Systematic Approach
   "Concept → Examples → Multiple Choice Questions → Student Produce Response → Practice Exams"

2. Complete content review and detailed explanations for all DSAT math topics, providing clarity and understanding.

3. Easy-to-understand problem-solving methods that facilitate a deep comprehension of mathematical concepts.

4. A reliable and effective reference guide for preparing for the DSAT exams as well as school exams.

A well−structured workbook is a cornerstone of a successful learning experience. It serves as a valuable guide, helping students navigate complex topics and develop their mathematical skills. I believe this workbook will not only aid in your preparation for the DSAT Math test but also ignite your curiosity and passion for mathematics.

Thank you for choosing this workbook as your study companion. I am confident that it will support your journey towards achieving your academic goals. Please feel free to reach out with any challenges, concerns, or successes you encounter along the way. Best of luck on your path to mastering the DSAT Math test!

Joseph Pak
JM EDU
B.A. Mathematics −University of Texas at Austin, 2024

Things to know about the DSAT test

1. The digital SAT is divided into two sections Reading and Writing, and Math.

2. Students have a total of 134 minutes to complete the test, with 64 minutes allocated for Reading and Writing (split into two 32—minute modules) and 70 minutes for Math (split into two 35—minute modules).

Component	Time Allotted(minutes)	Number of Questions/Tasks
Reading and Writing	64(two 32-minute modules)	54
Math	64(two 35-minute modules)	44
Total	134	98

3. There is a 10—minute break between the two sections.

4. The first module in each section includes a mix of easy, medium, and hard questions, and the difficulty of the second module depends on the student's performance in the first module.

5. The SAT provides 68% more time per question compared to the ACT.

6. Most questions are multiple choice, but some math questions require students to enter the answer.

7. There is no penalty for guessing on any questions.

CONTENTS

Chapter

I

Algebra

1. Linear Equations
2. Lines in the Coordinate Plane
3. Linear Inequalities and Absolute Value
4. System of Linear Equations and Inequalities

1. Linear Equations

01. Solutions of Linear Equations

In most cases, a linear equation has one solution. However, the equation sometimes has **infinitely many solutions or no solution.**

1. Linear Equation with Infinitely Many Solutions

If the equation is in the form of $ax=b$ and, $a=0$ and $b=0$,

then there are infinitely many solutions to the equation.

2. Linear Equation with No Solution

If the equation is in the form of $ax=b$ and, $a=0$ and $b \neq 0$,

then there are no solutions to the equation.

Example 1

Solve the equation $3(2x-5)+1=4(x+2)-18$.

Solution

$3(2x-5)+1=4(x+2)-18$	$\rightarrow$ Write original equation
$6x-15+1=4x+8-18$	$\rightarrow$ Remove parentheses
$6x-14=4x-10$	$\rightarrow$ Simplify each side
$6x-4x-14=4x-4x-10$	$\rightarrow$ Subtract $4x$ to each side
$2x-14=-10$	$\rightarrow$ Simplify
$2x-14+14=-10+14$	$\rightarrow$ Add 14 to each side
$2x=4$	$\rightarrow$ Simplify
$\dfrac{2x}{2}=\dfrac{4}{2}$	$\rightarrow$ Divide each side by 2
$x=2$	$\rightarrow$ Simplify

The solution is $x=2$

Example 2

Solve the equation $4+6x=2(3x+2)$.

$$4+6x=2(3x+2) \quad \rightarrow \text{Given}$$
$$4+6x=6x+4 \quad \rightarrow \text{Remove parentheses}$$
$$4+6x-6x=4 \quad \rightarrow \text{Subtract } 6x \text{ to each side}$$
$$6x-6x=4-4 \quad \rightarrow \text{Subtract } 4 \text{ to each side}$$
$$(6-6)x=4-4 \quad \rightarrow 6x-6x=(6-6)x$$
$$0{\cdot}x=0 \quad \rightarrow \text{Simplify}$$

This means that the equation is always true for all x.

Therefore, the equation has infinitely many solutions.

Example 3

Solve the equation $5x-4=5x+4$.

$$5x-4=5x+4 \quad \rightarrow \text{Given}$$
$$5x-5x-4=4 \quad \rightarrow \text{Subtract } 5x \text{ to each side}$$
$$5x-5x=4+4 \quad \rightarrow \text{Add } 4 \text{ to each side}$$
$$(5-5)x=4+4 \quad \rightarrow 5x-5x=(5-5)x$$
$$0{\cdot}x=8 \quad \rightarrow \text{Simplify}$$

This means that the equation is always false for all x.

Therefore, the equation has no solution.

02. Application of Linear Equations

The key to solving application problems is converting the words into mathematical equations. Refer to the following steps.

1. **Understand thoroughly what the problem is asking you to do.**
2. **Represent one of the unknown quantities with a variable.**
3. **Form an equation that will relate known quantities to the unknown quantities.**
4. **Solve the equation.**

Example 4

Two cars A and B started from the same point, traveling in opposite directions at 60 miles per hour and 70 miles per hour, respectively. After how many hours will they be 520 miles apart?

Solution

Let x be the time each car traveled. Then, the distance car A traveled is $60 \times x = 60x$ and the distance car B traveled is $70 \times x = 70x$, as shown in the figure below.

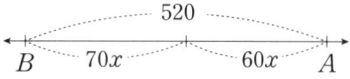

Since two cars are 520 miles apart, we have $60x + 70x = 520$. Now solve the equation for x.
$60x + 70x = 520$
$\qquad 130x = 520, \ x = 4$
Therefore, they will be 520 miles apart after 4 hours.

4 hours

Example 5

How many gallons of a 40% saline solution must be added to 10 gallons of a 13% saline solution to make a 25% saline solution?

Solution

Let x be the amount of a 40% saline solution. Create a table as shown below.

	40% saline solution	13% saline solution	25% saline solution
The amount of solution	x	10	$x+10$
The amount of salt	$\frac{40}{100}x=0.4x$	$\frac{13}{100}\cdot 10=1.3$	$\frac{25}{100}(x+10)=0.25(x+10)$

Because the sum of the salts of a 40% saline solution and a 13% saline solution is the same as that of a 25% saline solution, we have $0.4x+1.3=0.25(x+10)$. Now solve the equation for x.

$$0.4x+1.3=0.25(x+10)$$
$$(0.4x+1.3)\cdot 100=(0.25(x+10))\cdot 100$$
$$40x+130=25(x+10)$$
$$40x+130=25x+250$$
$$15x+130=250$$
$$15x=120, \quad x=8$$

8 gallons of a 40% saline solution

Multiple Choice **Questions**

0001

$$10-4(x+1)=2(x+5)$$

What is the solution to the given equation above?

(A) $\dfrac{2}{3}$

(B) $-\dfrac{2}{3}$

(C) $\dfrac{3}{2}$

(D) $-\dfrac{3}{2}$

0002

$$\dfrac{x+1}{2}-\dfrac{2x+5}{3}=\dfrac{3x-1}{4}$$

What is the solution to the given equation above?

(A) 1

(B) 2

(C) -1

(D) -2

0003

If $4a-\dfrac{2}{5}=3$, what is the value of $20a$?

(A) 11

(B) 13

(C) 15

(D) 17

0004

If $3x-4=-5$, what is the value of $12-9x$?

(A) $-\dfrac{1}{3}$

(B) 3

(C) -15

(D) 15

0005

If $x=-3$ is the solution to the equation $2(x-3k)+1=4k-3(4-x)$, what is the value of k?

(A) $\dfrac{8}{5}$

(B) $\dfrac{5}{8}$

(C) 5

(D) 8

0006

For what value of b does the equation $2(x-2)=3bx-7$ have no solutions for x?

(A) $\dfrac{3}{2}$

(B) $\dfrac{2}{3}$

(C) $-\dfrac{2}{3}$

(D) $-\dfrac{3}{2}$

0007

$$4ax-8=3(x+4)+5(x-2)$$

If the equation above has no solution, what is the value of a? (a is a constant)

(A) 1

(B) 2

(C) 3

(D) 4

0008

If $3a=\dfrac{4}{3}b$, which of the following is equal to $12b$ in terms of a?

(A) $9a$

(B) $18a$

(C) $27a$

(D) $36a$

0009

If the solution of $5x+3=12x-3(2x-2)$ is $x=a$ and the solution of $\dfrac{x-2}{3}=\dfrac{3x-1}{2}-6$ is $x=b$, what is the value of ab?

(A) -2

(B) 8

(C) -15

(D) 30

0010

If the equation $6(3x-2a)+4=-2(bx+5)-8x$ is true for all x, what is the value of $6a-b$?

(A) 5

(B) 10

(C) 15

(D) 20

0011

$$6x-4-3(3+ax)=-13$$

If the equation given above has exactly one solution, which of the following can NOT be the value of a?

(A) 1

(B) 2

(C) 3

(D) 4

0012

The equation $k-ky=4y$ has a solution for all values of k EXCEPT

(A) -4

(B) -2

(C) 0

(D) 2

0013

Which of the following equation has infinitely many solutions?

(A) $0.4x-0.9=0.2x+0.9$

(B) $\dfrac{6x+4}{5}=x+0.2$

(C) $\dfrac{1}{2}(4x+8)=-2(3-x)$

(D) $2(x+1)-\dfrac{5}{4}x=\dfrac{3x+8}{4}$

0014

$$3-\dfrac{5-3x}{4}=\dfrac{7}{8}+\dfrac{3}{4}x$$

Which of the following statements is true about the equation given above?

(A) The equation has one solution because only one value of x is true in the equation.

(B) The equation has no solution because the equation is always false for all x.

(C) The equation has infinitely many solutions because the equation is always true for all x.

(D) The number of the solutions to the equation is unknown.

0015

The perimeter of the rectangle is 64 inches. If the length of the rectangle is 4 inches less than twice the width, what is the area of the rectangle?

(A) 42

(B) 60

(C) 120

(D) 240

0016

A taxi charge $2.5 for the first 2 miles and $0.85 for each additional mile. If a customer rides in this taxi for n miles, where $n \geq 2$, which of the following represents the price that a customer must pay?

(A) $0.85n+0.8$

(B) $0.85n-1.2$

(C) $0.85n+2.5$

(D) $2.5n+0.85$

0017

Currently, John is 14 years old and his father is 38 years old. In how many years will his father be twice as old as John will be?

(A) In 10 years

(B) In 12 years

(C) In 16 years

(D) In 24 years

0018

Chris invests $5,000 in the bank that pays $x\%$ interest and $3,000 in stocks that pay an annual return of $y\%$. Suppose his annual income from both investments is $318, and the equation below represents this situation.

$$50 \cdot \frac{x}{100} + 30 \cdot \frac{y}{100} = 318$$

Which of the following is the best interpretation of the term $30 \cdot \frac{y}{100}$ in this context?

(A) The annual income from the bank.

(B) The annual income from stocks.

(C) The amount invested in the bank each year.

(D) The amount invested in stocks each year.

0019

Ben walks and jogs to work each day. He averages 3 miles an hour walking and 5 miles an hour jogging. The distance from home to work is 5 miles and Ben makes the trip in 1 hour 20 minutes. If the equation $3x + 5\left(\frac{4}{3} - x\right) = 5$ represents this situation, which of the following is the best interpretation of the expression $\frac{4}{3} - x$ in this context?

(A) The total distance Ben walked to work.

(B) The number of hours Ben walked to work.

(C) The total distance Ben jogged to work.

(D) The number of hours Ben jogged to work.

0020

Jason has some coins in his pocket consisting of nickels and dimes only. If the total value of the coins is $3.60 and there are 9 more nickels than dimes, which equation gives the number of nickels x in Jason's pocket?

(A) $10x + 5(x - 9) = 360$

(B) $10(x - 9) + 5x = 360$

(C) $10x + 5(x + 9) = 360$

(D) $10(x + 9) + 5x = 360$

15

0021

There are two different squares.
The length of one side of the larger square is 3 centimeters longer than the length of one side of the smaller square. If the sum of the perimeters of the two squares is 68 centimeters, what is the length of one side of the larger square?

(A) 9 centimeters

(B) 10 centimeters

(C) 11 centimeters

(D) 12 centimeters

0022

Two cars A and B are 340 miles apart and moving directly towards each other. Car A is moving at a speed of 64 miles per hour and car B at 72 miles per hour, respectively. If car B starts moving 1 hour later than car A, which equation represents the time t, in hours, it takes for car A to meet car B?

(A) $64t + 72t = 340$

(B) $64(t-1) + 72t = 340$

(C) $64t + 72(t-1) = 340$

(D) $72t - 64t = 340$

0023

Justin's science teacher distributes 65 balloons to his students in his laboratory. When he gives 4 balloons to each of his students, 1 balloon will remain. How many students are in the laboratory?

(A) 13 students

(B) 14 students

(C) 15 students

(D) 16 students

0024

John spent a total of $8.4 for fresh salmon and pork. The salmon cost 1.5 times as much per pound as the pork, and John bought 2 times as many pounds of pork as pounds of salmon. How much, in dollars, did the John spend on pork?

(A) $3.6

(B) $4.2

(C) $4.8

(D) $5.4

0025

Two planes, which are 1860 miles apart, fly toward each other. If their speeds differ by 80 miles per hour and they pass each other after 4 hours, what is the speed of faster plane?

(A) 112.5 miles per hour

(B) 192.5 miles per hour

(C) 232.5 miles per hour

(D) 272.5 miles per hour

0026

When a 20 centimeter candle is lit, the candle is shortened by 4 cm every 16 minutes. Which of the following represents the relationship between the length of a lit candle L and time T?

(A) $L+4T=80$

(B) $4L+T=80$

(C) $L+4T=20$

(D) $4L+T=20$

0027

$$5(2x-3)+2=6x-3(2-x)$$

What is the solution to the given equation above?

0028

If $\frac{3}{4}a+\frac{1}{2}=0$, what is the value of $3a+2$?

0029

If $\frac{4}{3}a-4=12$, what is the value of $4a$?

0030

For what value of a and b does the equation $\frac{ax+5}{2}-\frac{2}{3}=\frac{5}{6}x-\frac{1}{3}b$ have infinitely many solutions for x?

00**31**

$$4 - \frac{1}{6}(4x+5) = 2kx+3$$

If the equation above has no solution, what is the value of k? (k is a constant)

00**32**

Four more than twice a number is equal to three times the number minus two. What is the number?

00**33**

What number divided by 4 is equal to 3 more than twice that same number?

00**34**

How many liters of an 18% acid−solution must be added to 8 liters of a 12% acid−solution to make a 15% acid−solution?

00**35**

Linda drove at a rate of 55 miles per hour for 3 hours. He stopped for dinner then drove for another 2 hours to reach his destination. If the total distance she traveled is 275 miles, at what rate did Linda drive for the last two hours?

00**36**

There is a rectangle with length and width of 8 inches and 4 inches, respectively. If the length of the rectangle decreases by x inches and the width increases by 3 inches, the area of the rectangle increases by 10 square inches. What is the value of x?

00**37**

At a concert, adult tickets were sold at $27 each and students tickets at $19. If the total amount of revenue from tickets sold was $4,000 and there were 160 people in attendance, how many adult tickets were sold?

0038

Justin's science teacher distributes balloons to his students in his laboratory. If he gives each student 6 balloons, 3 balloons will remain. If he wishes to give each student 7 balloons, he will need 4 additional balloons. How many balloons does the teacher have?

0039

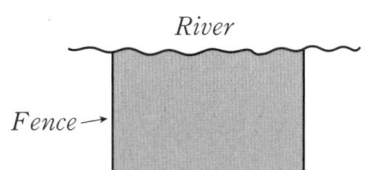

Paul has 74 feet of fencing and wants to fence off a rectangular field that borders a straight river, as shown in the figure above. If the length of the field is 14 feet more than three times the width, what is the length of the field if no fencing is needed along the river?

0040

A pharmacist has a 45% saline solution and a 20% saline solution. How much of 45% saline solution must be mixed to make 20 liters of a 30% saline solution?

0041

There are two candles A and B, each 25 cm and 30 cm long. Candle A shortens by 3 cm every 10 minutes, and Candle B shortens by 5 cm every 8 minutes. How many minutes later will both candles be the same length if they are lit at the same time?

2. Lines in the Coordinate Plane

01. Slope of a Line

1. $\text{Slope} = \dfrac{\text{difference in } y \text{ values}}{\text{difference in } x \text{ values}} = \dfrac{\Delta y}{\Delta x} = \dfrac{\text{rise}}{\text{run}}$, where $\Delta x \neq 0$

The slope, usually denoted by the letter m, of a line passing through the points

$(x_1,\ y_1)$ and $(x_2,\ y_2)$ is given by $m = \dfrac{\Delta y}{\Delta x} = \dfrac{y_2 - y_1}{x_2 - x_1}$, where $x_2 - x_1 \neq 0$

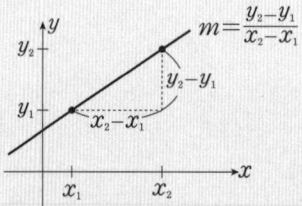

2. A line with a **positive slope** increases from left to right.

3. A line with a **negative slope** decreases from left to right.

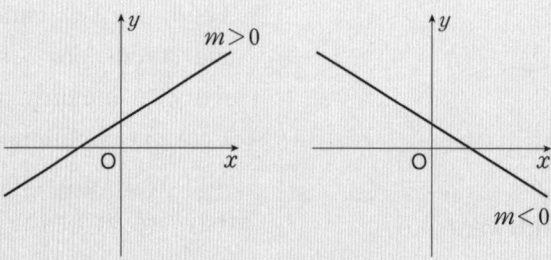

4. The **slope of the horizontal line** is always equal to **zero**.

5. The **slope of the vertical line** is always **undefined**.

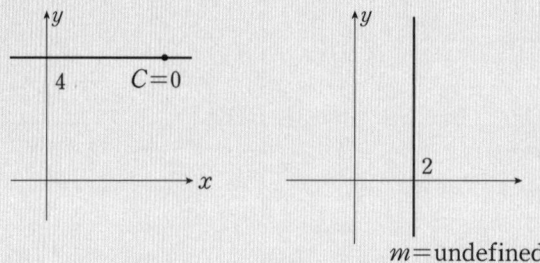

Example 1

Find the slope of the line that passes through the points $(1, 5)$ and $(5, 7)$.

Solution

Let $(x_1, y_1) = (1, 5)$ and $(x_2, y_2) = (5, 7)$.

The slope $m = \dfrac{y_2 - y_1}{x_2 - x_1} = \dfrac{7 - 5}{5 - 1} = \dfrac{2}{4} = \dfrac{1}{2}$.

The slope of the line is $\dfrac{1}{2}$.

02. Two Forms of Equation in Line

1. Point−Slope Form

The point−slope formula for finding the equation of a line is

$$y - y_1 = m(x - x_1)$$

where **m is the slope** and **(x_1, y_1) is a point on the line.**

2. Slope−Intercept Form

The slope−intercept form of the equation is

$$y = mx + b$$

where **m is the slope** and **b is the y−intercept** of the line.

Example 2

Write the equation of the line that passes through the points $(4, -3)$ and $(-2, 5)$.

Solution

First, we need to find the slope using the given points. Let $(x_1, y_1) = (4, -3)$ and $(x_2, y_2) = (-2, 5)$. Then the slope is

$$m = \frac{y_2 - y_1}{x_2 - x_1} = \frac{5 - (-3)}{-2 - 4} = \frac{8}{-6} = -\frac{4}{3}$$

Now, write the equation $y - y_1 = m(x - x_1)$ using one of the two points.

$$y - y_1 = m(x - x_1) \qquad \rightarrow \text{ The point−slope form}$$

$$y - (-3) = -\frac{4}{3}(x - 4) \quad \rightarrow (x_1, y_1) = (4, -3) \text{ and } m = -\frac{4}{3}$$

$$y + 3 = -\frac{4}{3}(x - 4) \quad \rightarrow \text{ Simplify the left side}$$

$$y + 3 = -\frac{4}{3}(x - 4)$$

Note You can also use the point $(x_2, y_2) = (-2, 5)$ to find the equation of the line.

Example 3

Find the equation of the line that has a slope of 4 and $y-$intercept -3.

Solution

$y=mx+b$ → The slope−intercept form
$y=4x-3$ → Substitute 4 for m and -3 for b

$$y=4x-3$$

03. Intersection of Two Lines

When two lines intersect at one point, the $x-$ and $y-$coordinates of the intersection point are the same as shown below.

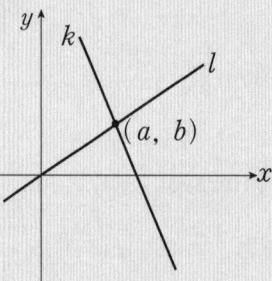

Intersection $(a,\ b)$ is on both lines k and l.

Example 4

Fine the intersection point of two lines $y=3x-4$ and $y=-2x+11$.

Solution

At the intersection point, two lines have the same $x-$ and $y-$coordinates. So, let

$$3x-4=-2x+11$$
$$5x=15,\ x=3$$

Now, substitute 3 for x in the equation of either line.

$$y=3x-4$$
$$y=3(3)-4=5$$

Therefore, the intersection point is $(3,\ 5)$.

04. Parallel and Perpendicular Lines

1. Parallel Lines

Two non−vertical lines are **parallel** when they have the **same slope** and different y−intercepts.

2. Perpendicular Lines

If two non−vertical lines are **perpendicular**, then the product of **their slopes is** -1.

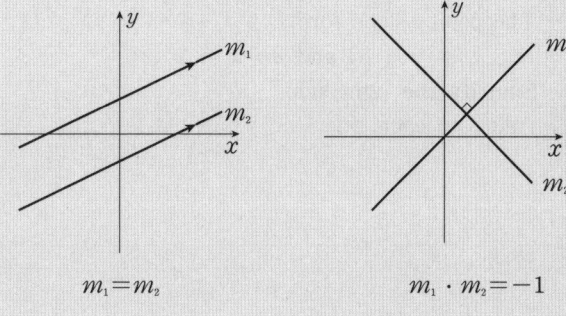

$$m_1=m_2 \qquad\qquad m_1 \cdot m_2 = -1$$

Example 5

Find the equation in slope−intercept form of the line that passes through $(3, -2)$ and is parallel to the line $y=\frac{5}{2}x+1$.

Solution

Step 1 The slope of the line $y=\frac{5}{2}x+1$ is $m=\frac{5}{2}$. The parallel lines have the same slope.

Step 2 Write an equation of the line in point−slope form that passes through $(x_1,\ y_1)=(3,\ -2)$ with slope $m=\frac{5}{2}$.

$$y-y_1=m(x-x_1) \qquad \rightarrow \text{ The point−slope form}$$
$$y-(-2)=\frac{5}{2}(x-3) \qquad \rightarrow (x_1,\ y_1)=(3,-2) \text{ and } m=\frac{5}{2}$$
$$y+2=\frac{5}{2}x-\frac{15}{2} \qquad \rightarrow \text{ Simplify each side}$$
$$y=\frac{5}{2}x-\frac{19}{2} \qquad \rightarrow \text{ Subtract 2 to each side}$$

$$y=\frac{5}{2}x-\frac{19}{2}$$

Example 6

Find the equation in slope−intercept form of the line that passes through $(-1, 5)$ and is perpendicular to the line $y=\frac{1}{2}x+3$.

Solution

Step 1 The slope of the line $y=\frac{1}{2}x+3$ is $m=-\frac{1}{2}$. The opposite(negative) reciprocal of $-\frac{1}{2}$ is 2.

Therefore, the perpendicular line has a slope of 2.

Step 2 Write an equation of the line in point−slope form that passes through $(x_1, y_1)=(-1, 5)$ with slope $m=2$.

$$y-y_1=m(x-x_1) \quad \rightarrow \text{The point−slope form}$$
$$y-5=2(x-(-1)) \quad \rightarrow (x_1, y_1)=(-1, 5) \text{ and } m=2$$
$$y-5=2x+2 \quad \rightarrow \text{Simplify the right side}$$
$$y=2x+7 \quad \rightarrow \text{Add 5 to each side}$$

$$y=2x+7$$

05. Applications

The key to solving application problems is converting the words into mathematical equations. Refer to the following steps.

1. Identify the meaning of the problem and set the variables x and y.

2. Establish an equation of the relationship between x and y.

3. Solve the equation.

4. Make sure that the solution you find fits the meaning of the problem.

Example 7

Hours Worked	Wage
10	$220
20	$400
30	$580
40	$760

The table above shows the amount of time Lillian works and her total wage.

① What equation in a point−slope form that gives Lillian's wage at any time?

② What does the slope represent?

③ What does the y−intercept represent?

Solution

① Let x be the number of hours and y be the total wage. Then we can use two points, such as $(x_1, y_1)=(10, 220)$ and $(x_2, y_2)=(20, 400)$ to find the slope

$$m=\frac{y_2-y_1}{x_2-x_1}=\frac{400-220}{20-10}=\frac{180}{10}=18.$$

Now, write the equation in point−slope form.
$$y-y_1=m(x-x_1)$$
$$y-220=18(x-10)$$

$$y-220=18(x-10)$$

② The slope with the units is

$$m=\frac{\$400-\$220}{(20-10)\text{hours}}=\frac{\$180}{10\ \text{hours}}=\$18/\text{hour}$$

Therefore, the meaning of the slope is her hourly pay rate (she earns $18 per hour).

③ The y−intercept is her total wage when she worked zero hours.
So it represents a fixed amount of income per pay period.

Practice **Problems**

00**42**

The slope of the line that passes through the points $(4, 3)$ and $(2, -1)$ is

(A) $\dfrac{5}{4}$

(B) $\dfrac{4}{5}$

(C) 2

(D) 3

00**43**

A line in the $xy-$plane passes through the point $(6, 2)$ and has a slope of $-\dfrac{2}{3}$. Which of the following points lies on the line?

(A) $(1, 4)$

(B) $(0, 5)$

(C) $(3, -4)$

(D) $(-3, 8)$

For questions 044~045, refer to the following graphs below

00**44**

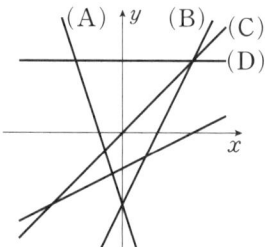

In the figure above, which line has the smallest slope?

00**45**

In the figure above, which line has the greatest slope?

00**46**

In the graph of $y=mx-4$, the value of y decreases by 6 units as the value of x increases by 3 units. What is the value of m?

(A) -2

(B) $-\dfrac{1}{2}$

(C) 2

(D) $\dfrac{1}{2}$

00**47**

The function f is defined by $f(x)=5x-7$. What is the value of $f(x)$ when $x=2$?

(A) 1

(B) 2

(C) 3

(D) 4

00**48**

The function g is defined by $g(x)=-2x+5$. What is the value of x when $g(x)=-11$?

(A) -3

(B) 8

(C) -17

(D) 27

00**49**

f is a linear function such that $f(-2)=5$ and $f(3)=20$. Which of the following equations defines f?

(A) $f(x)=3x+11$

(B) $f(x)=3x-17$

(C) $f(x)=-3x-1$

(D) $f(x)=-3x+29$

00**50**

Which point lies on the line defined by $4x-5y=-3$?

(A) $(-2,\ -1)$

(B) $(-1,\ -2)$

(C) $(2,\ 1)$

(D) $(1,\ 2)$

00**51**

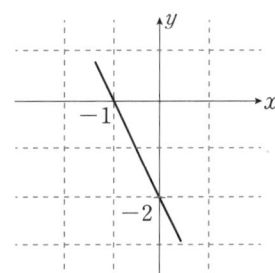

Which of the following is the equation of the line given above?

(A) $y=-2x-2$

(B) $y=-\dfrac{1}{2}x-2$

(C) $y=2x-1$

(D) $y=\dfrac{1}{2}x-1$

0052

$$y = 4x - 8$$

What is the x-intercept of the graph of the function above?

(A) $(0, 2)$

(B) $(2, 0)$

(C) $(0, 4)$

(D) $(4, 0)$

0053

The function f is defined by $f(x) = 3x - 12$. If the graph of f has an x-intercept at $(a, 0)$ and y-intercept at $(0, b)$, where a and b are constants, what is the value of ab?

(A) -36

(B) -48

(C) 36

(D) 48

For questions 054~055, refer to the following graph.

0054

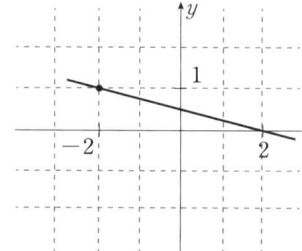

Which of the following is the equation of the line given above?

(A) $y = -4x + \dfrac{1}{2}$

(B) $y = -\dfrac{1}{4}x + \dfrac{1}{2}$

(C) $y = 4x + 1$

(D) $y = \dfrac{1}{4}x + 1$

0055

Which equation defines the line m when the line m is parallel to the line in the figure above and passes through the point $(2, 3)$?

(A) $y = -4x + \dfrac{5}{2}$

(B) $y = 4x + \dfrac{7}{2}$

(C) $y = -\dfrac{1}{4}x + \dfrac{5}{2}$

(D) $y = -\dfrac{1}{4}x + \dfrac{7}{2}$

0056

What is the y−intercept of the graph of $8x-12y=72$ in the coordinate plane?

(A) $(0, -9)$

(B) $(0, -6)$

(C) $(0, 6)$

(D) $(0, 9)$

0057

What is the y−intercept of the line which passes through the points $(3, -1)$ and $(6, 5)$?

(A) 17

(B) -7

(C) 5

(D) -5

0058

If a line has the equation $y=6$, then the slope of this line is

(A) 0

(B) 1

(C) -1

(D) Undefined.

0059

Find the equation of the line with x−intercept -2 and y−intercept 3.

(A) $3x-2y+6=0$

(B) $3x+2y-6=0$

(C) $-3x-2y-6=0$

(D) $2x+3y-4=0$

0060

If the slope of the line that passes through the points $(k+1, 4)$ and $(2, 3k-1)$ is 2, what is the value of k?

(A) -7

(B) 5

(C) $\dfrac{7}{5}$

(D) $-\dfrac{5}{7}$

0061

What is the slope of the line perpendicular to the equation $2x+4y-5=0$?

(A) 2

(B) -2

(C) $\dfrac{1}{2}$

(D) $-\dfrac{1}{2}$

0062

In the linear equation $y=-2.25x+14.57$, what does the number -2.25 indicate?

(A) y increases by 2.25 for every x increases by 1

(B) y decreases by 2.25 for every x increases by 1

(C) x increases by 2.25 for every y increases by 1

(D) x decreases by 2.25 for every y increases by 1

0063

Andrea is an urban planner. As an independent contractor, she charges a \$160 fee plus \$30 per hour for each contract with the city. Find the total amount she charges for 12 hours project.

(A) \$360

(B) \$520

(C) \$1920

(D) \$4800

0064

x	1	2	4	7
y	1	-1	-5	-11

The table above shows the coordinates of the selected points on a line in the plane. What is the value of x when $y=5$?

(A) -2

(B) -1

(C) 1

(D) 2

0065

Suppose the line k is horizontal that passes through the point $(4, -5)$. Which of the following is the equation of the line k?

(A) $x=4$

(B) $x=-5$

(C) $y=4$

(D) $y=-5$

0066

Which of the following is the intersection point of two lines $y=-\dfrac{1}{2}x+6$ and $y=3x-22$?

(A) $(6,\ 3)$

(B) $(7,\ -1)$

(C) $(8,\ 2)$

(D) $(9,\ 5)$

For questions 067~068, refer to the following graph.

0067

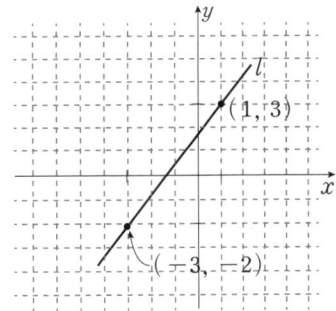

Which of the following is an equation of a line that is parallel to line l?

(A) $5x+4y=3$

(B) $4x+5y=3$

(C) $5x-4y=-3$

(D) $-5x-4y=-3$

0068

Which of the following is an equation of a line that is perpendicular to line l?

(A) $5x+4y=3$

(B) $4x+5y=3$

(C) $5x-4y=-3$

(D) $-5x+4y=-3$

0069

Which of the following is an equation of the line that passes through the $(0,\ 2)$ and is parallel to the line $x+2y=4$?

(A) $x+2y=2$

(B) $x+2y=4$

(C) $2x-y=2$

(D) $2x-y=4$

0070

Which of the following equation of the line passes through the point $(-3,\ 2)$ and is perpendicular to the line $2y-x+8=0$?

(A) $y=2x-7$

(B) $y=\dfrac{1}{2}x+\dfrac{7}{2}$

(C) $y=-2x-4$

(D) $y=-\dfrac{1}{2}x+\dfrac{1}{2}$

0071

Which equation represents the line that passes through $(2, 5)$ and is perpendicular to the graph of $y=-2x+3$?

(A) $x-2y=-8$

(B) $2x-y=-1$

(C) $2x-2y=-6$

(D) $2x+2y=14$

0072

In the $xy-$plane, two lines m and n are perpendicular. If the equation of line m is $3x-4y+1=0$, which of the following could be the equation of the n?

(A) $4x-3y+4=0$

(B) $4x+3y-1=0$

(C) $-3x+4y+2=0$

(D) $-3x-4y+1=0$

0073

If the graphs of two lines $f(x)=ax+b$ and $g(x)=cx+d$ are perpendicular to each other at some point, which of the following must be true?

(A) $a=c$

(B) $a+c=-1$

(C) $ac=-1$

(D) $ad-bc=0$

0074

The equation of line k is $3x+4y=11$, and the equation of line p is $4x-3y=9$. Which statement about the two lines is true?

(A) Lines k and p have the same $x-$intercept.

(B) Lines k and p have the same $y-$intercept.

(C) Lines k and p are parallel.

(D) Lines k and p are perpendicular.

0075

Two lines l and n are perpendicular and intersect at the origin. If line l passes through the point (a, b), which of the following could be the equation of line n?

(A) $y=-ax$

(B) $y=-\dfrac{ax+1}{b}$

(C) $y=-\dfrac{ax}{b}$

(D) $y=\dfrac{1-ax}{b}$

0076

Suppose that $f(x)=ax+1$ and $g(x)=bx-3$, for all real numbers a and b. Which of the following statement is true about the graph of $f+g$?

(A) Lines whose x−intercept is -2

(B) Lines whose y−intercept is -2

(C) Parabola whose x−intercept is -2

(D) Parabola whose y−intercept is -2

0077

At a video game center, g games are played by adding q quarters. If $g=2q+1$, how many additional quarters are needed to play 6 additional games?

(A) 3 quarters

(B) 6 quarters

(C) 9 quarters

(D) 12 quarters

0078

Customers rent certain equipment for an initial cost of \$24 and an additional fee of \$15 per day. Which of the following represents the total cost C to rent this equipment for x days?

(A) $C=15x-24$

(B) $C=15x$

(C) $C=15x+9$

(D) $C=15x+24$

For questions 079~080, refer to the following information.

Jamie plans to spend \$24 on apples and oranges at the food market. The graph below shows the possible combinations of apples and oranges he could purchase.

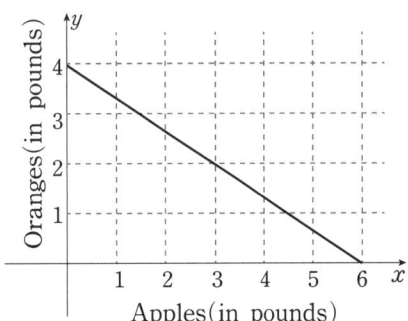

0079

What is the price of 1 pound of apple?

(A) \$2

(B) \$4

(C) \$6

(D) \$8

0080

Which of the following correctly expresses the relationship between the number of apples x and the number of oranges y?

(A) $4x+6y=24$

(B) $6x+4y=24$

(C) $2x+3y=24$

(D) $3x+2y=24$

For questions 081~083, refer to the following information.

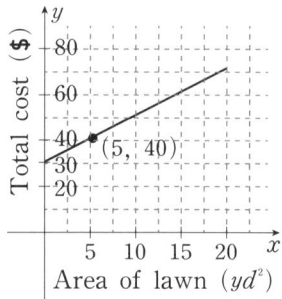

Area of lawn (yd^2)

Samuel is hiring a company to mow the lawn in his backyard. The company charges a one-time fee plus a certain amount per square yard of mowing. The graph above shows the relationship between the number of square yards of mowing and the total cost, in dollars.

0081

What is the best interpretation of the coordinate $(5, 40)$ in this context?

(A) The company charges $5 for the first 40 square yards

(B) If the company mows 5 square yards, it will charge $40

(C) For every 5 square yards the company mows, the cost the company charges increases by $40

(D) The company charges a total of $40 for each mowing every five days

0082

What is the best interpretation of the slope of the graph?

(A) The initial cost charged by the company

(B) The cost charged by the company per square yard

(D) The total cost that the company charges

(D) The minimum cost that the company charges

0083

Which of the following expressions represents the cost f, in dollars, that the company charges for mowing m square yards?

(A) $f(m)=3m+20$

(B) $f(m)=2m+30$

(C) $f(m)=5m+15$

(D) $f(m)=5m+40$

0084

To edit a college essay, Mr. Jackson charges $30 for the first 3 pages and $14 per page after the first 3 pages. Which of the following expressions represents the cost C, in dollars, Mr. Jackson charges after x hours of editing?

(A) $C=14x+30$

(B) $C=14x+12$

(C) $C=14x-12$

(D) $C=14x-30$

0085

The total cost y in dollars of renting a certain premium car for x days is given by equation $y=150+70x$. Which of the following best describes the slope of the graph of the equation in the coordinate plane?

(A) For every 70 days the car is rented, the price increases by $150

(B) For each additional day the car is rented, the price increases by $70.

(C) For each additional day the car is rented, the price increases by $150.

(D) For each additional day the car is rented, the price increases by $220.

0086

$$f(t)=-0.045t+1.25$$

The given linear function f models the annual percentage decrease in a particular baseball player's average fastball speed t years after 2008. What is the best interpretation of $f(10)=0.8$ in this context?

(A) 10 years after 2008, this baseball player's average fastball speed would be about 0.8 times his speed in 2008.

(B) The percentage decrease in average fastball speed of this baseball player over 10 years is 20%.

(C) 10 years after 2008, the percentage decrease in this baseball player's average fastball speed is 80% over the previous year.

(D) 10 years after 2008, this baseball player's average fastball speed decreased by 0.8 mph.

For questions 087~088, refer to the following information.

Renting a Lawn Mower

Days (d)	Cost in dollars (C)
3	$70
5	$130
7	$190

The data in the table shows the cost of renting a lawn mower by the day. Assume the cost increases constantly as the number of days a lawn mower is rented.

00**87**

Which of the following expressions represents the cost y, in dollars, to rent a lawn mower for x days?

(A) $y=30x+20$

(B) $y=30x-20$

(C) $y=60x+70$

(D) $y=60x-70$

00**88**

What is the cost if a lawn mower is rented for 10 days?

(A) $280

(B) $320

(C) $530

(D) $670

For questions 089~090, refer to the following information.

x (hours)	C ($)
1	13
2	19
4	31

The table above shows the cost, C, of renting a bicycle for x hours. The relationship between C and x is linear. Suppose the data are graphed on the coordinate plane.

00**89**

What is the value of the $y-$intercept?

(A) 6

(B) 7

(C) 9

(D) 13

00**90**

Which of the following best describes the slope of the graph of the equation in the coordinate plane?

(A) The cost of renting a bicycle increases by $6 per hour

(B) The cost of renting a bicycle increases by $7 per hour

(C) The total cost of renting a bike for 2 hours is $16

(D) The total cost of renting a bike for 4 hours is $24

0091

Which of the following equation is the perpendicular bisector of the line segment between points $A(-3, 1)$ and $B(2, -4)$?

(A) $x-y-1=0$

(B) $x+y-1=0$

(C) $2x-y-1=0$

(D) $x+2y+1=0$

0092

$$K=-0.004t+245$$

$$J=-0.0025t+625$$

Recently, low fertility rates in Korea and Japan have reached a very serious situation. The above two equations K and J model the number of babies under $1-$year$-$old (in thousand) in Korea and Japan t years after 2010, respectively. Which of the following best describes a comparison of the number of babies in these two countries?

(A) K decreases at a greater rate per year than J, and $K>J$ for all t.

(B) K decreases at a greater rate per year than J, and $K<J$ for all t.

(C) J decreases at a greater rate per year than K, and $K>J$ for all t.

(D) J decreases at a greater rate per year than K, and $K<J$ for all t.

0093

If f is a linear function such that $f(1)=-2$ and $f(3)=4$, what is the value of $f(0)$?

0094

If two graphs, $y=-4x+a$ and $y=bx-\dfrac{1}{2}$, are identical, what is the value of ab?

Qestions 095~096, refer to the following graph.

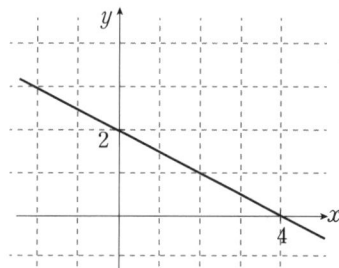

The graph above has the equation $y=mx+b$.

0095

Find the value of mb.

0096

If the equation of the line $y = ax + c$ has the x−intercept at $x = -2$ and is perpendicular to the line shown above, what is the value of $a + c$?

0097

If the slope and the y−intercept of the line $2ax - 5y = b$ is 2 and 6 respectively, what is the value of b?

0098

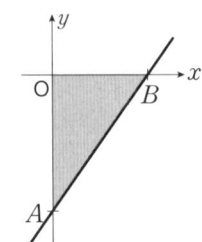

If the equation of the line that passes through A and B above is $7x - 5y = 21$, what is the area of $\triangle AOB$?

0099

What is the area bounded by three lines $y = x + 1$, $y = -x + 2$, and x−axis in the xy−plane?

0100

If the three points $(1,\ 4)$, $(-2,\ 3a+1)$, and $(2,\ 2a-3)$ lie on the same line, what is the value of a?

0101

Suppose the line passing through the origin also passes through the two points $(a-3,\ 4)$ and $(3a+2,\ -2)$. What is the value of a?

0102

The line k passes through the point $(4,\ 0)$ and is perpendicular to line $4x + 3y = 24$. What is the slope of line k?

Memo

3. Linear Inequalities and Absolute Value

01. Solving Linear Inequalities

1. Properties of Inequalities

Inequalities are governed by the following properties. Assume a, b, and c are real numbers.

Property	Examples
Converse Property: 1. If $a<b$, then $b>a$	1. If $2<5$, then $5>2$ 2. If $-3<4$, then $4>-3$
Transitivity Property: 1. If $a<b$ and $b<c$, then $a<c$ 2. If $a>b$ and $b>c$, then $a>c$	1. If $2<5$ and $5<7$, then $2<7$ 2. If $2>-1$ and $-1>-6$, then $2>-6$
Addition and Subtraction Properties: 1. If $a<b$, then $a\pm c<b\pm c$ 2. If $a>b$, then $a\pm c>b\pm c$	1. If $2<5$, then $2+3<5+3$ 2. If $4>2$ then $4-5>2-5$
Multiplication and Division Properties: 1. If $a<b$ and $c>0$, then $ac<bc$ and $\dfrac{a}{c}<\dfrac{b}{c}$ 2. If $a<b$ and $c<0$, then $ac>bc$ and $\dfrac{a}{c}>\dfrac{b}{c}$	1. If $1<3$ and $c=2$, then $1\cdot2<3\cdot2$ and $\dfrac{1}{2}<\dfrac{3}{2}$ 2. If $1<3$ and $c=-2$, then $1(-2)>3(-2)$ and $\dfrac{1}{-2}>\dfrac{3}{-2}$
Additive Inverse Property 1. If $a<b$, then $-a>-b$ 2. If $a>b$, then $-a<-b$	1. If $2<4$, then $-2>-4$ 2. If $3>-2$, then $-3<2$
Multiplicative Inverse Property 1. If $0<a<b$, then $\dfrac{1}{a}>\dfrac{1}{b}$	If $2<5$, then $\dfrac{1}{2}>\dfrac{1}{5}$

✔ These properties also hold true for inequalities involving $\leq$ and $\geq$.

2. Solving Linear Inequalities

Here are useful steps to solve more complicated inequality problems.

a. Remove parentheses, if there is(are) any.

b. Simplify each side of the inequality.

c. Move all the terms with the variable to one side and all the constants to the other using addition and subtraction.

d. Divide both sides by the variable's coefficient.

3. Compound Inequalities

A compound inequality is an inequality that combines two simple inequalities.

Example 1

Solve the inequality. $2(x-4)+3(1-2x) \geq 2x+13$

Solution

$2(x-4)+3(1-2x) \geq 2x+13$	$\rightarrow$ Given
$2x-8+3-6x \geq 2x+13$	$\rightarrow$ Remove parentheses
$-4x-5 \geq 2x+13$	$\rightarrow$ Simplify each side
$-6x-5 \geq 13$	$\rightarrow$ Subtract both sides by $2x$
$-6x \geq 18$	$\rightarrow$ Add both sides by 5
$x \leq -3$	$\rightarrow$ Divide both sides by -6. Change the direction of the inequality sign

The solution is $x \leq -3$

Example 2

Solve the inequality. $-5 < 2x-1 \leq 11$

Solution

$-5 < 2x-1 \leq 11$	$\rightarrow$ Given
$-5+1 < 2x-1+1 \leq 11+1$	$\rightarrow$ Add all three sides by 1
$-4 < 2x \leq 12$	$\rightarrow$ Simplify each side
$\dfrac{-4}{2} < \dfrac{2x}{2} \leq \dfrac{12}{2}$	$\rightarrow$ Divide all three sides by 2
$-2 < x \leq 6$	$\rightarrow$ Simplify each side

The solution is $-2 < x \leq 6$.

02. Absolute Value

1. If $|x| = a$, then $x = \pm a$, where a is positive number

2. If $|x| < a$, then $-a < x < a$, where a is positive number

$|x| < a$ means that x is restricted to points on the number line less than a units from 0 in either the positive or negative direction.

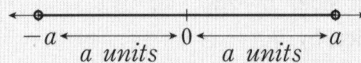

3. If $|x| > a$, then $x < -a$ or $x > a$, where a is positive number

$|x| > a$ means that x is restricted to points on the number line more than a units from 0 in either the positive or negative direction.

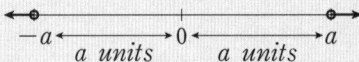

✔ These properties also hold true for inequalities involving $\leq$ and $\geq$.

Example 3

Solve the inequality.

① $|2x - 3| < 5$

② $\left|\dfrac{1}{2}x - 1\right| - 4 \geq 4$

Solution

①
$|2x - 3| < 5$	→ Given
$-5 < 2x - 3 < 5$	→ Write the inequality as a conjunction
$-2 < 2x < 8$	→ Add all three sides by 3
$-1 < x < 4$	→ Divide all three sides by 2

The solution is $-1 < x < 4$

②
$\left|\dfrac{1}{2}x - 1\right| - 4 \geq 4$	→ Given
$\left|\dfrac{1}{2}x - 1\right| \geq 8$	→ Add both sides by 4
$\dfrac{1}{2}x - 1 \leq -8$ or $\dfrac{1}{2}x - 1 \geq 8$	→ Write the inequality as a disjunction
$\dfrac{1}{2}x \leq -7$ or $\dfrac{1}{2}x \geq 9$	→ Add each side by 1
$x \leq -14$ or $x \geq 18$	→ Multiply each side by 2

The solution is $x \leq -14$ or $x \geq 18$

03. Graphing Linear Inequality

To graph a linear inequality, rearrange the equation for y first. Then, assume that the inequality to be the equal sign and then graph the line.

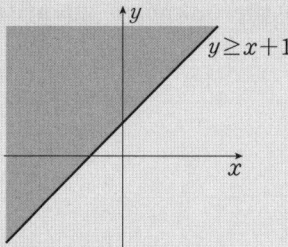

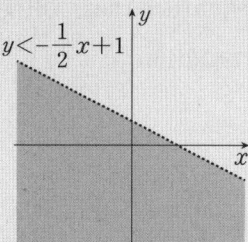

1. Every point on a solid line is a solution.

2. A solid line is used for inequalities with $\leq$ or $\geq$.

3. If $y >$ or $y \geq$, the region of the solution is above the line.

1. Every point on a dashed line is NOT a solution.

2. A dashed line is used for inequalities with $<$ or $>$.

3. If $y <$ or $y \leq$, the region of the solution is below the line.

Example 4

Graph the inequality $y \geq 2x - 4$.

Solution

Step 1 Graph $y = 2x - 4$ as a solid line

Step 2 Shade the area above the line since y is greater than or equal to $x - 2$.

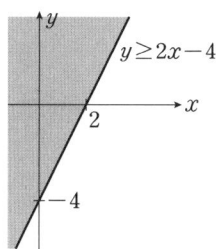

04. Applications

1. **Understand thoroughly what the problem is asking you to do.**

2. **Represent one of the unknown quantities with a variable.**

3. **Form an equation that will relate known quantities to the unknown quantities.**

4. **Solve the equation.**

Example 5

Daniel took a taxi. The taxi charges $4 for the first mile and $0.5 for every additional quarter mile. What is the maximum distance in miles she can travel if she has only $56?

Solution

Let x be the number of miles Jane travels after the first 1 mile. Since the taxi charges $0.5 for every additional quarter mile after the first mile, the taxi charges $2 for each additional mile. Then we have the following inequality:

$$4+2x \leq 56$$
$$2x \leq 52$$
$$x \leq 26$$

Therefore, the maximum distance she can travel is 27 miles (26 miles+first 1 mile).

Example 6

A company makes boxes of mechanical pencils. Each box should contain 160 pencils, plus or minus 4 pencils. What are the minimum and maximum numbers of mechanical pencils in each box?

Solution

Let x be the number of mechanical pencils in the box. Then the absolute value inequality that gives the solution x is

$$|x-160| \leq 4$$
$$-4 \leq x-160 \leq 4$$
$$156 \leq x \leq 164.$$

Therefore, the minimum and maximum numbers of mechanical pencils in each box is 156 and 164, respectively.

Practice **Problems**

0103

Which of the following numbers is NOT a solution of the inequality $3x - 5 \geq -2(4 - x) + 1$?

(A) -3

(B) -1

(C) 1

(D) 3

0104

$$|3x - 5| = 13$$

What is the negative solution to the given equation above?

(A) $-\dfrac{8}{3}$

(B) $-\dfrac{3}{8}$

(C) -3

(D) -6

0105

$$-8 \leq 6 - x \leq -4$$

Which of the following is the solution to the inequality given above?

(A) $10 \leq x \leq 14$

(B) $-14 \leq x \leq -10$

(C) $-14 \leq x \leq 10$

(D) $-10 \leq x \leq 14$

0106

$$-4 \leq \frac{4x - 2}{3} \leq 1$$

In the inequality given above, which of the following is true about the expression $6 - 12x$?

(A) $6 - 12x$ is greater than -9 but less than 36

(B) $6 - 12x$ is greater than 9 but less than 36

(C) $6 - 12x$ is greater than -36 but less than 9

(D) $6 - 12x$ is greater than -36 but less than -9

0107

In the xy-plane, which of the following points does NOT lie on the graph of the inequality $2|x| + |y| \geq 5$?

(A) $(-3, 0)$

(B) $(-1, -3)$

(C) $(0, -4)$

(D) $(3, -2)$

0108

How many positive integers are in the solution set of $|2x + 5| < 13$?

(A) 3

(B) 4

(C) 5

(D) 6

0109

For what value of x is $|2x-1|+2$ equal to 1?

(A) 0

(B) 1

(C) 2

(D) There is no such value of x.

0110

$$\frac{|x-2|}{2}+2 \leq 8$$

Which of the following is the solution to the inequality given above?

(A) $10 \leq x \leq 14$

(B) $-14 \leq x \leq -10$

(C) $-14 \leq x \leq 10$

(D) $-10 \leq x \leq 14$

0111

If a is a negative integer, then $-|a|=$

(A) a

(B) $-a$

(C) $\frac{1}{a}$

(D) $-\frac{1}{a}$

0112

If $|x+1|=4$, then which of the following could be $|x-4|$?

(A) 5

(B) 6

(C) 8

(D) 9

0113

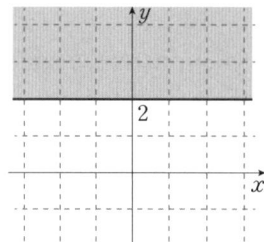

Which of the following inequalities represent the graph above?

(A) $y \leq 2$

(B) $y \geq 2$

(C) $x \leq 2$

(D) $x \geq 2$

0114

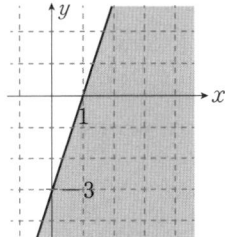

Which of the following inequalities represent the graph above?

(A) $y \leq \frac{1}{3}x - 3$

(B) $y \geq \frac{1}{3}x + 1$

(C) $y \leq 3x - 3$

(D) $y \geq 3x + 1$

0115

How many integer values of x satisfy the inequality $2x - 1 < 7$ and $2 - 3x < 11$?

(A) 4 integer values

(B) 5 integer values

(C) 6 integer values

(D) 7 integer values

0116

If the sum of a number and its square is greater than or equal to zero, which of the following CANNOT be the value of the number?

(A) $-\frac{3}{2}$

(B) -1

(C) $-\frac{1}{2}$

(D) 0

0117

If m is a positive integer, and if there are exactly m integers greater than m and less than $(m-1)^2$, which of the following could be m?

(A) 2

(B) 3

(C) 4

(D) 5

0118

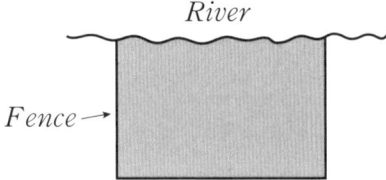

River

Fence →

Jack has 121 feet of fences and wants to fence off a rectangular field as shown in the figure above. If the length of the rectangular field is 4 feet less than three times the width x. Which of the following inequalities represent the situation for finding the maximum width above?

(A) $2x+(3x-4)\geq 121$

(B) $2x+(3x-4)\leq 121$

(C) $2x+(3x+4)\leq 121$

(D) $2x+(3x+4)\leq 121$

0119

In 2016, Country K had approximately 128 million trees. Starting in 2017, the country has been planting 8 million trees each year. At this rate, in which year will Country K first have more than 300 million trees?

(A) Year 2037

(B) Year 2038

(C) Year 2039

(D) Year 2040

0120

Mike received 82, 90, and 87 in his first three exams in his chemistry exams this semester. What is the minimum score Mike can get on the fourth exam to get an average of 85 or more?

(A) 77

(B) 79

(C) 81

(D) 83

0121

Suppose a car is allowed within 6 miles per hour at a speed limit of 60 miles per hour. If the car does not receive a ticket within this range, what is the maximum speed the car is allowed to run?

(A) 66 miles per hour

(B) 72 miles per hour

(C) 78 miles per hour

(D) 86 miles per hour

0122

A certain car averages 26 miles per gallon on the highway. The actual mileage varies from the average by at most 4 miles per gallon. Which of the following inequalities represents all possible gas mileage x, in gallons, of the car?

(A) $|x-4| \leq 26$

(B) $|x-4| \geq 26$

(C) $|x-26| \leq 4$

(D) $|x-26| \geq 4$

0123

The interior of Earth is chemically divided into layers. The mantle is the layer of the Earth that is more than 100 kilometers and less than 2900 kilometers below the Earth's surface. Which of the following inequalities describes all possible depth x, in kilometers, below the Earth's surface that are in the mantle?

(A) $|x+100| < 2,900$

(B) $|x-100| < 2,900$

(C) $|x+100| < 1,400$

(D) $|x-1,500| < 1,400$

0124

Andrea is considering accepting one of two sales positions. Company A offers a yearly salary of $39,000. Company B offers a yearly salary of $25,000 plus a 4% annual commission on sales. Which of the following statements about the amount of sales is true?

(A) Company B's salary is less than company A's salary when the amount of sales is over $35,000.

(B) Company B's salary is greater than company A's salary when the amount of sales is over $35,000.

(C) Company B's salary is less than company A's salary when the amount of sales is over $25,000.

(D) Company B's salary is greater than company A's salary when the amount of sales is over $25,000.

0125

Tom wants to make more than 12% brine by mixing 400g of 6% brine and 15% brine. How many grams of 15% brine does he need to mix?

(A) Between 500 grams and 600 grams of 15% brine.

(B) Between 600 grams and 700 grams of 15% brine.

(C) Between 700 grams and 800 grams of 15% brine.

(D) More than 800 grams of 15% brine.

0126

What is one possible solution to the inequality $|4x+1|-1 \le 2$?

0127

If $|3x-3|=18$, what is the positive value of $x-1$?

0128

$$|4x-3|=5$$

What is the sum of the solutions to the given equation above?

0129

$$-4 \le 2(3-x) < 10$$

What is the largest value of the solution for the given inequality above?

0130

If $4(2-y) \le 3y - \frac{1}{3}(y+6)$, what is the smallest possible value of $2y+1$?

0131

How many positive integers are in the solution set of $|4x-1|<5$?

0132

David and his two older sisters, Jenny and Ariel, are each two years apart in age. The sum of their ages is greater than the age of their mother, who is 54. What is the youngest age that David can be?

0133

Nick is a salesperson who sells furniture. He gets a base salary of $300 per week and a commission of 2% on every piece of furniture he sells. What is the total amount of furniture in dollars that Nick must sell to earn at least $800 a week?

0134

An online download movie club has a one−time registration fee of $15.5 and charges $2.25 for downloading each movie. If David has $100 to join the club and download movies, what is the maximum number of movies he can download?

0135

The local tennis club has a one−off registration fee of $20.5 and charges $6.50 per hour played. Jason's budget is $200. If he joins a tennis club and plays tennis, how many hours at most can he play?

0136

The company can produce bottled water using up to 2000 liters of water per day. If the volume of one bottle of water is 450 milliliters, which of the following is the largest bottled water a company can produce in a day?

4. System of Linear Equations and Inequalities

01. Solving System of Linear Equations

1. Definition

The general form of a system of linear equations in two variables is written as
$$\begin{cases} a_1 x + b_1 y = c_1 \\ a_2 x + b_2 y = c_2 \end{cases}$$

2. The solutions to the System

In most cases, a system of linear equation has one solution. However, the system sometimes has **infinitely many solutions or no solution**. The solution of a system of linear equations is the point of intersection of their graphs.

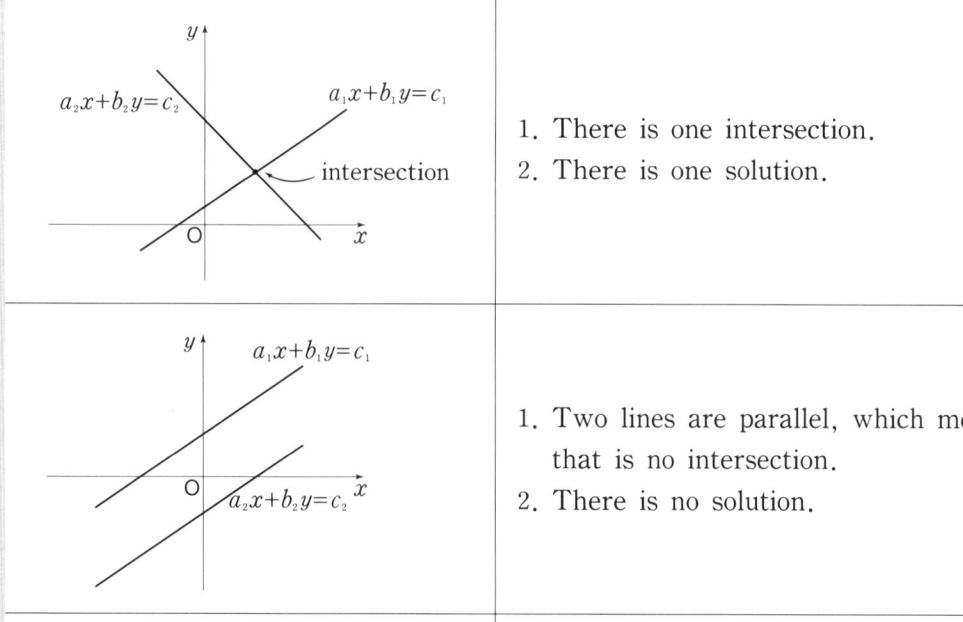

	1. There is one intersection. 2. There is one solution.
	1. Two lines are parallel, which means that is no intersection. 2. There is no solution.
	1. Since two lines are identical, there are infinitely many intersections. 2. There are infinitely many solutions.

3. Linear Systems with Infinitely Many Solutions

When one of the variables is eliminated, we have the equation $0 \cdot x = 0$ or $0 \cdot y = 0$.

If $\dfrac{a_1}{a_2} = \dfrac{b_1}{b_2} = \dfrac{c_1}{c_2}$, two equations are exactly equal so that there are infinitely many solutions to the system.

4. Linear Systems with No Solution

When one of the variables is eliminated, we have the equation $0 \cdot x \neq 0$ or $0 \cdot y \neq 0$.

If $\dfrac{a_1}{a_2} = \dfrac{b_1}{b_2} \neq \dfrac{c_1}{c_2}$, two lines are parallel, and there are no solution to the system.

Example 1

Solve the system.

(1) $\begin{cases} x - 2y = -6 \\ 2y - 2x = 9 \end{cases}$

(2) $\begin{cases} 4x + y = -5 \\ 3x - 2y = -12 \end{cases}$

(3) $\begin{cases} 2x - y = 2 \\ 4x - 2y = 4 \end{cases}$

(4) $\begin{cases} 2x + y = 1 \\ 6x + 3y = 4 \end{cases}$

Solution

(1) Solve the first equation for x.

$x - 2y = -6$

$x = 2y - 6$

Substitute $2y - 6$ for the other x

$2y - 2(2y - 6) = 9$

$2y - 4y + 12 = 9$

$-2y = -3, \quad y = \dfrac{3}{2}$

Now, substitute $\dfrac{3}{2}$ for y in $x = 2y - 6$.

$x = 2\left(\dfrac{3}{2}\right) - 6$

The solution is $\left(-3, \dfrac{3}{2}\right)$

(2) Multiply $4x + y = -5$ by 2 and then add.

$\begin{cases}(4x + y = -5) \cdot 2 \\ 3x - 2y = -12 \end{cases} \Rightarrow \begin{array}{r} 8x + 2y = -10 \\ - \underline{3x - 2y = -12} \\ 11x \quad\quad = -22 \\ x = -2 \end{array}$

Substitute -2 for x in $4x + y = -5$.

$4(-2) + y = -5$

$y = 3$

The solution is $(-2, 3)$

(3) Method 1:

$\begin{cases} 2x - y = 2 \quad \Rightarrow y = 2x - 2 \\ 4x - 2y = 4 \end{cases}$

Substitute $2x - 2$ for y in the second equation.

$4x - 2(2x - 2) = 4$

$4x - 4x + 4 = 4$

$4x - 4x = 4 - 4$

$0 \cdot x = 0$

Method 2:

From $\begin{cases} 2x - y = 2 \\ 4x - 2y = 4 \end{cases}$, we have $\dfrac{2}{4} = \dfrac{-1}{-2} = \dfrac{2}{4}$.

Therefore, the system has **infinitely many solutions.**

(4) Method 1:

$\begin{cases} 2x + y = 1 \quad \Rightarrow y = -2x + 1 \\ 6x + 3y = 4 \end{cases}$

Substitute $-2x + 1$ for y in the second equation.

$6x + 3(-2x + 1) = 4$

$6x - 6x + 3 = 4$

$6x - 6x = 4 - 3$

$0 \cdot x = 1 \rightarrow 0 \cdot x \neq 0$

Method 2:

From $\begin{cases} 2x + y = 1 \\ 6x + 3y = 4 \end{cases}$, we have $\dfrac{2}{6} = \dfrac{1}{3} \neq \dfrac{1}{4}$.

Therefore, the system has **no solution.**

02. System of Linear Inequalities

A system of linear inequalities in two variables consists of at least two linear inequalities in the same variables. **Solving systems of linear inequalities** means graphing each inequality, and then **finding the overlap** of the solutions.

Example 2

Graph the system of inequalities $\begin{cases} y \geq x+1 \\ y < -\dfrac{1}{2}x+1 \end{cases}$.

Solution

First, graph each inequality separately. The solution to the system is the region where the shadings from each inequality overlap one another.

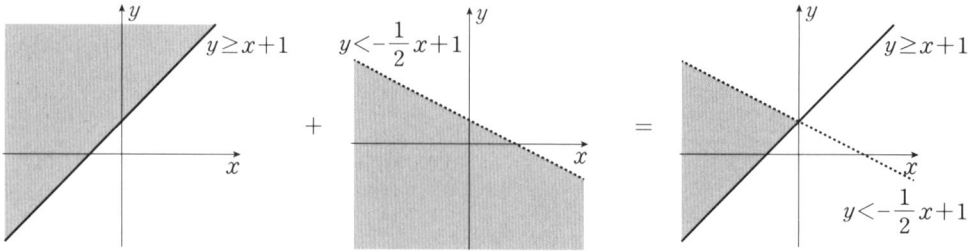

03. Application

The key to solving application problems is converting the words into mathematical equations. Refer to the following steps below.

1. **Understand thoroughly what the problem is asking you to do.**

2. **Represent unknown quantities with variables.**

3. **Form a system of equations that will relate known quantities to the unknown quantities.**

4. **Solve the system of equations.**

Example 3

Andrew is four years younger than twice Brian's. If the sum of their ages after 5 years is 45, how old are they now?

Solution

Let x and y be Andrew and Brian's current age, respectively. Then we have

$x=2y-4$ and $(x+5)+(y+5)=45$. Now, solve the system $\begin{cases} x=2y-4 \\ (x+5)+(y+5)=45 \end{cases}$.

$\begin{cases} x=2y-4 \\ (x+5)+(y+5)=45 \end{cases} \Rightarrow \begin{cases} x=2y-4 \\ x+y=35 \end{cases}$

Substitute $2y-4$ for x in the second equation.
$$(2y-4)+y=35$$
$$3y=39, \ y=13$$
Now, substitute 13 for y in the equation $x=2y-4$.
$$x=2(13)-4=22$$

Therefore, Andrew is now 22 years old and Brian is now 13 years old.

Example 4

The perimeter of rectangle is 64 inches. If the length of the rectangle is 4 inches less than twice the width, what is the area of the rectangle?

Solution

Let x and y be the width and length of the rectangle, respectively. Since the perimeter is 64 inches, $2x+2y=64$. Also, since the length of the rectangle is 4 inches less than twice

the width, $y=2x-4$. Now, solve the system $\begin{cases} 2x+2y=64 \\ y=2x-4 \end{cases}$.

$\begin{cases} 2x+2y=64 \\ y=2x-4 \end{cases} \Rightarrow \begin{cases} x+y=32 \\ y=2x-4 \end{cases}$

Substitute $2x-4$ for y in the first equation.
$$x+(2x-4)=32$$
$$3x=36, \ x=12$$
Now, substitute 12 for x in the equation $x+y=32$.
$$(12)+y=32, \ y=20$$

Therefore, the width is 12 inches and the length is 20 inches.

Practice **Problems**

0137

$$\begin{cases} 6x - 4y = -12 \\ 2x - y = -7 \end{cases}$$

If (x, y) is the solution to the given system of equations, what is the value of x?

(A) 8

(B) 12

(C) -8

(D) -12

0138

$$\begin{cases} x - 12y = 4 \\ 3x = 20y + 28 \end{cases}$$

In the system of equations above, what is the value of y in terms of x?

(A) $\dfrac{x}{16}$

(B) $\dfrac{x}{4}$

(C) $2x$

(D) $8x$

0139

$$\begin{cases} x - \dfrac{y}{3} = \dfrac{1}{3} \\ -\dfrac{x}{2} + \dfrac{2y}{5} = 1 \end{cases}$$

If (a, b) is the solution to the given system of equations, what is the value of $a + b$?

(A) 5

(B) 7

(C) 12

(D) 17

0140

$$\begin{cases} 2x - y = 9 \\ 3ax + ay = 11 \end{cases}$$

If the $x-$coordinate of the solution to the given system is 4, what is the value of a?

(A) 1

(B) 2

(C) 3

(D) 4

0141

$$\begin{cases} ax - by = 5 \\ bx + ay = -2 \end{cases}$$

If $x = 2$ and $y = -1$ is solution to the given system of equations, what is the value of a?

(A) $\dfrac{11}{4}$

(B) $\dfrac{12}{5}$

(C) $\dfrac{11}{6}$

(D) $\dfrac{12}{7}$

0142

$$\begin{cases} -x + 2y = 3 \\ 3x - 6y = -8 \end{cases}$$

How many solutions does the given system of equations have?

(A) Zero

(B) Exactly one

(C) Exactly two

(D) Infinitely many

0143

$$\begin{cases} x-4y=7 \\ 8y=2x-15 \end{cases}$$

How many solutions (x, y) are there to the system of equations above?

(A) Zero

(B) Exactly one

(C) Exactly two

(D) Infinitely many

0144

$$\begin{cases} 6x-by=-5 \\ -3x+5y=2 \end{cases}$$

If the system of equations given above has exactly one solution, which of the following could be the value of b? (b is a constant)

      I. 5   II. 10   III. 15

(A) I only

(B) II only

(C) I and II only

(D) I and III only

0145

$$\begin{cases} 3x-2y=14 \\ 2x+7y=19 \end{cases}$$

If the solution to the given system of equation is (x, y), what is the value of $5x+5y$?

(A) 5

(B) -5

(C) 33

(D) 47

0146

$$\begin{cases} x+4y=a \\ 2x=by+10 \end{cases}$$

If the system of equations given above has infinitely many solutions, which of the following is true for the values of a and b?

(A) $a=5$, $b=-8$

(B) $a=-5$, $b=8$

(C) $a=8$, $b=-5$

(D) $a=-8$, $b=5$

0147

$$4a-3b=13$$

One of the two equation in a linear system is given above. If the system has no solution, which of the following could the second equation in the system?

(A) $6b-8a=-26$

(B) $4a+3b=13$

(C) $2a+\dfrac{3}{2}b=6$

(D) $12a-9b=-13$

0148

$$\begin{cases} 2x+6y=a \\ 3x-by=6 \end{cases}$$

For which of the following values of a and b does the system of equations have no solution?

(A) $a\neq4,\ b=-9$

(B) $a=4,\ b\neq-9$

(C) $a=-9,\ b=4$

(D) $a\neq-9,\ b=4$

0149

If $3m-n+2k=7$, $m+n=3$, and $m-k=4$, what is the value of n?

(A) -1

(B) 0

(C) 1

(D) 2

0150

$$\begin{cases} x+ay=-3 \\ 3x+by=5 \end{cases}$$

If the ordered pair $(1,\ 2)$ is a solution to the system of equations above, which of the following is true?

(A) $a>0$

(B) $b<0$

(C) $a=2b$

(D) $a=-2b$

0151

$$\begin{cases} 2x-y=3 \\ -6x+3y=-9 \end{cases}$$

Which of the following points in terms of k, where k is a constant, lies on the graph of each equation above in the $xy-$plane?

(A) $(k,\ 2k-3)$

(B) $\left(2k,\ \dfrac{k+3}{2}\right)$

(C) $(2k-3,\ k)$

(D) $\left(\dfrac{k+3}{2},\ 2k\right)$

0152

If both systems $\begin{cases} 4x - ay = 7 \\ 5x + y = 13 \end{cases}$ and $\begin{cases} 2x - 3y = -5 \\ bx - 4y = 9 \end{cases}$ have the same solution, what is the value of ab?

(A) 3

(B) 3.5

(C) 4

(D) 4.5

0153

$$\begin{cases} 2x - 3y > -1 \\ -x + 5y \leq 3 \end{cases}$$

Which of the following points does not lies in the solution region of the system of inequalities above?

(A) $(1, \ 2)$

(B) $(1, \ -2)$

(C) $(-1, \ -2)$

(D) $(2, \ -1)$

0154

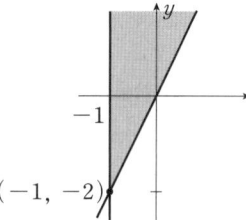

Which of the following inequalities represent the graph above?

(A) $\begin{cases} x \geq -1 \\ y \geq -2x \end{cases}$

(B) $\begin{cases} y \geq -1 \\ y \leq 2x \end{cases}$

(C) $\begin{cases} x \geq -1 \\ y \geq 2x \end{cases}$

(D) $\begin{cases} y \geq -1 \\ y \leq -2x \end{cases}$

0155

$$\begin{cases} 3x - 2y > -6 \\ y \geq 12 \end{cases}$$

The point $(a, \ 12)$ is a solution to the system of inequalities in the $xy-$plane. Which of the following could be the value of a?

(A) 2

(B) 4

(C) 6

(D) 8

0156

$$\begin{cases} 5x-2y>32 \\ 2x-3y<10 \end{cases}$$

The point $(8,\ y)$ is a solution to the system of inequalities in the $xy-$plane. Which of the following could be the value of y?

(A) 1

(B) 2

(C) 3

(D) 4

0157

$$\begin{cases} y>4x+1 \\ 3x+2>8 \end{cases}$$

Which of the following consists of the $y-$coordinates of all points satisfying the system of inequality above?

(A) $y>9$

(B) $y<9$

(C) $y>13$

(D) $y<13$

0158

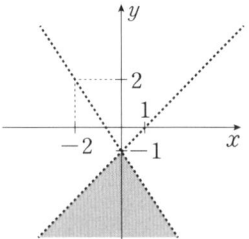

Which of the following inequalities represent the graph above?

(A) $\begin{cases} y<-\dfrac{3}{2}x-1 \\ y<x-1 \end{cases}$

(B) $\begin{cases} y>-\dfrac{3}{2}x-1 \\ y<x-1 \end{cases}$

(C) $\begin{cases} y>-\dfrac{3}{2}x-1 \\ y>x-1 \end{cases}$

(D) $\begin{cases} y<-\dfrac{3}{2}x-1 \\ y>x-1 \end{cases}$

0159

Mike, who runs the restaurant, ordered 20 packages of buns from a wholesaler. Some packages include 12 buns each, some of them 8 buns each. If he has a total of 188 buns, how many packages of 8 buns Mike ordered?

(A) 12 packages

(B) 13 packages

(C) 14 packages

(D) 15 packages

0160

Charles bought several dozen pencils and pens at the local mart. The pencils cost $4.50 per dozen, and the pens cost $6.50 per dozen. If Charles bought 8 dozen pencils and pens a total of $42, how many dozens of pencils did he buy?

(A) 2 dozens of pencils

(B) 3 dozens of pencils

(C) 4 dozens of pencils

(D) 5 dozens of pencils

0161

A small bakery in town sells only two croissants a butter croissant and a chocolate cream croissant. Three butter croissants and four chocolate cream croissants costs $16. Four butter croissants and two chocolate cream croissants costs $13. How much would it cost if a customer purchases two butter croissants and three chocolate cream croissants?

(A) $11

(B) $11.5

(C) $12

(D) $12.5

0162

An airplane flies with a tail wind from New York to Los Angeles, a distance of 2550 miles, in 5 hours. On the return trip against the same wind, the airplane flies back in 6 hours. If x is the speed of the airplane in still air and y is the speed of the wind, which of the following system of equations is correct?

(A) $\begin{cases} 5x+5y=2550 \\ 6x-6y=2550 \end{cases}$

(B) $\begin{cases} 5x-5y=2550 \\ 6x+6y=2550 \end{cases}$

(C) $\begin{cases} 5x+5y=1275 \\ 6x-6y=1275 \end{cases}$

(D) $\begin{cases} 5x-5y=1275 \\ 6x+6y=1275 \end{cases}$

0163

A chemist has a 16% saline solution and a 25% saline solution. He wants to make 36 liters of a 20% saline solution by mixing a 16% solution and a 25% solution. If a and b are the liters of a 16% and 25% saline solution, respectively, which of the following system of equations is correct?

(A) $\begin{cases} a-b=36 \\ 0.16a+0.25b=0.2 \end{cases}$

(B) $\begin{cases} a-b=36 \\ 16a+25b=20(a-b) \end{cases}$

(C) $\begin{cases} a+b=36 \\ 0.16a+0.25b=a+b \end{cases}$

(D) $\begin{cases} a+b=36 \\ 16a+25b=20(a+b) \end{cases}$

0164

This week, Emily can work up to 32 hours and must earn at least $600 to pay for her apartment rent. She earns $18 an hour doing math tutoring and $15 an hour serving in a restaurant. If x represents hours worked as math tutor and y represents hours worked in restaurants, which of the following systems of inequality represents the situation?

(A) $\begin{cases} x+y \leq 32 \\ 18x+15y \geq 600 \end{cases}$

(B) $\begin{cases} x+y \geq 32 \\ 18x+15y \leq 600 \end{cases}$

(C) $\begin{cases} x+y \leq 32 \\ 15x+18y \geq 600 \end{cases}$

(D) $\begin{cases} x+y \geq 32 \\ 15x+18y \leq 600 \end{cases}$

0165

There are m men and w women in a bus. If 4 women get off the bus, the number of men is twice the number of women. Which of the following equations represent the relationship between m and w?

(A) $w = \dfrac{m+4}{2}$

(B) $w = \dfrac{m+8}{2}$

(C) $w = 2m-4$

(D) $w = 2(m-4)$

0166

$$\begin{cases} ax+y=2 \\ 3x-by=1 \end{cases}$$

If the solution to the given system of equations is $(1, 3)$, what is the value of $a+b$?

0167

$$\begin{cases} 3x+y=4 \\ 2x-5y=14 \end{cases}$$

If (x, y) satisfies the system of equations above, what is the value of y?

0168

$$\begin{cases} x=ay+2 \\ 3x-4y=5 \end{cases}$$

For what value of a does the given system have no solution?

0169

$$\begin{cases} 2(x-3)+3y=-9 \\ 2(5-y)-x=11 \end{cases}$$

If (x, y) is the solution to the given system of equations, what is the value of $x+y$?

0170

$$\begin{cases} x+\dfrac{y-1}{3}=1 \\ \dfrac{2x+6}{5}-\dfrac{y+2}{2}=2 \end{cases}$$

If (x, y) is the solution to the given system of equations, what is the value of x?

0171

$$\begin{cases} 15a-28b=123 \\ 13a-27b=123 \end{cases}$$

If (a, b) is the solution to the given system of equations, what is the value of $a-b$?

0172

$$\begin{cases} y=(4a+b)x+5 \\ y=ax-(3b+7) \end{cases}$$

If the graphs of the two equations above are identical, what is the value of ab?

0173

$$7x+2y=4x+y=2x-y-4$$

If (x, y) is the solution to the given equation above, what is the value of $x+y$?

0174

$$\begin{cases} y\geq-2 \\ x\geq1 \\ 2x+y\leq6 \end{cases}$$

For the system of linear inequalities above, find the area of the solution region.

0175

The perimeter of the rectangle is 24 feet. When the rectangle is doubled in length and tripled in width, the perimeter of the new rectangle will be 10 feet greater than twice the perimeter of the original rectangle. Find the width of the original rectangle.

0176

Kevin is 22 years older than his son, Paul. If Kevin is twice as old as Paul in 7 years, how old is Paul now?

0177

If 4 burgers and 3 soft drinks cost $26 and 3 burgers and 6 soft drinks cost $27, how much is a burger and soft drink combined?

0178

Admission tickets for adults and students at the museum were sold for $15 and $9 respectively. If the total revenue of the tickets sold was $2,250 and there were 170 attendees, how many adult tickets were sold?

0179

202 people have a seminar with 60 tables. Some of the tables can seat 2 people each, while others can seat 4 people each. Assuming all tables are full and everyone attends the seminar, how many tables exactly are tables for two?

II

Advanced Math

1. Operations with Polynomials

01. Multiplication of Polynomials

1. Binomial × Binomial

$$(a+b)(c+d)=\overset{①}{(\overline{a\times c})}+\overset{②}{(\overline{a\times d})}+\overset{③}{(\overline{b\times c})}+\overset{④}{(\overline{b\times d})}$$

$$\qquad\qquad\quad \text{First}\qquad \text{Outer}\qquad \text{Inner}\qquad \text{Last}$$

$$=ac+ad+bc+bd$$

2. Binomial × Trinomial

$$(a+2)(a+1)=\overset{①}{(\overline{a\times a})}+\overset{②}{(\overline{a\times 1})}+\overset{③}{(\overline{2\times a})}+\overset{④}{(\overline{2\times 1})}$$

$$=a^2+a+2a+2=a^2+3a+2$$

3. Special Cases

(1) $(a+b)^2=a^2+2ab+b^2 \quad \rightarrow \quad (\varDelta+O)^2=\varDelta^2+2\varDelta O+O^2$

(2) $(a-b)^2=a^2-2ab+b^2 \quad \rightarrow \quad (\varDelta-O)^2=\varDelta^2-2\varDelta O+O^2$

(3) $(a+b)(a-b) \quad \rightarrow \quad (\varDelta-O)^2=\varDelta^2-2\varDelta O+O^2$

4. Multiplication by Grouping

If the expression has a common part (usually a binomial), then use the substitution to multiply the polynomials.

Example 1

Multiply the polynomials.

(1) $(2a+3)(a-4)$

(2) $(4a-1)^2$

(3) $(5x-3)(5x+3)$

(4) $(x+y+2)(x+y-2)$

Solution

(1) $(2a+3)(a-4)=(2a\times a)+(2a\times -4)+(3\times a)+(3\times -4)$
$\qquad\qquad\qquad =2a^2-8a+3a-12=2a^2-5a-12$

(2) $(4a-1)^2=(4a)^2-2(4a)(1)+1^2=16a^2-8a+1$

(3) $(5x-3)(5x+3)=(5x)^2-3^2=25x^2-9$

(4) $(x+y+2)(x+y-2) \quad \rightarrow \quad$ Let $x+y=A$
$\quad =(A+2)(A-2)=A^2-2^2$
$\quad =(x+y)^2-2^2$
$\quad =x^2+2xy+y^2-4$

Example 2

$$(x-a)(2x+3)=2x^2+bx-12$$

Find the value of a and b in the equation given above.

Solution

$$(x-a)(2x+3)=2x^2+3x-2ax-3a$$
$$=2x^2+(3-2a)x-3a$$

Since $2x^2+(3-2a)x-3a=2x^2+bx-12$,

$3a=12$ and $3-2a=b$

$a=4$ $3-2(4)=b,\ b=-5$

$$a=4,\ b=-5$$

02. Factoring Polynomials

First, if each term in the polynomial has a greatest common factor, the factors are grouped together and factored.

1. Binomial: $a^2-b^2=(a-b)(a+b)$

2. Trinomial: $x^2+(a+b)x+ab$

$$x^2+\underline{(a+b)}x+\underline{ab}=(x+a)(x+b)$$ → The coefficient of x^2 is 1.

Find a and b such that

(1) Their product is equal to the constant term ab.

(2) Sum of a and b is equal to coefficient of x.

3. Trinomial: $acx^2+(ad+bc)x+bd$

$acx^2+(ad+bc)x+bd$ → The coefficient of x^2 is <u>NOT</u> 1.

$$
\begin{array}{lll}
ax & b \to & bcx \\
cx & d \to & \underline{(+)\ adx} \\
& & (ad+bc)x
\end{array}
$$

$$\Rightarrow (ax+b)(cx+d)$$

If you multiply in the diagonal direction as shown above, the sum of the two terms is the same as the middle term.

4. Factoring by Grouping

Polynomials with four terms can usually be factored by grouping terms.

Example 3

Factor the polynomial.

(1) $2x^2-4x$

(2) $4a^2-25$

(3) $x^2-3x-10$

(4) $2x^2+3x-2$

(5) $3(x+2)^2+48(x+2)$

(6) a^3+2a^2-4a-8

Solution

(1) $2x^2-4x=2x(x-2)$

(2) $4a^2-25=(2a)^2-5^2=(2a-5)(2a+5)$

(3) Two integers whose product is -10 and whose sum is -3 are -5 and 2.
$$x^2-3x-10=(x-5)(x+2)$$

(4) $(\underbrace{2x^2+3x-2}_{2\times-2=-4}) \rightarrow -4=-1\times4 \Rightarrow -1+4=3$

$$\begin{array}{cc} 2x & -1 \rightarrow & -x \\ x & 2 \rightarrow & (+)\ \underline{\quad 4x} \\ & & 3x \end{array}$$

$$2x^2+3x-2=(2x-1)(x+2)$$

(5) $3(x+2)^2+48(x+2)=3A^2+48A \qquad \rightarrow$ Let $x+2=A$
$$=3A(A+16)=3(x+2)(x+2+16)$$
$$=3(x+2)(x+18)$$

(6) $a^3+2a^2-4a-8=(a^3+2a^2)-(4a+8) \quad \rightarrow$ Group the first two and the last two terms
$$=a^2(\underline{a+2})-4(\underline{a+2}) \qquad \rightarrow \text{Find the common factor}$$
$$=(a+2)(a^2-4) \qquad \rightarrow \text{Factor out } (a+2)$$
$$=(a+2)(a-2)(a+2)$$
$$=(a+2)^2(a-2)$$

Practice **Problems**

0180

$2(3x^2+2)-6(x^2-3x)$

Which of the following is equal to the expression above?

(A) 20

(B) $18x+4$

(C) $-18x+4$

(D) $22x$

0181

$(4x^2-2+5x)+2(3x^2+3x-7)$

Which of the following is equal to the expression above?

(A) $10x^2+11x+12$

(B) $10x^2+11x-16$

(C) $-2x^2-x-16$

(D) $-2x^2-x+12$

0182

$x+3-\dfrac{3(2-x)}{5}$

Which of the following is equal to the expression above?

(A) $\dfrac{2x+9}{5}$

(B) $\dfrac{2x+21}{5}$

(C) $\dfrac{8x+9}{5}$

(D) $\dfrac{8x+21}{5}$

0183

$(x^2-1)(2x+3)$

Which of the following is equal to the expression above?

(A) $2x^2-3$

(B) $2x^3-3$

(C) $2x^2-x-3$

(D) $2x^3+3x^2-2x-3$

0184

$(3a+2)(4+a-a^2)$

Which of the following is equal to the expression above?

(A) $-3a^3+5a^2+10a-8$

(B) $-3a^3-5a^2+10a+8$

(C) $-3a^3+a^2+14a+8$

(D) $-3a^3-a^2+11a+8$

0185

$3x^4-12x^2$

Which of the following is equal to the expression above?

(A) $3x(x-2)(x+2)$

(B) $3x(x^2+4)$

(C) $3x^2(x-2)(x+2)$

(D) $3x^2(x^2+4)$

0186

Which expression is equivalent to $6xy^3 - 54xy$?

(A) $6xy(y^2)$

(B) $6xy(9y^2)$

(C) $6xy(y^2 - 8)$

(D) $6xy(y-3)(y+3)$

0187

Which of the following is equal to
$(4x-3)(4x+3) - 4(2x-1)^2$?

(A) $16x - 5$

(B) $16x - 13$

(C) $8x^2 + 16x - 9$

(D) $8x^2 - 16x - 13$

0188

$x(3a - 2b) + 4y(2b - 3a)$

Which of the following is equal to the expression above?

(A) $(3a - 2b)(x - 4y)$

(B) $(3a - 2b)(x + 4y)$

(C) $(2b - 3a)(x - 4y)$

(D) $(2b - 3a)(x + 4y)$

0189

Which of the following is equal to
$\dfrac{3(2a^2 + a - 1)}{2} + \dfrac{3a - a^2 + 1}{6}$?

(A) $\dfrac{17a^2 + 12a - 8}{2}$

(B) $\dfrac{17a^2 + 12a - 8}{6}$

(C) $\dfrac{5a^2 + 6a - 2}{2}$

(D) $\dfrac{5a^2 + 6a - 2}{6}$

0190

If $\dfrac{x - 2y}{3} - \dfrac{3x + 2y}{4} = ax + by$, what is the value of $a + b$?

(A) $\dfrac{3}{4}$

(B) 4

(C) $-\dfrac{19}{12}$

(D) -4

0191

If $ax^2 - c = (2x + a)(x + b)$, what is the value of $a + b + c$?

(A) 3

(B) 4

(C) 5

(D) 6

0192

If $m=x-1$, then which of the following is $1-2x+x^2$ in terms of m?

(A) m^2

(B) m^2-2

(C) m^2-m-2

(D) $2-m^2$

0193

If the expression $4ab^2\left(\dfrac{a^2}{2}-3b\right)$ is equal to $ma^3b^2-12ab^3$, where m is a constant, what is the value of m?

(A) $\dfrac{1}{2}$

(B) 2

(C) 4

(D) 8

0194

If the coefficient of y of $(3+2y)(ay^2-3y+b)$ is 8, what is the value of b?

(A) 8

(B) 8.5

(C) 9

(D) 9.5

0195

$$(ax^2+3x-4)(2x-b)=10x^3+11x^2-5x-4$$

If the equation above is true for all x, where a and b are constants, what is the value of $a+b$?

(A) 1

(B) 2

(C) 3

(D) 4

0196

$$(x+1)(x^2-2x+3)$$

If the expression above can be written as ax^3+bx^2+cx+d, where a, b, c, and d are constants, what is the value of c?

(A) 1

(B) 2

(C) 3

(D) 4

0197

Suppose that $A=x^2-2x+3$, $B=3x^2-2$, and $C=2x^2+x$. If $3A-B+2C=ax^2+bx+c$, what is the value of $a+b+c$?

(A) 8

(B) 9

(C) 10

(D) 11

0198

$$6x^3 - 13x^2y + 6xy^2$$

Which of the following is equal to the expression above?

(A) $(3x^2 - 2y)(2x - 3y)$

(B) $x(3x - 2y)(2x - 3y)$

(C) $(6x^2 - 3y)(x - 2y)$

(D) $x(6x - 3y)(x - 2y)$

0199

$$\frac{a^2 - 16}{a - 4} = b^2 - 16$$

In the equation above, a and b are constants and $a \neq 4$. Which of the expressions is equal to a?

(A) $b^2 - 20$

(B) $b^2 - 12$

(C) $b - 12$

(D) $b - 20$

0200

$$a(x - y) + b(y - x)$$

Which of the following is equal to the expression above?

(A) $(x - y)(a - b)$

(B) $(x - y)(a + b)$

(C) $(y - x)(a - b)$

(D) $(y - x)(a + b)$

0201

$$x^3 - 2x^2 - 9x + 18$$

One of the factors from the expression above is $x + a$, where a is a positive constant. What is the value of a?

(A) 2

(B) 3

(C) 6

(D) 9

0202

$$2a^4 - 32b^4 = 2(a - 2b)(a + 2b)(a^2 + mb^2)$$

Which of the following is value of m in the expression above?

(A) -2

(B) 2

(C) -4

(D) 4

0203

If $3a - 2b = 4$ and $9a^2 - 4b^2 = 24$, what is the value of $6a + 4b$?

(A) 6

(B) 8

(C) 10

(D) 12

0204

In the polynomial $2x^3 - kx^2 - 8x + 4k$, where k is a constant, which of the following is NOT a factor of this polynomial ?

(A) $x - 2k$

(B) $2x - k$

(C) $x - 2$

(D) $x + 2$

0205

If $a^2 - b^2 = 2$ and the value of $a - b$ is between -2 and 0, then which of the following must be the value of $a + b$?

(A) Less than -2

(B) Between -2 and -1

(C) Less than -1

(D) Between -1 and 0

0206

In some expression, $a^2 - 3a - 2$ should be added to A, but subtracted from A by mistake. If the resulting expression is $4a^2 + 5a - 4$, which of the following is the expression A?

(A) $3a^2 + 8a - 2$

(B) $5a^2 + 2a - 6$

(C) $6a^2 - a - 8$

(D) $6a^2 + 2a - 2$

0207

A rectangular garden is a feet wide. The length of the floor is 12 feet longer than the width. Which of the following represents the perimeter (in feet) of a garden in terms of a?

(A) $2a + 12$

(B) $4a + 24$

(C) $2a + 24$

(D) $a^2 + 12a$

0208

A badminton court shaped like a rectangle has a width of $2k + 1$ feet. If the length of the court is 5 feet longer than twice the width, which expression gives the area, $A(k)$ of the tennis court in square feet?

(A) $A(k) = 8k^2 + 18k + 7$

(B) $A(k) = 16k^2 + 16k + 6$

(C) $A(k) = 20k^2 + 20k + 5$

(D) $A(k) = 40k^2 + 40k + 10$

For questions 209~210, refer to the following figure below.

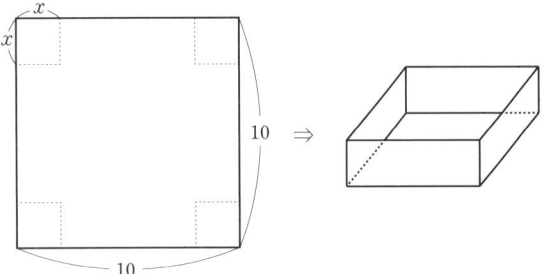

The open box is made by removing and folding the four identical corners of a square sheet as shown above.

0209

Which of the following quantities is represented by $4x(10-2x)$?

(A) The area of four squares removed from the sheet

(B) The area of the bottom of the box

(C) The area of four faces of the box

(D) The surface area of the open box

0210

Which of the following represents the volume V of the box in terms of x?

(A) $V=x(10-x)^2$

(B) $V=2x(10-x)^2$

(C) $V=x(10-2x)^2$

(D) $V=2x(10-2x)^2$

0211

The unit of the side of the cube is a. The new cube is formed with each side 4 units longer than the original cube's side. Which of the following represents the volume V of the new cube in terms of a?

(A) $V=a^3+12a^2+48a+64$

(B) $V=a^3+48a^2+12a+64$

(C) $V=a^3-48a^2+12a-64$

(D) $V=a^3-12a^2+48a-64$

0212

$$6(2a^3-a^2+4)-3(4a^3-3a^2-4a+2)$$

If the above expression is equal to $ma^2+na+18$, what is the value of $m+n$?

0213

If $(3a^2-4a+6)-2(a^2-2a+5)=5$, what is one possible value of $3a+10$?

0214

$$\frac{3x-1}{2}+\frac{x+2}{3}=\frac{ax+b}{c}$$

If the equation above is true for all x, what is the value of $a+b+c$?

0215

If $(x-a)(2x+3)=2x^2+bx-12$, what is the value of $a+b$?

0216

If $(3x+1)(x-2)=ax^2+bx+c$ for all x, what is the value of $a+b+c$?

0217

$$(x-3)(x^2-x+1)$$

If the expression above can be written as ax^3+bx^2+cx+d, where a, b, c, and d are constants, what is the value of $a+b+c+d$?

0218

$$(2x^2+ax-b)(4x+3)=8x^3+14x^2+2x-3$$

If the equation above is true for all x, where a and b are constants, what is the value of $a+b$?

0219

If $(x-3)(5x+a)=5x^2-11x+b$, what is the value of b?

0220

If the sum of $5x^2-6x+3$ and $(2x+1)(x-2)$ can be written in the form ax^2+bx+c, then what is the value of $a+b+c$?

0221

If $x^2=3$ and $y^2=5$, what is the value of $\left(\dfrac{2x}{3}-\dfrac{y}{5}\right)\left(\dfrac{2x}{3}+\dfrac{y}{5}\right)$?

0222

$$x^2+4x+3=(x+1)^2+m(x+1)+n$$

For all values of x, the above expression is always true and m and n are constants. What is the value of n?

0223

If $x+y=4$ and $x-y=-3$, what is the value of $x^2(x-y)+y^2(y-x)$?

0224

If $a+b=8$ and $ab=6$, what is the value of a^2+b^2?

0225

If the value of x^2-x-12 when $x=\sqrt{3}+4$ is equal to $a+b\sqrt{c}$, what is the value of a?

0226

If $9y^2-16x^4=-8$ and $4x^2-3y=2$, what is the value of $3y+4x^2$?

0227

One of the factors of $2x^3-18x$ is $x+k$, where k is a positive integer. What is the value of k?

0228

One of the factors of $6x^3+5x^2-6x$ is $x+m$, where m is a positive constant. What is the value of m?

For questions 229~230, refer to the following expression below.

$$x=1-\sqrt{2},\ y=1+\sqrt{2}$$

0229

Find the value of b if $x^2-y^2=a\sqrt{b}$, where b is the smallest integer.

0230

Find the value of $x^2-2xy+y^2$.

2. Quadratic Equations

01. Solving by finding Square Roots

1. Solving by finding Square Roots

Every positive number has two square roots a positive square root and a negative square root.

(1) $ax^2=b$, where $\left(\dfrac{b}{a}\geq 0\right)$.

$\Rightarrow x^2=\dfrac{b}{a}$, $x=\pm\sqrt{\dfrac{b}{a}}$

(2) $(x+a)^2=b$, where $(b\geq 0)$.

$\Rightarrow x+a=\pm\sqrt{b}$, $x=-a\pm\sqrt{b}$

2. Solving by Factoring

(1) Write the quadratic function in standard form. $\Rightarrow ax^2+bx+c=0$

(2) Factor the left side of a quadratic equation. $\Rightarrow a(x-\alpha)(x-\beta)=0$

(3) Use Zero–Product Property:

$a(x-\alpha)(x-\beta)=0$	$a(x-\alpha)^2=0$
$x-\alpha=0$ or $x-\beta=0$	$x-\alpha=0$
$x=\alpha$ or $\quad x=\beta$	$x=\alpha$

3. Using the Quadratic Formula

The solutions to the equation $x^2+bx+c=0$ $(a\neq 0)$ are $x=\dfrac{-b\pm\sqrt{b^2-4ac}}{2a}$.

Example 1

Solve the equation.

(1) $2(x+1)^2+3=15$

(2) $x^2-4=4x+1$

Solution

(1) $2(x+1)^2+3=15$

$\quad 2(x+1)^2=12$

$\quad (x+1)^2=6$

$\quad\quad x+1=\pm\sqrt{6}$

$\quad\quad\quad x=-1\pm\sqrt{6}$

$\quad\quad\quad\quad x=-1-\sqrt{6}$ and $x=-1+\sqrt{6}$.

(2) $\quad\quad x^2-4=4x+1$

$\quad\quad x^2-4x-5=0$

$\quad (x-5)(x+1)=0$

$\quad x-5=0$ or $x+1=0$

$\quad\quad\quad x=5$ or $x=-1$

Example 2

Which of the following is the solution of the equation $x^2+3x-1=0$?

(A) $x=\dfrac{3\pm\sqrt{5}}{2}$ (B) $x=\dfrac{-3\pm\sqrt{5}}{2}$ (C) $x=\dfrac{3\pm\sqrt{13}}{2}$ (D) $x=\dfrac{-3\pm\sqrt{13}}{2}$

Solution

The equation is in appropriate form $ax^2+bx+c=0$. Since the coefficients can be identified as $a=1$, $b=3$,

and $c=-1$, substitute these values into the formula $x=\dfrac{-b\pm\sqrt{b^2-4ac}}{2a}$.

$$x=\frac{-3\pm\sqrt{(3)^2-4(1)(-1)}}{2(1)}$$

$$=\frac{-3\pm\sqrt{9+4}}{2}=\frac{-3\pm\sqrt{13}}{2}$$

The answer is D.

02. Solutions and Coefficients

1. Discriminant

In quadratic formula $x=\dfrac{-b\pm\sqrt{b^2-4ac}}{2a}$, the part b^2-4ac is called the discriminant D, and this is to determine the nature of the solutions of a quadratic equation.

Let $ax^2+bx+c=0\,(a\neq 0)$ be a quadratic equation with real coefficients.
1. $D=b^2-4ac>0 \rightarrow$ There are two real solutions.
2. $D=b^2-4ac=0 \rightarrow$ There is one real solution.
3. $D=b^2-4ac<0 \rightarrow$ There is no real solution.

2. The Sum and Product of the Solutions

Let the solutions of the quadratic equation, $ax^2+bx+c=0$ $(a\neq 0)$, be α and β. Then

(1) The sum of solutions $\alpha+\beta=-\dfrac{b}{a}$

(2) The product of solutions $\alpha\beta=\dfrac{c}{a}$

Example 3

Without solving the equation $2x^2=5x-4$, determine the nature of its solutions.

Solution

$2x^2=5x-4$

$2x^2-5x+4=0 \rightarrow a=2$, $b=-5$, and $c=4$

$D=b^2-4ac=(-5)^2-4(2)(4)=25-32=-7<0$

There is no real solution.

Example 4

Find the values of k for which the equation $x^2-6x+k=0$ has two real solutions.

Solution

$x^2-6x+k=0 \rightarrow a=1$, $b=-6$ and $c=k$
$D=(-6)^2-4(1)(k)>0$
$\quad\quad\quad 36-4k>0$, $k<9$

$k<9$

Example 5

Find the sum and product of solutions of the equations $3x^2-4x+5=0$.

Solution

$3x^2-4x+5=0 \rightarrow a=3$, $b=-4$ and $c=5$

Sum of the solutions: $-\dfrac{b}{a}=-\dfrac{-4}{3}=\dfrac{4}{3}$

Product of the solutions: $\dfrac{c}{a}=\dfrac{5}{3}$

The sum is $\dfrac{4}{3}$ and the product is $\dfrac{5}{3}$.

03. Applications

Solve the application problems using quadratic equations in the following order.

1. Let x be the unknown needed to be solved in the problem.

2. Write a quadratic equation.

3. Solve the equation to find the solution.

4. Make sure the solution you find fits the meaning of the problem.

Example 6

Find two consecutive positive odd integers whose product is 255.

Solution

Let x and $x+2$ be two consecutive positive odd integers. Then we have
$$x(x+2)=255$$
$$x^2+2x-255=0$$
$$(x+17)(x-15)=0$$
$$x=-17 \text{ or } x=15$$
Since $x>0$, $x=15$. So two integers are $x=15$ and $x=17$.

Two integers are 15 and 17.

Example 7

At noon, John left school walking at 6 km per hour due south; an hour later, Chris left school walking at 5 km per hour due east. After how many hours will the boys be 13 km apart?

Solution

Let John left school x hours ago. Then, Chris left school $x-1$ hours ago.

	John	Chris
Rate	6	5
Time	x	$x-1$
Distance	$6x$	$5(x-1)$

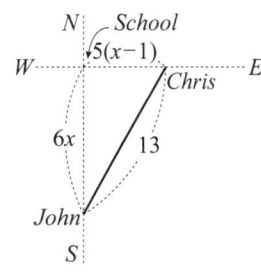

By the Pythagorean Theorem, we have

$$(6x)^2+(5(x-1))^2=13^2$$
$$36x^2+25x^2-50x+25=169$$
$$61x^2-50x-144=0$$
$$(61x+72)(x-2)=0$$
$$x=-\frac{72}{61} \text{ or } x=2$$

Since the time must be positive, $x=2$.

The boys will be 13 km apart in 2 hours

0231

Which of the following quadratic equations does NOT have $x=-2$ as the solution?

(A) $x^2+4x+4=0$

(B) $x^2+2x=0$

(C) $2x^2+5x+2=0$

(D) $2x^2-5x+2=0$

0232

If $x^2-12x+36=0$, what is the value of $x-6$?

(A) -12

(B) -6

(C) 0

(D) 6

0233

$$x^2-3x+1=0$$

Which of the following is the solution to the equation above?

(A) $x=\dfrac{3\pm\sqrt{5}}{2}$

(B) $x=\dfrac{-3\pm\sqrt{5}}{2}$

(C) $x=-3-\sqrt{5}$

(D) $x=3-\sqrt{5}$

0234

If the quadratic equation $2x^2-4x-1=0$ is solved by using quadratic formula, the solution is $x=a\pm\dfrac{\sqrt{b}}{c}$, where a, b, and c are positive integers. Find the value of abc.

(A) 8

(B) 12

(C) 16

(D) 20

0235

$$x^2+6x-6=0$$

What is the sum of the solutions to the equation above?

(A) -6

(B) 6

(C) -3

(D) 3

0236

$$2(x+1)^2+3=15$$

What is the sum of the solutions to the equation above?

(A) -1

(B) -2

(C) $-1-2\sqrt{6}$

(D) $-2-\sqrt{6}$

0237

If $(2a-5)^2-7(2a-5)+10=0$, what is the value of $5-2a$?

(A) 2

(B) 4

(C) -4

(D) -5

0238

For which of the following equations is the sum of its solutions a positive number?

(A) $x^2+4x=0$

(B) $x^2+x+3=0$

(C) $x^2-x+3=0$

(D) $3-4x-x^2=0$

0239

If the sum of solutions of the quadratic equation $2x^2-6x+9=0$ is one of the solution of the quadratic equation $5x^2+(a-2)x-3=0$, what is the value of a?

(A) -10

(B) 10

(C) -12

(D) 12

0240

If $2x$ is subtracted from x^2, the result is 8. Find all possible values of x.

(A) $x=-4$ only

(B) $x=-2$ only

(C) $x=-4$ and $x=2$

(D) $x=-2$ and $x=4$

0241

$$x^2+4mx-4=0$$

If one of the solutions to the quadratic equation above is $x=4$, what is the value of m?

(A) $-\dfrac{3}{4}$

(B) $\dfrac{3}{4}$

(C) $-\dfrac{4}{3}$

(D) $\dfrac{4}{3}$

0242

If $x=3$ is the solution of both $x^2-4x+m=0$ and $2x^2+nx-7=0$, what is the value of $m+n$?

(A) $-\dfrac{1}{4}$

(B) $-\dfrac{1}{2}$

(C) $-\dfrac{2}{3}$

(D) -2

0243

$$(x-3)(x+2)=-2x(x-2)$$

How many distinct real solutions does the above equation have?

(A) Zero

(B) Exactly one

(C) Exactly two

(D) Infinitely many

0244

$$4x^2-8x+5=0$$

How many distinct real solutions does the above equation have?

(A) Zero

(B) Exactly one

(C) Exactly two

(D) Infinitely many

0245

If the quadratic equation

$$4(x+3)(x-4)=\frac{1}{2}(2x+1)(x-2)+\frac{3}{2}x$$

is written as $ax^2+bx+c=0$, what is the value of $a+b+c$?

(A) 40

(B) 46

(C) -46

(D) -48

0246

If $f(x)=8-2x^2$ and $g(x)=2x^2-8$, for what real numbers x does $f(x)=g(x)$?

(A) 2 only

(B) 4 only

(C) 2 and -2 only

(D) 4 and -4 only

0247

If $2x^2-16x=0$ and x is a positive integer, which of the following is equal to x?

(A) $\sqrt{4x}$

(B) $4\sqrt{x}$

(C) $2\sqrt{2x}$

(D) $4\sqrt{x}$

0248

If the solution to the quadratic equation

$$2x^2+mx-4=0 \text{ is } x=\frac{1\pm\sqrt{n}}{2},$$

where m and n are integers, what is the value of $m+n$?

(A) -11

(B) -7

(C) 7

(D) 11

0249

$\frac{1}{2}x^2+4x-3a=0$

If the equation above has exactly one solution, what is the value of $3a$?

(A) $-\frac{8}{3}$

(B) $\frac{8}{3}$

(C) -8

(D) 8

0250

For which of the following values of k does the equation $2x^2-kx+8=0$ have more than one real solution?

(A) $|k|>8$

(B) $|k|<8$

(C) $|k|>64$

(D) $|k|<64$

0251

$5x^2-kx+4=0$

If the equation above has no real solutions, which of the following must be true?

(A) $k>20$

(B) $k<20$

(C) $k^2>80$

(D) $k^2<80$

0252

For which of the following values of m and n does the equationm $mx^2-4x-n=0$ have only one real zero?

(A) $m=1,\ n=0$

(B) $m=1,\ n=4$

(C) $m=2,\ n=2$

(D) $m=2,\ n=-2$

0253

Which of the following(s) must be true for all real values?

   I. $x^2-x>0$

   II. $x^2-2x+1>0$

   III. $x^2+x+1>0$

(A) I only

(B) II only

(C) III only

(D) II and III only

0254

The quadratic equation $2x^2+24x+k=0$, where k is a constant, has no real solutions if $b<k$. What is the least possible value of b?

(A) 36

(B) 72

(C) 108

(D) 144

0255

The sum of a negative number and its square is 6. What is the number?

(A) -4

(B) -3

(C) -2

(D) -1

0256

The product of two consecutive positive even integers is 6 more than three times their sum. Which of the following is the smaller integer?

(A) 4

(B) 6

(C) 8

(D) 10

0257

If the square of the sum of a number and its reciprocal is 4, which of the following could be this number?

(A) -1 only

(B) 0 only

(C) 1 only

(D) -1 or 1

0258

Two runners Nick and Jeff leave the same position at right angles at the same time. Jeff runs 1 mile per hour faster than Nick. If they are $2\sqrt{13}$ miles apart after 2 hours, which is the following is true?

(A) The speed of Nick is 3 miles per hour

(B) The speed of Jeff is 3 miles per hour

(C) The speed of Nick is 4 miles per hour

(D) The speed of Jeff is 4 miles per hour

0259

There are two different squares. The length of one side of the large square is 2 inches longer than the length of one side of the small square. If the sum of the areas of the two squares is 100 square inches, which of the following must be true?

(A) The length of one side of the small square is 6 inches.

(B) The length of one side of the small square is 7 inches.

(C) The length of one side of the large square is 6 inches.

(D) The length of one side of the large square is 7 inches.

For questions 260~261, refer to the following expression below.

0260

A ball is thrown vertically upward from the ground and the height of the ball in feet at x seconds is given by $-16x^2 + 28x$.

After how many seconds does the ball hit the ground?

(A) $\frac{5}{4}$ seconds

(B) $\frac{7}{4}$ seconds

(C) 2 seconds

(D) $\frac{5}{2}$ seconds

0261

After how many seconds does the ball reaches 12 feet above the ground?

(A) 1 second

(B) 2 seconds

(C) 3 seconds

(D) 4 seconds

0262

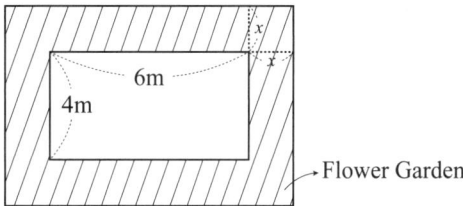

Flower Garden

A pond measuring 6 meters by 4 meters is surrounded by a flower garden of uniform width, as shown in Figure above. If the area of the flower garden is 144 square meters, what is the width of the flower garden?

(A) 3 meters

(B) 3.5 meters

(C) 4 meters

(D) 4.5 meters

0263

Two bicycles start out at the same point. One bicycle starts out going south at 6 mph. One hour later, the second bicycle starts going west at 8 mph. How long after the second bicycle starts travelling does it take for the two bicycles to be 45 miles apart?

(A) 3 hours and 2 minutes

(B) 3 hours and 28 minutes

(C) 3 hours and 54 minutes

(D) 4 hours and 7 minutes

0264

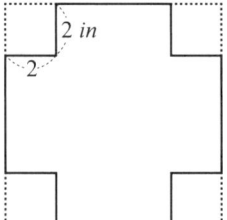

A square piece of cardboard was used to construct a box by cutting 2—inch squares out of each corner and turning up the flaps, as shown in Figure above. Find the length of one side of the square if the box has a volume of 128 cubic inches.

(A) 4

(B) 8

(C) 12

(D) 16

0265

$$x^2 + 4x = 32$$

Given the equation above, what is the value of the smaller solution subtracted from the larger solution?

0266

$$(x+1)^2 - 4(x+1) - 5 = 0$$

What is the positive solution to the equation above?

0267

If k is a solution of the equation $x^2 - 3x - 10 = 0$ and $k > 0$, what is the value of k?

0268

If the solution to the quadratic equation $x^2-2x+a=0$ is $x=1\pm\sqrt{7}$, what is the value of a?

0269

One of the two solutions to the quadratic equation $(x-2)(x+3)=2(x-2)(2x+1)$ is $x=2$. What is the value of the other solution?

0270

Find the values of k for which the equation $3x^2-6x-k=0$ has exactly one real solution.

0271

$$2x^2-14x+a=0$$

The equation above has 2 real solutions. What is the greatest possible value of k, if $a<k$?

0272

What is the greater of the two solutions of the equation $3x^2-20x+12=0$?

0273

If one of the solutions to the equation $x^4-9x^2+20=0$ is $\sqrt{a}$, where a is positive constant, what is the value of a?

0274

What is the sum of the solutions of
$(x-4)^2=(2x+3)^2$?

0275

If the larger of the two solutions of quadratic equation $x^2+5x-14=0$ is also the solution of quadratic equation $5x^2-2x-a=0$, what is the value of a?

0276

$$2x^2+3ax+a+\frac{1}{8}=0$$

Find the value of a, where $a>0$,
if the quadratic equation has only one real solution.

0277

Suppose the length of a rectangle is twice its width. If the area of this rectangle is 450 square meters, what is the length of the rectangle?

0278

A rectangle has an area of 36 square centimeters and a perimeter of 30 centimeters. Find the difference between the length and the width of the rectangle.

0279

David and his family are planning a transcontinental trip by train. Each ticket costs $340, and the number of tickets David's family needs is x. If it is modeled by the equation $3x^2-13x-10=0$, where $x>0$, what is the total cost of the tickets?

0280

Christina tries to distribute 300 marbles equally to the students in his Algebra class. If the number of marbles each student receives is 5 less than the number of students, find the number students.

0281

When Jenny opened the Digital SAT workbook, the product of two pages was 210. Find the sum of two pages.

0282

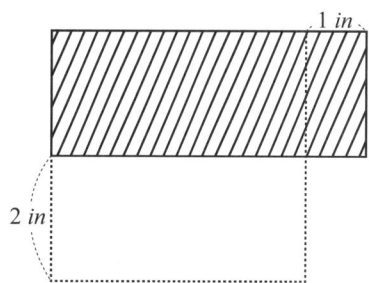

Suppose that one side of the square is increased by 1 inch, but the other side is decreased by 2 inches, as shown in Figure above. If the area of the resulting rectangle is 70 square inches, what is the length of one side of the original square?

0283

Two bicycles leave the same intersection. One bicycle travels north and the other travels east. When the bicycle traveling north had gone 12 miles, the distance between the bicycles was 3 miles more than twice the distance traveled by bicycle heading east. Find the distance between the bicycles at this moment.

3. Quadratic Functions

01. Definition of Quadratic Functions

A **quadratic function** is a polynomial function of the form $y=ax^2+bx+c$ where a, b, and c are constant and $a \neq 0$. The graph of a quadratic function is U−shaped and is called a **parabola**. The lowest or highest point of the graph of a quadratic function is called the vertex and vertical line through the vertex is called the **axis of symmetry**. The x−intercept(s) of the quadratic function is often called **zero(s) or root(s)**.

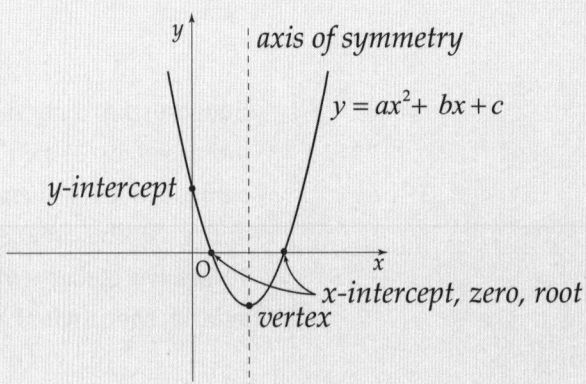

02. The Graph of $y=ax^2+bx+c$

1. **Axis of symmetry** $\left(x=-\dfrac{b}{2a} \right)$:

   The axis of symmetry is the midpoint of two zeros.

2. y−**intercept**: $(0,\ c)$

3. If $a>0$, the parabola **opens upward**; if $a<0$, the parabola opens downward.

4. If $a<0$, then $y\left(-\dfrac{b}{2a} \right)$ is a **maximum** value of y.

5. If $a>0$, then $y\left(-\dfrac{b}{2a} \right)$ is a **minimum** value of y.

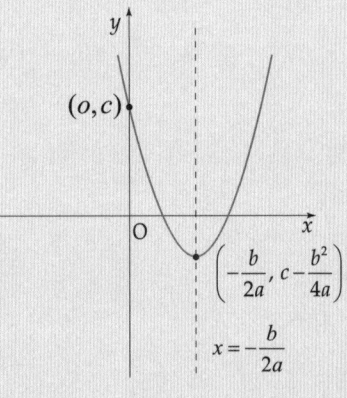

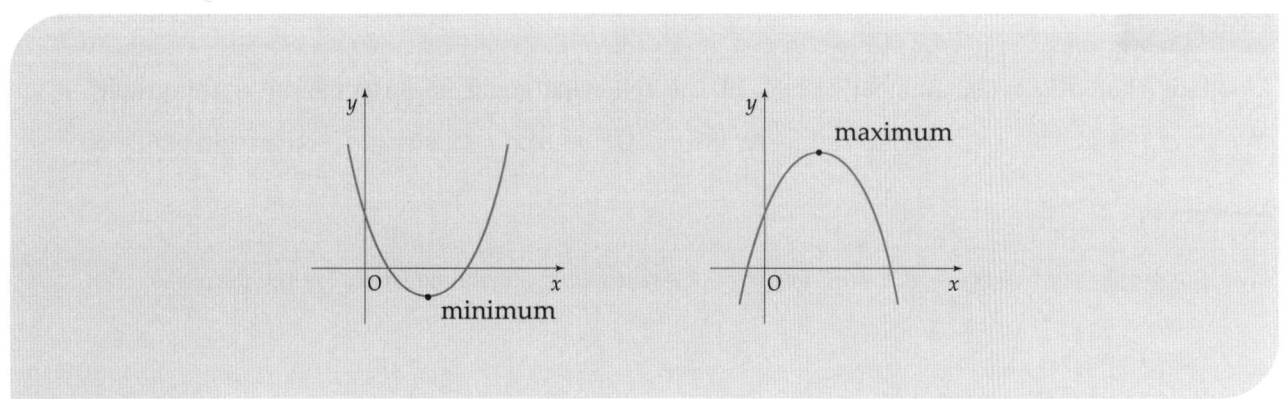

Example 1

For examples 1-3, refer to the following graph.

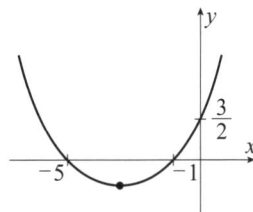

Find the equation of the axis of symmetry.

Solution

Since the axis of symmetry is the midpoint of two zeros,

$$x = \frac{-1+(-5)}{2} = -3$$

$$x = -3$$

Example 2

If the graph shown above is $y = ax^2 + bx + c$, which of the following is true?

(A) $a > 0,\ c > 0$ (B) $a < 0,\ c > 0$ (C) $a < 0,\ c < 0$ (D) $a > 0,\ c < 0$

Solution

The graph opens upward: $a > 0$

The y-intercept is above the x-axis: $c > 0$

Therefore, the correct answer is A.

The answer is A.

Example 3

Assuming that a is a real number, which of the following could be an equation of the graph?

(A) $y=a(x^2+4x-5)$　　　(B) $y=a(x^2+6x+5)$　(C) $y=a(x^2-4x+5)$　　(D) $y=a(x^2-6x-5)$

Solution

Since the graph has two zeros at $x=-5$ and $x=-1$, we could write the equation for the graph as

$$y=a(x+5)(x+1)$$
$$=a(x^2+6x+5)$$

Therefore, the correct answer is B.

The answer is B.

Example 4

Find the minimum or maximum of the quadratic function $y=5x^2-10x+3$.

Solution

Since $a=5>0$, the function has the minimum value.
The axis of symmetry is

$$x=-\frac{b}{2a}=-\frac{-10}{2\cdot5}=1.$$

So the minimum value is
$$y(1)=5(1)^2-10(1)+3=-2.$$

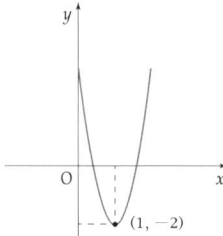

The minimum value of the function is -2

03. The Graph of $y=a(x-h)^2+k$

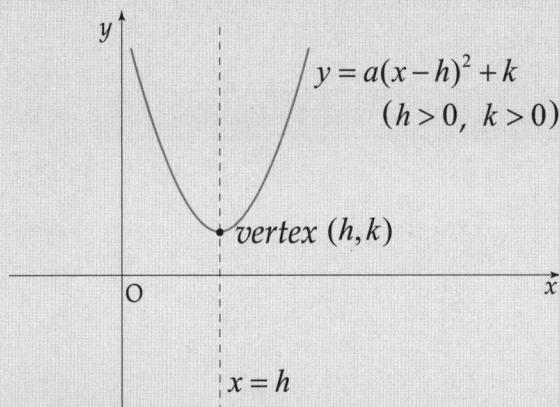

$$y = a(x-h)^2 + k$$
$$(h > 0, \ k > 0)$$

vertex (h, k)

$x = h$

1. The equation $y=a(x-h)^2+k$ is called a standard form or vertex form of the quadratic function.

2. The vertex is $(h, \ k)$.

3. If $a<0$, then **y is a maximum** value of y; If $a>0$, then **y is a minimum** value of **y**.

4. The graph of $y=a(x-h)^2+k$ is the graph of $y=ax^2$ translated(shifted) horizontally by h units and vertically by k units.

Example 5

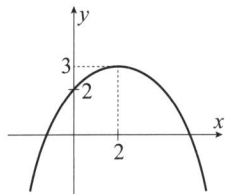

Which of the following is an equation of the graph above?

(A) $y=-4(x-2)^2+3$ (B) $y=-\dfrac{1}{4}(x-2)^2+3$

(C) $y=-4(x+2)^2+3$ (D) $y=-\dfrac{1}{4}(x+2)^2+3$

Solution

The graph has the vertex $(2, 3)$. So, we can write the function
$$y=a(x-2)^2+3$$
Now substitute $(0,2)$ to find a.
$$2=a(0-2)^2+3, \ a=-\frac{1}{4}$$
Thus, $y=-\dfrac{1}{4}(x-2)^2+3$

The answer is B.

04. Quadratic Functions and Discriminant

By using discriminant $D=b^2-4ac$, we can determine the number of zeros of the quadratic function. For the quadratic function $y=ax^2+bx+c$,

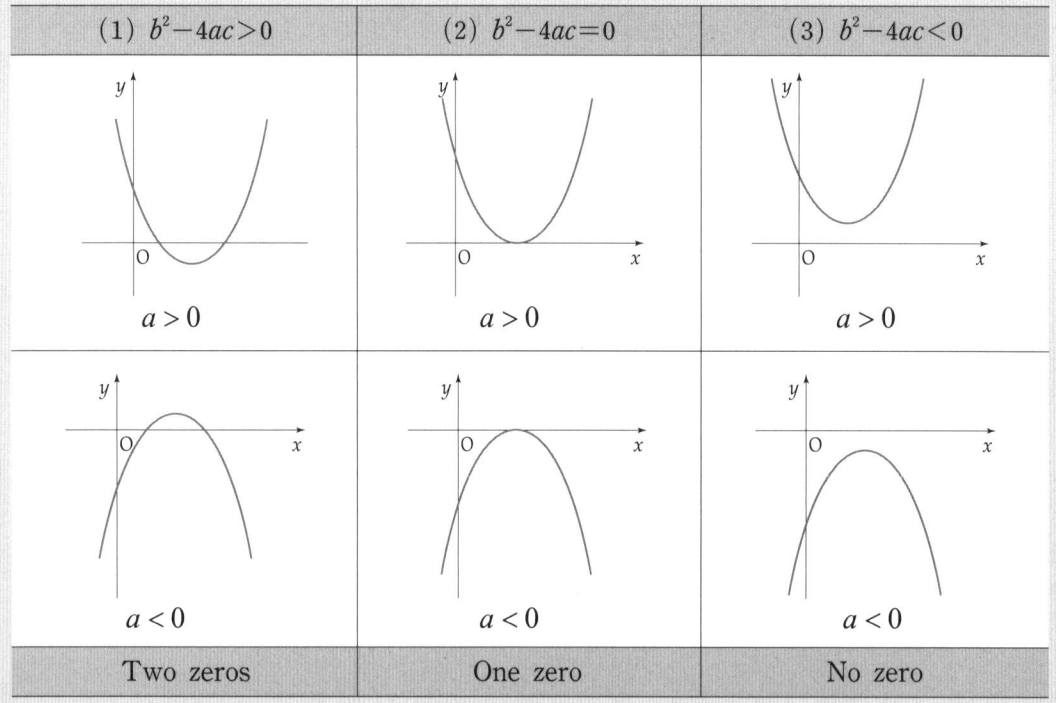

(1) $b^2-4ac>0$	(2) $b^2-4ac=0$	(3) $b^2-4ac<0$
$a>0$	$a>0$	$a>0$
$a<0$	$a<0$	$a<0$
Two zeros	One zero	No zero

Example 6

Determine the number of zeros of the quadratic function.

(1) $y=x^2-4x+4$

(2) $y=-3x^2+7x-1$

Solution

(1) $y=x^2-4x+4$
   $D=b^2-4ac$
   $=(-4)^2-4\cdot1\cdot4$
   $=16-16=0$
   Since $D=0$, there is one zero.

   There is one zero

(2) $y=-3x^2+7x-1$
   $D=b^2-4ac$
   $=7^2-4(-3)(-1)$
   $=49-12=37>0$
   Since $D>0$, there are two zeros.

   There are two zeros

05. Applications

Many applications involve solving for the maximums or minimums of quadratic functions. The maximum or minimum of the quadratic function is the vertex of the parabola, and this vertex can be found using the equation of the axis of symmetry or by method of completing the square.

Example 7

There are two numbers with a sum of 10. Find the two numbers when the product of these two numbers is maximized.

Solution

Let x be one of two numbers. Then, the other number is $10-x$. Also, let y be the product of these two numbers. Then, we have $y=x(10-x)$ and we need to find the vertex of this function.

Method 1
$$y=x(10-x)=-x^2+10x$$
$$=-(x^2-10x+5^2-5^2)$$
$$=-(x-5)^2+25$$

Method 2

Since $y=x(10-x)$ has two zeros $x=0$ and $x=10$, the axis of symmetry is $x=\dfrac{0+10}{2}=5$ and

$y(5)=5(10-5)=25$.

So, y is maximum when $x=5$ and the maximum value is 25.
Therefore, two numbers are $x=5$ and $10-x=10-5=5$.

5 and 5

Example 8

A ball is thrown vertically upward from the top of a 96-foot building. If the height h, in feet, of the ball from the ground after t seconds is given by $h=-16t^2+80t+96$, after how many second does the ball reaches the maximum height in the air? What is the maximum height of the ball?

Solution

Using the axis of symmetry $t=-\dfrac{b}{2a}=-\dfrac{80}{2(-16)}=\dfrac{5}{2}$,

the maximum height of the ball is

$$h\left(\frac{5}{2}\right)=-16\left(\frac{5}{2}\right)^2+80\left(\frac{5}{2}\right)+96=196$$

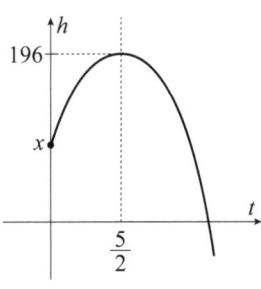

The ball reaches its maximum height of 196 feet after $\dfrac{5}{2}$ seconds

Practice **Problems**

0284

Which of the following points is NOT on the graph of quadratic function $y=2x^2-3$?

(A) $(0, -3)$

(B) $(1, -1)$

(C) $(2, 5)$

(D) $(-1, 1)$

0285

If the quadratic function $y=\frac{9}{2}x^2$ passes through the point $(a, 72)$, what is the value of a? (a is a positive constant.)

(A) 2

(B) 3

(C) 4

(D) 5

0286

$$f(x)=a(x+3)^2-4$$

In quadratic function above, if $f(-1)=8$, what is the value of $f(-4)$?

(A) -2

(B) -1

(C) 1

(D) 2

0287

If the graph of quadratic function $y=ax^2$ opens downward and passes through the point $(3, -6)$, which of the following points is also on the graph of $y=ax^2$?

(A) $\left(1, -\frac{2}{3}\right)$

(B) $\left(2, \frac{8}{3}\right)$

(C) $(-3, -8)$

(D) $(-4, 10)$

0288

The graph of $y=ax^2+5x-2$ passes through the point $(-1, -3)$. What is the value of a?

(A) 1

(B) 2

(C) 3

(D) 4

0289

Which of the following quadratic functions has the vertex $(-3, -2)$ and $y-$intercept 16.

(A) $y=\frac{1}{2}(x+3)^2-2$

(B) $y=\frac{1}{2}(x-3)^2-2$

(C) $y=2(x+3)^2-2$

(D) $y=2(x-3)^2-2$

0290

If the graph of the quadratic function $y=-\dfrac{1}{2}(x-1)^2$ is shifted k units up, then the graph passes through the point $(3, 4)$. What is the value of k?

(A) 3

(B) 4

(C) 5

(D) 6

0291

$$f(x)=-4x^2$$

If the graph of the quadratic function is translated 1 unit to the left and 2 units up, then which of the following must be the equation of a new quadratic function?

(A) $y=-4(x-1)^2+2$

(B) $y=-4(x+1)^2+2$

(C) $y=-4(x-1)^2-2$

(D) $y=-4(x+1)^2-2$

0292

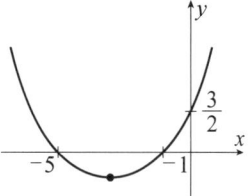

If the graph of the quadratic function $y=a(x-h)^2+k$ is shown above, which of the following must be true about the signs of a, h, and k?

(A) $a<0$

(B) $k>0$

(C) $h<0$

(D) Not enough information is provided

0293

The graph of quadratic function $f(x)=a(x-m)(x-n)$, where a, m and n are constants, opens downward and has the vertex at (h, k). If both h and k are positive, which of the following could be true?

(A) $a>0$, $m>0$, $n<0$

(B) $a>0$, $m<0$, $n>0$

(C) $a<0$, $m>0$, $n>0$

(D) $a<0$, $m<0$, $n<0$

0294

If $a>0$, $h>0$, $k<0$, which of the following could be the graph of
$y=a(x-h)^2+k$?

(A)

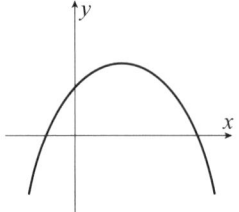

(B)

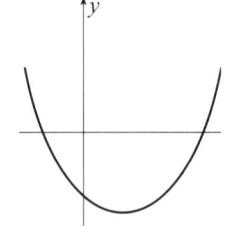

(C)

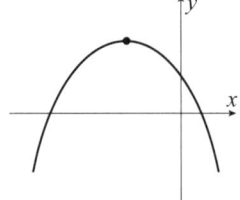

(D)

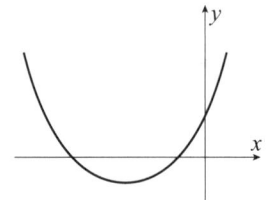

0295

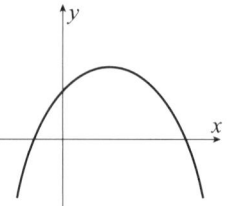

The graph of the quadratic function f is shown above. Which of the following could be the graph of $y=f(x)-3$?

(A)

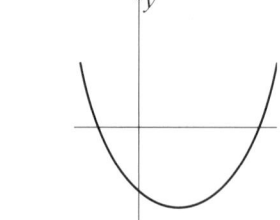

(B)

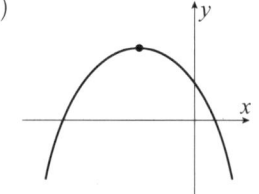

(C)

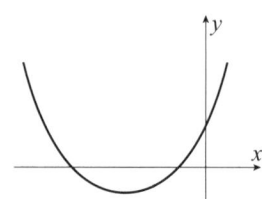

(D)

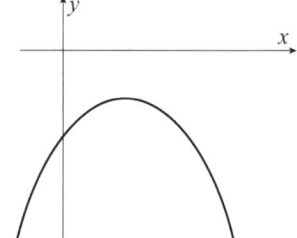

0296

If the graph of the quadratic function $y=3x^2-2$ is shifted 4 unit to the right and 2 units up, what is the coordinate of the vertex of the new function?

(A) $(4, 2)$

(B) $(2, 2)$

(C) $(4, 0)$

(D) $(2, 0)$

0297

If a function f has a vertex at $(2, 3)$ and x−intercepts at $(-1, 0)$ and $(a, 0)$, what is the value of a?

(A) 3

(B) 4

(C) 5

(D) 6

For questions 298~299, refer to the following graph below.

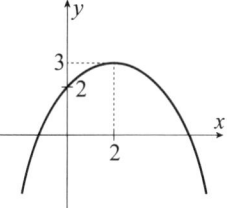

0298

If the y−intercept of the graph above is 2, what is the equation of the graph shown above?

(A) $y=-2x^2+x+2$

(B) $y=-2x^2+4x+2$

(C) $y=-\dfrac{x^2}{4}+x+2$

(D) $y=-\dfrac{x^2}{4}+4x+2$

0299

If the graph of the quadratic function above is shifted 3 units to the left and 1 unit up, which of the following is the function of the new graph?

(A) $y=-2(x+1)^2+2$

(B) $y=-2(x-5)^2+4$

(C) $y=-\dfrac{1}{4}(x+1)^2+4$

(D) $y=-\dfrac{1}{4}(x-5)^2+2$

0300

For the function $y = -2x^2 + 8x - 3$, find the maximum value of the function.

(A) -3

(B) -5

(C) 3

(D) 5

0301

The graph of a quadratic function $y = x^2 - x - 6$ intersects the x-axis at two different points. What is the distance between two zeros?

(A) 5

(B) 6

(C) 7

(D) 8

0302

Which of the following is NOT true about the graph of $y = 2(x-2)^2 - 5$?

(A) The graph opens upward

(B) The equation of the axis of symmetry is $x = 2$

(C) The vertex of the graph is at $(2, -5)$.

(D) The graph is shifted 2 units to the left and 5 units down from the graph of $y = 2x^2$

For questions 303~304, refer to the following graph below.

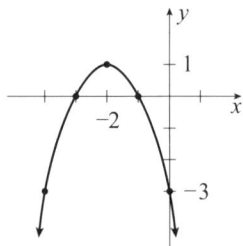

0303

Which of the following is an equation of the quadratic function graphed above?

(A) $y = -(x+2)^2 + 1$

(B) $y = -(x-2)^2 - 3$

(C) $y = -\frac{1}{2}(x-2)^2 - 3$

(D) $y = -\frac{1}{2}(x+2)^2 + 1$

0304

Which of the following is NOT true about the graph above?

(A) The zeros are -3 and -1

(B) The vertex is $(-2, 1)$

(C) The range is the set of real numbers greater than or equal to 1

(D) The y-intercept is at -3

0305

x	-1	0	2	3	5
y	0	-3	-3	0	

A quadratic function describes the relationship between x and y in the table above. What value of y corresponds to a x value of 5?

(A) 9

(B) 10

(C) 11

(D) 12

0306

If the graph of $y=ax^2-4x-5$ does not intersect the $x-$axis, which of the following must be true?

(A) $a>-\dfrac{4}{5}$

(B) $a<-\dfrac{4}{5}$

(C) $a^2>\dfrac{4}{5}$

(D) $a^2<\dfrac{4}{5}$

0307

The graph of the quadratic function $y=4x-x^2$ is shown above. If the graph has the vertex at B and passes through two zeros A and C, what is the area of triangle ABC?

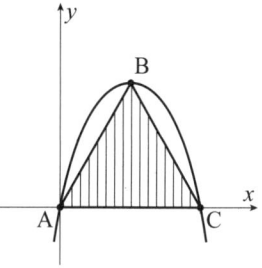

(A) 4

(B) 8

(C) 10

(D) 12

For questions 308~309, refer to the following graph below.

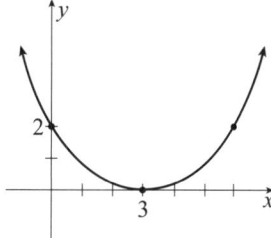

0308

The $y-$intercept of the graph shown is $(0, k)$. What is the value of k?

(A) 2

(B) 3

(C) 6

(D) 8

0309

An equation for the graph of the quadratic function $y=\dfrac{2}{9}(x-3)(x-a)$ is given above. What is the value of a?

(A) -3

(B) 3

(C) -6

(D) 6

0310

If the graph of the quadratic function $y=a(x-h)^2+k$ is shown above, which of the following must be true about the signs of a, h, and k?

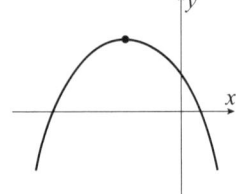

(A) $a>0$, $h>0$, $k>0$

(B) $a>0$, $h<0$, $k>0$

(C) $a<0$, $h>0$, $k>0$

(D) $a<0$, $h<0$, $k>0$

0311

If the graph of the quadratic function $y=4x^2-6x+b$ intersects the x−axis at one point, what is the value of b?

(A) 18

(B) 9

(C) $\dfrac{9}{2}$

(D) $\dfrac{9}{4}$

0312

If the quadratic function $y=ax^2+bx+c$ opens downward and has 1 real zero, which of the following must be true?

(A) $a>0$, $b^2-4ac>0$

(B) $a<0$, $b^2-4ac>0$

(C) $a>0$, $b^2-4ac=0$

(D) $a<0$, $b^2-4ac=0$

0313

What is the range of the function $y=-x^2+5x+2$?

(A) $y\le\dfrac{5}{2}$

(B) $y\ge\dfrac{5}{2}$

(C) $y\le\dfrac{33}{4}$

(D) $y\ge\dfrac{33}{4}$

0314

A parabola is symmetric about the line $x=-4$ and passes through the origin. Which of the following must be the zero of this parabola?

(A) $(-8, 0)$

(B) $(-6, 0)$

(C) $(-2, 0)$

(D) $(4, 0)$

0315

A parabola is symmetric about the line $x=2$ and passes through the point $(4, 2)$. Which of the following points must be on this parabola?

(A) $(0, 0)$

(B) $(0, 2)$

(C) $(-2, 0)$

(D) $(-2, 2)$

0316

The graph of $y=ax^2+bx+c$ cannot have points in the first or second quadrants if

(A) $a>0$ and $b^2-4ac>0$

(B) $a<0$ and $b^2-4ac>0$

(C) $a<0$ and $b^2-4ac<0$

(D) $a>0$ and $b^2-4ac<0$

0317

The quadratic function $y=ax^2+bx+c$ opens upward and has 2 real zero. If $D=b^2-4ac$, which of the following must be true?

(A) $a>0$, $D>0$

(B) $a<0$, $D>0$

(C) $a>0$, $D=0$

(D) $a<0$, $D=0$

0318

Jason wants to make a rectangular garden. One side is his house wall. He has 28 meters of fence that he will use to surround the other three sides. If $A(x)$ is the area of the garden, in square meters, and x is the width, in meters, which of the following represents the area of the rectangle?

(A) $A(x)=x(28-2x)$

(B) $A(x)=\frac{x}{2}(28-x)$

(C) $A(x)=x(2x-28)$

(D) $A(x)=\frac{x}{2}(x-28)$

0319

A soccer ball is kicked vertically upward at a height of 12 feet from the ground and the height g, in feet, of the soccer ball from the ground after t seconds is given by $g(t) = -16(t-2)^2 + 76$. Which of the following is the best interpretation of the vertex of the graph of $y = g(x)$?

(A) The height of the soccer ball is 12 feet before the ball is kicked.

(B) The minimum of the soccer ball is 2 feet after 76 seconds.

(C) The maximum of the soccer ball is 76 feet after 2 seconds.

(D) The time it takes for a soccer ball to hit the ground is 76 seconds.

0320

When a factory produces x products a day, the profit, in hundred dollars, is $-\dfrac{x^2}{2} + 12x - 40$. The factory manager is contemplating how many products should be produced per day to achieve maximum profit. Which of the following statements is true about the maximum daily profit?

(A) When producing 12 products in the factory, the maximum daily profit is $3,200

(B) When producing 12 products in the factory, the maximum daily profit is $3,600

(C) When producing 15 products in the factory, the maximum daily profit is $3,200

(D) When producing 15 products in the factory, the maximum daily profit is $3,600

0321

A ball is thrown vertically upward from ground. If the height h, in meters, of the ball from the ground after t seconds is given by $h = -4.9t^2 + 19.6t$, what is the maximum height of the ball?

(A) 11.8 meters

(B) 13.8 meters

(C) 14.4 meters

(D) 19.6 meters

For the questions 322~324, A ball is thrown vertically upward from the top of a 96—foot building. The height h in feet of the ball from the ground after t seconds is given by $h=-16t^2+80t+96$.

0322

Which number represents the height, in feet, from which the ball was thrown?

(A) -16

(B) 80

(C) 96

(D) None of the above

0323

After how many seconds does the ball hit the ground?

(A) 6 seconds

(B) 7 seconds

(C) 8 seconds

(D) 9 seconds

0324

After how many seconds does the ball pass the top of the building on its way down?

(A) 3 seconds

(B) 4 seconds

(C) 5 seconds

(D) 6 seconds

0325

$$h(t)=-\frac{1}{2}gt^2+v_0t+h_0$$

The function h above gives the height, in meters, of an object propelled vertically for time t seconds, where $t \geq 0$. The object's initial velocity, v_0, is 68.6 meters per second and its initial height, h_0, is 6 meters. What is the maximum height of the object if g stands for gravity and its measure is always 9.8 meters per second per second?

(A) 246.1 meters

(B) 253.5 meters

(C) 258.7 meters

(D) 260.4 meters

0326

$$h = -16t^2 + 64t + 8$$

The function h above gives the height, in feet, of a baseball thrown from the platform after t seconds. Which of the following best interprets the number 8 in the equation?

(A) The initial height at which the baseball was thrown

(B) The maximum height of the baseball

(C) The time the baseball reached its maximum height

(D) The time at which the baseball hit the ground

0327

Suppose you have a cake that sells 30 pieces a day if you sell it for $5 per piece. If you raise the price of cake by x per piece, you sell $2x$ pieces less. If y is the revenue, in dollars, which of the following must be true?

(A) $y = (5 - 2x)(30 + x)$

(B) $y = (5 - x)(30 + 2x)$

(C) $y = (5 + 2x)(30 - x)$

(D) $y = (5 + x)(30 - 2x)$

0328

A rectangle is to be inscribed under the curve $y = 4 - x^2$ and above the x-axis. What dimensions will produce a rectangle with the largest area?

(A) $\dfrac{3\sqrt{2}}{3}$ and $\dfrac{7}{3}$

(B) $\dfrac{3\sqrt{3}}{3}$ and $\dfrac{7}{3}$

(C) $\dfrac{2\sqrt{3}}{3}$ and $\dfrac{8}{3}$

(D) $\dfrac{4\sqrt{2}}{3}$ and $\dfrac{8}{3}$

0329

An open box (no top) with a square base has a volume of 6 cubic inches. The material used to build the base cost $4 per square inch and the material used to build the sides cost $2 per square inch. To the nearest dollar, what is the minimum cost for the materials need to make the box?

(A) $38

(B) $40

(C) $42

(D) $44

0330

The graph of the quadratic function f has the vertex $(2, 5)$ and passes through the point $(3, 3)$. Which of the following equations represents the graph of function f?

(A) $f(x)=2(x-2)^2+5$

(B) $f(x)=-2(x-2)^2+5$

(C) $f(x)=2(x-3)^2+3$

(D) $f(x)=-2(x-3)^2+3$

0331

If the quadratic function $y=ax^2$ passes through the point $(-2, 32)$ and $\left(\frac{1}{2}, b\right)$, what is the value of $a+b$?

0332

If the graph of the quadratic function $y=2x^2$ is shifted 3 units to the right, then the graph passes through the point $(a, 8)$. Find the possible value of a.

0333

$$y=-3x^2-6x+m+1$$

If the quadratic function above has the maximum value of 12, what is the value of m?

0334

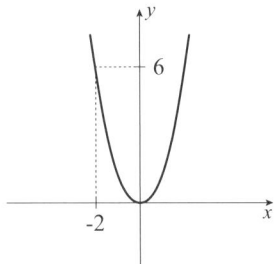

If the graph of quadratic function $y=ax^2$ above passes through the point $(4, m)$, what is the value of m?

0335

The graph of a quadratic function $y=ax^2+bx+c$ intersects the x−axis at $(-6, 0)$ and $(2, 0)$. What is the value of the x−coordinate of this graph's line of symmetry?

0336

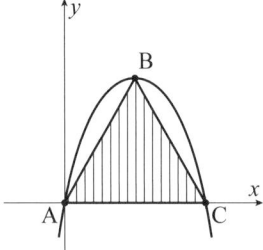

The graph of the quadratic function $y=6x-x^2$ is shown above. If the graph has the vertex at B and passes through two zeros A and C, what is the area of triangle ABC?

0337

If the graph of the function $y=5(x+2)^2-1$ shifts h units horizontally and k units vertically, then the function of the graph is $y=5(x-1)^2-4$. What is the value of $h+k$?

0338

If the quadratic function $y=-\frac{1}{2}x^2-6x+k$ intersects the $x-$axis at two points, the distance between two points is 8. What is the value of k?

0339

There are two numbers with a difference of 6. Find the smaller number when the product of these two numbers is minimized.

0340

Eugene wants to make a rectangular henhouse using 52−inch wire. Suppose that one side of the henhouse is the wall. If he uses all of the 52−inch wire to surround the other three sides, what is the maximum area of the henhouse that can be made?

0341

If $x+2y=12$, what is the maximum value of xy?

0342

If $2x-y=4$, what is the minimum value of $2xy$?

0343

A ball is thrown vertically upward from ground. The height h, in feet, of the ball from the ground after t seconds is given by $h=-16t^2+80t$. After how many second does the ball reaches the maximum height?

0344

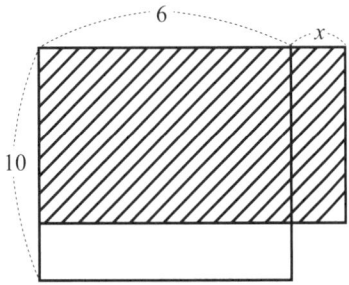

There is a rectangle with length 10 and width 6. If we increase the width by x and decrease the length by x to create a new rectangle as shown in Figure above, what is the maximum area of the new rectangle?

0345

Find the maximum area of the triangle whose sum of base and height is 16.

0346

There are two numbers with a difference of 6. When the product of two numbers is minimum, what is the larger of the two numbers?

0347

Jason has a certain product that sells 12 products for $8 every day. If Jason drops the price by $x per product, he sells $2x$ products more. Then, how much should he sell a product to maximize profit?

Memo

4. Exponentials and Radicals

01. Exponents and Radical Expressions

1. Basic Law of Exponents

Let $a>0$, $b>0$ and m, n be real numbers.

(1) $a^m \cdot a^n = a^{m+n}$

(2) $a^m \div a^n = \dfrac{a^m}{a^n} = a^{m-n}$

(3) $(a^m)^n = a^{mn}$

(4) $(ab)^m = a^m b^m$

(5) $\left(\dfrac{a}{b}\right)^m = \dfrac{a^m}{b^m}$ $(b \neq 0)$

2. Zero and Negative Exponents

Let $a \neq 0$ and m be positive number.

(1) $a^0 = 1$

(2) $a^{-m} = \dfrac{1}{a^m}$

Note 0^0 and 0^m is not defined.

3. Radicals ⇒ Rational Exponents

Let $a>0$, $n \geq 2$, and m, n be integers.

(1) $\sqrt[n]{a} = a^{\frac{1}{n}}$

(2) $\sqrt[n]{a^m} = a^{\frac{m}{n}}$

(3) $\dfrac{1}{\sqrt[n]{a^m}} = \dfrac{1}{a^{\frac{m}{n}}} = a^{-\frac{m}{n}}$

4. Transformation of Exponents

Let $a>0$, $b>0$ and m, n be real numbers.

(1) If $a^m = b^n$, then $(a^m)^{\frac{1}{m}} = (b^n)^{\frac{1}{m}} \Rightarrow a = b^{\frac{n}{m}}$

(2) If $a^m = b^n = k$, then $(a^m)^{\frac{1}{n}} = (b^n)^{\frac{1}{n}} \Rightarrow b = a^{\frac{m}{n}}$

Example 1

Which of the following is equivalent to $b\sqrt{a^3 b}$

(A) $(ab)^{\frac{3}{2}}$　　(B) $a^{\frac{2}{3}}b^{\frac{3}{2}}$　　(C) $a^{\frac{2}{3}}b^2$　　(D) $\dfrac{1}{a^{\frac{2}{3}}b^2}$

Solution

The expression $\sqrt{a^3 b} = \sqrt{a^3}\sqrt{b} = a^{\frac{3}{2}}b^{\frac{1}{2}}$. Therefore,

$b\sqrt{a^3 b} = b \cdot a^{\frac{3}{2}}b^{\frac{1}{2}} = a^{\frac{3}{2}}b^{\frac{1}{2}+1}$

$\quad = a^{\frac{3}{2}}b^{\frac{3}{2}} = (ab)^{\frac{3}{2}}$

The answer is A.

02. Exponential Equations

1. Assume $a > 0$ and $a \neq 1$

If $a^m = a^n$, then $m = n$.

2. Assume $a > 0$, $a \neq 1$, $b > 0$, and $b \neq 1$.

If $a^m = b^m$, then $a = b$ or $m = 0$.

Example 2

$3(2^{x-2}) = 48$

(A) 3   (B) 4   (C) 5   (D) 6

Solution

$$3(2^{x-2}) = 48$$
$$2^{x-2} = 16 \quad \rightarrow \text{Divide by 3}$$
$$2^{x-2} = 2^4 \quad \rightarrow 16 = 2^4$$
$$x - 2 = 4 \quad \rightarrow \text{One-to-one property}$$
$$x = 6 \quad \rightarrow \text{Solve for } x$$

The answer is D.

03. Exponential Functions

1. Definition

A basic exponential functionfwith baseahas the form

$$y = a^x \quad (a > 0, \ a \neq 1)$$

and the domain is considered to be the set of all real numbers.

2. The Graph of $y = a^x$ ($a > 0$, $a \neq 1$)

(1) The graph passes through the point $(0, 1)$ and $(1, a)$.

(2) The horizontal asymptote is x-axis($y = 0$).

(3) When $a > 1$, y increases as x increases.

When $0 < a < 1$, y decreases as x increases.

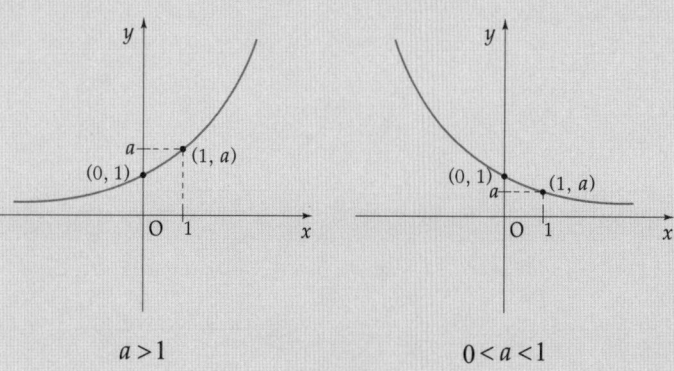

$a > 1$ $0 < a < 1$

Example 3

Which of the following is a function of the graph above?

(A) $y=3^x-2$ (B) $y=3^x+1$

(C) $y=2^x+3$ (D) $y=2^{x+1}-1$

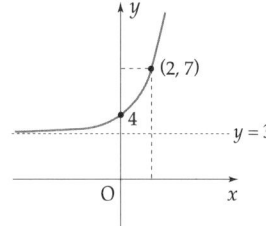

Solution

Given a graph, the best way to find a function is to substitute the given coordinates. The graph above passes through $(2, 7)$ and $(0, 4)$.

(A) $(0, 4)-4\neq3^0-2$, $4\neq-1$ → $(0, 4)$ is NOT on the graph
$(2, 7)-7=3^2-2$, $7=7$ → $(2, 7)$ is on the graph
(B) $(0, 4)-4=3^0+1$, $4=4$ → $(0, 4)$ is on the graph
$(2, 7)-7\neq3^2+1$, $7\neq10$ → $(2, 7)$ is NOT on the graph
(C) $(0, 4)-4=2^0+3$, $4=4$ → $(0, 4)$ is on the graph
$(2, 7)-7=3^2-2$, $7=7$ → $(2, 7)$ is on the graph
(D) $(0, 4)-4\neq3^0-2$, $4\neq-1$ → $(0, 4)$ is NOT on the graph
$(2, 7)-7=3^2-2$, $7=7$ → $(2, 7)$ is on the graph

Therefore, only the graph of $y=2^x+3$ passes through the points $(2, 7)$ and $(0, 4)$.

The answer is C.

116 II. Advanced Math

04. Radical Equations

A radical equation is an equation that contains radical with a variable in the radicand. $x-3=\sqrt{2x-1}$ and $\sqrt{2x-1}-4=0$ are radical equations for instance. To solve radical equations, we need to eliminate the radicals and obtain a polynomial equation. However, solving the radical equation sometimes yields an extraneous solution.

An extraneous solution is a solution that emerges from the process of solving the equation but is not a valid solution to the equation. When solving the radical equation, we always need to check for an extraneous solution.

Example 4

$$\sqrt{2x+9}=x+3$$

What are all possible solutions to the given equation above?

(A) 0 and -4 (B) 0 and 4   (C) -4 only   (D) 0 only

Solution

$\sqrt{2x+9}=x+3$	→ Isolate the radical term
$(\sqrt{2x+9})^2=(x+3)^2$	→ Square both sides to eliminate the radical
$2x+9=x^2+6x+9$	→ Expand
$x^2+4x=0$	→ Simplify
$x(x+4)=0$	→ Factor
$x=0$ or $x=-4$	→ Solve for x

Check $x=0$ in the original equation.
$$\sqrt{2\cdot 0+9}=0+3$$
$$\sqrt{9}=3$$
$$3=3$$
→ Solution checks.

Check $x=-4$ in the original equation.
$$\sqrt{2(-4)+9}=(-4)+3$$
$$\sqrt{1}=-1$$
$$1\neq -1$$
→ Extraneous solution

Therefore, the only solution is $x=0$.

The answer is D.

Practice **Problems**

0348

Which of the following is equal to the expression $16\sqrt[3]{4}$?

(A) $4^{\frac{2}{3}}$

(B) $4^{\frac{8}{3}}$

(C) $2^{\frac{8}{3}}$

(D) $2^{\frac{14}{3}}$

0349

$$4^{\frac{1}{5}}\sqrt[3]{2}$$

Which of the following is equal to the expression above?

(A) $2^{\frac{2}{15}}$

(B) $2^{\frac{11}{15}}$

(C) $4^{\frac{2}{15}}$

(D) $4^{\frac{11}{15}}$

0350

Which of the following is equal to the expression $8^{\frac{4}{3}}$?

(A) $8\sqrt{2}$

(B) 16

(C) $16\sqrt{2}$

(D) 32

0351

Which of the following is equal to the expression $k^{\frac{5}{4}}$?

(A) $\sqrt[16]{k^{25}}$

(B) $\sqrt[5]{k^{25}}$

(C) $\sqrt[20]{k^{25}}$

(D) $\sqrt[4]{k^{25}}$

0352

If the expression $a^{\frac{7}{3}}$ is equivalent to $a^x \cdot \sqrt[3]{a^y}$, what is the value of $x+y$? (Both x and y are positive integers, and $y > x$)

(A) 2

(B) 3

(C) 4

(D) 5

0353

Which of the following is equal to the expression $3^{-\frac{3}{4}}$?

(A) $-\sqrt[4]{27}$

(B) $-\sqrt[3]{81}$

(C) $\dfrac{1}{\sqrt[4]{27}}$

(D) $\dfrac{1}{\sqrt[3]{81}}$

0354

$$3^{\frac{2}{n}} \sqrt[n]{5}$$

In the expression above, n is a positive integer. Which of the following is equal to the expression above?

(A) $\sqrt[n]{15}$

(B) $\sqrt[n]{45}$

(C) $15^{\frac{3}{n}}$

(D) $45^{\frac{2}{n}}$

0355

$$\left(\frac{1}{\sqrt[3]{b}}\right)^{m}$$

In the expression above, b and m are positive integers. Which of the following is equal to the expression above?

(A) $b^{\frac{m}{3}}$

(B) $b^{-\frac{m}{3}}$

(C) $b^{m-\frac{1}{3}}$

(D) $b^{\frac{1}{3}-m}$

0356

If $a \neq 0$, then $\dfrac{(a^{3-b})^{2}}{a^{6}} = ?$

(A) a^{2b}

(B) $\dfrac{a^{2b}}{a^{3}}$

(C) $\dfrac{a^{3}}{a^{2b}}$

(D) $\dfrac{1}{a^{2b}}$

0357

$$a^{\frac{3}{4}} b^{\frac{1}{2}}$$

In the expression above, a and b are positive integers. Which of the following is equal to the expression above?

(A) $\sqrt[4]{a^{3}b}$

(B) $\sqrt[4]{a^{3}b^{2}}$

(C) $\sqrt{a^{3}b}$

(D) $\sqrt{a^{3}b^{2}}$

0358

If $3^{x} = 9^{y} = \dfrac{1}{81}$, what is the value of $x - y$?

(A) -6

(B) -2

(C) 2

(D) 4

0359

If $\sqrt[3]{0.024} = a\sqrt[3]{b}$, what is the value of $\dfrac{b}{a}$? (b is the smallest possible positive integer)

(A) 15

(B) 18

(C) 24

(D) 28

0360

If $\sqrt{2}=a$, $\sqrt{3}=b$, and $\sqrt{5}=c$, which of the following is equal to $\sqrt{360}$?

(A) a^2bc^3

(B) a^3bc^2

(C) a^2b^3c

(D) a^3b^2c

0361

If $2^n+2^{n+1}=k$, then what is the value of 2^{n+2} in terms of k?

(A) k

(B) $5k$

(C) $\dfrac{3k}{2}$

(D) $\dfrac{4k}{3}$

0362

$$(1+2\sqrt{2})(1-\sqrt{2})$$

Which of the following expression is equal to the expression above?

(A) -3

(B) $-3+\sqrt{2}$

(C) $3-\sqrt{2}$

(D) $3-2\sqrt{2}$

0363

If the expression $(\sqrt{3}-2\sqrt{7})^2$ can be written as $a+b\sqrt{c}$, where c is the smallest possible integer, what is the value of $a+b+c$?

(A) 16

(B) 24

(C) 36

(D) 48

0364

Which expression is equivalent to the expression $(\sqrt{x}-1)(2-\sqrt{x})$, where x is positive constant?

(A) $3\sqrt{x}$

(B) $-2-x$

(C) $5\sqrt{x}-2$

(D) $3\sqrt{x}-x-2$

0365

$$\dfrac{\sqrt{2}}{\sqrt{3}-2}$$

Which of the following expression is equal to the expression above?

(A) $2\sqrt{2}-\sqrt{6}$

(B) $-2\sqrt{2}+\sqrt{6}$

(C) $-\sqrt{6}+2\sqrt{2}$

(D) $-\sqrt{6}-2\sqrt{2}$

0366

Which expression is equivalent to the expression $(\sqrt{2}a+\sqrt{2}b)^2$, where a and b are positive constants?

(A) $2a+2b$

(B) $2a+2\sqrt{ab}+2b$

(C) $2a+4\sqrt{ab}+2b$

(D) $(2(\sqrt{a}+\sqrt{b}))^2$

0367

Which expression is equivalent to the expression $(\sqrt{a}-\sqrt{2y})^{\frac{2}{3}}$, where x and y are positive constants?

(A) $\sqrt{a-2ay+2y}$

(B) $\sqrt{a-2\sqrt{2ay}+2y}$

(C) $\sqrt[3]{a-2ay+2y}$

(D) $\sqrt[3]{a-2\sqrt{2ay}+2y}$

0368

The product of the square root of a positive real number and its reciprocal is

(A) -1

(B) 1

(C) Less than -1

(D) Greater than 1

0369

x	0	1	3	4
$f(x)$	3	6	24	48

The table above gives the values of the exponential function f at selected values of x. If the function can be written as $f(x)=ab^x$, where a and b are positive constants, what is the value of $a+b$?

(A) 4

(B) 5

(C) 6

(D) 7

For questions 370−371, refer to the following graph below.

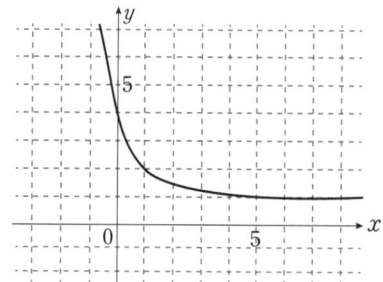

0370

The graph of $y=3^{a-x}+1$ is shown above, where a is a positive constant. What is the value of a?

(A) 0

(B) 1

(C) 2

(D) 3

0371

What is the x−intercept of the graph shown?

(A) 1

(B) 2

(C) 4

(D) Does not exist

For questions 372−373, refer to the following graph below.

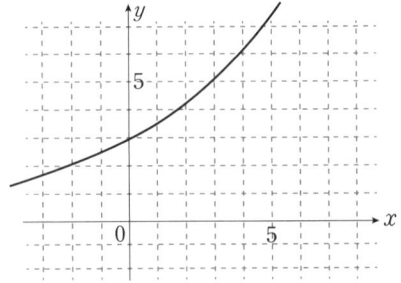

0372

What is the y−intercept of the graph shown?

(A) $(0, -3)$

(B) $(-3, 0)$

(C) $(0, 3)$

(D) $(3, 0)$

0373

Which of the following could be the equation of the graph above?

(A) $y=-\left(\dfrac{2}{3}\right)^{x}+4$

(B) $y=\left(\dfrac{2}{3}\right)^{x}+2$

(C) $y=-\left(\dfrac{3}{2}\right)^{x}+4$

(D) $y=\left(\dfrac{3}{2}\right)^{x}+2$

0374

If the graph of the exponential function $y=a^{x}$ passes through the points $(2, 4)$ and $\left(k, \dfrac{1}{8}\right)$, what is the value of k?

(A) -2

(B) 2

(C) -3

(D) 3

0375

If $f(x)=a^{x}$ where $a>0$, and if $f(4)=\dfrac{16}{81}$, what is the value of $f(6)$?

(A) 0.059

(B) 0.088

(C) 0.132

(D) 0.197

0376

If the function g is defined by
$g(x)=4(1.5)^{x+1}$, what is the value of $g(2)$?

(A) 4

(B) 9

(C) 13.5

(D) 20.25

0377

$$2^{2x-3}-32=0$$

What is the solution to the equation above?

(A) 4

(B) -4

(C) 5

(D) -5

0378

$$64^{2x+1}=\frac{1}{256}$$

What is the solution to the equation above?

(A) $-\frac{6}{7}$

(B) $-\frac{7}{6}$

(C) $-\frac{2}{3}$

(D) $-\frac{3}{2}$

0379

The equation $a^b=c^d$ relates to positive
numbers a, b, c, and d. Which equation
correctly expresses c in terms of a, b, and d?

(A) $c=a^{\frac{b}{d}}$

(B) $c=a^{b-d}$

(C) $c=a^{\frac{d}{b}}$

(D) $c=a^{d-b}$

0380

$$\sqrt{(2x+1)^2}=5$$

What are all possible solutions to the equation
above?

(A) -3

(B) 2

(C) 3

(D) -3 and 2

0381

$$\sqrt{x-3}-x=-5$$

What are all possible solutions to the equation
above?

(A) 4

(B) 7

(C) 4 and 7

(D) -4 and -7

0382

$$\sqrt{(x-4)^2}=x-4$$

Which of the following CAN NOT be the solution to the equation above?

(A) 3

(B) 4

(C) 5

(D) 6

0383

$$\sqrt{2x-k}=k$$

If k is a constant and $k<0$, how many solution(s) doe the equation above have?

(A) No solution

(B) 1 solution

(C) 2 solutions

(D) Infinitely many solutions

0384

For the function f, the value of $f(x)$ increases by 0.2% for every increase in the value of x by 1. Which of the following equations represents the function f?

(A) $f(x)=0.02x+50$

(B) $f(x)=0.002x+50$

(C) $f(x)=50(1.02)^x$

(D) $f(x)=50(1.002)^x$

0385

The number of bacteria in a culture is 100 at the beginning of experiment. If the number of bacteria increases at a rate of 9% per hour, which of the following equation models the number of bacteria y in a culture after x hours?

(A) $y=0.09x+100$

(B) $y=1.09x+100$

(C) $y=100(1.09)^x$

(D) $y=100x^{1.09}$

0386

Suppose the value of an Italian antique increases exponentially. Which of the following statements must be true about the value of the antique?

(A) Each year, the price of antique increases by $60 compared to the previous year.

(B) Each year, the price of antique delcreases by $60 compared to the previous year.

(C) Each year, the price of antique increases by 6% compared to the previous year.

(D) Each year, the price of antique decreases by 6% compared to the previous year.

0387

Suppose the population of California grows 5% every decade. After a century, the population of California will be how many times the size of the population today?

(1 decade=10 years, 1 century=100 years)

(A) 1.25

(B) 1.47

(C) 1.63

(D) 1.94

For questions 388−389, refer to the following information below.

0388

$$S(t)=2,000(1.02)^{\frac{t}{2}}$$

The given function S models the number of squirrels in a national park, where t represents the number of years after 2022.

Which of the following is the best interpretation of the number 1.02 in this context?

(A) The model predicts that the number of squirrels grow by approximately 40 every year.

(B) The model predicts that the number of squirrels grow by approximately 40 every two years.

(C) The model predicts that the number of squirrels grow by approximately 2% every year.

(D) The model predicts that the number of squirrels grows by approximately 2% every two years.

0389

Which of the following equations best models the number of squirrels m months after 2022?

(A) $S(m)=2,000\left(\dfrac{1.02}{12}\right)^{\frac{m}{2}}$

(B) $S(m)=\dfrac{2,000}{12}(1.02)^{\frac{m}{2}}$

(C) $S(m)=2,000(1.02)^{\frac{m}{24}}$

(D) $S(m)=2,000(1.02)^{24m}$

0390

If the value of a new truck was $28,000 5 years ago, and by now the value was halved. If the value of this car had decreased by the same percent each year, which of the following is closest to the annual percent decrease over the last 5 years?

(A) 10%

(B) 11%

(C) 12%

(D) 13%

0391

Linear Function: $y=\frac{3}{2}x-1$

Exponential Function: $y=2^x-2$

Which of the following is true about two functions given above?

(A) The exponential function is greater than the linear function for all x

(B) The exponential function is less than the linear function for all x

(C) The exponential function is greater than the linear function on the interval $0<x<2$

(D) The exponential function is less than the linear function on the interval $0<x<2$

0392

If $2^{\frac{3}{2}}\cdot 3=\sqrt{x}$, what is the value of x?

0393

$$\left(\sqrt[3]{a^2}\right)^n=a^{12},$$

In the expression above, $a\geq 0$ and n is a positive integer. What is the value of n?

0394

$$\sqrt[3]{50}=2^a5^b$$

In the expression above, a and b are positive numbers. What is the value of $a+b$?

0395

What is the value of $(\sqrt{2}-\sqrt{3})(\sqrt{2}+\sqrt{3})$?

0396

If the expression $\dfrac{1}{1+\sqrt{2}}$ can be written as $a+\sqrt{b}$, where b is positive integer, what is the value of $a+b$?

0397

If $\sqrt{4-2xy}=x-y$, what is the value of x^2+y^2?

0398

$$3^{x+1}=9\sqrt{27}$$

What is the solution to the equation above?

0399

If $2^{1-2x}=4^{1+2x}$, what is the value of x?

0400

$$2^{x^2-4x}=\left(\dfrac{1}{2}\right)^{x+2}$$

Find one possible solution to the equation above.

0401

$$(x^2)^3\times(xy^2)^4\times x^3y=x^a y^b$$

What is the value of $a-b$ in the equation above? (a and b are positive integers)

0402

If $3^x+3^x+3^x=3^{2x-1}$ for all x, then what is the value of x?

0403

$$f(x)=4(5)^{2x}-3$$

What is the y-intercept of the graph of f in the xy-plane?

0404

x	0	1	2	3
$f(x)$	18	10	6	4

The table above gives the values of the exponential function f at selected values of x. If the function can be written as $f(x)=4\left(\dfrac{1}{2}\right)^{x-h}+k$, where h and k are positive constants, what is the value of hk?

0405

If the graph of the exponential function $y=a^{x-1}+2$ passes through the points $(2,\ 4)$ and $\left(m,\ \dfrac{9}{4}\right)$, what is the value of m?

0406

$$B(t)=1{,}200(2)^{\frac{2t}{150}}$$

The function B give the number of bacteria t seconds after first being observed. How many minutes does it take for the number of bacteria to double?

Memo

5. More about Polynomials and Equations

01. Dividing Polynomials

1. Division Algorithm

Let $f(x)$ and $d(x)$ be polynomials with degree of d, $d \neq 0$, less than or equal to the degree of f. Then there exist a quotient $q(x)$ and remainder $r(x)$ such that

$$\underbrace{f(x) = d(x) \cdot q(x) + r(x)}_{\text{Polynomial Form}} \Leftrightarrow \underbrace{\frac{f(x)}{d(x)} = q(x) + \frac{r(x)}{d(x)}}_{\text{Fraction Form}}$$

2. Long Division

Polynomials can be divided by using long division. It closely resembles the division of integers.

$$
\begin{array}{r}
212 \\
13\overline{)2759} \\
26 \\
\hline
159 \\
13 \\
\hline
29 \\
26 \\
\hline
3
\end{array}
\qquad \Rightarrow \qquad
\begin{array}{r}
2x^2 + x + 2 \\
x+3\overline{)2x^3 + 7x^2 + 5x + 9} \\
2x^3 + 6x^2 \\
\hline
x^2 + 5x + 9 \\
x^2 + 3x \\
\hline
2x + 9 \\
2x + 6 \\
\hline
3
\end{array}
$$

> Quotient
> Dividend
> $(x+3) \times 2x^3$
> Subtract
> $(x+3) \times x$
> Subtract
> $(x+3) \times 2$
> Remainder

Therefore, $\dfrac{2x^3 + 7x^2 + 5x + 9}{x+3}$ can be written as $2x^2 + x + 2 + \dfrac{3}{x+3}$.

3. Synthetic Division

There is a shortcut for long division, which is a lot simpler and easier. It is called synthetic division. However, this method can be only used when divisor is linear.

$$\frac{2x^3 + 7x^2 + 5x + 9}{x+3} \qquad \Rightarrow$$

$$
\begin{array}{r|rrrr}
 & 2 & 7 & 5 & 9 \\
 & & + & + & + \\
-3 & \downarrow & -6\downarrow & -3\downarrow & -6\downarrow \\
\hline
 & 2 & 1 & 2 & \boxed{3}
\end{array}
$$

Quotient $\rightarrow \qquad 2x^2 \quad 1x \quad 2$

Quotient: $2x^2 + x + 2$
Remainder: 3

Example 1

$$\frac{x^3-6x^2+3x-4}{x+2}$$

Which of the following is equivalent to the expression above?

(A) $x^2-8x+19-\dfrac{42}{x+2}$

(B) $x^2-4x+11-\dfrac{26}{x+2}$

(C) $x^2-8x+19$

(D) $x^2-4x+11$

Solution

Method 1: Long Division

$$
\begin{array}{r}
x^2-8x+19 \\
x+2\overline{)x^3-6x^2+\ 3x-4} \\
\underline{x^3+2x^2} \\
-8x^2+\ 3x-4 \\
\underline{-8x^2-16x} \\
19x-4 \\
\underline{19x+38} \\
-42
\end{array}
$$

Method 2: Synthetic Division

$$
\begin{array}{r|rrrr}
& 1 & -6 & 3 & -4 \\
-2 & & -2 & 16 & -38 \\
\hline
& 1 & -8 & 19 & \boxed{-42}
\end{array}
$$

Quotient: $x^2-8x+19$

Remainder: -42

Therefore, $\dfrac{x^3-6x^2+3x-4}{x+2}=x^2-8x+19-\dfrac{42}{x+2}$

The answer is A.

02. Remainder and Factor Theorem

1. Remainder Theorem

Let the quotient and remainder be $q(x)$ and R, respectively. The remainder theorem states that $f(a)=R$ when a polynomial $f(x)$ is divided by $x-a$.

$$\frac{f(x)}{x-a} \Rightarrow f(a)=R$$

2. Factor Theorem

The theorem states that a polynomial $f(x)$ has a factor $x-a$ if and only if $f(a)=0$.

In other words, if $f(a)=0$, then $x-a$ is a factor of $f(x)$.

Example 2

For a polynomial $f(x)$, the value of $f(-1)=3$. Which of the following is true about $f(x)$?

(A) $x-1$ is a factor of $f(x)$.

(B) $x+1$ is a factor of $f(x)$.

(C) The remainder when $f(x)$ is divided by $x-1$ is 3.

(D) The remainder when $f(x)$ is divided by $x+1$ is 3.

Solution

$f(-1)=3$ means that the remainder is 3 when the polynomial $f(x)$ is divided by $x+1$.
Therefore, the correct answer is D.

The answer is D.

03. Rational Expressions

1. Definition

A rational expression is one that can be expressed as a quotient of polynomials. For example, $\dfrac{1}{x+3}$ and $\dfrac{x+1}{x-2}$ are rational expressions.

2. Simplifying Rational Expression

Let A, B, and $C(B \neq 0,\ C \neq 0)$ be nonzero real numbers or variable expressions.

$\dfrac{A\cancel{C}}{B\cancel{C}} = \dfrac{A}{B}$ ⇒ Divide out common factor C

3. Multiplication of Rational Expressions

Let A, B, C, 0 and $D(B \neq 0,\ D \neq 0)$ be nonzero real numbers or variable expressions.

$\dfrac{A}{B} \times \dfrac{C}{D} = \dfrac{AC}{BD}$ ⇒ (Denominator × Denominator) and (Numerator × Numerator)

4. Division of Rational Expressions

Let A, B, C, and $D(B \neq 0,\ D \neq 0)$ be nonzero real numbers or variable expressions.

$\dfrac{A}{B} \div \dfrac{C}{D} = \dfrac{A}{B} \times \dfrac{D}{C} = \dfrac{AD}{BC}$ ⇒ Convert division to multiplication

5. Addition and Subtraction of Rational Expressions

(1) When denominator is identical, simply add or subtract numerators.

$\dfrac{A}{B} + \dfrac{C}{B} = \dfrac{A+C}{B},\quad \dfrac{A}{B} - \dfrac{C}{B} = \dfrac{A-C}{B}$

(2) When denominator is NOT identical, find the least common denominator (LCD) and then add or subtract numerators.

$\dfrac{A}{B} + \dfrac{C}{D} = \dfrac{AD}{BD} + \dfrac{BC}{BD} = \dfrac{AD+BC}{BD},\quad \dfrac{A}{B} - \dfrac{C}{D} = \dfrac{AD}{BD} - \dfrac{BC}{BD} = \dfrac{AD-BC}{BD}$

Example 3

Simplify the expression.

(1) $\dfrac{x^2-x-6}{x^2-3x}$

(2) $\dfrac{x-3}{x-4} \times \dfrac{x^2-16}{5x-15}$

(3) $\dfrac{2x-12}{x^2-4} \div \dfrac{x^2-5x-6}{3x-6}$

(4) $\dfrac{x-4}{x} + \dfrac{x+3}{x+2}$

(1) $\dfrac{x^2-x-6}{x^2-3x}=\dfrac{(x-3)(x+2)}{x(x-3)}=\dfrac{x+2}{x}$

(2) $\dfrac{x-3}{x-4}\times\dfrac{x^2-16}{5x-15}=\dfrac{x-3}{x-4}\times\dfrac{(x-4)(x+4)}{5(x-3)}$

$\qquad\qquad\qquad=\dfrac{1}{1}\times\dfrac{x+4}{5}=\dfrac{x+4}{5}$

(3) $\dfrac{2x-12}{x^2-4}\div\dfrac{x^2-5x-6}{3x-6}=\dfrac{2x-12}{x^2-4}\times\dfrac{3x-6}{x^2-5x-6}$

$\qquad\qquad\qquad=\dfrac{2(x-6)}{(x-2)(x+2)}\times\dfrac{3(x-2)}{(x-6)(x+1)}$

$\qquad\qquad\qquad=\dfrac{2}{x+2}\times\dfrac{3}{x+1}$

$\qquad\qquad\qquad=\dfrac{6}{(x+2)(x+1)}$

(4) $\dfrac{x-4}{x}+\dfrac{x+3}{x+2}=\dfrac{(x-4)(x+2)}{x(x+2)}+\dfrac{(x+3)x}{(x+2)x}$

$\qquad\qquad\qquad=\dfrac{x^2-2x-8+x^2+3x}{x(x+2)}$

$\qquad\qquad\qquad=\dfrac{2x^2+x-8}{x(x+2)}$

04. Rational Equations

Equations that contain rational expressions are called rational equations. To solve a rational equation, refer to the following steps.

1. Find least common denominator (LCD).

2. Multiply both sides of the equation by LCD.

3. Solve the resulting polynomial equation.

4. Check the solution(s) to make sure there isn't an extraneous solution. In rational equations, the extraneous solution is the value that makes denominator equal to zero.

Example 4

$$\dfrac{1}{x-1}+\dfrac{4}{x+2}=2$$

What are all possible solutions to the given equation above?

(A) $-\dfrac{1}{2}$ and 2 (B) $\dfrac{1}{2}$ and -2 (C) $-\dfrac{1}{2}$ only   (D) 2 only

$$\left(\frac{1}{x-1}+\frac{4}{x+2}\right)(x-1)(x+2) \rightarrow \text{Multiply by LCD } (x-1)(x+2)$$

$$(x+2)+4(x-1)=2x^2+2x-4$$

$$5x-2=2x^2+2x-4$$

$$2x^2-3x-2=0$$

$$(2x+1)(x-2)=0$$

$$2x+1=0 \text{ or } x-2=0$$

$$x=-\frac{1}{2} \text{ or } x=2$$

Check the solution $\dfrac{1}{-\frac{1}{2}-1\neq0}+\dfrac{4}{-\frac{1}{2}+2\neq0}=2$ and $\dfrac{1}{2-1\neq0}+\dfrac{1}{2+2\neq0}=2$

When we substitute the solution back into the original equation, each denominator is not equal to zero. Therefore, both $x=-\frac{1}{2}$ and $x=2$ are solutions to the equation.

The answer is A.

05. System of Nonlinear Equations

A nonlinear system is a system with one or more nonlinear equations. In particular, a system consisting of one linear equation and one quadratic equation is presented in the exam. To solve this system, we usually apply a substitution method. Here are some examples of graphical interpretation of solutions in nonlinear systems.

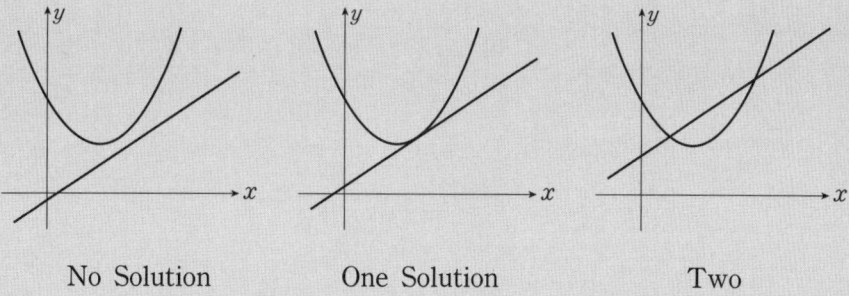

No Solution   One Solution   Two

Example 5

$$y=x^2-3$$
$$2x+y=5$$

What are all possible solutions for the given system above?

(A) $(-2, -7)$ and $(3, 6)$ 　　　　(B) $(-4, 13)$ and $(2, 1)$

(C) $(-2, 9)$ and $(3, -1)$ 　　　　(D) $(-3, 6)$ and $(3, -1)$

Substitute $y=x^2-3$ into the equation $2x+y=5$.

$$2x+(x^2-3)=5$$
$$2x+x^2-3=5$$
$$x^2+2x-8=0$$
$$(x+4)(x-2)=0, \ x=-4 \text{ or } x=2$$

Substitute $x=-4$ and $x=2$ into either equation.

$$x=-4; \ 2(-4)+y=5 \qquad\qquad x=2-2(2)+y=5$$
$$-8+y=5, \ y=13 \text{ and} \qquad\qquad 4+y=5, \ y=1$$

Therefore, the solutions are $(-4, \ 13)$ and $(2, \ 1)$.

The answer is B.

Memo

0407

$$\frac{x^4-5}{x^2+2}$$

Which of the following is equivalent to the expression above?

(A) $x^2+x-2-\dfrac{1}{x^2+2}$

(B) $x^2+x+1-\dfrac{2}{x^2+2}$

(C) $x^2-2-\dfrac{1}{x^2+2}$

(D) $x^2+1-\dfrac{2}{x^2+2}$

0408

$$\frac{x^3+4x^2-9x+2}{x+3}$$

Which of the following is equivalent to the expression above?

(A) $x^2+x-12+\dfrac{38}{x+3}$

(B) $x^2-x+12-\dfrac{38}{x+3}$

(C) $x^2-4x+3+\dfrac{9}{x+3}$

(D) $x^2+4x-3-\dfrac{9}{x+3}$

0409

$$\frac{4x(x+2)-3(x+2)}{5x+10}$$

Which of the following is equivalent to the expression above?

(A) $\dfrac{4x-3}{x+2}$

(B) $\dfrac{4x-3}{5}$

(C) $\dfrac{x+2}{5x+10}$

(D) $\dfrac{1}{5}$

0410

$$f(x)=2x^2+11x+12$$

$$g(x)=3x^2+11x-4$$

Which of the following expressions is equivalent to $\dfrac{f(x)}{g(x)}$, where $g(x)\neq0$?

(A) $\dfrac{2x+1}{3x-1}$

(B) $\dfrac{2x+1}{3x+1}$

(C) $\dfrac{2x+3}{3x-1}$

(D) $\dfrac{2x+3}{3x+1}$

0411

When a number is divided by 9, the remainder is 4. What is the remainder when three times that number is divided by 9?

(A) 1

(B) 2

(C) 3

(D) 4

0412

For a polynomial $P(x)$, the value of $P(3)=0$. Which of the following is true about $P(x)$?

(A) $x+3$ is a factor of $P(x)$

(B) $x-3$ is a factor of $P(x)$

(C) The remainder when $P(x)$ is divided by x is 3

(D) The remainder when $f(x)$ is divided by x is -3

0413

If $\dfrac{x-1}{x+1}+\dfrac{3}{2x+3}=\dfrac{ax^2+bx+c}{(x+1)(2x+3)}$, where $x\neq -1$ and $x\neq -\dfrac{3}{2}$, what is the value of $a+b+c$?

(A) 5

(B) 6

(C) 7

(D) 8

0414

If $\dfrac{2x-4}{x+3}-\dfrac{x+1}{3x-1}=\dfrac{ax^2+bx+c}{3x^2+8x-3}$, where $x\neq -1$ and $x\neq -\dfrac{3}{2}$, what is the value of b?

(A) -5

(B) -18

(C) 3

(D) 1

0415

$$2-\dfrac{x-4}{x-1}$$

Which of the following is equivalent to the expression above?

(A) $\dfrac{x+2}{x-1}$

(B) $\dfrac{2x+1}{x-1}$

(C) 6

(D) 5

0416

$$\dfrac{2}{x-2}-\dfrac{x-1}{x}$$

Which of the following is equivalent to the expression above?

(A) $\dfrac{x^2-x-2}{x(x-2)}$

(B) $\dfrac{x^2-x-2}{x(x-2)}$

(C) $\dfrac{x^2-5x-2}{x(x-2)}$

(D) $-\dfrac{x^2-5x+2}{x(x-2)}$

5. More about Polynomials and Equations 139

0417

Which of the following is the reciprocal of $\dfrac{1}{a}-\dfrac{1}{b}$?

(A) $\dfrac{a-b}{ab}$

(B) $\dfrac{b-a}{ab}$

(C) $\dfrac{ab}{a-b}$

(D) $\dfrac{ab}{b-a}$

0418

$$\dfrac{\dfrac{m}{n}-l}{\dfrac{r}{s}}$$

If each letter in the expression above represents a positive integer, which of the following operations will have the effect of reducing the value of the entire expression to exactly $\dfrac{1}{4}$ of its original value?

    I. Dividing n by 4

    II. Multiplying r by 4

    III. Dividing s by 4

(A) I only

(B) II only

(C) III only

(D) II and III only

0419

$$\dfrac{2}{x+4}=8x+32$$

In the equation above, which of the following is a possible value of $x+4$?

(A) -1

(B) -0.25

(C) -0.5

(D) 0

0420

If $1+\dfrac{2}{x}=2+\dfrac{4}{x}$ where $x\neq0$, what is the value of $1+\dfrac{2}{x}$?

(A) -1

(B) 0

(C) 1

(D) 2

0421

$$\dfrac{x^2-x-6}{x+2}=0$$

What is the solution to the equation above?

(A) -2

(B) 0

(C) 2

(D) 3

0422

$$\frac{5}{x-3}-2=\frac{30}{x^2-9}$$

What are all possible solutions to the equation above?

(A) $-\frac{1}{2}$

(B) 3

(C) $-\frac{1}{2}$ and 3

(D) No solution

0423

$$\frac{5}{x^2-2x}+\frac{2}{x}=\frac{5}{x^2-2x}$$

What are all possible solutions to the equation above?

(A) 2

(B) 5

(C) 2 and 5

(D) No solution

0424

If $\frac{1}{k}=\frac{1}{a}+\frac{1}{b}+\frac{1}{c}$, and none of a, b, c, and k are zero, then $k=?$

(A) $a+b+c$

(B) $\dfrac{1}{a+b+c}$

(C) $\dfrac{a+b+c}{abc}$

(D) $\dfrac{abc}{ab+bc+ac}$

0425

Which of the following is a value of x for which the expression is $\dfrac{2x}{x^3+x^2-6x}$ undefined?

(A) -2

(B) 0

(C) 3

(D) 6

0426

What are all possible values of m for which the expression $\dfrac{3x^2-27}{m^2-16}$ is undefined?

(A) 3 only

(B) 4 only

(C) 3 and -3

(D) 4 and -4

0427

$$y=x+1$$
$$y=x^2-1$$

Which of the followings is the set of all ordered pairs that satisfy the system above?

(A) $\{(-1,\ 0)\}$

(B) $\{(2,\ 3)\}$

(C) $\{(1,\ 2),\ (2,\ 3)\}$

(D) $\{(-1,\ 0),\ (2,\ 3)\}$

0428

$$x+y=-1$$
$$y=x^2-4x+1$$

The solution to the system of equations above is (x, y). What are all possible value of y?

(A) 2

(B) -3

(C) 2 and -3

(D) -2 and -3

0429

$$y=x^2+8$$
$$y=2(4-3x)$$

The graphs of the given equations in the $xy-$plane intersect at the point (x, y). What is one possible value of y?

(A) 26

(B) 32

(C) 44

(D) 50

0430

$$y=3x^2-2x$$
$$y=2x^2+24$$

The graphs of the given equations in the $xy-$plane intersect at the point (x, y). If $x<0$, what is the value of x?

(A) -4

(B) -3

(C) -2

(D) -1

0431

$$a^2-2ab+b^2=16$$
$$2b-a=6$$

If the solution to the system of equations above is (a, b), which of the following could be the value of a?

(A) 2

(B) 4

(C) 6

(D) 14

0432

$$y = x^2 - 2x + 5$$

$$2x - y = -1$$

How many solutions does the system of equations above have?

(A) Zero

(B) Exactly one

(C) Exactly two

(D) Infinitely many

0433

$$y = 3x^2$$

$$8x - y = k$$

In the given system of equations, k is a positive constant. The system has exactly one distinct real solution. What is the value of k?

(A) 16

(B) 8

(C) 4

(D) $\frac{16}{3}$

0434

In the $xy-$plane, the points M and N lie on the intersection of the graph of $f(x) = 2x + 4$ and $g(x) = x^2 + 1$, respectively. What is the slope of $\overline{MN}$?

(A) 0

(B) 1

(C) 2

(D) 3

0435

In the $xy-$plane, which of the following lines has two intersections with the graph of $y = x^2 + 2x + 3$?

(A) $y = 2x - 1$

(B) $y = 2x$

(C) $y = 4x + 3$

(D) $y = 4x - 5$

0436

James can paint his house in 14 hours less time than John, his younger brother, can. Together they can paint the house in 24 hours. Which of the following equation models the number of hours x for James to paint the house?

(A) $\dfrac{1}{x}+\dfrac{1}{x+14}=1$

(B) $\dfrac{1}{x-14}+\dfrac{1}{x}=1$

(C) $\dfrac{1}{x}+\dfrac{1}{x+14}=\dfrac{1}{24}$

(D) $\dfrac{1}{x-14}+\dfrac{1}{x}=\dfrac{1}{24}$

0437

Min's motorcycle can travel 30 miles against the wind in the same amount of time that it takes him to cover 60 miles with the wind. If the speed of the wind is 3 miles per hour, which of the following equation models the speed of Min's motorcycle x in miles per hour when he travels with wind?

(A) $\dfrac{60}{x+3}+\dfrac{30}{x-3}=1$

(B) $\dfrac{60}{x+3}-\dfrac{30}{x-3}=1$

(C) $\dfrac{60}{x-3}-\dfrac{30}{x+3}=1$

(D) $\dfrac{60}{x+3}=\dfrac{30}{x-3}$

0438

David rode his rollers skate 24 miles from his house to the park. On his way back, he borrowed a bicycle from his friend. Going twice as fast on the bicycle, the return trip took 2 hours less. What is his average speed for the entire trip?

(A) 6 miles per hour

(B) 7 miles per hour

(C) 8 miles per hour

(D) 9 miles per hour

0439

$$\frac{2}{2x-3}-2=\frac{ax+b}{cx+d}$$

If the equation above is true for all x where $x\neq\frac{3}{2}$, what is the value of $a+b+c+d$?

0440

Given the equation

$$\frac{10}{(2x-1)(x+2)}=\frac{a}{2x-1}+\frac{b}{x+2},$$

find the value of $a+b$.

0441

Given the equation

$$\frac{12}{x^2-4}=\frac{a}{x-2}+\frac{b}{x+2} \text{ where } x\neq\pm2,$$

find the value of $a+b$.

0442

Find the remainder when $x^4-4x^3+x^2+2x-3$ is divided by $x-2$.

0443

The graph of the function f and g are defined by $f(x)=3x^2-7x+2$ and $g(x)=3x+10$, respectively. What is the value of k such that $f(k)=g(k)$ where $k>0$?

0444

$$2y^2-y-2x=8$$

$$3y-2x=8$$

The solution to the system of equations above is (x, y). If $y>0$, what is the value of y?

0445

$$y = 8x^2 + 32$$
$$y = 40x - a$$

In the given system of equations, a is a positive constant. The system has exactly two distinct real solutions. If $b > a$, what is the least value of b?

0446

A positive integer is 2 greater than the other. When the reciprocal of the larger number subtracted from the reciprocal of the smaller one, the result is $\frac{1}{4}$. What is the value of the smaller integer?

0447

Eric can complete his backyard work in 3 hours. If his son works together, they will be able to finish the work in 2 hours. How long would the yard work take if his son was working alone?

0448

One day, Andy drove 50 miles from home to work. When he returned home, he increased his average speed 10 miles per hour higher than the speed on the way to work. If this reduced his return time by 10 minutes, what was his average speed going to work?

Memo

6. Representation of Functions

01. End Behavior

The graph of the polynomial function $f(x) = a_n x^n + a_{n-1} x^{n-1} + \cdots + a_1 x + a_0$ eventually increases or decreases in the following manner.

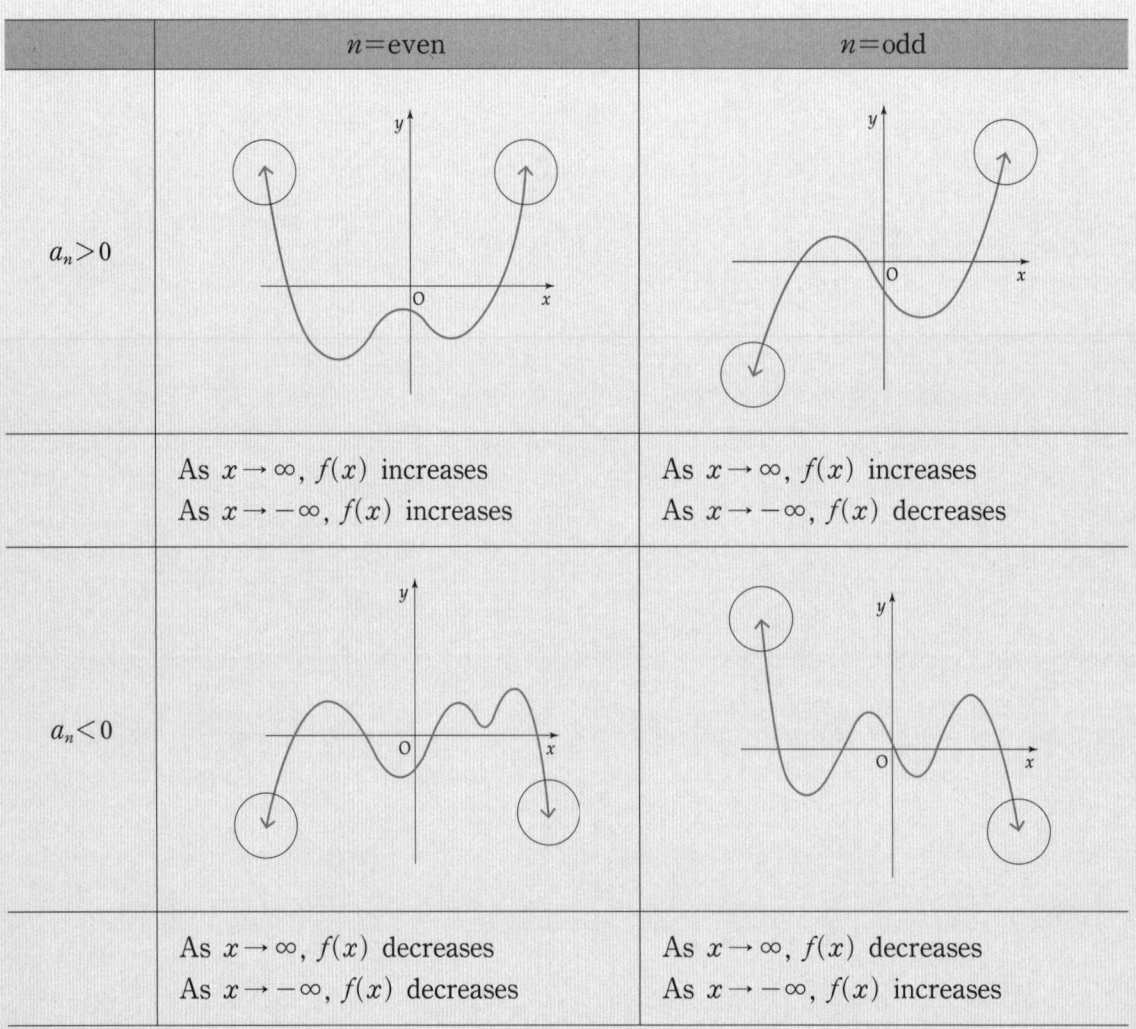

	$n=$even	$n=$odd
$a_n > 0$	As $x \to \infty$, $f(x)$ increases As $x \to -\infty$, $f(x)$ increases	As $x \to \infty$, $f(x)$ increases As $x \to -\infty$, $f(x)$ decreases
$a_n < 0$	As $x \to \infty$, $f(x)$ decreases As $x \to -\infty$, $f(x)$ decreases	As $x \to \infty$, $f(x)$ decreases As $x \to -\infty$, $f(x)$ increases

02. The x-intercept

The x-intercepts of the graph of f, often called zeros, correspond to values of x such that $f(x) = 0$, which corresponds to where the graph intersects the x-axis. If the function f has the factor $(x-a)^r$ and $r > 1$, **the graph touches** the x-axis **if r is even and passes though** the x-axis **if r is odd**.

For examples 1~2, refer to the following graph.

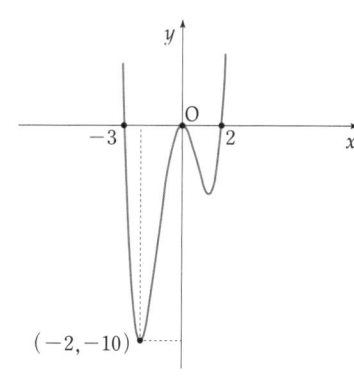

Example 1

Assuming that a is a real number, which of the following could be a function of the graph?

(A) $f(x)=ax(x+3)(x-2)$

(B) $f(x)=ax^2(x+3)(x-2)$

(C) $f(x)=ax(x+3)^2(x-2)$

(D) $f(x)=ax(x+3)(x-2)^2$

Solution

The given graph has three $x-$intercepts at $x=-3$, $x=0$, and $x=2$. For $x=-3$ and $x=2$, the graph passes through the $x-$axis. For $x=0$, the graph touches the $x-$axis.
This means that the factors $x+3$ and $x-2$ must have an odd degree, and the factor x must have even degree.
Therefore, a possible function among the answer choices is B.

The answer is B.

Example 2

If the function $g(x)=b$ and there are 3 solutions that satisfy $g(x)=f(x)$, which of the following could be the value of b? (b is a real number)

(A) 1   (B) -1 (C) -3 (D) -5

Solution

The number of solutions that satisfy $g(x)=f(x)$ is the number of intersections of two graphs.
The graph of $g(x)=b$ is a horizontal line, so when $b=-3$, there are 3 solutions as shown below.

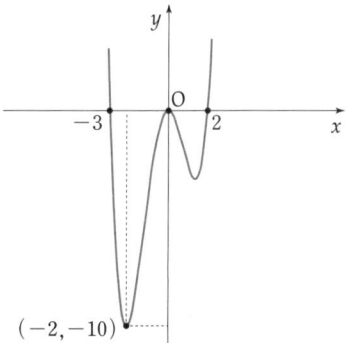

The answer is C.

02. Function Notation

1. Function Notation

$f(a)=b$ means that when x is a, the value of y is equal to b.

2. Function Operations

Given two functions f and g, following operations can be defined.

(1) Sum: $\quad\quad\quad\quad\quad\quad\quad$ $(f+g)(x)=f(x)+g(x)$

(2) Difference: $\quad\quad\quad\quad\quad$ $(f-g)(x)=f(x)-g(x)$

(3) Product: $\quad\quad\quad\quad\quad\quad$ $(fg)(x)=f(x)\cdot g(x)$

(4) Quotient: $\quad\quad\quad\quad\quad\quad$ $\left(\dfrac{f}{g}\right)(x)=\dfrac{f(x)}{g(x)}$, $g(x)\neq0$

(5) Composition of Functions: $f\circ g=(f\circ g)(x)=f(g(x))$

$\quad\quad\quad\quad\quad\quad\quad\quad\quad\quad g\circ f=(g\circ f)(x)=g(f(x))$

3. Symmetry of the Functions

For all x, symmetries are defined for functions as follows.

(1) Symmetric about the $x-$axis: $f(x)=-f(x)$

(2) Symmetric about the $y-$axis: $f(x)=f(-x)$

(3) Symmetric about the origin: $f(x)=-f(-x)$

4. Translation

Suppose $y=f(x)$ defines any function and $h>0$, $k>0$.

Then, vertical and horizontal translations are represented as follows.

(1) Vertical Translation

$\quad$① Shifts k units upward $\quad\quad \to g(x)=f(x)+k$

$\quad$② Shifts k units downward $\quad \to g(x)=f(x)-k$

(2) Horizontal translation

$\quad$① Shifts h units to the right $\to g(x)=f(x-h)$

$\quad$② Shifts h units to the left $\to g(x)=f(x+h)$

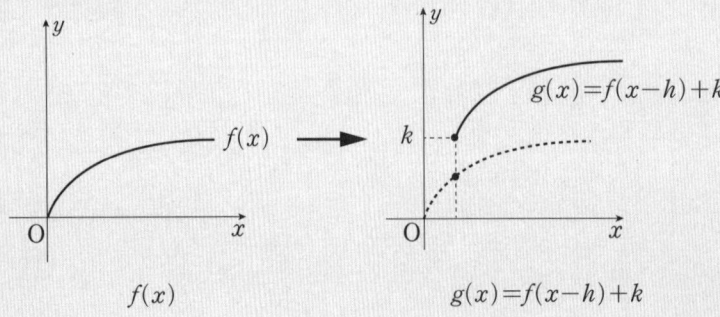

$f(x)$ $\quad\quad\quad\quad\quad\quad\quad\quad$ $g(x)=f(x-h)+k$

Example 3

If $f(x)=2^x-1$ and $g(x)=\dfrac{x}{x-2}$, then what is the value of $f(g(1))$?

(A) $\dfrac{3}{2}$ (B) 1 (C) 0 (D) $-\dfrac{1}{2}$

Solution

$g(1)=\dfrac{1}{1-2}$ and $f(g(1))=f(-1)=2^{-1}-1$

$\quad\ =-1$ $=\dfrac{1}{2}-1=-\dfrac{1}{2}$

The answer is D.

Example 4

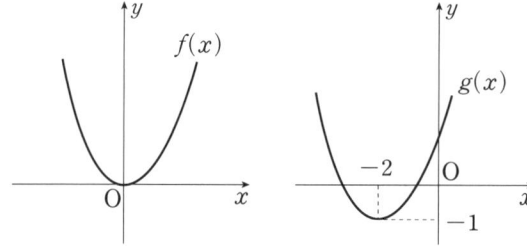

Given the graph of $f(x)$ and $g(x)$, which of the following is true?

(A) $g(x)=f(x+2)-1$ (B) $g(x)=f(x-2)+1$

(C) $g(x)=f(x+1)-2$ (D) $g(x)=f(x-1)+2$

Solution

The graph of $g(x)$ shifts the graph of $f(x)$ 2 units to the left and 1 unit up, so $g(x)=f(x+2)-1$.

The answer is A.

0449

The function f is defined by $f(x)=2x-1$. Which of the following values is equal to $f(1)+2f(2)$?

(A) 4

(B) 5

(C) 6

(D) 7

0450

If $f(x)=3-2x^2$ and $x<0$, for what value of x is $f(x)=0$?

(A) $-\dfrac{\sqrt{3}}{2}$

(B) $-\dfrac{\sqrt{3}}{4}$

(C) $-\dfrac{\sqrt{6}}{2}$

(D) $-\dfrac{\sqrt{6}}{4}$

0451

If $f(x)=2^x-1$ and $g(x)=\dfrac{x}{x-2}$, then what is the value of $f(g(0))$?

(A) 1

(B) $\dfrac{1}{2}$

(C) 0

(D) $-\dfrac{1}{2}$

0452

If $f(x)=\sqrt{1-2x}$ and $g(x)=x^2-5$, then what is the value of $f(g(1))$?

(A) 3

(B) 4

(C) 5

(D) $f(g(1))$ is not defined.

0453

x	$f(x)$
0	-2
1	2
2	4
3	5
4	0

If a function f is defined by the table above, what is the value of $f(f(1))$?

(A) 0

(B) 2

(C) 4

(D) 5

0454

The function f is defined by

$f(x)=\dfrac{a}{x-1}+x-1$ and $f(2)=2f(-1)$.

What is the value of a?

(A) $-\dfrac{5}{2}$

(B) -2

(C) $\dfrac{3}{2}$

(D) 5

0455

If $f(x)=x^2-x-1$, which of the following is equal to $f(x+h)-f(x)$?

(A) $2xh+h^2$

(B) $2xh+h^2-h$

(C) $2x-1$

(D) $2x-1-h$

0456

If $f(x)=2x+1$ and $g(x)=x^2-2$, then what is the value of $g\!\left(f\!\left(\dfrac{x}{2}\right)\right)$?

(A) x^2+2x-1

(B) x^2+2x+3

(C) $\dfrac{x^2}{4}+x-1$

(D) $\dfrac{x^2}{4}-x+1$

0457

If $f(x)=x-4$ and $g(x)=2(x-2)$, then which of the following expresses $g(x)$ in terms of $f(x)$?

(A) $g(x)=f(x-2)$

(B) $g(x)=f(x+2)$

(C) $g(x)=2f(x)-4$

(D) $g(x)=2f(x)+4$

0458

If $f(x)=x^2-1$ and $g(x)=2x-3$, what are all value of a such that $f(g(2))=g(f(a))$?

(A) $\dfrac{\sqrt{5}}{2}$ only

(B) $\dfrac{\sqrt{10}}{2}$ only

(C) $\dfrac{\sqrt{5}}{2}$ and $-\dfrac{\sqrt{5}}{2}$

(D) $\dfrac{\sqrt{10}}{2}$ and $-\dfrac{\sqrt{10}}{2}$

0459

Which of the following must be true about the graph of the function $f(x)=-x^4+5x^3+x$?

I. It eventually increases as x increases

II. It eventually increases as x decreases

III. It eventually decreases as x increases

IV. It eventually decreases as x decreases

(A) I and II only

(B) I and III only

(C) II and III only

(D) III and IV only

0460

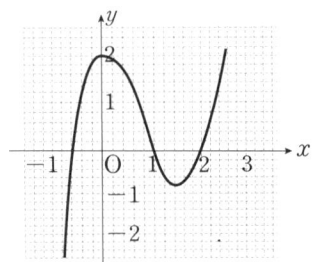

Which of the following functions could represent the graph above?

(A) $y=-(x-1)(x-2)(2x+1)$

(B) $y=(x-1)(x-2)(2x+1)$

(C) $y=-(x+1)(x+2)(2x-1)$

(D) $y=(x+1)(x+2)(2x-1)$

0461

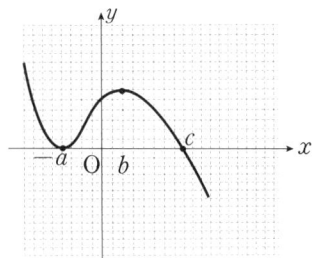

The graph of the function f given by $f(x)$ is shown above, where a, b, and c are constants. Which of the following could be the equation of $f(x)$?

(A) $f(x)=-(x+a)(x-b)(x-c)$

(B) $f(x)=(x-a)(x+c)^2$

(C) $f(x)=(x+a)^2(x-c)$

(D) $f(x)=-(x+a)^2(x-c)$

For questions 462−463, refer to the following information.

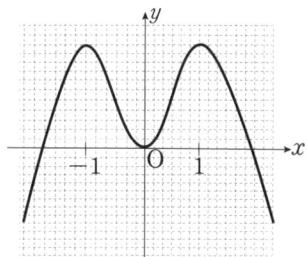

The graph of $f(x)=ax^4+bx^3+cx^2+dx+e$ is shown above.

0462

Which of the following must be true?

(A) $a>0$ and $e\neq0$

(B) $a<0$ and $e\neq0$

(C) $a>0$ and $e=0$

(D) $a<0$ and $e=0$

0463

If the function $h(x)=b$ and there are exactly 3 solutions that satisfy $f(x)=h(x)$, which of the following could be the value of b? (b is a real number)

(A) -1

(B) 0

(C) 1

(D) No such value of b exists.

0464

Let f be a polynomial function such that the graph of $y=f(x)$ in the $xy-$plane contains the points $(-2, 2)$, $(0, 3)$, and $(1, -2)$. Which of the following must be true about the zeros of f?

(A) f has exactly one zero

(B) f has exactly two zeros

(C) f has a zero between $x=-2$ and $x=0$

(D) f has a zero between $x=0$ and $x=1$

0465

How many distinct real zeros does the function $f(x)=(x^2+2.5)(x-4)(x+1)$ have?

(A) One

(B) Two

(C) Three

(D) Four

0466

$$f(x)=(x-5)(x-3)(x-2)$$

The function f is defined above. What is an $x-$intercept of the graph f?

(A) $(-2, 0)$

(B) $(3, 0)$

(C) $(0, -5)$

(D) $(0, 2)$

Practice **Questions**

0467

Which of the following function has exactly two $x-$intercepts?

(A) $f(x)=(x^2-16)(x+3)$

(B) $f(x)=(x^2+16)(x-4)$

(C) $f(x)=(x^2-16)(x-4)^2$

(D) $f(x)=(x^2+x-12)(x-1)^2$

For questions 468−470, refer to the function f below.

$$h(x)=(x-2)(x-1)$$

0468

Which of the following is the factor of function h?

(A) x

(B) $x+1$

(C) $x-2$

(D) $x+2$

0469

Which table of values represents $y=h(x)+4$?

(A)

x	y
0	-2
1	0
2	4

(B)

x	y
0	2
1	4
2	8

(C)

x	y
0	-6
1	-4
2	0

(D)

x	y
0	6
1	4
2	4

0470

How many distinct real zeros does the function $y=(x-2)h(x)$ have?

(A) 1

(B) 2

(C) 3

(D) 4

0471

Which of the following functions have zeros at -2 and 1?

I. $f(x)=\dfrac{x^2+x-2}{x-2}$

II. $g(x)=\dfrac{x^3+x^2-2x}{x+2}$

III. $g(x)=\dfrac{x+1}{x^2+x-2}$

(A) I only

(B) II only

(C) III only

(D) I and II only

0472

x	-2	-1	0	1
$f(x)$	0	6	4	0

Suppose f is a polynomial with degree 3. Based on the table above, which of the following could be f?

(A) $x(x-2)(x+2)$

(B) $(x-1)\left(x-\dfrac{1}{2}\right)(x+2)$

(C) $(x-2)(x-1)(x+2)$

(D) $(x-1)\left(x-\dfrac{1}{2}\right)\left(x+\dfrac{1}{2}\right)$

0473

If $f(x)=x^2-3x+7$ and $f(k)=2$, which of the following must be true?

(A) There is exactly 1 solution of k to the equation.

(B) There are exactly 2 solution of k to the equation.

(C) There is no solution of k to the equation.

(D) There are infinitely many solutions of k to the equation.

0474

Which of the following functions transforms $y=f(x)$ by shifting it 2 units to the left and 3 units up?

(A) $y=f(x+2)+3$

(B) $y=f(x-2)+3$

(C) $y=f(x+3)+2$

(D) $y=f(x-3)+2$

0475

The graph of $y=f(x)$ passes through the point $(-2, 4)$. If the graph of $y=f(x)$ is shifted 2 units to the right and 1 unit down, which point must it go through?

(A) $(-4, 3)$

(B) $(-4, 5)$

(C) $(0,3)$

(D) $(0, 0)$

For questions 476−477, refer to the function f below.

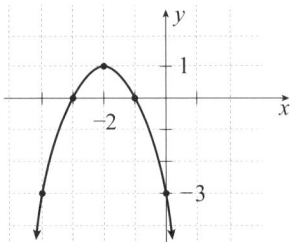

The graph of function f is shown above in the $xy-$plane.

0476

If the function h (not shown) is defined by $h(x)=f(x)-4$, what is the maximum value of the function h?

(A) -7

(B) -6

(C) -4

(D) -3

0477

If the function g (not shown) is defined by $g(x)=f(x-3)+1$, what is the $y-$intercept of the function g?

(A) -2

(B) -1

(C) 0

(D) 1

0478

In the $xy-$plane, the graph of $y=-(x+3)^2+2$ is shifted 1 unit to the left and 2 units down. Which of the following is an equation for the resulting graph?

(A) $y=-(x+2)^2$

(B) $y=-(x+4)^2$

(C) $y=-(x+2)^2+4$

(D) $y=-(x+4)^2+4$

0479

Which of the following translation of the graph of $f(x)=-x^2$ would result in the graph of $g(x)=-x^2+2x+k$, where k is a real number such that $k>0$?

(A) 1 unit to the right and $k+1$ units up

(B) 1 unit to the right and $k+1$ units down

(C) 2 units to the left and $k-1$ units up

(D) 2 units to the left and $k-1$ units down

0480

If f and g are polynomial functions defined for all real numbers and $g(x)=f(x)(2x-1)+k$ for all x, then which of the following is equivalent to k?

(A) $g(-1)$

(B) $g\left(-\dfrac{1}{2}\right)$

(C) $g(0)$

(D) $g\left(\dfrac{1}{2}\right)$

0481

The relationship between the Fahrenheit(F) scale and the Celsiu s(C) scale is $F=\dfrac{9}{5}C+32$. At which of the following temperature does the Celsius temperature equal to twice that of the Fahrenheit temperature?

(A) $-12.31°$F

(B) $-8.45°$F

(C) $-4.86°$F

(D) $2.69°$F

0482

If $f(x)=ax^3+bx^2+cx+d$ such that $f(0)=2$, $f(1)=2$ and $f(-1)=-2$, what is the value of $a+c$?

0483

If $f(x)=\sqrt{x-1}$ and $g(x)=3x+2$, for what value of x is $f(g(x))=1$?

0484

If the function $y=4x-1$ is shifted 4 units to the right, what is the $y-$intercept of the shifted function?

0485

The function g is defined as $g(x)=(x-m)(x-n)$, where m and n are integers and $m<n$. If $g(-4)>0$ and $g(2)<0$, what is one possible value of m?

0486

$$f(x)=x^3+2x^2-7x+4$$

If one of the zeros of the function f above -4, what is the other zero of the function f?

0487

x	$f(x)$
-2	1
-1	2
0	0
1	-3
2	-2

A function f is defined by the table above. What is the values of $f(f(-1))=$?

0488

If the function f is symmetric about the line $x=1$ and $f(0)=-2$, then what is the value of $f(2)$?

III

Problem Solving and Data Analysis

1. Ratio and Proportion

01. Ratio and Proportion

1. The **ratio of a to b** can be often expressed as $a : b$ or $\dfrac{a}{b}$. An equation stating that two ratios are equal such as $a : b = c : d$ or $\dfrac{a}{b} = \dfrac{c}{d}$ is called a **proportion**.

   Using the cross product, the proportion can be written as :
   $$\frac{a}{b} = \frac{c}{d} \;\Rightarrow\; ad = bc \text{ or } bc = ad$$

2. The Ratio of Similar Figures

   If the ratio of two figures that are similar to each other is $a : b$, then

   (1) The ratio of area is $a^2 : b^2$

   (2) The ratio of volume is $a^3 : b^3$

Example 1

Solve the equation $\dfrac{2x+1}{4} = \dfrac{x-4}{3}$.

Solution

$$\frac{2x+1}{4} = \frac{x-3}{3}$$
$$3(2x+1) = 4(x-4)$$
$$6x+3 = 4x-16$$
$$2x = -19,\; x = -\frac{19}{2}$$

$$x = -\frac{19}{2}$$

Example 2

The ratio of boys to girls in my Algebra 1 class is 3 to 2. If there are 12 boys, how many girls are there?

Solution

Letting b be the number of boys and g be the number of girls, we have $\dfrac{b}{g} = \dfrac{3}{2}$.

Since there are 12 boys, we have

$$\frac{12}{g} = \frac{3}{2}$$
$$3g = 24,\; g = 8$$

There are 8 girls.

Example 3

The side length of square ABCD is three times the side length of square EFGH. If the area of EFGH is 12cm^2, what is the area of square ABCD?

Solution

Let x be the area of square ABCD. Since the side length of square ABCD to the side length of square EFGH is $3 : 1$, we have

$$\frac{\text{Area of ABCD}}{\text{Area of EFGH}} = \frac{x}{12} = \frac{3^2}{1^2}$$

$$x = 9 \cdot 12 = 108$$

The area of square ABCD is 108cm^2.

02. Direct Proportion

Two variable quantities are in direct proportion when they increase or decrease in constant ratio.

In this case, we can use a proportion to solve the problem. For example, if a donut costs $2 at your school cafeteria, you will have to pay $4 for two donuts, $6 for three donuts, and so on.

Number of donuts (x)	1	2	3	4	...
Total cost (y)	$2	$4	$6	$8	...

As we see from the table, the constant ratio of the total cost to the number of donuts is $\frac{y}{x} = \frac{2}{1} = \frac{4}{2} = \frac{6}{3} = \frac{8}{4} = 2$. This constant ratio is called the **constant of proportionality**.

If x and y are directly proportional, then the ratio $\frac{y}{x} = k$ or $y = kx$ for some nonzero constant k.

Example 4

If x and y are directly proportional and $x = 4$ when $y = 10$, then what is x when y is 16?

Solution

Method 1
Since x and y are directly proportional, we have

$$\frac{y}{x} = \frac{10}{4}, \ \frac{y}{x} = \frac{5}{2}$$

Since y is 16, we have

$$\frac{16}{x} = \frac{5}{2}$$

$$5x = 32, \ x = \frac{32}{5}$$

Method 2
Using the equation $y = kx$ for some nonzero constant k, we have

$$y = kx$$

$$10 = k \cdot 4, \ k = \frac{5}{2}$$

Since y is 16, we have

$$y = \frac{5}{2}x$$

$$16 = \frac{5}{2}x, \ x = \frac{32}{5}$$

$$x = \frac{32}{5}$$

Example 5

If a 5 feet tall person casts a six feet shadow, how tall is the person who casts nine feet shadow?

Solution

Let p be the height of the person and s the length of shadow. Since the height of a person is directly proportional to the length of its shadow, we have

$$\frac{p}{s} = \frac{5}{6}$$

Since s is 9, we have the following :

$$\frac{p}{9} = \frac{5}{6}$$

$$6p = 45, \quad p = \frac{15}{2} = 7.5$$

The height of the person is 7.5 feet.

03. Inverse Proportion

Two variable quantities are in inverse proportion when their product is constant. If two quantities x and y are inversely proportional, then an increase in x causes a proportional decrease in y and vice−versa. That is, $xy = k$ or $y = \dfrac{k}{x}$, where k is a constant called the **constant of proportionality**. For example, a driver is traveling for a fixed distance of 100 miles. If the driver takes 1 hour to cover the distance at 100 mi/h, he will take 2 hours to cover the same distance at 50 mi/h and 4 hours to cover it at 25 mi/h, and so on.

Speed (mi/h)	100	50	25	10	...
Time (h)	1	2	4	10	...

If a driver halves his speed, the time taken for him to cover the same distance is doubled. If he quartered his speed, the time is quadrupled. That is, if x is the speed and y the time taken, we can say that $xy = k$ and $k = 100 \cdot 1 = 50 \cdot 2 = 25 \cdot 4 = 10 \cdot 10 = 100$. Therefore, the speed and the time taken are inversely proportional.

Example 6

If x and y are inversely proportional and $x=4$ when $y=15$, then what is y when x is 12?

Solution

Method 1

Since x and y are inversely proportional, we have

$$xy=4 \cdot 15, \quad xy=60$$

Since x is 12, we have the following :

$$xy=k$$
$$12y=60, \ y=5$$

Method 2

Using the equation $y=\dfrac{k}{x}$ for some nonzero constant k, we have

$$y=\dfrac{k}{x}$$
$$15=\dfrac{k}{4}, \ k=60$$

Since x is 12, we have the following :

$$y=\dfrac{k}{x}, \ y=\dfrac{60}{12}=5$$

$$y=5$$

Example 7

Suppose 16 pumps can empty a take filled with water in 12 hours. In how many hours could 24 pumps have emptied the same tank?

Solution

Let x be the number of pumps and y the amount of time in hours to finish the whole job. The number of pumps working and the time it takes to do the whole job are in inverse proportion. So we have

$$xy=16 \cdot 12, \ xy=192$$

Since x is 24, we have

$$xy=192$$
$$24y=192, \ y=8$$

The job will take 8 hours.

Practice **Problems**

0489

$$\frac{2}{3x+1}=\frac{3}{x-4}$$

Which of the following is the solution to the given equation above?

(A) $-\frac{11}{7}$

(B) $-\frac{7}{11}$

(C) $-\frac{5}{6}$

(D) $-\frac{6}{5}$

0490

If $\frac{4x}{3y}=\frac{2}{3}$, what is the value of $\frac{y}{x}$?

(A) 0.25

(B) 0.5

(C) 1

(D) 2

0491

If y varies inversely as x, and $y=4$ and $x=10$, what is the value of x when $y=12$?

(A) $\frac{2}{5}$

(B) $\frac{10}{3}$

(C) 30

(D) 40

0492

If $\frac{4a+9b}{7b-6a}=\frac{3}{2}$, which of the following is equal to the ratio of a to b?

(A) $\frac{6}{13}$

(B) $\frac{9}{13}$

(C) $\frac{6}{19}$

(D) $\frac{3}{26}$

0493

$$A : \frac{x-4a}{3}=4-x$$
$$B : \frac{x+5a}{4}=\frac{2x}{3}$$

If the ratio of the solutions of equation A to equation B is $2 : 3$, what is the value of a?

(A) 2

(B) 3

(C) 4

(D) 5

0494

The equation $\dfrac{3}{8a} = \dfrac{5b}{4c}$ relates to positive numbers a, b, and c. Which equation correctly expresses c in terms of a and b?

(A) $480ab$

(B) $\dfrac{10ab}{3}$

(C) $\dfrac{10b}{3a}$

(D) $\dfrac{3a}{10b}$

0495

The equation $\dfrac{5c}{4a-1} = \dfrac{b}{a}$ relates to positive numbers a, b, and c. Which equation correctly expresses a in terms of b and c?

(A) $\dfrac{4b-5c}{b}$

(B) $\dfrac{5c-4b}{b}$

(C) $\dfrac{b}{5c-4b}$

(D) $\dfrac{b}{4b-5c}$

0496

If milk is on sale at 2 half−gallons for $7, how much is 5 half−gallons of milk?

(A) $16

(B) $16.5

(C) $17

(D) $17.5

0497

The ratio of boys to girls in the school is 4 to 3. There are a total of 105 students in the school. How many boys are in the school?

(A) 40

(B) 45

(C) 60

(D) 65

0498

Three kilograms of apples cost $4 on the market. At this rate, how much does k kilograms of apples cost in terms of k?

(A) $3k-4$

(B) $4k-3$

(C) $\dfrac{3k}{4}$

(D) $\dfrac{4k}{3}$

0499

A certain city has a land area of 48 square miles and a population of 384. What is the number of people in $4m$ square miles in this city?

(A) $\dfrac{m}{4}$

(B) $\dfrac{m}{2}$

(C) $32m$

(D) $64m$

0500

Sally is a high school softball player. One of her goals during the offseason is to hit 1,040 batting balls. If she hits 80 batting balls every 3 days, how many days will it take her to hit 1,040 batting balls?

(A) 36

(B) 39

(C) 41

(D) 43

0501

One pack of one company's vitamin C powder is enough for 4 children under the age of 10 to consume for d days. Adults consume twice as much vitamin C as children under the age of 10. Which equation represents the total number of days, A, if 8 adults consume 1 packet of vitamin C powder?

(A) $A(x) = \dfrac{d}{2}$

(B) $A(x) = \dfrac{d}{4}$

(C) $A(x) = \dfrac{d}{2} - 4$

(D) $A(x) = \dfrac{d}{4} - 2$

0502

The ratio of girls to boys in the 9th grade is 4 to 5. If there are 162 students in the class, how many more boys are there than girls?

(A) 18

(B) 19

(C) 20

(D) 21

0503

A basketball player decided to donate $2,000 for every five 3—pointers he makes. How many 3—pointers does he need to make to reach the $1.2 million donation?

(A) 1250

(B) 2500

(C) 3000

(D) 5000

0504

The time to complete a project varies inversely with the number of students. A group of 4 students can complete the project in 8 hours. Assuming that all students work on a project at the same rate, how long will it take 5 students to complete the project?

(A) 5 hours

(B) $\dfrac{28}{5}$ hours

(C) 6 hours

(D) $\dfrac{32}{5}$ hours

0505

Jennifer and Jeff currently weigh 120 and 130 pounds, respectively. If the ratio of Jennifer's weight to Jeff's weight is the same as the ratio of Jeff's weight to Chris' weight, how many pounds does Chris weigh?

(A) 140.83 lbs

(B) 142.26 lbs

(C) 146.42 lbs

(D) 148.65 lbs

For questions 506~507, refer to the following.

A bag contains only black, white, and blue balls. The ratio of black balls to white balls to blue balls is 2 : 1 : 3.

0506

If there is a total of 42 balls in the bag, how many blue balls are in the bag?

(A) 7

(B) 12

(C) 21

(D) 28

0507

If there are 48 black balls in the bag, how many balls are there in the bag?

(A) 72

(B) 96

(C) 120

(D) 144

0508

On a local map of certain region, 1 inch represents a half mile. If a ranch is represented on the map by a rectangle that has sides of length 2.5 inches and 4 inches, what is the actual area of the ranch in square miles?

(A) $2.5mi^2$

(B) $5mi^2$

(C) $7.5mi^2$

(D) $10mi^2$

0509

David spent $250 of his paycheck and deposited the remaining $70 in his savings account. If the amount he spends is proportional to the amount he saves, how much of a $960−paycheck will he spend?

(A) $740

(B) $750

(C) $760

(D) $770

0510

In a scale drawing of a rectangular parking lot, the parking lot is x inches wide and 5 inches long. If the actual parking lot is 120 feet long, which of the following functions A can represent the area (in square feet) of the actual parking lot?

(A) $A(x)=120x$

(B) $A(x)=2880x$

(C) $A(x)=\dfrac{120}{x}$

(D) $A(x)=\dfrac{2880}{x}$

0511

If the radius of sphere A is twice as long as the radius of sphere B, then what is the ratio of the volume of sphere A to the volume of sphere B?

(A) $\dfrac{1}{2}$

(B) $\dfrac{1}{8}$

(C) 2

(D) 8

0512

Triangle A and Triangle B are similar. The length of each side of triangle A is 4 times the length of the corresponding side of triangle B. How many times the area of triangle A is the area of triangle B?

(A) 4

(B) 16

(C) 32

(D) 64

0513

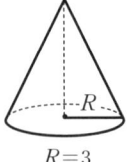 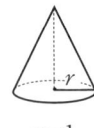

$R=3$ $r=1$

If the two cones in Figure above are similar and if the volume of the larger cone is 81 cubic inches, what is the volume of the smaller cone?

(A) 3 cubic inches

(B) 6 cubic inches

(C) 9 cubic inches

(D) 18 cubic inches

0514

There are two similar cones with a length ratio of $1:2$. Which of the following is true?

(A) The surface area of the large cone is twice the surface area of the small cone.

(B) The surface area of the large cone is 4 times the surface area of the small cone.

(C) The volume of the large cone is twice the volume of the small cone.

(D) The volume of the large cone is 4 times the volume of the small cone.

0515

A cylindrical tank has a radius to height ratio of $3:5$. If the height of the tank increases by 10 units, how much must the radius increase or decrease to maintain this ratio?

(A) It must decrease by 6 units.

(B) It must increase by 6 units.

(C) It must decrease by 18 units.

(D) It must increase by 18 units.

0516

If $\dfrac{a-b}{x+y}=\dfrac{3}{4}$, what is the value of $\dfrac{4a-4b}{3x+3y}$?

0517

The equation $\dfrac{12k}{9m}=\dfrac{8n}{6}$ can be written as $m=\dfrac{ak}{n}$, where a, k, m, and n are positive constants. What is the value of a?

0518

Pens are to be removed from a pencil case that contains 20 black pens and 20 blue pens. What is the number of pens that could be removed so that the ratio of black pens to blue pens left in the pencil case will be 5 to 4?

0519

Six people together can paint a house in 36 hours. In how many hours could 8 people have painted the same house? (Assume that all people paint a house at the same rate.)

0520

On Friday night, 680 adults and children came to a certain movie theater. If the ratio of adults to children was 13 to 7, how many adults came to the movie theater?

0521

The Empire State Building in New York is 381 meter tall. The Trump Tower in New York is 202 meter tall. Suppose a sculptor is asked to build a small−scale replica of each. If he make the Empire State Building 2.5 meters tall, what would be the height of the Trump Tower replica?

0522

Suppose 16 pumps can empty a tank filled with water in 12 hours. In how many hours could 24 pumps have emptied the same tank?

0523

A particular dish requires 3 scoops of rice for every $\frac{2}{3}$ tablespoon of sugar. According to this recipe, how much rice should the cook use if he used 3 tablespoons of sugar?

0524

K−Pencil Inc. is a company that manufactures pencils. The company's pencil−making machine produces 5 pencils every 2 minutes. If your company has 4 machines and all machines make pencils at the same speed, what is the total number of pencils that can be produced in 16 minutes?

0525

If the radius of sphere A is twice as long as the radius of sphere B, then what is the ratio of the volume of sphere A to the volume of sphere B?

0526

Points A, B, and C are three vertices of a triangle. If each vertex's $x-$and $y-$coordinates are doubled, a new triangle is formed. The area of the new triangle is how many times the area of the triangle ABC?

2. Unit Conversion and Percentage

01. Unit Conversion

Unit Conversion is the conversion between different units of measurement for the same quantity, typically through multiplicative conversion factors. A conversion factor is a ratio of quantities that is equal to 1. For example, 1 foot equals 12 inches, so we can write

$$\frac{1 \text{ foot}}{12 \text{ inches}}=1 \text{ or } \frac{12 \text{ inches}}{1 \text{ foot}}=1$$

The relationship between units is given in the test problem.

Example 1

Convert 48 inches into feet. (1 ft=12 in)

Solution

Since there are 12 inches in 1 foot, we have

$$48 \text{ in}=48 \text{ in}\times\frac{1 \text{ ft}}{12 \text{ in}}=4 \text{ ft}$$

48 inches are equal to 4 feet.

Example 2

1 cup (c)	= 8 fluid ounces (oz)
1 pint (pt)	= 2 cups
1 quart (qt)	= 2 pints
1 gallon (gal)	= 4 quarts

Using the information given in the table above, how many cups are in 2 gallons?

Solution

Conversion factors are very useful in that we can use more than one at the same time, as shown below.

$$2 \text{ gal}=2 \text{ gal}\times\frac{4 \text{ qt}}{1 \text{ gal}}\times\frac{2 \text{ qt}}{1 \text{ qt}}\times\frac{2 \text{ c}}{1 \text{ pt}}$$
$$=(2\times4\times2\times2) \text{ c}$$
$$=32 \text{ c}$$

There are 32 cups in two gallons.

02. Percentage

Percent means parts per 100 and it is often denoted using "%". A **percentage** is just a number or <u>ratio</u> expressed as a <u>fraction</u> of 100. Here are some examples of percent and percentage.

$$17\% = \frac{17}{100}, \quad 25\% = \frac{25}{100} = \frac{1}{4}, \quad 300\% = \frac{300}{100} = 3$$

In general, we can write $a\% = \frac{a}{100}$. In reverse, $a = a \times 100\%$.

Example 3

What is 40% of 240?

Solution

Method 1

Let x be the number of 40% of 240.
Then, the ratio of x to 240 equals the ratio of 60 to 100. So, we have

$$\frac{x}{240} = \frac{40}{100}$$
$$\frac{x}{240} = \frac{2}{5}$$
$$5x = 480, \quad x = 96$$

Method 2

We can calculate in a simple manner as shown below.
$$40\% \text{ of } 240 = 240 \times \frac{40}{100} = 96$$
or
$$40\% \text{ of } 240 = 240 \times 0.4 = 96$$

40% of 240 is 96.

Example 4

What percent of 120 is 56?

Solution

Let 56 be $x\%$ of 120, then the ratio of 56 to 120 equals to the ratio of x to 100. Therefore, we have

$$\frac{56}{120} = \frac{x}{100}$$
$$\frac{7}{15} = \frac{x}{100}$$
$$15x = 700, \quad x = \frac{140}{3}$$

56 is $\frac{140}{3}\%$ of 120.

Example 5

There are 35 passengers in a bus, in which 14 of them are men. What percent of the passengers in a bus are women?

Solution

Since 14 of 35 passengers are men, 21 of 35 passengers are women. Now, we need to find out 21 is what percent of 35.

$$\frac{21}{35} = \frac{x}{100}$$

$$\frac{3}{5} = \frac{x}{100}$$

$$5x = 300, \quad x = 60$$

60% of the passengers in a bus are women.

03. Percent of Change

A percent of change shows how much a quantity has increased or decreased in comparison with the original amount. Thus, we have the following :

$$\text{Percent of change, } p = \frac{\text{Amount of increase or decrease}}{\text{Original amount}} \times 100\%$$

If the new amount is greater than the original amount, then the percent of change is called a percent of increase. If the new amount is less than the original amount, then the percent of change is called a percent of decrease.

Example 6

What is the percent of increase from 12 to 18?

Solution

$$p = \frac{\text{Amount of increase or decrease}}{\text{Original amount}} \times 100\% = \frac{18-12}{12} \times 100\%$$

$$= \frac{6}{12} \times 100\% = 50\%$$

The percent of increase is 50%.

Example 7

Sam has 320 songs in his cellular phone. If he deletes 30% of the songs, how many songs are left?

Solution

Let's find the amount of decrease, 30% of 320.

Decrease=30% of 320=320×0.3=96

Now, we need to subtract 96 from the original amount.

So, there are 320−96=224 songs left on Sam's cellular phone.

224 songs left.

Practice **Problems**

0527

A car is traveling at a speed of 60 miles per hour. What is the car's speed in meters per second? (1 mi=1.609 km)

(A) 26.82 meters per second

(B) 27.03 meters per second

(C) 27.78 meters per second

(D) 28.87 meters per second

0528

A recipe calls for 2 cups of flour. If 1 cup of flour weighs 120 grams, what is the weight of the flour needed for the recipe in kilograms?

(A) 0.24 kg

(B) 0.48 kg

(C) 1.20 kg

(D) 2.40 kg

0529

A cylindrical tank has a diameter of 10 feet and a height of 20 feet. If the tank is filled with water up to a height of 15 feet, what is the volume of the water in gallons?

$$(1 \text{ gal}=0.134 \text{ ft}^3) \text{ (Use } \pi=3.14)$$

(A) 2,799 gallons

(B) 8,787 gallons

(C) 33,511 gallons

(D) 37,680 gallons

0530

A parcel delivery service charges $2.50 per pound for packages weighing up to 5 pounds and $3.00 per pound for packages weighing over 5 pounds. If a package weighs 7 pounds, what is the cost of shipping in dollars?

(A) $16.50

(B) $18.50

(C) $21.00

(D) $22.50

0531

A rectangular garden measures 20 feet by 30 feet. If the garden is to be covered with grass at a rate of $0.50 per square foot, what is the cost of covering the garden in dollars?

(A) $300

(B) $450

(C) $600

(D) $750

0532

If the size of the parking lot is 270 square feet, how many square yard is it?

$$(1 \text{ yard}=3 \text{ feet})$$

(A) 30 square yard

(B) 90 square yard

(C) 810 square yard

(D) 2430 square yard

0533

Jason averaged 60 miles per hour on a trip. Which of the following is Jason's speed in feet per second? (1 mile=5280 feet)

(A) 76 feet per second

(B) 80 feet per second

(C) 84 feet per second

(D) 88 feet per second

0534

Rick is a long—distance runner. He runs at a constant speed of 16 miles per hour. If Rick runs 4 hours every day, how many days will it take him to run 320 miles at this rate?

(A) 0.83 day

(B) 2 days

(C) 4 days

(D) 5 days

0535

If Nick drove 90 miles at a three—quarter mile per minute, how many hours did he drive?

(A) 1.5 hours

(B) 2 hours

(C) 2.5 hours

(D) 3 hours

0536

If one US dollar is equal to 130 Japanese yen, how many dollars can you buy with 5200 yen?

(A) $38

(B) $40

(C) $45

(D) $52

0537

Kevin traveled to Thailand with 4000 US dollars. The exchange rate at this time is 36.04 baht per US dollar. He exchanged all his dollars into baht and spent 80% of the money. At the end of the trip, he exchanged the baht he has left back into dollars at a rate of $1=35.95 baht. Approximately, how much does he get in dollars?

(A) $798

(B) $800

(C) $802

(D) $804

0538

Jenny bought the drone for shooting at Walmart for $89 plus 8% tax. Andrew ordered the same product online for 1300 pesos plus a shipping fee of 250 pesos when the exchange rate is $1=19.32 Mexican pesos. Which of the following statements is true?

(A) Jenny paid about $12 more than Andrew.

(B) Jenny paid about $16 more than Andrew.

(C) Andrew paid about $12 more than Jenny.

(D) Andrew paid about $16 more than Jenny.

0539

A tire with a 2 feet radius is rotating at a rate of 40 miles per hour. What is the approximate revolutions per minute of the tire? (1 mile=5280 feet)

(A) 280

(B) 300

(C) 312

(D) 320

0540

What percent of 240 is 60?

(A) 22%

(B) 25%

(C) 27%

(D) 29%

0541

27 is 150% of what number?

(A) 16

(B) 17

(C) 18

(D) 19

0542

If p percent of 240 is 108, what is p percent 340?

(A) 153

(B) 135

(C) 180

(D) 306

0543

The expression $0.4m$ represents the result of decreasing a positive number m by what percent?

(A) 4%

(B) 6%

(C) 40%

(D) 60%

0544

The number k is 150% greater than the number m. What is the value of m in terms of k?

(A) $1.15k$

(B) $2.25k$

(C) $\dfrac{k}{1.15}$

(D) $\dfrac{k}{2.5}$

0545

Nick's weight has decreased by 3.5%. If Nick's original weight is m, which of the following expression represents Nick's current weight?

(A) $0.35m$

(B) $0.65m$

(C) $0.035m$

(D) $0.965m$

0546

A dress that normally costs $86.50 is on sale for 20% off. What is the sale price of the dress?

(A) $68.4

(B) $69.2

(C) $70.6

(D) $71.4

For questions 547~548, refer to the following information below.

A total of 400 people participated in the marathon. During the race, 36 people gave up due to injuries and 24 people gave up due to physical exhaustion.

0547

What percentage of the total number of students who completed the marathon race?

(A) 80%

(B) 82.5%

(C) 85%

(D) 87.5%

0548

If the number of people who gave up from injuries is b times the number of people who gave up from physical exhaustion, what is the value of b?

(A) 1.5

(B) 2

(C) 2.5

(D) 3

0549

A beauty shop buys best treatment shampoos for $6.00 per bottle and marks up the price by 45%. For what price does the beauty shop sell each bottle of shampoo?

(A) $8.7

(B) $9.5

(C) $10.5

(D) $11.6

0550

Jenny invests $3,800 in Bank M, which pays 2.5% interest annually. She also invests $5,000 in Bank N, which pays 3% interest annually. If no withdrawals are made from both bank accounts, which of the following gives the sum of the amounts in both bank accounts after 1 year?

(A) $3800(0.025)+5000(0.03)$

(B) $3800(0.25)+5000(0.3)$

(C) $3800(1.025)+5000(1.03)$

(D) $3800(1.25)+5000(1.3)$

0551

Jason bought a shirt and a pair of pants for his homecoming party. The sum of the prices before the sales tax was $76. There was an 8% sales tax on the shirt and a 5% sales tax on the pants. If the total amount Jason paid including the sales tax was $81, which of the following is true about the price of each item?

(A) The shirt is $36 and the pair of pants is $40.

(B) The shirt is $40 and the pair of pants is $36.

(C) The shirt is $38.88 and the pair of pants is $42.4.

(D) The shirt is $43.2 and the pair of pants is $38.16.

For questions 552~553, refer to the following information below.

	2021	2022
Profit	26	27
Total number of Employee	120	132

The above table displays the total number of employees and profit, in million dollars, of the growing company in the technology sector.

0552

Assuming the number of employees increases at the same rate each year, how many more employees does the company expect to hire in the year 2023?

(A) Approximately 10 employees

(B) Approximately 11 employees

(C) Approximately 12 employees

(D) Approximately 13 employees

0553

If a company's goal in 2023 is to increase profits by $3 million over 2022, what percentage should the company's profits grow in 2023 compared to 2022?

(A) 11.11%

(B) 12.03%

(C) 12.87%

(D) 13.06%

0554

Mrs. Kaup works at local dealership as an accountant. She plans to purchase a new car priced at $24,000. She will receive a 20% employee discount and then will have to pay a 6% sales tax. How much does she have to pay for the car including sales tax?

(A) $19,200

(B) $20,352

(C) $22,485

(D) $25,440

0555

A chemist mixed some 20%−saline solution with some 35%−saline solution to obtain 8 liters of a 25%−saline solution. Which of the following is closest to the amount the chemist used in the mixture with a 20%−saline solution?

(A) 4.8 liters

(B) 5.1 liters

(C) 5.3 liters

(D) 5.6 liters.

0556

Suppose the number of bacteria increases by 20.6% every day. How many times the number of bacteria today is the number of bacteria yesterday?

(A) 0.206

(B) 1.0206

(C) 1.206

(D) 2.206

0557

The car dealer receives a salary of $300 per week plus a commission of 0.5% of total sales. Which of the following represents a car dealer's weekly income as total sales x?

(A) $300 + \dfrac{5}{100}x$

(B) $300 + \dfrac{0.5}{100}x$

(C) $\dfrac{5}{100}(300 + x)$

(D) $\dfrac{0.5}{100}(300 + x)$

0558

A store has an item marked down by $13 with an additional discount of 20% of the marked−down price. If the final price was $28, what was the original?

(A) $52

(B) $50

(C) $48

(D) $46

0559

A small bakery in town sells only two croissants: a butter croissant and a chocolate cream croissant. Three butter croissants and four chocolate cream croissants costs $16. Four butter croissants and two chocolate cream croissants costs $13. The bakery offers a 10% discount to customers who purchase a dozen or more croissants. If a customer buys a dozen butter croissants and half a dozen chocolate cream croissants, how much should the bakery charge the customer?

(A) $35.1

(B) $36.6

(C) $39

(D) $41.4

0560

In Elementary School A, there were some boys and girls last year, and the total number of students was 820. This year, the number of boys increased by 10% and the number of girls decreased by 8% compared to last year. As a result, the total number of students increased by 19. What is the number of boys in the school this year?

(A) 270

(B) 350

(C) 470

(D) 517

0561

A company has 24,000 tablets PCs in stock, of which 55 percent are 10 inches and 45 percent are 8 inches in size. The entire tablet PCs are either black or white in color. If 18,000 of the tablet PCs are black and 9,500 of the black tablet PCs are 10 inches, how many of the tablet PCs are both white and 8 inches?

(A) 2,300

(B) 3,700

(C) 6,000

(D) 8,500

0562

A car is traveling at a speed of 65 miles per hour. What is the speed of the car in meters per second? (1 mile=1.6 km)

0563

Convert 45 US dollars into Korean won given that 1000 won=$0.75

0564

At one particular time, the speed of a car was measured at 67 miles per hour. What is the equivalent speed of the car in feet per second? Round your answer to two decimal places. (1 mile=5280 feet)

0565

1 cup (c)	=8 fluid ounces (oz)
1 pint (pt)	=2 cups
1 quart (qt)	=2 pints
1 gallon (gal)	=4 quarts

A dripping faucet wastes 2 fluid ounces of water in one hour. How much water, in gallons, is wasted in three days?

0566

A single cornfield in Michigan is 2,500,000 square feet. What is the area in square miles of this cornfield? (1 mile=5,280 feet)

0567

The maximum speed of a red−tailed hawk is 180 kilometers per hour. If a red−tailed hawk flies at maximum speed to hunt a snake 2 kilometers away, how many seconds does it take?

0568

A rectangular swimming pool measures 50 feet by 25 feet. If the pool is filled to a depth of 10 feet, what is the number of thousands of gallons of water in the pool? (Assume 1 cubic foot of water is approximately 7.48 gallons.)

0569

The number c is 60% less than the number p. The number p is 60% greater than 60. What is the value of c?

0570

As soon as a new car is purchased and driven away from the dealership, it's value depreciate. Daniel bought a new 2022 Camry for $32,000. Next day, the value of the car was $30,000. What was the percent decrease in the value of the car?

0571

Christian buys a suit that is on sale for 20% off its original price. Luckily, the store was offering an additional 12% off the sale price. If Christian paid $281.6 for the suit, what was the original price of the suit?

0572

The list price of a particular item is set by adding a 20% profit to the original price of the item. Selling it at a discount of $2 from the list price resulted in a 10% profit from the original price. What is the original price of this item?

0573

Mr. Henderson wants to make 1.5 liters of 35% orange juice by mixing 20% orange juice and 60% orange juice. How many milliliters of a 60% orange juice does he need to add?
(Note : 1 liter is equal to 1,000 milliliters)

0574

Bike rentals offer low−cost daily flat−rate rentals of mountain bikes and standard bikes. All bikes must be returned before 6pm before the shop closes. Mountain bikes are 50% more expensive than standard bikes. And on weekends, due to a large number of customers, they offer rentals at a price that is 20% higher than the rental price on weekdays. If David's family paid $80 to rent two mountain bikes and one standard bike for the weekend, how much would it cost to rent a mountain bike for a weekday?

3. Data Analysis

01. Graphical Display of the Distribution

1. **Frequency Table**: This shows the distribution of a categorical variable in raw counts. For example, the table below shows the distribution of the favorite colors for 50 adults.

Favorite Color	Frequency
Yellow	10
Pink	15
Blue	8
Green	17
Total	50

2. **Bar Graph**: This is a chart or graph that presents categorical variables. The vertical axis labels frequency and the horizontal axis labels the possible values that could be listed in any order.

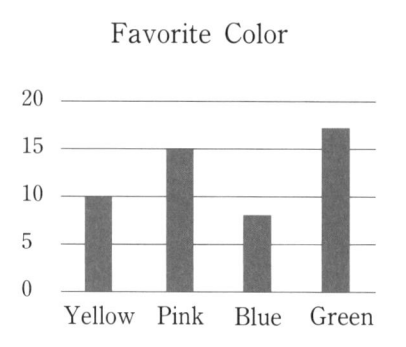

3. **Dot Plot**: Each data value is shown as a dot above its location on a number line. The horizontal axis must be labeled and marked with a scale. For example, the Algebra 1 test score of a class can be represented in the dot plot below.

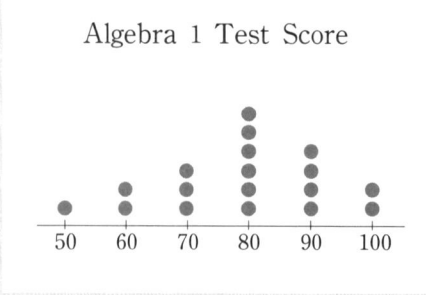

4. **Stem Plot**: Typically, stems represent ten's place and leaves represent one's place, but other place values can be also used. For example, the data below is the number of pencils that 15 elementary school students have at home, and can be represented by the stem plot below.

13, 15, 19, 22, 23, 24, 26, 26, 27, 28, 30, 31, 34, 49, 51

1	359	Key: 419
2	2346678	represents
3	014	49 pencils
4	9	
5	1	

5. **Two—Way Table**: This displays frequencies for two categorical variables. One category is represented by rows and a second category is represented by columns. For example, the table below shows the distribution of the favorite colors for 50 men and women.

	Favorite Color				
	Yellow	Pink	Blue	Green	Total
Men	4	5	6	9	24
Women	6	10	2	8	26
Total	10	15	8	17	50

02. Positional Statistics

1. **Percentile**: A percentile provides information about how the data are spread over the interval from the smallest value to the largest values. The pth percentile of a data set is a value such that at least p percent of the values take on this value or less.

2. **Five Number Summary**

   (1) Minimum: The lowest value

   (2) Lower Quartile(Q_1): The middle value of the lower half (25th percentile)

   (3) Median: The middle value when they are in order (50th percentile)

   (4) Upper Quartile(Q_3): The middle value of the upper half (75th percentile)

   (5) Maximum: The highest value

3. **Range**: The difference between the maximum and minimum value

4. **Interquartile Range(IQR)**: The difference between the first and third quartile(Q_3-Q_1).

5. **Box Plot**: A graphical representation of the fiver number summary.

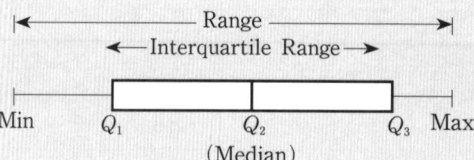

Example 1

$$A=\{10,\ 39,\ 35,\ 11,\ 25,\ 15,\ 42,\ 18,\ 27,\ 40,\ 30\}$$

Find the median, interquartile range, and range in the data set given above.

Solution

First, list each data value in order from least to greatest.

$$\underbrace{10,\ 11,\ 15,\ 18,\ 25}_{5\ datas},\ 27,\ \underbrace{30,\ 35,\ 39,\ 40,\ 42}_{5\ datas}$$

Since there are 11 numbers, the median is 27 (6th from the left or right).

$$\underbrace{10,\ 11,}_{2\ datas}\ \boxed{15},\ \underbrace{18,\ 25}_{2\ datas} \quad \rightarrow \text{15 is the lower quartile (the median of first 5 data)}$$

$$\underbrace{30,\ 35,}_{2\ datas}\ \boxed{39},\ \underbrace{40,\ 42}_{2\ datas} \quad \rightarrow \text{39 is the upper quartile (the median of last 5 data)}$$

The Interquartile range is $39-15=24$.

The range is the difference between the maximum and minimum value, so

$$42-10=32$$

Median$=27$, Interquartile Range$=24$, Range$=32$

03. Value-Based Statistics

1. **Mean**: The sum of values divided by the number of values (the average).

2. **Standard Deviation**: A measure of the typical distance of the values from the mean.

3. **Variance**: The square of the standard deviation.

4. **Median vs. Mean**

   (1) **Median** is a resistant measure of center. If the highest value increases (or the lowest value decreases) drastically, the median does not change.

   (2) **Mean** is NOT a resistant measure of center. It gets pulled towards extreme values.

Example 2

Daniel's test grades are 84, 87, 96, and 89. What score must he get on the fifth (last) test in order to get an average of 90 for the semester?

Solution

Let x be the score of the fifth test. Then we have

$$\frac{84+87+96+89+x}{5} = 90$$

$$\frac{356+x}{5} = 90$$

$$356 + x = 450, \quad x = 94$$

David must score 94 on his fifth test.

Example 3

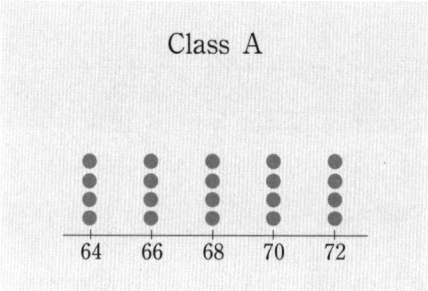

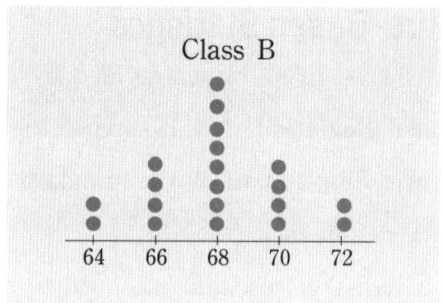

The two dot plots above show the weight distributions, in kilograms, of students in two different classes of 20 students each. Which of the following statements is true?

(A) The standard deviation of student weight in Class A is equal to that of student weight in Class B.

(B) The standard deviation of student weight in Class A is less than that of student weight in Class B.

(C) The standard deviation of student weight in Class A is greater than that of student weight in Class B.

(D) There is not enough information to compare the standard deviation.

Solution

Class A has a mean of 68 kilograms, the data values are evenly distributed, and many data values do not come close to the mean value. In Class B, the mean is also 68 kilograms, and the data values are more closely clustered around the mean. Therefore, the standard deviation of the data values in Class A is greater than the standard deviation of the data values in Class B.

The answer is C.

Practice **Problems**

0575

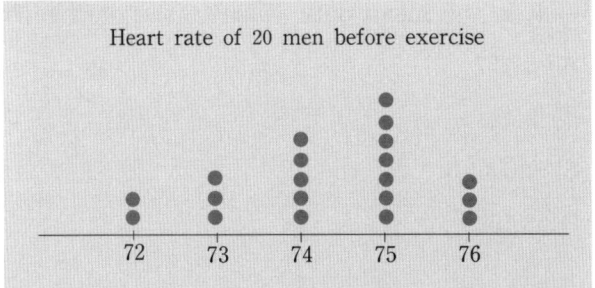

Heart rate of 20 men before exercise

The heart rates were recorded for 20 men before exercise. The dot plot above shows the results. What is the median number of the heart rates?

(A) 73.5

(B) 74

(C) 74.5

(D) 75

0576

```
5 | 2  7
6 | 3  7  9
7 | 1  3  5  6
8 | 0  4  4  7  9
9 | 0  0  1  3
```
    5 | 2 represent 52

The stem−and−leaf plot above shows the final exam scores for a group of students. What is the median score for this group?

(A) 76

(B) 78

(C) 80

(D) 82

For questions 577−578, refer to the following information.

    72, 78, 80, 80, 82, 85, 86,

    88, 89, 90, 91, 93, 98, 99

The data above shows the math scores for a class of 14 students.

0577

What is the median score?

(A) 78

(B) 80

(C) 87

(D) 92

0578

What is the mean score?

(A) 86

(B) 86.5

(C) 87

(D) 87.5

For questions 579–580, refer to the following information.

Data Value	Frequency
0	4
1	3
2	5
3	2

The frequency table above summarizes the 14 data values in a data set.

0579

What is the maximum data value in the data set?

(A) 2

(B) 3

(C) 4

(D) 5

0580

What is the median data value in the data set?

(A) 1

(B) 1.5

(C) 2

(D) 2.5

0581

What is the mean data value in the data set?

(A) 1.357

(B) 2.333

(C) 2.500

(D) 3.167

0582

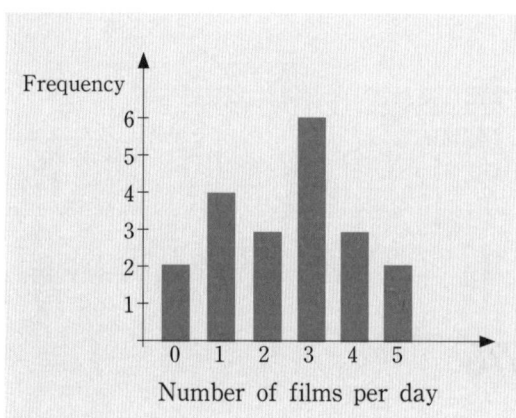

The bar chart in the Figure above shows the number of films are released over a period of time. What is the mean of films released per day?

(A) 2

(B) 2.5

(C) 3

(D) 3.5

0583

	Favorite Color			
	Yellow	Pink	Blue	Green
Male	4	5	6	9
Female	6	10	2	8
Total	10	15	8	17

The table above is a survey of the favorite colors of 50 males and females. What is the fraction of the males whose favorite color is blue?

(A) $\frac{1}{4}$

(B) $\frac{3}{8}$

(C) $\frac{8}{25}$

(D) $\frac{12}{25}$

For questions 584−585, refer to the following information.

	With soda	Without soda
With fries	54	18
Without fries	25	7

The table above shows whether a customer ordered a soda and fries when ordering a hamburger at a local hamburger restaurant in one day.

0584

What is the probability that a randomly selected customer ordered both soda and fries that day?

(A) $\frac{27}{52}$

(B) $\frac{3}{4}$

(C) $\frac{54}{79}$

(D) $\frac{25}{32}$

0585

What is the probability that a randomly selected customer order soda given that the customer did not order fries?

(A) $\frac{27}{52}$

(B) $\frac{3}{4}$

(C) $\frac{54}{79}$

(D) $\frac{25}{32}$

0586

	Political Opinion		
	Conservative	Independent	Liberal
Male	17	45	19
Female	4	30	25

The table above is a survey of the political opinion of 140 males and females. If one person who responded to the survey is selected at random, which of the following statements results in the greatest value?

(A) The probability that the person's political opinion is independent, given that the person is male

(B) The probability that the person's political opinion is independent, given that the person is female

(C) The probability that the person is male given that the person's political opinion is independent

(D) The probability that the person is female given that the person's political opinion is independent

0587

There is a group of 5 people with a mean age of 37. A 43−year−old person joins the group. What is the mean age of the 6 people in the group?

(A) 38

(B) 43

(C) 47

(D) 51

0588

If $\dfrac{3x+3y+3z}{9}=k$, what is the mean of x, y, and z in terms of k?

(A) $\dfrac{k}{9}$

(B) $\dfrac{k}{3}$

(C) k

(D) $3k$

0589

The mean of the ages of 12 men is x and the mean of the ages of 16 women is y. What is the total average of all the ages combined?

(A) $28(x+y)$

(B) $\dfrac{12x+16y}{28}$

(C) $14\left(\dfrac{x}{12}+\dfrac{y}{16}\right)$

(D) $\dfrac{16x+12y}{28}$

0590

Eric averaged a 88 on his first four quizzes. What score will he need on this 5th quiz to increases his average to a 90?

(A) 95

(B) 96

(C) 97

(D) 98

0591

$$A = \{1, 1, 3, 3, 4, 6\}$$

The mean and median of the data set above is 3. Which of the following numbers can be added to the set so that the value of mean and median would NOT be changed?

(A) 2

(B) 3

(C) 4

(D) 5

0592

15 employees at a certain company earn annual salaries. The mean salary is \$35,624, and the median salary is \$39,687. If a new employee joins the company and earns an annual salary of \$38,000, which of the following must be true?

(A) The new median salary will be greater than \$39,687

(B) The new median salary will be less than \$39,687

(C) The new mean salary will be greater than \$35,624

(D) The new mean salary will be less than \$35,624

0593

The water park is only open 90 days a year. The company that operates the water park wants an average of 4,000 visitors per day. If an average of 3800 visitors visited the water park in the last 50 days, how many people, on average, should visit the water park per day for the remaining 40 days to achieve your company's goals?

(A) 4100

(B) 4175

(C) 4250

(D) 4325

0594

Number of Credits	Frequency
10	2
11	4
12	7
13	5
14	2
15	1

The table above shows the number of credits enrolled for 21 students enrolled in college classes. Which of the following lists the mean, median, and mode of age in order?

(A) mode<median<mean

(B) mode<mean<median

(C) median=mode<mean

(D) mean<mode= median

For questions 595−596, refer to the following information.

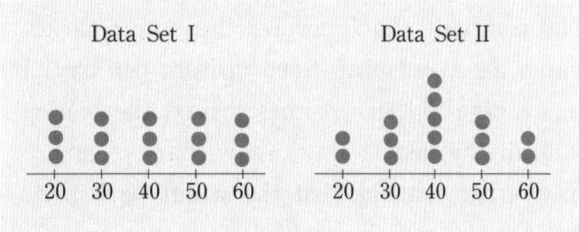

0595

The dot plots shown each represent a data set. Which of the following statements best compares the means and medians of the two data sets?

(A) Both data sets have the same mean and median.

(B) Both data sets have the same mean, but the median of data set I is less than the median of data set II.

(C) Both data sets have the same median, but the mean of data set I is less than the mean of data set II.

(D) Both data sets have the same median, but the mean of data set I is greater than the mean of data set II.

0596

Which of the following statements best compares the standard deviations of the two data sets?

(A) The standard deviation of data set I is equal to the standard deviation of data set II.

(B) The standard deviation of data set I is greater than the standard deviation of data set II.

(C) The standard deviation of data set I is less than the standard deviation of data set II.

(D) There is not enough information to compare the standard deviation.

0597

A teacher recorded the final exam scores of 26 students. Later, the teacher discovered that the highest score was mistakenly recorded as 10 times the actual score. However, after correcting the error, the corrected score is still greater than any other scores. What should remain the same after correcting the score?

(A) Mean

(B) Median

(C) Range

(D) Standard Deviation

0598

Data Set 16, 20, 24, 28, 32

In the data set above, if each data is increases by 5, which of the following is true?

I. The mean will increase by 5.

II. The median will increase by 5.

III. The standard deviation will increase by 5.

(A) I only

(B) II only

(C) III only

(D) I and II only

0599

Data Set X

Data Set Y

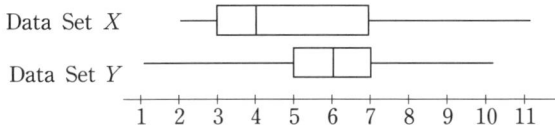

The boxplots for data set X and data set Y are shown above. Which of the following is true about X and Y?

(A) The range of Y is greater than the range of X.

(B) At least 50% of the data in Y are greater than 50% of the data in X.

(C) The median of Y is less than the median of X.

(D) The mean of Y is less than the mean of X.

0600

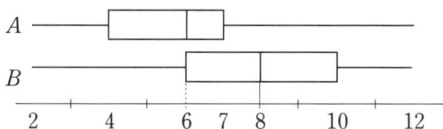

In the figure above, which of the following is NOT true?

(A) The median of A is 6

(B) The median of A is less than the median of B

(C) The range of A is equal to the range of B

(D) The standard deviation of A is greater than the standard deviation of B

For questions 601−603, refer to the following information.

```
1 | 2  2  3  5  7
2 | 0  1  2  4  6  6  7
3 | 1  1  1  2  5  7  7  8  8
4 | 0  3  4  5  7
5 | 0
```

    5 | 2   represent 52

The stem−and−leaf plot above shows the number of sit−ups by students in gym class.

0601

What is the median number of sit−ups?

0602

How many students recorded 20 or more sit−ups but less than 30?

0603

If it is said that 20 or more sit−ups is pass, how many students did not pass?

0604

179	168	174
177	180	172
183	182	170

The height of each of the 9 students, in centimeter, is given in the data set above. How large is the range of the data set than the interquartile range of the data set?

0605

Four numbers have a mean of 16. When a fifth number is included, the mean is doubled. What is the fifth number?

0606

There are twenty numbers that have a mean of 16. If 36 and 50 are removed from the twenty numbers, what is the mean of the remaining numbers?

0607

Waiting time (minutes)	Frequency
5	6
10	7
15	4
20	2
25	1

The frequency distribution table above shows the waiting time for 20 students in Jason's class to enter the art museum. What is the average time students waited?

For questions 608−609, refer to the following information.

	Own a car	Do not own a car
11th grade	170	65
12th grade	190	25

A survey of all 11th and 12th graders of high school asked whether they owned a car. The results of the survey are shown in the table above.

0608

If one of the students in 11th or 12th grade is randomly chosen, what is the probability that the student owned a car?

0609

If one of the students who owned a car is selected at random, what is the probability that the students is in 12th grade?

For questions 610−611 , refer to the following information.

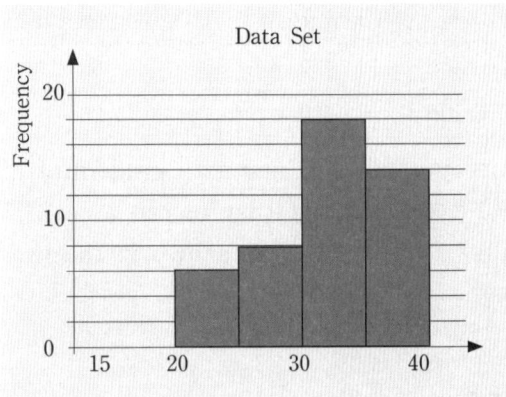

A data sets of 46 integers each are summarized in the histogram shown. In each histogram, the first interval represents the frequency of integers greater than or equal to 15 but less than 20. The second interval represents the frequency of integers greater than or equal to 20 but less than 25, and so on.

0610

What is the largest possible mean of data set?

0611

What is the smallest possible median of data set?

Memo

4. Designing Studies

01. Sample Survey

A goal in the design of sample surveys is to obtain a sample that is representative of the population so that precise inferences can be made.

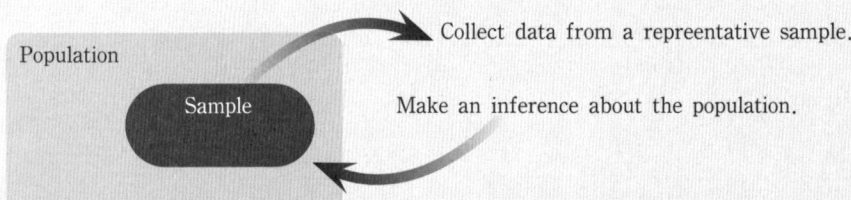

1. **Population**: The entire group of individuals that we hope to learn something about.

2. **Parameter**: Characteristic of the population.

3. **Sample**: A subset of the population that actually gets examined. We use information from a sample to draw conclusions about the entire population.

4. **Statistic**: Characteristic of the sample.

5. **Sample Survey**: A study that uses an organized plan to choose a sample that represents some specific population

6. A good sample is representative of the population. It would provide a good estimate of the value of interest.

7. A biased(bad) sample over−or under−represents a portion of the population. It would consistently overestimate or underestimate the value of interest.

For examples 1−2, refer to the following information.

David wants to know how strongly La Porte residents support the La Porte high school football team. He visited a restaurant in La Porte city and conducted a survey of 35 people randomly selected.

Example 1

The sample for the survey is

(A) All people who attended the football game the day the survey was conducted.

(B) The 35 people who took part in the survey and gave their opinions.

(C) All La Porte high school students.

(D) All La Porte residents.

Solution

The sample for the survey is the 35 people who took part in the survey and gave their opinions. The survey only includes the 35 people who were randomly selected at the restaurant in La Porte city, not all La Porte residents or high school students.

The answer is B.

Example 2

The population for this survey is

(A) All people who attended the football game the day the survey was conducted.

(B) The 35 people who took part in the survey and gave their opinions.

(C) All La Porte high school students.

(D) All La Porte residents.

Solution

The population for this survey is the group of interest that David wants to generalize the results to. In this case, David wants to know how strongly La Porte residents support the La Porte high school football team. Therefore, the population for this survey is all La Porte residents.

The answer is D.

Example 3

A company wants to know if their customers are satisfied with their new product. A sample of 500 customers who have purchased the new product was randomly selected. Among the selected customers, 350 people answered that they were satisfied with the new product. Which of the following is the largest population to which the results of the survey can be generalized?

(A) The 350 customers who were satisfied with the new product

(B) The 500 customers who were surveyed

(C) All customers who have purchased the new product

(D) All customers who have ever purchased any product from the company

Solution

The survey was conducted to measure the satisfaction level of customers who have purchased the new product. Therefore, the results of the survey can be generalized to all customers who have purchased the new product, which is the population of interest.

The answer is C.

Example 4

A survey of 500 randomly selected students at a college found that 420 owned an iPad. If the college has 35,000 students, approximately how many students would own an iPad?

(A) 26,600 students

(B) 28,000 students

(C) 28,700 students

(D) 29,400 students

Solution

To estimate the number of students who own an iPad in the college, we can set up a proportion

$$\frac{420}{500} = \frac{x}{35000},$$

where x represents the number of students who own an iPad. Solving for x, we have

$$x = \frac{420}{500} \cdot 35000 = 29,400$$

Therefore, approximately 29,400 students would own an iPad.

The answer is D.

02. Estimating with Confidence

1. Margin of Error: Statistical values obtained from sample should account for how far the actual values are from the estimates. To describe the accuracy of an estimate, statisticians use the margin of error.

   (1) The larger the standard deviation, the larger the margin of error. The smaller the standard deviation, the smaller the margin of error.

   (2) Increasing the sample size usually reduces the margin of error.

2. Confidence Interval: Estimated value from the sample ± margin of error. It gives an interval of plausible values for a population parameter.

3. Confidence Level: The overall success rate of the method for calculating the confidence interval. If the confidence level is 90%, then approximately 90% of the confidence intervals produced should capture the true population parameter.

Example 5

Which of the following is the most plausible value for the true mean annual salary of software developers, based on a random sample of 300 software developers with a mean salary of $120,000 and a margin of error of $4,000 at a 95% confidence level?

(A) $114,000

(B) $117,000

(C) $125,000

(D) $130,000

Solution

The margin of error of $4,000 at a 95% confidence level means that we can be 95% confident that the true population mean salary lies within $4,000 of the sample mean salary of $120,000. So, we can construct a confidence interval as follows:

$$\text{Sample mean} \pm \text{Margin of error } \$120{,}000 \pm \$4{,}000$$

This gives us a range of $116,000 to $124,000. Since we are asked for the most plausible value for the true mean salary, the best answer choice is (B) $117,000, which is inside the range and therefore more likely to be the true mean.

The answer is B.

Example 6

A random sample of 200 customers at a grocery store shows that the average amount spent on groceries per visit is $75, with a margin of error of $5 at a 95% confidence level. Which of the following is the most reasonable claim about the average amount spent on groceries per visit?

(A) The average amount spent on groceries per visit is about $71.25.

(B) The average amount spent on groceries per visit is between $70 and $80.

(C) The average amount spent on groceries per visit is exactly $75.

(D) The average amount spent on groceries per visit cannot be estimated with the given information.

Solution

The most reasonable claim about the average amount spent on groceries per visit is option (B), which states that the average amount spent on groceries per visit is between $70 and $80. This is because the sample mean of $75 is within the margin of error of $5, indicating that the true population mean is likely to fall within the range of $70 to $80 with 95% confidence.

The answer is B.

03. Scatterplot

1. **Scatterplot**: A type of data display that shows the relationship between two numerical variables. Both horizontal and vertical axes are labeled as number lines—each point displays two measurements for the same subject.

2. **Explanatory Variable**

   The variable that is in control of the other

   Independent and predictor variable

   Chosen for the x−axis in the scatterplot

3. **Response Variable**

   The variable that changes according to the explanatory

   Dependent and outcome variable

   Represented on the y−axis of the scatterplot

4. **Types of Scatterplots**

   Most scatterplots are linear models. However, not all scatterplots are linear. There are also quadratic and exponential models.

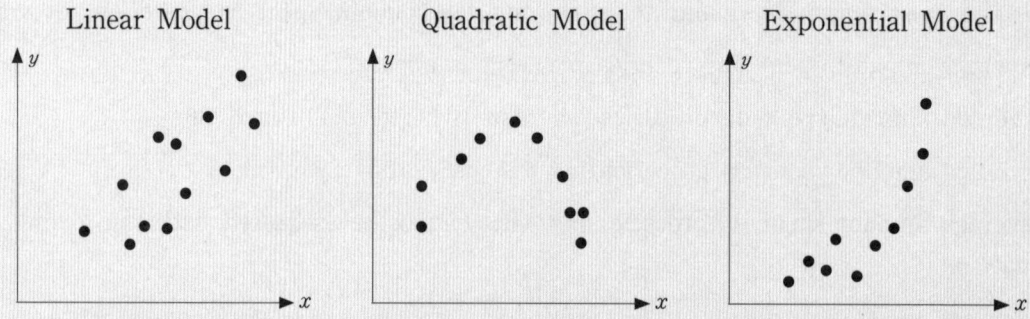

04. Regression Line

1. **Regression Line**: A linear model that describes how a response variable, y, changes as an explanatory variable, x, changes–we predict y for a given x. This line is also called the line of best fit.

2. **Regression Equation**: $\hat{y}=b_0+b_1x$, where

   x=the actual x value, y=the actual y value

   $\hat{y}$=the predicted y value, b_0=y−intercept, b_1=slope

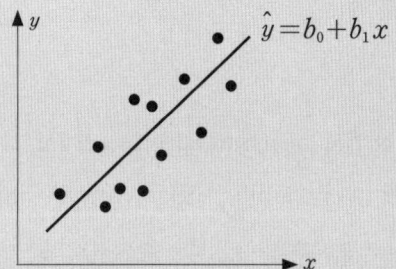

For examples $7-9$, refer to the following information.

The scatterplot shows the relationship between two variables, x and y. A line of best fit is also shown below.

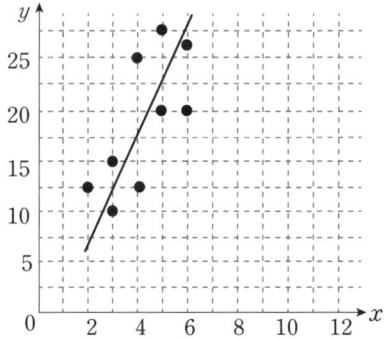

Example 7

Which of the following is closest to the equation of the line of best fit above?

(A) $y=2x+3.5$

(B) $y=2x-2.5$

(C) $y=5x-2.5$

(D) $y=5x+3.5$

It seems like the line passes through two points $(2, 7.5)$ and $(6, 27.5)$. Then the slope is

$$m = \frac{27.5 - 7.5}{6 - 2} = \frac{20}{4} = 5$$

Now using the equation of the line $y - y_1 = m(x - x_1)$ with the point $(2, 7.5)$, we have

$$y - 7.5 = 5(x - 2) \qquad \rightarrow (x_1, y_1) = (4, -3) \ and \ m = 5$$
$$y - 7.5 = 5x - 10$$
$$y = 5x - 2.5$$

The answer is C.

Example 8

Which of the following statements is the best interpretation for the slope of the line of best fit?

(A) For every 1 unit increase in the x variable, the y variable increases by 2 units, on average.

(B) For every 2 units increase in the y variable, the x variable increases by 1 units, on average.

(C) For every 1 unit increase in the x variable, the y variable increases by 5 units, on average.

(D) For every 5 unit increase in the y variable, the x variable increases by 1 units, on average.

Solution

Answer (C) is the best interpretation for the slope of the line of best fit. It means that for every 1 unit increase in the x variable, the y variable increases by 5 units, on average

The answer is C.

Example 9

For how many of the data points is the actual $y-$value at least 4 less than the $y-$value predicted by the line of best fit?

Solution

Based on the given graph, the vertical scale is such that one unit on the grid paper corresponds to 2.5 units in the actual values of the dependent variable. Using this scale, it can be observed that there are two data points for which the actual $y-$values are at least 4 units less than the $y-$values predicted by the line of best fit. These points correspond to $x-$values of 4 and 6.

The answer is 2.

Memo

Practice **Problems**

0612

The county board of education in a particular city wants to know if residents are in favor of building a new high school library.
A sample of 200 residents in the city was randomly selected. Among the selected residents, 120 people answered in favor when asked whether they supported the construction of the new library. Which of the following is the largest population to which the results of the survey can be generalized?

(A) The 120 residents who responded that they support the construction of the new library

(B) The 200 residents who were surveyed

(C) All high school students in the city

(D) All residents in the city

0613

The state government wants to know the percentage of students who have a part−time job while studying. A sample of 1,000 students was randomly selected from universities in that state. Among the selected students, 600 reported having a part−time job. Which of the following is the largest population to which the results of the survey can be generalized?

(A) The 600 students who reported having a part−time job

(B) The 1,000 students who were surveyed

(C) All students who attend a particular university in the state

(D) All students who attend universities in the state

0614

A high school has 250 senior students. A random sample of senior students was asked if they would be willing to enroll in an after−school SAT program. 42% of those surveyed said they would be interested in enrolling in the SAT program. Based on this survey, which of the following best estimates the total number of senior students who will be enrolled in a program of study?

(A) 105

(B) 140

(C) 170

(D) 210

0615

A survey of 500 randomly selected employees at a company found that 300 had used the company's wellness program in the past year. If the company has 28,000 employees, approximately how many employees would have used the wellness program in the past year?

(A) 10,500 employees

(B) 11,200 employees

(C) 16,800 employees

(D) 17,500 employees

0616

A survey of 1,200 randomly selected adults in a certain country found that 480 had traveled abroad in the past year. If the country has a population of 4.5 million adults, approximately how many adults would have traveled abroad in the past year?

(A) 1 million adults

(B) 1.2 million adults

(C) 1.4 million adults

(D) 1.8 million adults

0617

Which of the following is the most plausible value for the true mean of the weight of a certain type of laptop in general, based on a random sample of 50 laptops with a mean weight of 4.3 pounds and a margin of error of 0.2 pounds at a 95% confidence level?

(A) 3.8 pounds

(B) 4.0 pounds

(C) 4.2 pounds

(D) 4.6 pounds

0618

In a particular city, a survey of 700 randomly selected residents found that 69% of them support a new tax policy. The estimate had a margin of error of 3% at the 95% confidence level. If the city has a population of 200,000 residents, which of the following best estimates the number of residents who support the new tax policy, at the 95% confidence level?

(A) Between 132,000 to 144,000 residents

(B) Between 136,000 to 142,000 residents

(C) Exactly 138,000 residents

(D) Approximately 190,000 residents

0619

Based on a random sample of air quality measurements, environmental scientists estimate that a certain city has an annual average PM2.5 concentration of $12.5\mu g/m^3$ with a margin of error of $1.2\mu g/m^3$ at a 95% confidence level. Which of the following is the most reasonable claim for the city's average annual PM2.5 concentration?

(A) The annual average PM2.5 concentration is between $11.3\mu g/m^3$ and $13.7\mu g/m^3$.

(B) The annual average PM2.5 concentration is exactly $12.5\mu g/m^3$.

(C) The annual average PM2.5 concentration is higher than $13.7\mu g/m^3$.

(D) The annual average PM2.5 concentration is lower than $11.3\mu g/m^3$.

0620

In a survey of 2,000 randomly selected households in a certain city, those surveyed spent an average of $180 per month on electricity bills. The estimates had a margin of error of $5 at the 90% confidence level. Which of the following is a reasonable claim to make based on this sample?

(A) All households in the city spent between $175 and $185 per month on electricity bills.

(B) 90% of households in the city spent between $175 and $185 per month on electricity bills.

(C) It is plausible that the average monthly spending of households in the city is between $175 and $185 on electricity bills.

(D) Between 85% and 95% of households in the city spent $185 per month on electricity bills.

0621

In a particular city, a survey of 700 randomly selected residents found that 60% of them support a new tax policy. The estimate had a margin of error of 5% at the 95% confidence level. If the city has a population of 250,000 residents, which of the following best estimates the number of residents who support the new tax policy, at the 95% confidence level?

(A) Between 132,000 to 144,000 residents

(B) Between 1625,500 to 137,500 residents

(C) Exactly 150,000 residents

(D) Approximately 150,000 residents

0622

A random sample of 600 employees at a company included 84 employees who reported that they were planning to leave their job within the next six months, with a margin of error of 130 employees and a confidence level of 90%. If the company has 13,000 employees, how many employees are planning to leave their job within the next six months, with a 90% confidence level?

(A) 1,300 to 1,820 employees

(B) 1,690 to 1,950 employees

(C) 1,495 to 2,015 employees

(D) 1,560 to 2080 employees

For questions 623−627 , refer to the following information.

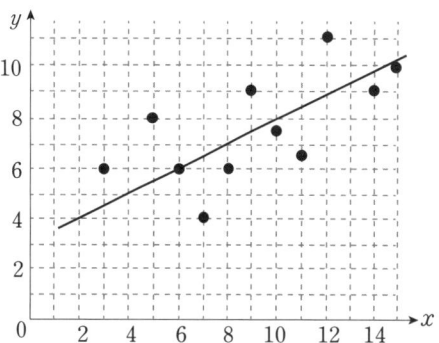

The scatterplot shows the relationship between two variables, x and y. The line of best fit is shown above.

0623

Which of the following could be the equation of the line of best fit above?

(A) $y = \frac{1}{3} x + 4$

(B) $y = \frac{1}{2} x + 3$

(C) $y = x + 2$

(D) $y = 2x + 1$

0624

For how many data points, the actual $y-$value is greater than the $y-$value predicted by the line of best fit by 2 or more?

(A) 1

(B) 2

(C) 3

(D) 4

0625

What is the predicted value of y when the value of x is 2?

0626

For what fraction of the data points in the scatterplot is the predicted $y-$value by the line of best fit less than the actual $y-$value?

0627

What is the difference between the predicted $y-$value and the actual $y-$value when $x=11$?

(A) -1

(B) -2

(C) 1

(D) 2

For questions $628-629$, refer to the following information.

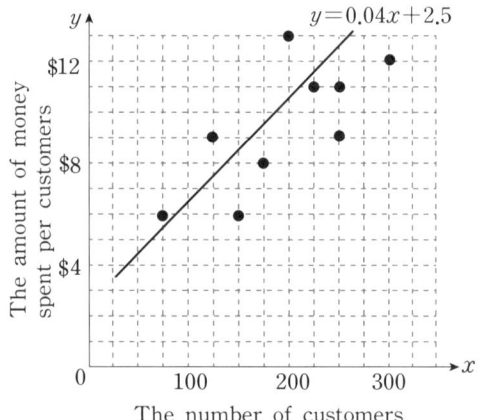

A convenience store recorded the number of customers in the store and the amount of money spent per customer for several days. The scatter plot above shows the data and the line of best fit.

0628

According to the line of best fit, if the store has 225 customers, how much money would the store expect to make per customer?

(A) $10.5

(B) $11

(C) $11.5

(D) $12

0629

Which of the following statements is the best interpretation for the slope of the line of best fit in this situation?

(A) The average amount of money spent per customer increases by $0.04 for every additional customer in the store.

(B) The average number of customers in the store increases by 1 for every $0.04 increase in money spent per customer.

(C) The average amount of money spent per customer decreases by $0.04 for every additional customer in the store.

(D) The average number of customers in the store decreases by 1 for every $0.04 increase in money spent per customer

0630

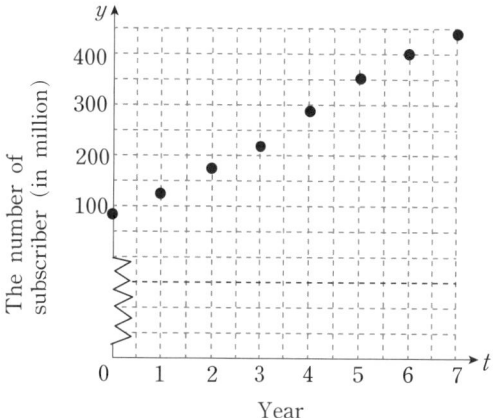

The scatterplot above shows the number of subscribers to a music streaming service, where t represents years since 2015. Which of the following is closest to the yearly increase in subscribers to the music streaming service from 2015 to 2022?

(A) 25 millions

(B) 50 millions

(C) 75 millions

(D) 85 millions

For questions 631−633, refer to the following information.

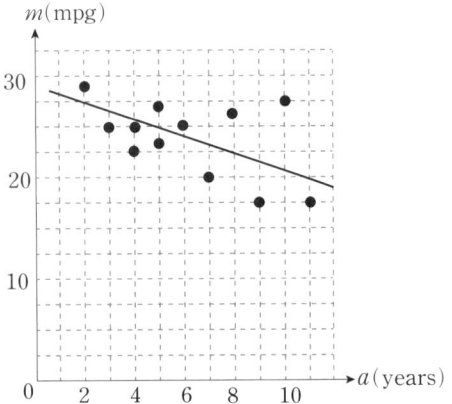

The scatterplot to the left shows the ages of various cars plotted against their corresponding gas mileage, where a is the age of the car, in years, and m is the gas mileage, in miles per gallon (mpg). A line that approximates the data is shown on the graph.

0631

Which of the following statements is the best interpretation for the slope of the line of best fit in this situation?

(A) The gas mileage of a car decreases by 0.8 mpg for each additional year of age.

(B) The gas mileage of a car decreases by 1 mpg for each additional 0.8 years of age.

(C) The age of a car decreases by 0.8 years for each additional 1 mpg decrease in gas mileage.

(D) The age of a car decreases by 1 year for each additional 0.8 mpg decrease in gas mileage

0632

Which of the following functions best describes the relationship shown?

(A) $3a+m=79$

(B) $3a-m=79$

(C) $5a+6m=170$

(D) $5a-6m=174$

0633

What is the difference between the actual miles per gallon (mpg) of the car and the predicted mpg from the best—fit line when the car's age is 7 years?

(A) 1 mile per gallon

(B) 2 miles per gallon

(C) 3 miles per gallon

(D) 4 miles per gallon

Memo

IV

Geometry and Trigonometry

1. Plane Geometry

01. Triangles

1. Isosceles Triangle

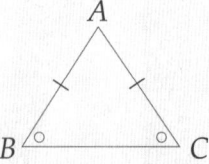

(1) AB≅AC and ∠B≅∠C

(2) Two of the three sides and angles are equal.

2. Equilateral Triangle

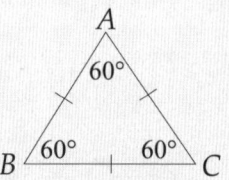

(1) AB≅AC≅BC and ∠A≅∠B≅∠C=60°

(2) Area$=\dfrac{\sqrt{3}}{4}s^2$

3. Exterior Angle Theorem

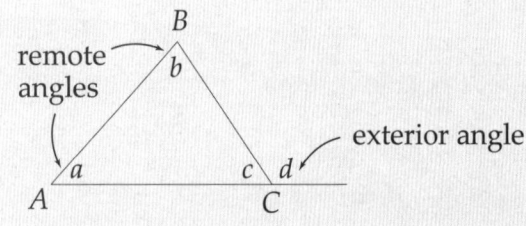

$\angle d = \angle a + \angle b$

4. Pythagorean Theore

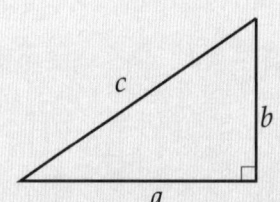

In any right triangle, $a^2+b^2=c^2$

5. Special Right Triangles

(1) 45°−45°−90° Triangle

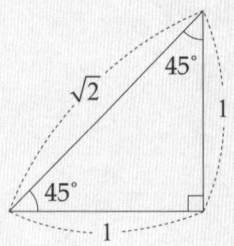

(2) 30°−60°−90° Triangle

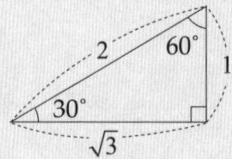

Example 1

Find the value of x in the figure below.

(1)

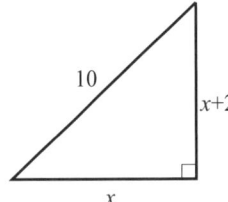

(2)

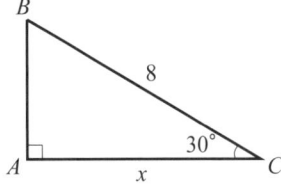

Solution

(1) Using the Pythagorean theorem,
$$x^2+(x+2)^2=10^2$$
$$x^2+x^2+4x+4=100$$
$$2x^2+4x-96=0$$
$$x^2+2x-48=0$$
$$(x+8)(x-6)=0, \ x=-8 \ \text{or} \ x=6$$
Since $x>0$, $x=6$.

$$x=6.$$

(2) $\angle B=180°-30°-90°=60°$
$\triangle ABC$ is $30°-60°-90°$ triangle.
$$AC : BC=\sqrt{3} : 2$$
$$\frac{\sqrt{3}}{2}=\frac{x}{8}$$
$$2x=8\sqrt{3}, \ x=4\sqrt{3}$$

$$x=4\sqrt{3}$$

02. Congruence and Similarity

1. Angles and Parallel Lines

Suppose two lines l and k are parallel, and the line m is a transversal.

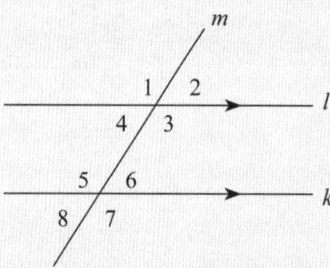

(1) Vertical Angles: $\angle 1 \cong \angle 3$, $\angle 2 \cong \angle 4$, $\angle 5 \cong \angle 7$, $\angle 6 \cong \angle 8$

(2) Corresponding angles: $\angle 1 \cong \angle 5$, $\angle 2 \cong \angle 6$, $\angle 3 \cong \angle 7$, $\angle 4 \cong \angle 8$

(3) Alternate interior angles: $\angle 3 \cong \angle 5$, $\angle 4 ? \angle 6$

(4) Alternate exterior angles: $\angle 1 \cong \angle 7$, $\angle 2 \cong \angle 8$

(5) Consecutive interior angles: $\angle 3 + \angle 6 = 180°$, $\angle 4 + \angle 5 = 180°$

2. Congruent Triangles

If two triangles $\triangle ABC$ and $\triangle DEF$ are congruent, all the corresponding pairs of sides and angles are equal and we write $\triangle ABC \cong \triangle DEF$. The condition for two triangles to be congruent is one of SSS, SAS, ASA, or AAS congruence.

(1) SSS Congruence   (2) SAS Congruence

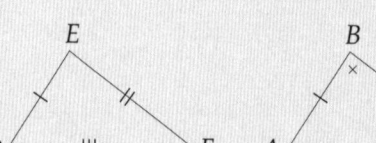   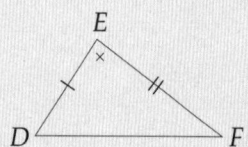

(3) ASA Congruence   (4) AAS Congruence

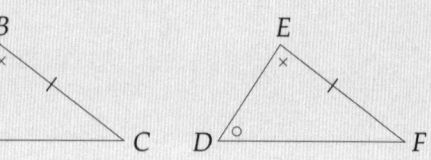

3. Similar Triangles

If two triangles △ABC and △DEF are similar, all the corresponding angles are congruent and the corresponding sides are proportional and we write △ABC~△DEF.
The condition for two triangles to be congruent is one of AA, SSS, or SAS similarity.

(1) AA Similarity

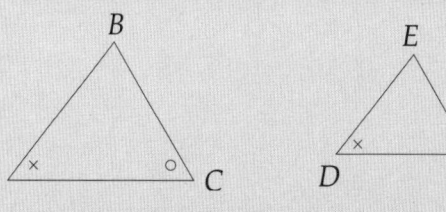

(2) SSS Similarity

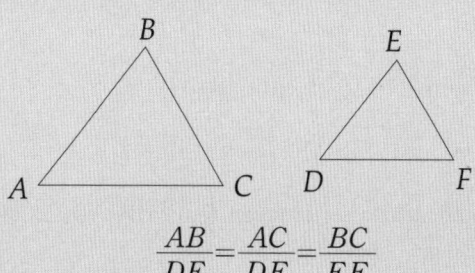

$$\frac{AB}{DE} = \frac{AC}{DF} = \frac{BC}{EF}$$

(3) SAS Similarity

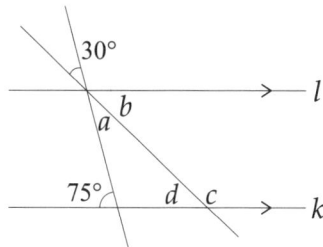 $$\frac{AB}{DE} = \frac{AC}{DF}$$

Example 2

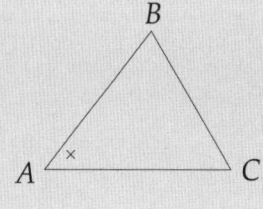

If two lines l and k are parallel in the figure above, what is the value of a, b, c, and d?

Solution

$a=30°$ (vertical angles)
$a+b=75°$ (alternate interior angles)
$\quad b=75°-a=75°-30°=45°$ and $d=b$ (alternate interior angles)
$$d=45°$$
$d+c=180°$ (supplementary angles)
$\quad c=180°-d=180°-45°=135°$

$$a=30°,\ b=45°,\ c=135°,\ d=45°$$

Example 3

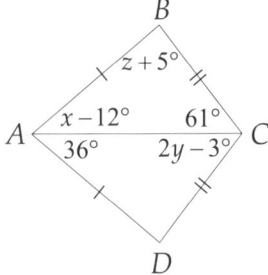

Find the value of x, y, and z.

Solution

In $\triangle ABC$ and $\triangle ADC$, it is given that $AB\cong AD$, $BC?DC$ and $AC\cong AC$. So we conclude that $\triangle ABC\cong\triangle ADC$ by SSS congruence. Therefore, we have

$$\begin{array}{cc} \angle BAC\cong\angle DAC & \angle BCA\cong\angle DCA \\ x-12°=36°,\ x=48° \quad\text{and}\quad & 61°=2y-3°,\ y=32° \end{array}$$

In $\triangle ABC$, $z+5°=180°-(48°-12°)-61°$
$\qquad\qquad z+5°=83°,\ z=78°$

$$x=48°,\ y=32°,\ z=78°$$

Example 4

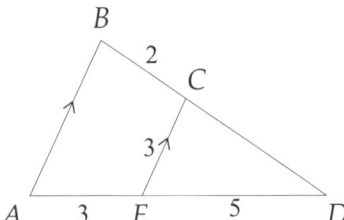

In the figure above, if sides AB and EC are parallel, what are the lengths of sides AB and CD?

Solution

Since $AB \parallel EC$, we have $\angle ABD\cong\angle ECD$ and $\angle BAD?\angle CED$ → corresponding angles
So $\triangle ABD\sim\triangle ECD$ by AA similarity and we have

$$\frac{AB}{EC}=\frac{AD}{ED} \qquad\qquad \frac{AD}{ED}=\frac{BD}{CD}$$
$$\frac{AB}{3}=\frac{3+5}{5},\ AB=\frac{24}{5} \quad\text{and}\quad \frac{3+5}{5}=\frac{2+CD}{CD}$$
$$8CD=10+5CD,\ CD=\frac{10}{3}$$

$$AB=\frac{24}{5},\ CD=\frac{10}{3}$$

03. Quadrilaterals

1. Parallelogram

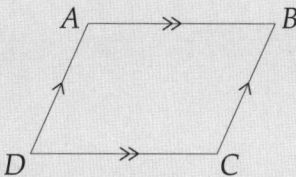

(1) AB ∥ DC and AD ∥ BC

(2) AB≅DC and AD≅BC

(3) ∠A≅∠C and ∠B≅∠D

(4) Area=bh

2. Trapezoid

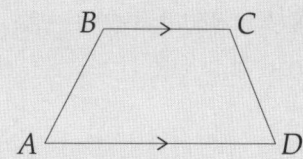

(1) BC ∥ AD

(2) If BA≅CD, the trapezoid is called an isosceles trapezoid (∠B≅∠C and ∠A≅∠D)

(3) ∠A+∠B=180° and ∠C+∠D=180°

(4) Area=$\frac{1}{2}(b_1+b_2)h$

3. Rectangle

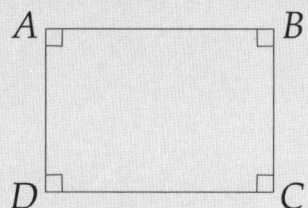

(1) ∠A≅∠B≅∠C≅∠D=90°

(2) AB≅DC and AD≅BC

(3) Area=lw

4. Square

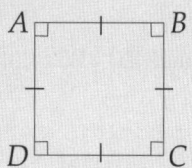

(1) ∠A≅∠B≅∠C≅∠D=90°

(2) AB≅BC≅CD≅AD

(3) Area=s^2

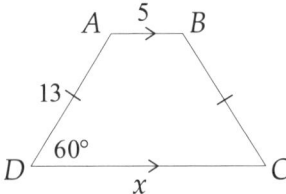

An isosceles trapezoid ABCD is given above.

Example 5

What is the value of x?

Solution

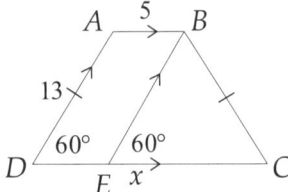

If we draw BE ‖ to AD, then AB≅DE=5 and ∠ADE≅∠BEC=60°.
Since AD≅BC, BC=13 and ∠BCE=60°.
In ΔBEC, ∠EBC=180°−60°−60°=60°.
So, ΔBEC is an equilateral triangle and ED≅BC=13.
Finally, x=DE+ED=5+13=18.

$$x=18$$

Example 6

Find the area of the trapezoid ABCD.

Solution

Since ΔBEF is a 30°−60°−90° triangle, BF=$\frac{13}{2}\sqrt{3}$. Therefore, the area of the trapezoid ABCD is

$$\text{Area}=\frac{1}{2}(b_1+b_2)h=\frac{1}{2}(5+18)\cdot\frac{13\sqrt{3}}{2}=\frac{299\sqrt{3}}{4}$$

$$\text{Area}=\frac{299\sqrt{3}}{4}$$

04. Polygons

1. The Name of the Polygon

Polygons are classified by the number of sides they have.

Number of Sides	Polygon
3	Triangle
4	Quadrilateral
5	Pentagon
6	Hexagon
7	Heptagon
8	Octagon
n	$n-$gon

2. Regular Polygon

A polygon that is equiangular (all angles are equal in measure) and equilateral (all sides have the same length). Here are some regular polygons.

(1) The sum of the measures of the angles with n sides: $180° \times (n-2)$

(2) The measure of each angle with n sides: $\dfrac{180° \times (n-2)}{n}$

Example 7

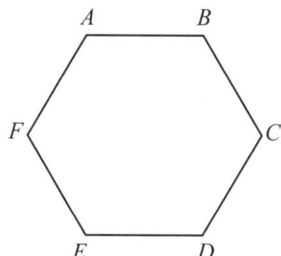

A regular hexagon ABCDEF with side length 4 is shown above. Find each of the followings.

(1) The sum of the measures of the angles.

(2) The measure of each angle.

(3) The area of the hexagon

Solution

(1) $180° \times (n-2) = 180° \times (6-2) = 720°$

(2) $\dfrac{180° \times (n-2)}{n} = \dfrac{180° \times (6-2)}{6} = \dfrac{720°}{6} = 120°$

(3)

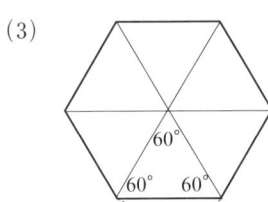

A regular hexagon is made up of 6 regular triangles as shown above. So, the area of the hexagon is 6 times the area of an equilateral triangle with side length 4.

$$\text{Area}=6\cdot\left(\frac{\sqrt{3}}{4}\cdot 4^2\right)=24\sqrt{3}$$

$$\text{Area}=24\sqrt{3}$$

05. Volume of solids

1. Prism

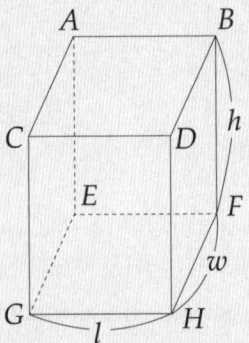

$$\text{Volume}=\text{Base}\times\text{Height}=lwh$$

2. Pyramid

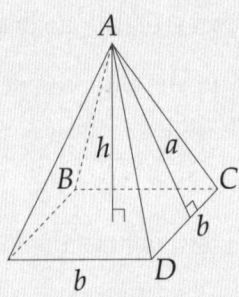

$$\text{Volume}=\frac{1}{3}\times\text{Base}\times\text{Height}=\frac{1}{3}b^2h$$

3. Cylinder

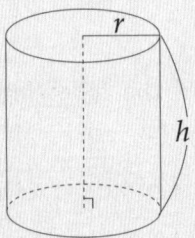

$$\text{Volume}=\text{Base}\times\text{Height}=\pi r^2h$$

4. Cone

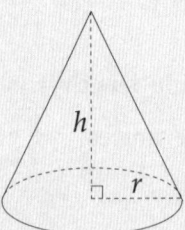

$$\text{Volume}=\frac{1}{3}\times\text{Base}\times\text{Height}=\frac{1}{3}\pi r^2h$$

5. Sphere

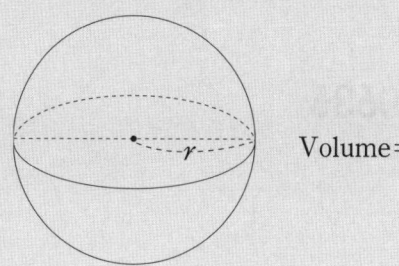

$$\text{Volume} = \frac{4}{3}\pi r^3$$

Example 8

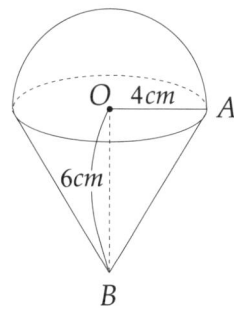

If the figure given above consists of a hemisphere(half of a sphere) of radius 4 and a cone of radius 4 and height of 6, what is the volume of the figure above?

Solution

Volume of the hemisphere: $V_H = \frac{1}{2}\cdot\frac{4}{3}\pi(4)^3 = \frac{128}{3}\pi$

Volume of the cone: $V_C = \frac{1}{3}\cdot\pi(4)^2\cdot 6 = 32\pi$

Therefore, the volume of the figure above is

$$V = V_H + V_C$$
$$= \frac{128}{3}\pi + 32\pi = \frac{224}{3}\pi$$

$$V = \frac{224}{3}\pi$$

Practice **Problems**

0634

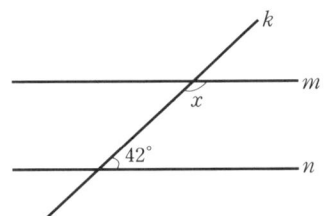

In the figure shown, line m is parallel to line n. What is the value of x?

(A) 42°

(B) 48°

(C) 132°

(D) 138°

0635

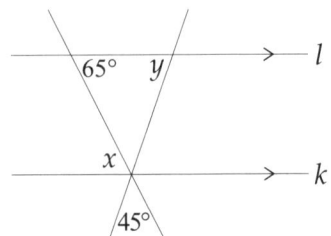

If line l is parallel to line k in the figure above, what is the value of $x+y$?

(A) 110°

(B) 125°

(C) 135°

(D) 140°

0636

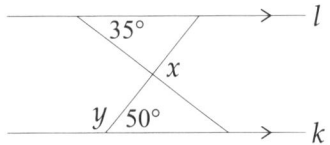

If line l is parallel to line k in the figure above, which of the following is equal to the value of $x+y$?

(A) 195°

(B) 215°

(C) 225°

(D) 230°

0637

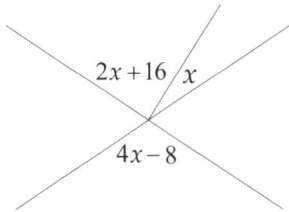

In the figure above, what is the value of $2x+16$?

(A) 42°

(B) 48°

(C) 56°

(D) 64°

0638

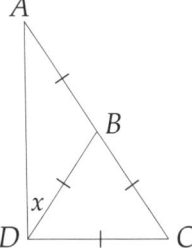

In the figure above, ABD is an isosceles triangle and BCD is an equilateral triangle. Which of the following is equal to x?

(A) 25°

(B) 30°

(C) 35°

(D) 40°

0639

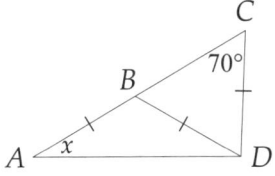

In the figure above, ABD and BCD are both isosceles triangles. Which of the following is equal to x?

(A) 25°

(B) 30°

(C) 35°

(D) 40°

0640

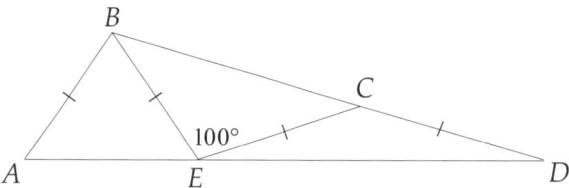

If the lengths of sides AB, BE, CE, and CD are all equal to each other in the figure above, what is the measure of angle ABE?

(A) 45°

(B) 50°

(C) 55°

(D) 60°

0641

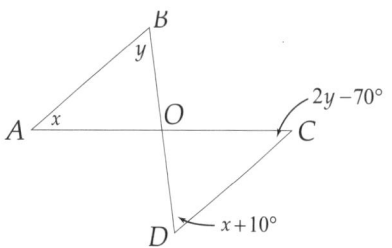

If O is the midpoint of sides AC and BD in the figure above, what is the value of $x+y$?

(A) 110°

(B) 115°

(C) 120°

(D) 125°

0642

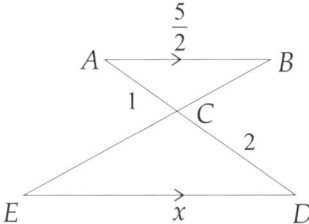

In the figure above, sides AB and ED are parallel. What is the value of x?

(A) 3

(B) 4

(C) 5

(D) 6

0643

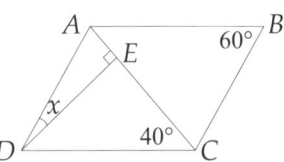

A parallelogram ABCD is given above. What is the value of x?

(A) 5°

(B) 10°

(C) 15°

(D) 20°

0644

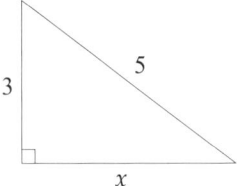

What is the value of x in the right triangle above?

(A) 3

(B) 4

(C) 5

(D) 6

0645

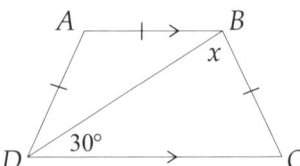

An isosceles trapezoid ABCD is given above. If the lengths of sides AB, AD, and BC are all equal to each other, what is the value of x?

(A) 75°

(B) 80°

(C) 85°

(D) 90°

0646

In a rectangle whose length is three times its width, its area is 48 square centimeters. What is the length, in centimeters, of a length of the rectangle?

(A) 4 centimeters

(B) 8 centimeters

(C) 12 centimeters

(D) 16 centimeters

0647

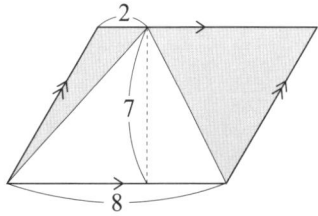

Which of the following is equal to the area of the shaded region?

(A) 28

(B) 30

(C) 32

(D) 34

0648

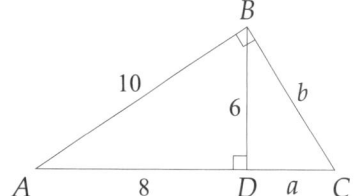

In the figure above, ABC, ABD, and CBD are all right triangles. Which of the following is equal to $a+b$?

(A) $\dfrac{23}{2}$

(B) 12

(C) $\dfrac{25}{2}$

(D) 13

0649

What is the area of the equilateral triangle that has vertices $(0, 0)$ and $(12, 0)$?

(A) $28\sqrt{3}$

(B) $32\sqrt{2}$

(C) $36\sqrt{3}$

(D) $38\sqrt{2}$

For questions 650−651, refer to the following information.

For a particular rectangle, the length is 1.5 times the width and x represents the width of the rectangle.

0650

What is the area of the rectangle in terms of x?

(A) $5x$

(B) $6x$

(C) $1.5x^2$

(D) $2.25x^2$

0651

What is the perimeter of the rectangle in terms of x?

(A) $3x$

(B) $5x$

(C) $\dfrac{2x^2}{3}$

(D) $\dfrac{3x^2}{2}$

0652

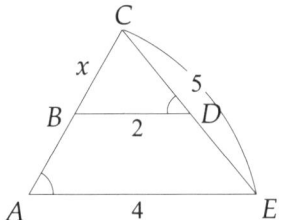

What is the value of x in the figure above?

(A) 1.5

(B) 2

(C) 2.5

(D) 3

0653

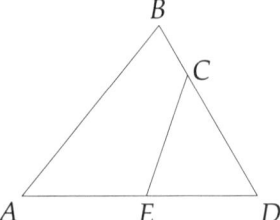

In the figure above, triangle ABD is similar to triangle CED. Angles A and B correspond to angles DCE and DEC, respectively. If angle A measures 45 degrees and angle D measures 75 degrees, what is the measure of angle DEC?

(A) 45 degrees

(B) 60 degrees

(C) 75 degrees

(D) 80 degrees

0654

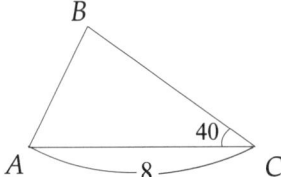

Triangle ABC shown above is similar to triangle DEF (not shown) such that $\angle A$ and $\angle B$ correspond to $\angle D$ and $\angle E$, respectively. The length of each side of triangle ABC is twice as long as the length of the corresponding side of triangle DEF. Which of the following statements is true?

(A) $\angle D = 40°$

(B) $\angle F = 50°$

(C) $EF = 16$

(D) $DF = 4$

For questions 655−656 , refer to the following information.

In triangles ABC and DEF, angles A and D are each 36°, and angles C and F are each 47°.

0655

Which additional information is needed to determine whether triangle ABC is similar to triangle DEF?

(A) The measure of angle B

(B) The length of side AC

(C) The measure of angle B and angle E

(D) No additional information is needed

0656

Which additional information is needed to determine whether triangle ABC is congruent to triangle DEF?

(A) The measure of angle B and angle E

(B) The length of side BC and DF

(C) The length of side AC and DF

(D) No additional information is needed

0657

In triangles ABC and DEF, sides AB and DE are 12 centimeters each, and sides BC and EF are 9 centimeters each. Which of the following is NOT additional information needed to determine whether triangle ABC is congruent to triangle DEF?

(A) The measure of angle B and angle E

(B) The measure of angle C and angle F

(C) The length of side AC and DF

(D) Triangles ABC and DEF are already congruent without any additional information.

0658

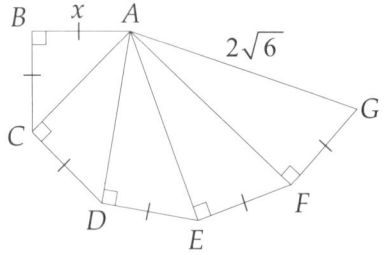

In the figure above, side AG has length $2\sqrt{6}$.

If the lengths of sides AB, BC, CD, DE, EF, and FG are all equal, what is the value of x?

(A) 2

(B) 3

(C) 4

(D) 5

0659

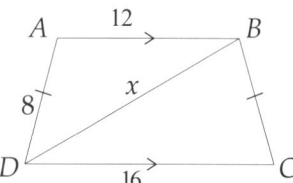

An isosceles trapezoid ABCD is given above. What is the value of x?

(A) 14

(B) 15

(C) 16

(D) 17

0660

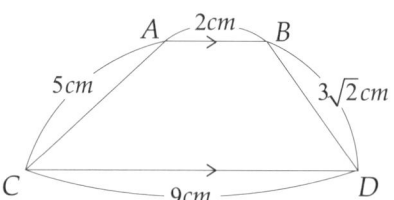

Which of the following is equal to the area of trapezoid ABCD given above?

(A) 14 square centimeters

(B) $\frac{29}{2}$ square centimeters

(C) 16 square centimeters

(D) $\frac{33}{2}$ square centimeters

0661

The measures of the angles of a pentagon are in the ratio of 2:3:4:5:6. What is the number of degrees in the measure of the smallest angle?

(A) 48°

(B) 54°

(C) 60°

(D) 62°

0662

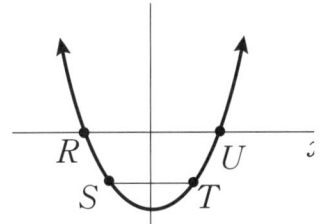

In Figure above, points R,S,T, and U lie on the parabola of equation $y=x^2-8$. If $\overline{ST}$ is parallel to the x-axis and $\overline{ST}=4$, what is the area of trapezoid RSTU?

(A) 19.31

(B) 26.45

(C) 32.12

(D) 38.62

0663

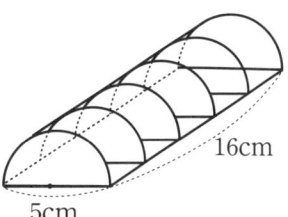

In cold winter, crops are grown in greenhouses, as shown in the figure above. What is the volume of the greenhouse above?

(A) 50π cubic meters

(B) 75π cubic meters

(C) 100π cubic meters

(D) 125π cubic meters

0664

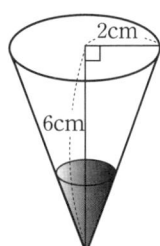

Water is being poured into the empty cone-shaped funnel at a constant rate of 1.6π cubic inches per second, as shown in the figure above. How many seconds does it take to fill the funnel with water?

(A) 4 seconds

(B) 4.5 seconds

(C) 5 seconds

(D) 5.5 seconds

0665

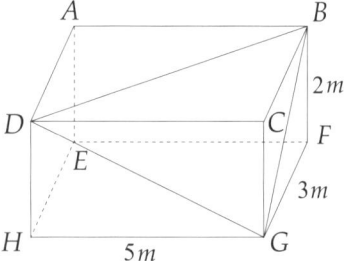

Given the rectangular prism above, what is the volume of the pyramid BCDG in cubic meters?

(A) 5 cubic meters

(B) 6 cubic meters

(C) 7 cubic meters

(D) 8 cubic meters

0666

If the volume of a sphere is the same numerical value as its surface area, what is the radius of this sphere?

(A) 3

(B) 4

(C) 5

(D) 6

0667

The volume of a right circular cylinder is 86 cubic inches. For a smaller right circular cylinder, the radius is decreased by 30% and the height is decreases by 20%. What is the volume of the smaller cylinder?

(A) 33.71 cubic inches

(B) 48.16 cubic inches

(C) 60.20 cubic inches

(D) 68.80 cubic inches

0668

John wants to paint the ceiling and walls of his rectangular room. If the length of John's room is 16 feet long by 14 feet wide by 9 feet high, how many square feet must be painted?

(A) 540 square feet

(B) 764 square feet

(C) 988 square feet

(D) 1212 square feet

0669

If the surface area of a cube is x^2, then what is the volume of this cube in terms of x?

(A) $\dfrac{\sqrt{6}x^3}{6}$

(B) $\dfrac{x^3}{6}$

(C) $\dfrac{x^3}{36}$

(D) $\dfrac{\sqrt{6}x^3}{36}$

0670

A company makes tomato soup in cylindrical cans with a height of 8 cm and a volume of 216 cubic centimeters. If the company reduces the volume of the can, how many centimeters will the height of the can be reduced if it's volume is reduced to 189 cubic centimeters and the base area remains the same?

(A) 7 centimeters

(B) 6 centimeters

(C) 5 centimeters

(D) 4 centimeters

0671

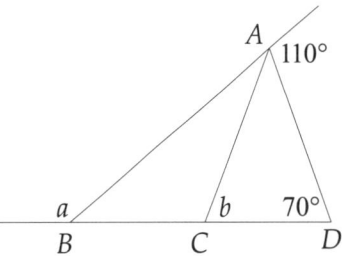

If angle BAC and angle CAD are equal in triangle ABD in the figure above, then what is the value of $a+b$?

0672

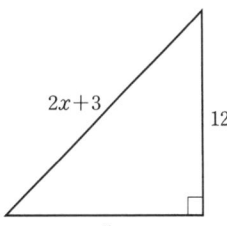

What is the value of x in the right triangle above?

0673

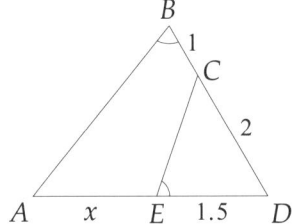

What is the value of x in the figure above?

0674

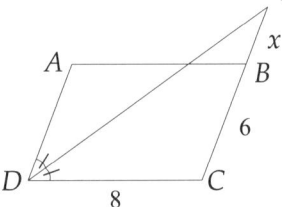

A parallelogram ABCD is given above. What is the value of x?

0675

What is the area of a regular hexagon with side length 4?

0676

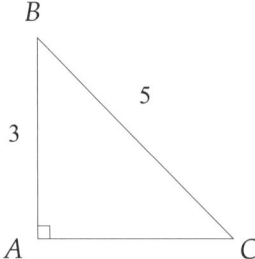

Triangle ABC above is similar to triangle DEF(not shown). If DE=9, what is the area of the triangle DEF?

For questions 677−678, refer to the following information.

The side length of an equilateral triangle ABC is 8 inches. The perimeter of equilateral triangle DEF is three times the perimeter of equilateral triangle ABC.

0677

How many times the area of equilateral triangle DEF is the area of equilateral triangle ABC?

0678

What is the area of an equilateral triangle DEF in square centimeters?

0679

Triangle ABC is similar to triangle DEF such that angles A and B correspond to angles D and E, respectively. If measure of angle A is 15 degrees and AC=2DF, what is the measure of angle D in degrees?

0680

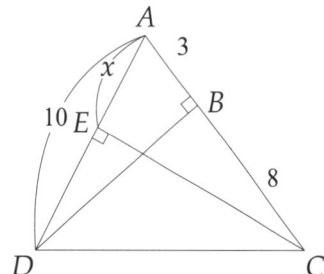

What is the value of x in the figure above?

0681

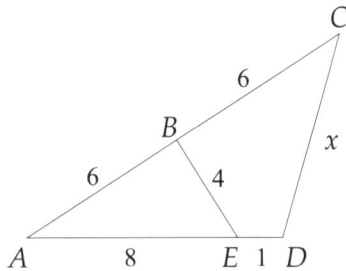

What is the value of x in the figure above?

0682

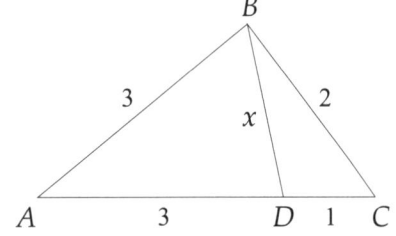

What is the value of x in the figure above?

0683

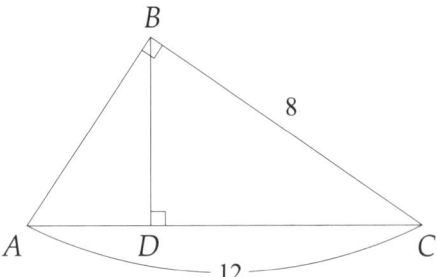

In the figure above, side BD is perpendicular to side AC and side AB is perpendicular to side BC. What is the measure of side BD?

0684

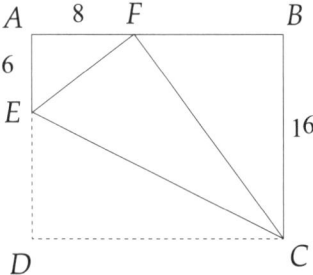

A piece of rectangular paper is folded as shown above. What is the measure of side FC?

0685

A trapezoid has one base longer than the other by 4 inches. If the height of the trapezoid is 8 inches and the area is 64 square inches, what is the length of the longer side of the trapezoid?

0686

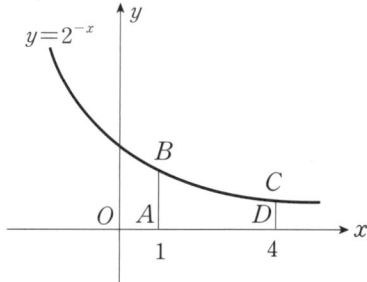

In the figure above, what is the area of trapezoid ABCD?

0687

A rhombus with each side of 4 centimeters is graphed in the xy-plane and diagonals of a rhombus intersect at the origin. All four vertices of the rhombus lie on the coordinate axes. If the longer diagonal of the rhombus is twice as long as its shorter diagonal, what is the sum of the y-coordinates of the vertices of the rhombus?

0688

What is the volume of the sphere with the radius 3 inches?

0689

If two concentric spheres (with the same center but different radii) have radii of 4 and 2 respectively, what is the volume of the space formed between the spheres?

0690

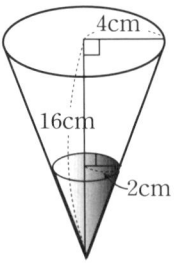

A cone—shaped cup above is filled with juice. First, Sam drank half the full height of the cup as pictured above, and then Eugene drank the remaining juice. How many times the amount of juice Sam drank was the amount of juice Eugene drank?

For questions 691—692, refer to the following information.

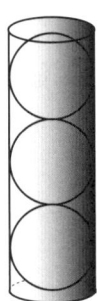

Three tennis balls fit into a cylinder—shaped barrel with a volume of 48π cubic centimeters as shown in the figure above. (Ignore the thickness of the barrel)

0691

What is the volume of a tennis ball in a barrel?

0692

What is the volume of the empty space around the tennis balls?

0693

A cone−shaped cup with a radius of 3 inches and a height of 12 inches is filled with water and poured into an empty cylinder with a radius 6 inches and a height 12 inches. What is the height of the water in the cylinder?

0694

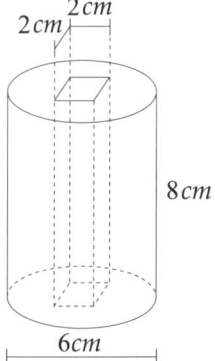

If the surface area of the figure above is $a+b$ π, what is the value of $b-a$?

0695

A right triangle has two legs with 12 inches and 18 inches long. If the length of the hypotenuse of this triangle can be written as $a\sqrt{b}$ inches (where b is a smallest integer), what is the value of $a+b$?

2. Circle Theorem

01. Circumference and Area

1. Introduction

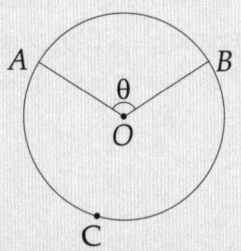

Chord: $\overline{AD}=AD$

Major Arc: $\overset{\frown}{ACB}$

Minor Arc: $\overset{\frown}{AB}$

Circumference: Length around a circle

Sector: Shaded region

2. Circumference and Area

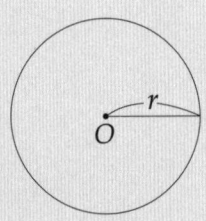

Circumference: $C=2\pi r$

Area of a circle: $A=\pi r^2$

Arc length: $l=2\pi r\times\dfrac{\theta^\circ}{360^\circ}$

Area of a sector: $A=\pi r^2\times\dfrac{\theta^\circ}{360^\circ}$

Example 1

In each of the following, find the value of x.

(1)

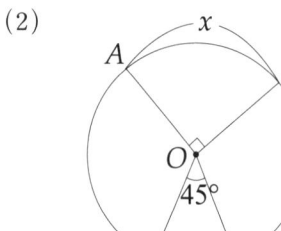

(2)

Solution

(1) <u>Method 1</u>

$$2\pi = 2\pi r \cdot \frac{40^\circ}{360^\circ}, \ r = 9$$

$$6\pi = 2\pi(9) \cdot \frac{x^\circ}{360^\circ}, \ x = 120^\circ$$

<u>Method 2</u>

Using the ratio,

$$\frac{40^\circ}{x} = \frac{2\pi}{6\pi}, \ x = 120^\circ$$

$$x = 120^\circ$$

(2) <u>Method 1</u>

$$4 = 2\pi r \cdot \frac{45^\circ}{360^\circ}, \ r = \frac{16}{\pi}$$

$$x = 2\pi \left(\frac{16}{\pi}\right) \cdot \frac{90^\circ}{360^\circ} = 8$$

<u>Method 2</u>

Using the ratio,

$$\frac{x}{4} = \frac{90^\circ}{45^\circ}, \ x = 8$$

$$x = 8$$

02. Arcs and Angles

1. Arc Measure: The measure of an arc is the measure of its central angle.

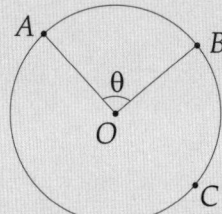

$$\to \ \overset{\frown}{AB} = \theta$$

$$\overset{\frown}{ACB} = 360^\circ - \theta$$

2. Inscribed Angle

(1) An angle subtended at a point on the circle by two given points on the circle.

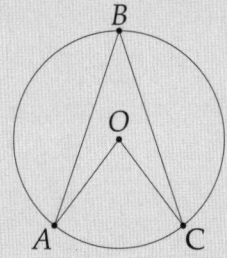

$\to$ ∠ABC is an inscribed angle.

$$\angle ABC = \frac{\overset{\frown}{AC}}{2} \ \text{ or } \ \angle ABC = \frac{\angle AOC}{2}$$

(2) If two or more inscribed angles of a circle intercept congruent arcs, then the angles are congruent.

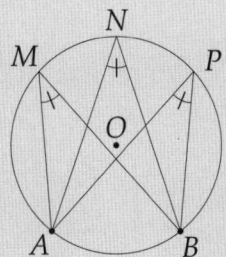

$\to$ ∠AMB ≅ ∠ANB ≅ ∠APB

Example 2

Find the value of x in each figure.

(1)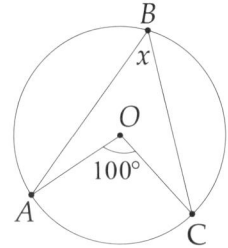

(2)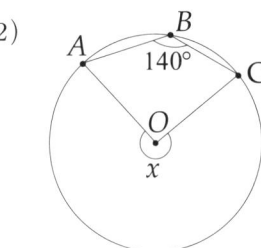

(1) $x = \frac{1}{2} \cdot 100° = 50°$

$x = 50°$

(2) $140° = \frac{x}{2}$, $x = 280°$

$x = 280°$

03. Circle and its Chordss

1. If a segment from the center is perpendicular to a chord, then it bisects the chord.

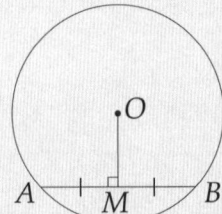

→ If $AB \perp OM$,

then $AM \cong BM$

2. If two arcs are congruent, their corresponding chords are congruent.

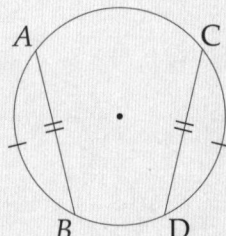

→ If $\overarc{AB} \cong \overarc{CD}$,

then $AB \cong CD$

3. If two chords are equidistant from the center, then they are congruent.

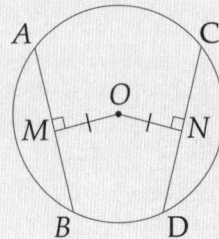

→ If $OM \cong ON$,

then, $AB \cong CD$

Example 3

Find the length of side AB in each figure.

(1)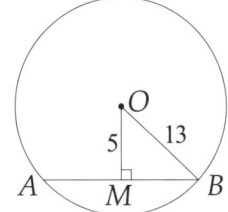

(2)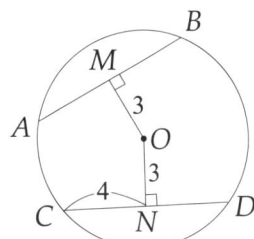

Solution

(1) In a right triangle $\triangle BOM$, $BM=\sqrt{13^2-5^2}=12$.
   Since $AM\cong BM, AB=2BM=2\cdot12=24$.

$$AM=24$$

(2) Since $OM\cong ON$, $AB\cong CD$.
   $AB=2CN=2\cdot4=8$

$$AB=8$$

04. Tangents

1. A line is tangent to a circle if it intersects a circle in exactly one point and this point is called a point of tangency. A tangent line to a circle is always perpendicular to the radius drawn to the point of tangency.

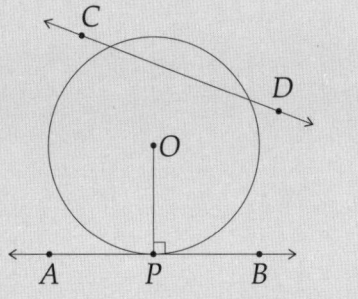

Tangent line: $\overline{AB}$

→ Point of tangency: P

$\overline{AB}\perp OP$

2. If two segments from the same exterior point are tangent to a circle, then they are congruent.

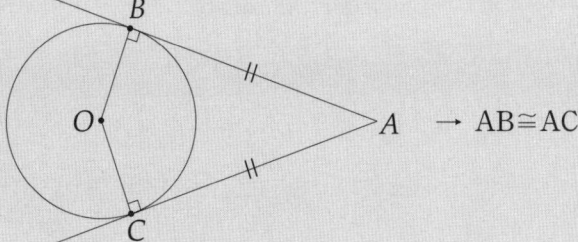

→ $AB\cong AC$

Example 4

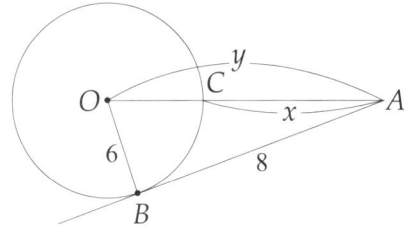

Find the value of x and y in the figure above.

Solution

Since $AB \perp OB$, $y = \sqrt{8^2 + 6^2} = 10$. Also $OB \cong OC = 6$,

$$x + OC = y$$
$$x + 6 = 10, \quad x = 4$$

$$x=4, \quad y=10$$

05. Equation of a Circle

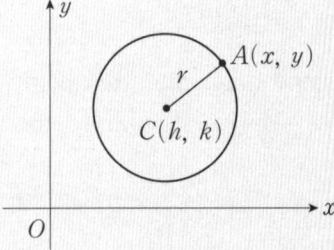

1. $x^2 + y^2 = r^2$ → Center: $(0, 0)$, Radius: r
2. $(x-h)^2 + (y-k)^2 = r^2$ → Center: (h, k), Radius: r

Example 5

Find the center and radius of the circle $x^2 + y^2 - 2y = 3$.

Solution

First rewrite the equation of the circle in $(x-h)^2 + (y-k)^2 = r^2$ by completing the square.

$$x^2 + y^2 - 2y = 3$$
$$x^2 + y^2 - 2y + 1 = 3 + 1$$
$$x^2 + (y-1)^2 = 4$$

Center $(0, 1)$, Radius 4

Memo

For questions 696−698, refer to the following information.

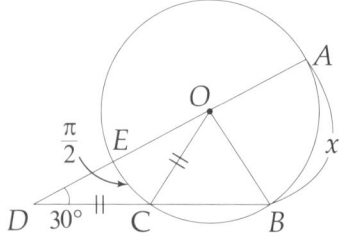

The circle shown has center O, CD≅CO, DO=$6\sqrt{3}$, $\overset{\frown}{CE}=\frac{\pi}{2}$, and $\angle CDO=30°$.

0696

What is the radius of the circle?

(A) 3

(B) $3\sqrt{2}$

(C) $3\sqrt{3}$

(D) 6

0697

What is the area of the triangle BCO?

(A) $\frac{9\sqrt{3}}{4}$

(B) 12

(C) $\frac{9\sqrt{3}}{2}$

(D) 9

0698

Which of the following is equal to the arc length x?

(A) $\frac{3\pi}{4}$

(B) π

(C) $\frac{5\pi}{4}$

(D) $\frac{3\pi}{2}$

0699

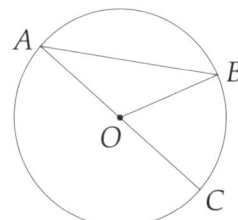

The circle shown has center O. If the length of arc AB is twice long as the length of arc BC, what is the measure of angle ABO?

(A) 20°

(B) 25°

(C) 30°

(D) 35°

0700

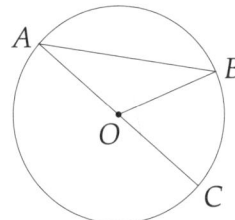

The circle shown has center O and radius 6. If the ratio of angles AOB to BOC to COA is 3 to 2 to 4, what is the area of sector BOC?

(A) 5π

(B) 6π

(C) 7π

(D) 8π

0701

A circle with a radius of 6 inches and center O (now shown) has points A, B, and C on its circumference. If the area of sector AOB is 24π, what is the central angle of sector AOB, measured in radians?

(A) $\frac{5\pi}{6}$

(B) π

(C) $\frac{5\pi}{4}$

(D) $\frac{4\pi}{3}$

0702

The pendulum swings through an angle of $\frac{2\pi}{3}$ and the tip sweeps out an arc of 8π inches. What is the length of a pendulum?

(A) 10 inches

(B) 11 inches

(C) 12 inches

(D) 13 inches

0703

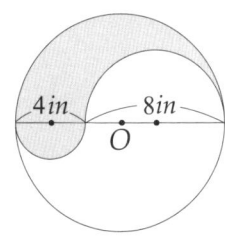

The circle shown has center O. Which of the following is equal to the shaded area in the figure above?

(A) 12

(B) 14

(C) 12π

(D) 14π

0704

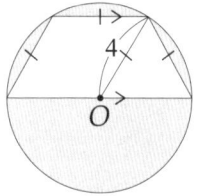

An isosceles trapezoid is inscribed in a circle with center O as shown in the figure above. Which of the following is equal to the shaded area?

(A) $16\pi - 12\sqrt{3}$

(B) π

(C) $\dfrac{5\pi}{4}$

(D) $\dfrac{3\pi}{2}$

0705

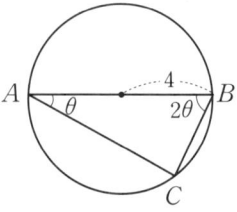

The triangle ABC is inscribed in a circle with center O as shown in the figure above. If angle ACB is right angle, what is the area of triangle ABC?

(A) 6

(B) 12

(C) $8\sqrt{3}$

(D) $12\sqrt{2}$

0706

A sector of a circle has an arc length of 2π inches and an area of 6π square inches. What is the angle of this sector in degree measure?

(A) 30°

(B) 45°

(C) 60°

(D) 90°

0707

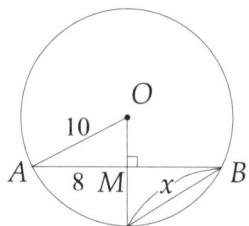

If the circle has center O and side AB is perpendicular to side OM in the figure above, what is the value x in the figure above?

(A) $3\sqrt{5}$

(B) $4\sqrt{5}$

(C) $3\sqrt{6}$

(D) $4\sqrt{6}$

0708

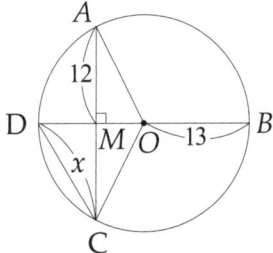

If the circle has center O and side AC is perpendicular to side BD in the figure above, what is the length of x?

(A) 16

(B) $4\sqrt{13}$

(C) 18

(D) $4\sqrt{15}$

0709

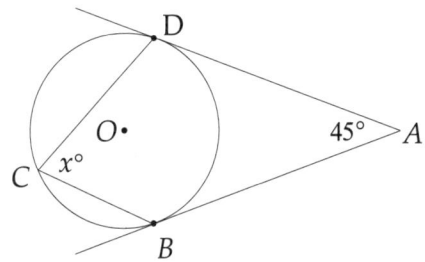

If two sides AB and AD are tangent to a circle with center O, what is the value of x in the figure above?

(A) 60°

(B) 62.5°

(C) 65°

(D) 67.5°

0710

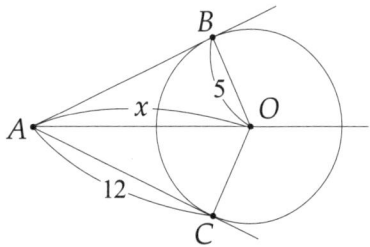

If two sides AB and AC are tangent to a circle with center O, what is the length of x?

(A) 13

(B) 14

(C) 15

(D) 16

0711

What are the coordinates of the center of the circle defined by the equation $(x+3)^2+(y-2)^2=16$?

(A) $(3, \ -2)$

(B) $(-2, \ 3)$

(C) $(-3, \ 2)$

(D) $(3, \ 4)$

0712

Which of the following points does NOT lie on the circle in the $xy-$plane whose equation is $(x+1)^2+(y-3)^2=25$?

(A) $(-4, -1)$

(B) $(0, -2)$

(C) $(2, -1)$

(D) $(3, 6)$

0713

$$x^2+y^2-6x+8y=0$$

What is the radius of a circle given by the equation above?

(A) 4

(B) 5

(C) 6

(D) 7

0714

$$2x^2+2y^2+8x-16y=0$$

What is the area of a circle given by the equation above?

(A) 20π

(B) 40π

(C) 60π

(D) 80π

0715

Which of the following points lies inside of the circle $(x-2)^2+y^2=16$?

(A) $(0, 4)$

(B) $(-2, 0)$

(C) $(-2, -4)$

(D) $(2, -3)$

0716

$$2x^2+2y^2+12x-6y+1=0.$$

What is the coordinates (x, y) of the center of the circle given by the equation above?

(A) $(6, -3)$

(B) $(-6, 3)$

(C) $\left(3, -\dfrac{3}{2}\right)$

(D) $\left(-3, \dfrac{3}{2}\right)$

0717

In the $xy-$plane, the circle whose equation is $(x+2)^2+(y-4)^2=16$ is translated 3 units to the left and 4 units down. What is the equation of the translated circle?

(A) $(x+5)^2+(y-8)^2=16$

(B) $(x+5)^2+y^2=16$

(C) $(x-2)^2+(y-6)^2=16$

(D) $(x-1)^2+(y-8)^2=16$

0718

Which of the following could be the coordinates of the center of a circle tangent to the line $y=-2$ and y axis?

(A) $(0, 0)$

(B) $(1, -3)$

(C) $(0, -2)$

(D) $(1, 1)$

0719

Which of the following equations represents a circle that intersects the x-axis at exactly one point?

(A) $(x-12)^2+(y+18)^2=36$

(B) $(x+6)^2+(y-12)^2=36$

(C) $(x-6)^2+(y+18)^2=36$

(D) $(x+18)^2+(y-6)^2=36$

0720

If a circle with center (h, k) in the second quadrant is tangent to the x-axis and the line $x=1$, then what does k equal in terms of h?

(A) $-h$

(B) $h+1$

(C) $h-1$

(D) $1-h$

0721

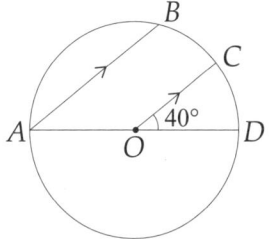

If the circle has center O, sides AB and OB are parallel in the figure above. If the length of the arc CD is 4, then, what is the length of arc AB?

0722

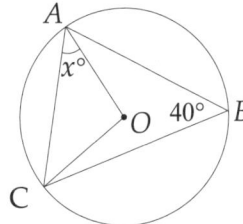

The circle shown has center O. What is the value of x?

0723

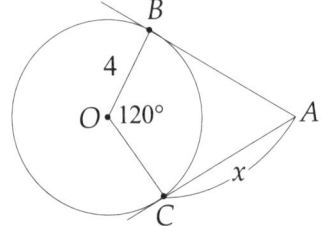

What is the value of x if two sides AB and AC are tangent to a circle with center O?

0724

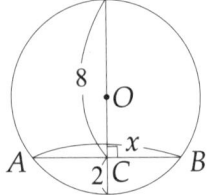

If the circle has center O and AC is perpendicular to OC in the figure above, what is the length of x?

0725

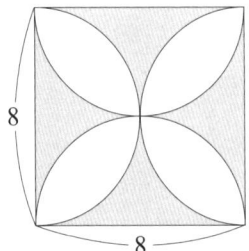

If the area of the shaded region in the figure above is $a+b\pi$, what is the value of $a+b$?

0726

Points A and B lie on a circle with radius 6 inches, and arc length of AB is $\frac{3\pi}{4}$.

The length of arc AB is what fraction of the circumference of the circle?

0727

In xy−plane, point $(-1, 4)$ is on a circle given by the equation $(x-h)^2+(y-3)^2=5$. If $h>0$, What is the value of h?

0728

If the circumference of the circle in the xy−plane with equation $x^2+y^2+4x-6y=3$ is $c\pi$, what is the value of c?

0729

If k is a positive integer, what is the value of k so that the radius of the circle $x^2+y^2+2x-ky=4$ has radius 3?

0730

The line $x=4$ passes through a circle whose radius is 3 and center is $(6, 2)$. If the y−coordinates of the points of intersections are in the form $a\pm\sqrt{b}$, what is the value of $a+b$?

3. Trigonometry

01. Radian Measure

Along with degree, radian is another unit used to measure angles. One radian is the measure of an angle θ when the radius is equal to the length of a corresponding arc.

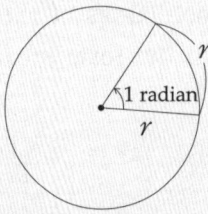 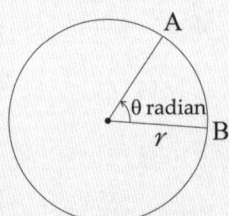

1. θ rad $= \dfrac{\widehat{AB}}{r}$

2. π rad $= 180°$ $\rightarrow$ 1 rad $= \dfrac{180°}{\pi}$, $1° = \dfrac{\pi \text{ rad}}{180}$

3. To convert degrees to radians $\rightarrow$ (Measure of degree) $\times \dfrac{\pi \text{ rad}}{180°}$

4. To convert radians to degrees $\rightarrow$ (Measure of radian) $\times \dfrac{180°}{\pi \text{ rad}}$

Degree	0°	30°	45°	60°	90°	180°	270°	360°
Radian	0	$\dfrac{\pi}{6}$	$\dfrac{\pi}{4}$	$\dfrac{\pi}{3}$	$\dfrac{\pi}{2}$	π	$\dfrac{3\pi}{2}$	2π

When no units of angle measure are specified, it is indicative of radian measure. For example, if we write $\theta = \pi$, we mean that $\theta = \pi$ radians.

Example 1

① Rewrite $225°$ in radian measure.

② Rewrite $\dfrac{3\pi}{4}$ in degree measure.

Solution

① $225° = 225° \times \dfrac{\pi}{180°} = \dfrac{5\pi}{4}$ $\quad \rightarrow$ Multiply by $\dfrac{\pi}{180°}$

$$225° = \dfrac{5\pi}{4}$$

② $\dfrac{3\pi}{4} = \dfrac{3\pi}{4} \times \dfrac{180°}{\pi} = 135°$ $\quad \rightarrow$ Multiply by $\dfrac{180°}{\pi}$

$$\dfrac{3\pi}{4} = 135°$$

02. Trigonometric Ratios

1. Trigonometric Ratios

(1) A ratio of the length of two sides of a right triangle. The most common ratios are sine, cosine, and tangent. Their abbreviations are sin, cos, and tan, respectively.

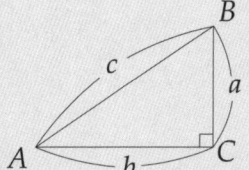

$$\sin A = \frac{a}{c} = \frac{\text{opposite leg}}{\text{hypotenuse}}, \quad \cos A = \frac{b}{c} = \frac{\text{adjacent leg}}{\text{hypotenuse}},$$

$$\text{and} \quad \tan A = \frac{a}{b} = \frac{\text{opposite leg}}{\text{adjacent leg}}$$

If we use a different angle, then the adjacent and opposite legs reverse.

(2) The value of a trigonometric ratio depends only on the measure of the angle. It does not depend on the size of the triangle.

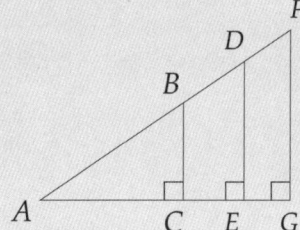

$$\rightarrow \quad \sin A = \frac{BC}{AB} = \frac{DE}{AD} = \frac{FG}{AF}$$

(3) SOH−CAH−TOA

This is a way of remembering how to compute the **sine**, **cosine**, and **tangent** of an **angle**. O, A, and H stand for opposite leg, adjacent leg, and hypotenuse, respectively.

$$S = \frac{O}{H} \quad \Big| \quad C = \frac{A}{H} \quad \Big| \quad T = \frac{O}{A}$$

(4) Trigonometric Ratios of Special Angles

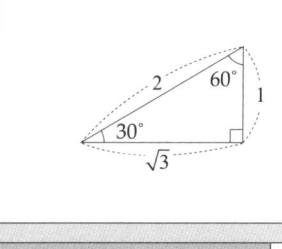 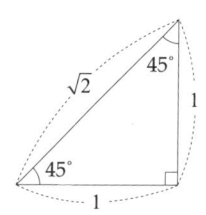 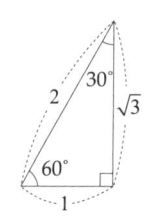

θ (degree, radians)	$30°, \dfrac{\pi}{6}$	$45°, \dfrac{\pi}{4}$	$60°, \dfrac{\pi}{3}$
$\sin \theta$	$\dfrac{1}{2}$	$\dfrac{1}{\sqrt{2}}$	$\dfrac{\sqrt{3}}{2}$
$\cos \theta$	$\dfrac{\sqrt{3}}{2}$	$\dfrac{1}{\sqrt{2}}$	$\dfrac{1}{2}$
$\tan \theta$	$\dfrac{1}{\sqrt{3}} = \dfrac{\sqrt{3}}{3}$	1	$\sqrt{3}$

Example 2

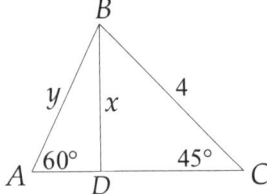

Find x and y using trigonometric ratios in the figure above.

Solution

In $\triangle CBD$, $\sin C = \dfrac{BD}{BC}$

$\qquad \sin 45° = \dfrac{x}{4}$

$\qquad \dfrac{\sqrt{2}}{2} = \dfrac{x}{4}$ and

$\qquad x = 4 \cdot \dfrac{\sqrt{2}}{2} = 2\sqrt{2}$

In $\triangle ABD$, $\sin A = \dfrac{BD}{AB}$

$\qquad \sin 60° = \dfrac{x}{y}$

$\qquad \dfrac{\sqrt{3}}{2} = \dfrac{x}{y}$

$\qquad y = \dfrac{2}{\sqrt{3}} \cdot x = \dfrac{2\sqrt{3}}{3} \cdot 2\sqrt{2} = \dfrac{4\sqrt{6}}{3}$

$$x = 2\sqrt{2}, \ y = \dfrac{4\sqrt{6}}{3}$$

Example 3

In a triangle ABC, angle A measures 30 degrees, angle B measures 60 degrees, and side AC measures 10 units. What is the length of side AB?

Solution

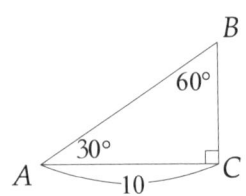

In $\triangle ABC$, $\cos 30° = \dfrac{AC}{AB}$

$\qquad \dfrac{\sqrt{3}}{2} = \dfrac{10}{AB}$

$\qquad AB = 10 \cdot \dfrac{2}{\sqrt{3}} = 10 \cdot \dfrac{2\sqrt{3}}{3} = \dfrac{20\sqrt{3}}{3}$

$$AB = \dfrac{20\sqrt{3}}{3}$$

03. Unit Circle

The unit circle is a circle whose radius is 1 and whose center is at the origin of a rectangular coordinate system. The following discussion sets the stage for defining the trigonometric functions using the unit circle. Let P(x, y) be the intersection of the terminal side. Then a right triangle with angle θ and two legs (x and y) is created as shown in the figure below.

We define six trigonometric functions as follows.

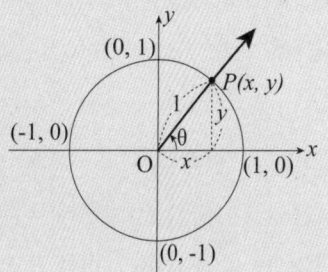

Word	Symbol	Definition
Sine	sin	$\sin\theta = \dfrac{y}{1} = y$
Cosine	cos	$\cos\theta = \dfrac{x}{1} = x$
Tangent	tan	$\tan\theta = \dfrac{y}{x}$

Example 4

Find the sine, cosine, and tangent of angle θ.

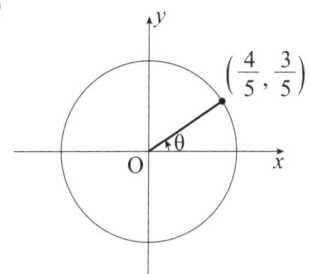

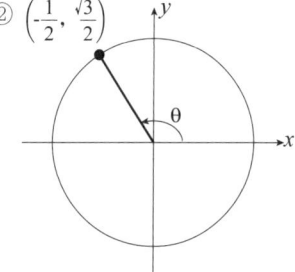

Solution

Remember that the $x-$and $y-$coordinates of the unit circle are the cosines and sines of the given angle, respectively.

① $\sin\theta = y = \dfrac{3}{5}$

$\cos\theta = x = \dfrac{4}{5}$

$\tan\theta = \dfrac{y}{x} = \dfrac{\dfrac{3}{5}}{\dfrac{4}{5}} = \dfrac{3}{4}$

$\qquad \sin\theta = \dfrac{3}{5}, \ \cos\theta = \dfrac{4}{5}, \ \tan\theta = \dfrac{3}{4}$

② $\sin\theta = y = \dfrac{\sqrt{3}}{2}$

$\cos\theta = x = -\dfrac{1}{2}$

$\tan\theta = \dfrac{y}{x} = \dfrac{\dfrac{\sqrt{3}}{2}}{-\dfrac{1}{2}} = -\sqrt{3}$

$\qquad \sin\theta = \dfrac{\sqrt{3}}{2}, \ \cos\theta = -\dfrac{1}{2}, \ \tan\theta = -\sqrt{3}$

04. Cofunction Identity

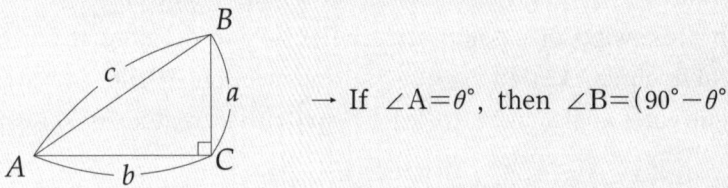 → If $\angle A = \theta°$, then $\angle B = (90° - \theta°)$

1. $\sin(90° - \theta°) = \dfrac{b}{c} = \cos\theta°$, $\cos(90° - \theta°) = \dfrac{a}{c} = \sin\theta°$

2. If $\sin A = \cos B$, then $\angle A + \angle B = 90°$

   If $\cos A = \sin B$, then $\angle A + \angle B = 90°$

This is also true when the angle is in radians.

Example 5

In a right triangle with an acute angle θ, if $\sin(\theta) = 0.6$, what is the value of $\cos(90° - \theta)$?

(A) 0.4　　　　　(B) 0.6　　　　　(C) 0.8　　　　　(D) 1.0

Solution

Since $\cos(90° - \theta) = \sin(\theta)$ by cofunction identity, $\cos(90° - \theta) = 0.6$.

The answer is B.

Practice **Problems**

0731

What is the degree measure of an angle with a measure of $\frac{2\pi}{3}$ radians?

(A) 60°

(B) 90°

(C) 120°

(D) 150°

0732

What is the radian measure of an angle with a measure of 225°?

(A) $\frac{7\pi}{6}$

(B) $\frac{5\pi}{4}$

(C) $\frac{4\pi}{3}$

(D) $\frac{3\pi}{2}$

0733

If the measure of angle A is $\frac{5\pi}{4}$ and the measure of angle B is $\frac{11\pi}{12}$, how much greater is the measure of angle A then the measure of angle B in degrees?

(A) 60°

(B) 75°

(C) 90°

(D) 105°

0734

In a right triangle, if one acute angle measures 30 degrees and the length of the hypotenuse is 10 units, what is the length of the longer leg?

(A) 5 units

(B) $5\sqrt{2}$

(C) $5\sqrt{3}$ units

(D) 8 units

0735

In triangle ABC, angle B is a right angle. If $\cos A = \frac{5}{13}$, what is the value of $\sin C$?

(A) $\frac{5}{13}$

(B) $\frac{12}{13}$

(C) $\frac{5}{12}$

(D) $\frac{13}{12}$

0736

In triangle ABC, angle A measures 90 degrees, and side AC has a length of 10 units. If $\sin B = 0.8$, what is the length of side BC?

(A) 12.5

(B) 16

(C) 16.5

(D) 20

0737

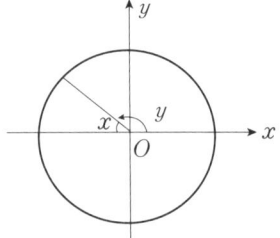

A circle with a radius of 5 is given above. If $\sin x = \frac{3}{5}$, what is the value of $\cos y$?

(A) $\frac{3}{5}$

(B) $\frac{4}{5}$

(C) $-\frac{3}{5}$

(D) $-\frac{4}{5}$

0738

In a right triangle with an acute angle θ, if $\cos(\theta) = 0.8$, what is the value of $\sin(90° - \theta)$?

(A) 0.2

(B) 0.4

(C) 0.6

(D) 0.8

0739

What expression is equivalent to $\sin 44°$?

(A) $\cos 44°$

(B) $\cos 46°$

(C) $\tan 44°$

(D) $\tan 46°$

0740

If $\cos \theta = -\frac{1}{3}$ and θ is in quadrant II, what is the value of $\sin \theta$?

(A) $-\frac{2\sqrt{2}}{3}$

(B) $-\frac{3\sqrt{2}}{4}$

(C) $\frac{2\sqrt{2}}{3}$

(D) $\frac{3\sqrt{2}}{4}$

0741

If $\tan \theta = 2$ and $\sin \theta < 0$, what is the value of $\cos \theta$?

(A) $-\sqrt{5}$

(B) $-\frac{\sqrt{5}}{5}$

(C) $\frac{\sqrt{5}}{2}$

(D) $\frac{2\sqrt{5}}{5}$

0742

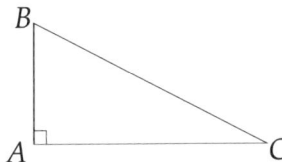

In triangle ABC above, point D (not shown) lies on BC. Which of the following must be true?

(A) $\sin(\angle BAD) + \cos(\angle CAD) = 1$

(B) $\sin(\angle BAD) - \cos(\angle CAD) = 0$

(C) $\sin(\angle ADB) = \cos(\angle ADC)$

(D) $\sin(\angle ADB) = -\cos(\angle ADC)$

0743

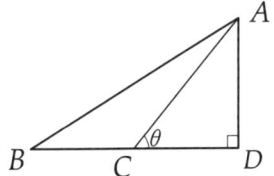

In the figure above, the length of side AB is 5, the length of side BC is 2, and C is the midpoint of side BD. What is the value of $\sin\theta$?

(A) $3\sqrt{3}$

(B) $\sqrt{13}$

(C) $\dfrac{\sqrt{13}}{3\sqrt{3}}$

(D) $\dfrac{3\sqrt{3}}{\sqrt{13}}$

0744

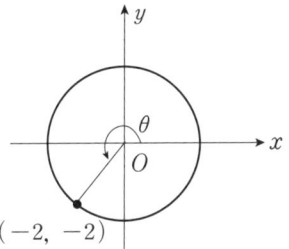

In the figure above, what is the radian measure of θ?

(A) $\dfrac{7\pi}{6}$

(B) $\dfrac{5\pi}{4}$

(C) $\dfrac{4\pi}{3}$

(D) $\dfrac{3\pi}{2}$

0745

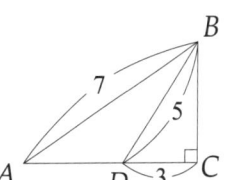

What is the value of the tangent of angle A in the figure above?

(A) $\dfrac{4}{5}$

(B) $\dfrac{4}{7}$

(C) $\dfrac{\sqrt{33}}{7}$

(D) $\dfrac{4}{\sqrt{33}}$

For questions 746—747, refer to the following information.

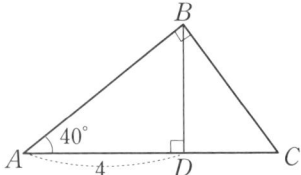

In the figure above, ABC, ABD, and CBD are all right triangles, and the length of side AD is equal to the length of side BC.

0746

Which expression is equal to the length of side BD?

(A) $4 \tan 40°$

(B) $4 \sin 50°$

(C) $4 \cos 40°$

(D) $\dfrac{\cos 50°}{4}$

0747

Which of the following is equal to the value of the cosine of angle C?

(A) $\cos \angle CBD$

(B) $\cos \angle A$

(C) $\sin \angle ABD$

(D) $\sin \angle DBC$

For questions 748—749, refer to the following information.

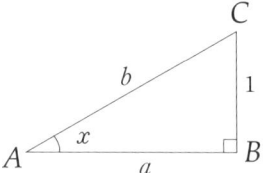

Triangle ABC is given above.

0748

Which of the following expression could be $a+b$?

(A) $\sin x + \cos x$

(B) $\dfrac{1}{\sin x} + \dfrac{1}{\cos x}$

(C) $\dfrac{1+\sin x}{\cos x}$

(D) $\dfrac{1+\cos x}{\sin x}$

0749

If the measure of angle x is 30 degrees, what is the value of b ?

(A) 1

(B) $\sqrt{2}$

(C) $\sqrt{3}$

(D) 2

For questions 750−753, refer to the following information.

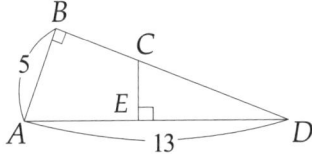

Triangle ABD is a right triangle and side CE is perpendicular to side AD as shown in the figure above.

0750

What is the length of side BD?

(A) 8

(B) 9

(C) 11

(D) 12

0751

What is the value of the sine of angle DCE?

(A) $\frac{5}{12}$

(B) $\frac{5}{13}$

(C) $\frac{12}{13}$

(D) $\frac{13}{12}$

0752

If the length of side CD is 6.5 inches, what is the length of side ED, in inches?

(A) 6

(B) 7

(C) 8

(D) 9

0753

What is the ratio of the area of triangle ABD to the area of triangle CED?

(A) 2

(B) 4

(C) 6

(D) 8

0754

Rick is standing 365 feet from the base of a building. If he measures the angle of elevation from the ground to the top of the building to be 16 degrees, which of the following express the height of the building?

(A) $365\sin 16°$

(B) $\dfrac{365}{\sin 16°}$

(C) $365\tan 16°$

(D) $\dfrac{365}{\cos 16°}$

0755

Emily who is about 5.6 feet tall is standing 200 feet from the base of a building. If she measures the angle of elevation from the top of her head to the top of the building to be 32 degrees, how tall is the building?

(A) 119.37 feet

(B) 124.97 feet

(C) 130.57 feet

(D) 145.12 feet

0756

A 6 feet tall person starts to walk directly toward a vertical building that is 45 feet tall. What is the distance the person traveled if the angle of elevation from the person's head to the top of the building changes from 15 degrees to 20 degrees?

(A) 26.43 feet

(B) 29.87 feet

(C) 35.7 feet

(D) 38.4 feet

0757

A balloon is hovering 600 feet above the ground. The balloon is observed by Tim riding a motorcycle as he looks upwards at an angle of 16 degrees. After 30 seconds, Tim has to look at an angle of 42 degrees to see the balloon. How fast was the motorcycle traveling?

(A) 45.12 feet per second

(B) 47.54 feet per second

(C) 49.37 feet per second

(D) 51.04 feet per second

0758

A surveyor determines the angle of elevation of a mountain from ground to be 12 degrees. If the surveyor gets in the car and drives away 1000 feet from the mountain, then the measure of the angle of elevation becomes 9 degrees. What is the height of the mountain?

(A) 459.46 feet

(B) 574.32 feet

(C) 597.24 feet

(D) 621.46 feet

0759

An angle measure of 90° is equal to an angle measure of $\frac{\pi}{a}$ radians. What is the value of a?

0760

$\frac{2\pi}{15}$ radians is equivalent to an angle measure of x degrees. What is the value of x?

0761

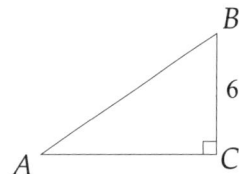

If $\sin A = \frac{3}{5}$ in the figure above, then what is the value of AC?

For questions 762−763, refer to the following information.

Triangle ABC has right angle C and $\cos A = \frac{3}{5}$

0762

What is the value of $\sin B$?

0763

What is the value of tan A?

0764

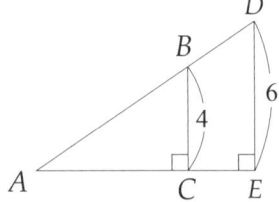

If the side BC is parallel to the side DE and $\tan A = \dfrac{3}{4}$ in the figure above, what is the value of side CE?

0765

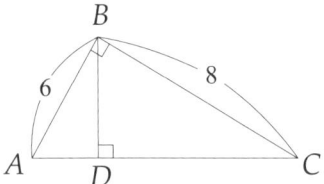

If triangle ABC is a right triangle and side BD is perpendicular to side AC as shown in the figure above, what is the value of $\sin \angle CBD$?

0766

A person is standing $80\sqrt{3}$ meters from the rocket launch point, where the rocket is launched vertically. What is the height of the rocket when the angle between the ground and the person's line of sight is 60 degrees?

0767

A passenger in an airplane flying at an altitude of 2400 feet sees two mountains directly to the east of the plane. The angles of depression to the mountains are 18 degrees and 31 degrees, respectively. How far apart are the mountains to the nearest feet?

Memo

Math
22 Questions

For multiple-choice questions, solve each problem, choose the correct answer from the choices provided, and then circle your answer in this book. Circle only one answer for each question. If you change your mind, completely erase the circle. You will not get credit for questions with more than one answer circled, or for questions with no answers circled.

For student-produced response questions, solve each problem and write your answer next to or under the question in the test book as described below.

- Once you've written your answer, circle it clearly. You will not receive credit for anything written outside the circle, or for any questions with more than one circled answer.

- If you find **more than one correct answer**, write and circle only one answer.

- Your answer can be up to 5 characters for a **positive** answer and up to 6 characters (including the negative sign) for a **negative** answer, but no more.

- If your answer is a **fraction** that is too long (over 5 characters for positive, 6 characters for negative), write the decimal equivalent.

- If your answer is a **decimal** that is too long (over 5 characters for positive, 6 characters for negative), truncate it or round at the fourth digit.

- If your answer is a **mixed number** (such as $3\frac{1}{2}$), write it as an improper fraction (7/2) or its decimal equivalent (3.5).

- Don't include **symbols** such as a percent sign, comma, or dollar sign in your circled answer.

CONTINUE ➡

1

Consider the system of linear equations

I. $2x+3y=10$ II. $4x-6y=15$

Which of the following could be true about the system of equations?

(A) The system has one solution.

(B) The system has exactly two solutions.

(C) The system has infinitely many solutions.

(D) The system has no solution.

2

The equation $m=5{,}000c+10{,}000$ approximates the value (in dollars) of a rare gem based on carat weight c. What is the increase in carat weight required to increase the value by $25,000?

(A) 1 carat

(B) 2 carats

(C) 3 carats

(D) 5 carats

3

A shipping company charges a flat rate of $20 for the first package, and then an additional $12 for each additional package. If p represents the number of packages sent, which of the following functions gives the total cost $C(p)$, in dollars, of shipping p packages?

(A) $C(p)=20p+12$

(B) $C(p)=12p+8$

(C) $C(p)=12p-20$

(D) $C(p)=12p+20$

4

A scientist is studying the decay of a radioactive substance. The amount of the substance, $A(t)$, in grams, after t minutes can be modeled by the function $A(t)=100(0.6)^{0.05t}$. Which of the following describes the meaning of the exponent 0.6 in the context described?

(A) Initial amount of the substance.

(B) The proportion of the initial amount of the substance that remains after 0.05 minutes.

(C) The proportion of the initial amount of the substance that remains after 1 minute.

(D) The proportion of the initial amount of the substance that remains after 20 minutes.

CONTINUE

5

$$g(x)=5(0.8)^x+5$$

The function g is show above. What is the y-intercept of the graph of $y=g(x)$ in the xy-plane?

6

Consider the function $f(x)=a(x+3)(x-5)$, where a is a constant. The graph of this function is a parabola that opens upwards. If the vertex of the parabola is located at $(1, -15)$, what is the value of a?

7

In laboratory experiments, certain types of bacteria initially have 1,200 colonies. Over time, the number of colonies decreases exponentially. Each hour for the next 10 hours, the number of colonies will decrease by approximately 35% from the previous hour. Which function g best models this situation, where $g(t)$ is the approximate number of colonies after t hours?

(A) $g(t)=1,200(0.65)^{\frac{t}{10}}$

(B) $g(t)=1,200(0.65)^t$

(C) $g(t)=1,200(0.35)^{\frac{t}{10}}$

(D) $g(t)=1,200(0.35)^t$

8

Consider the expression $3x^2+8x-16$. Which of the following is a factor of the given expression?

(A) $3x-4$

(B) $2x-5$

(C) $x-2$

(D) $4x+5$

9

In the xy-plane, the graph of the equation $y=3x+5$ intersects the graph of the equation $y=2x^2$ at two points. What is the sum of the x-coordinates of the two points?

(A) 1

(B) 1.5

(C) 2

(D) 2.5

10

Which expression is equivalent to the expression $(2\sqrt{a}+\sqrt{2b})^2$, where a and b are positive constants?

(A) $4a+2b$

(B) $4a+\sqrt{8ab}+2b$

(C) $4a+8\sqrt{ab}+2b$

(D) $4a+4\sqrt{2ab}+2b$

CONTINUE

11

A ball is thrown upward from the ground. The function $h(t) = -9.8t^2 + 29.4t$ models the height of the ball above the ground, in meters, t seconds after the ball is thrown. According to the model, how many seconds does it take the ball to reach its maximum height?

12

In a certain city, the number of bicycles rented in the month of July was 1200. The number of bicycles rented in the month of August was 900. Bicycle rentals in August were what percent less than bicycle rentals in July to the nearest percent?

(A) 20%   (B) 25%   (C) 30%   (D) 35%

13

$$\sqrt{(4x-3)^2} = x$$

What is the sum of all solutions to the equation above?

14

A Ferris wheel has a radius of 12 meters. The Ferris wheel makes one complete revolution in 90 seconds. What is the approximate speed of the Ferris wheel to the nearest kilometer per hour?

(1 kilometer = 1000 meters)

(A) 2 km/hr

(B) 3 km/hr

(C) 4 km/hr

(D) 5 km/hr

15

According to a recipe for a fruit smoothie, 4 servings call for 2 cups of milk. If a restaurant plans to make eight dozen servings of the smoothie, how many cups of milk should they use?

16

At a department store, all items are on sale with a 30% discount. Mark bought several items and paid $245.00, including 8% tax on the discounted price. What was the total price of the items, in the nearest dollar, before the discount?

CONTINUE

17

Major	Undergraduate	Graduate
Chemistry	60	35
Biology	160	100
Economics	120	85

Data from a random sample of 500 students at a university are listed in the table above. The table indicates the number of students in 3 academic majors and whether each student is an undergraduate or graduate student. No student is enrolled in more than one major. If a student is selected at random, what is the probability that the selected student is an undergraduate, given that the student is majoring in Economics?

(A) 0.366   (B) 0.415

(C) 0.585   (D) 0.632

18

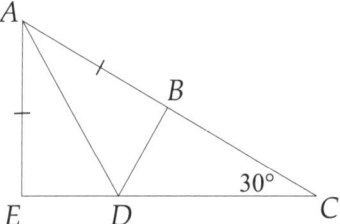

In the figure above, sides AE and AB are perpendicular to sides ED and BD, respectively. Also, side AE has the same length as side AB. What is the measure of angle ADE?

(A) 40°   (B) 50°

(C) 60°   (D) 70°

19

The graph of $x^2+y^2-x+3y=\dfrac{15}{4}$ in the $xy-$plane is a circle. What is the length of the circle's diameter?

20

$$85,\ 92,\ 78,\ 102,\ 88,\ 95,\ 80,\ 90,\ 85,\ 98$$

In a basketball tournament, the total points scored by 10 teams were recorded as shown above. Later, it was discovered that the reported scores of these 10 teams were 3 points greater than their actual scores. Which of the following statistics will remain unchanged if the total points are reported using the corrected scores?

(A) Mean

(B) Median

(C) Range

(D) Standard deviation

CONTINUE

21

In a city, a survey was conducted among 800 residents to determine how many of them had visited the newly opened art museum in the last month. The results showed that 480 residents had visited the museum during that time. If the city's population is 60,000, approximately how many residents would be expected to have visited the museum in the last month?

(A) 14,400 residents

(B) 16,800 residents

(C) 24,000 residents

(D) 36,000 residents

22

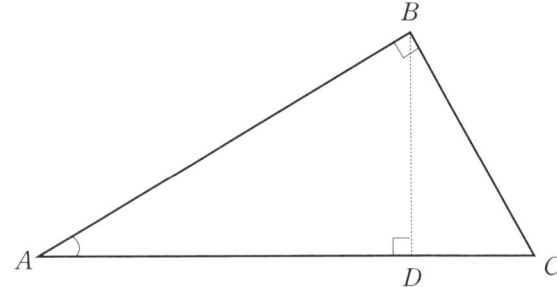

Which of the following is equal to the value of the sine of angle A?

(A) $\cos\angle CBD$

(B) $\cos\angle A$

(C) $\sin\angle ABD$

(D) $\sin\angle DBC$

Math
22 Questions

For multiple-choice questions, solve each problem, choose the correct answer from the choices provided, and then circle your answer in this book. Circle only one answer for each question. If you change your mind, completely erase the circle. You will not get credit for questions with more than one answer circled, or for questions with no answers circled.

For student-produced response questions, solve each problem and write your answer next to or under the question in the test book as described below.

- Once you've written your answer, circle it clearly. You will not receive credit for anything written outside the circle, or for any questions with more than one circled answer.

- If you find **more than one correct answer**, write and circle only one answer.

- Your answer can be up to 5 characters for a **positive** answer and up to 6 characters (including the negative sign) for a **negative** answer, but no more.

- If your answer is a **fraction** that is too long (over 5 characters for positive, 6 characters for negative), write the decimal equivalent.

- If your answer is a **decimal** that is too long (over 5 characters for positive, 6 characters for negative), truncate it or round at the fourth digit.

- If your answer is a **mixed number** (such as $3\frac{1}{2}$), write it as an improper fraction (7/2) or its decimal equivalent (3.5).

- Don't include **symbols** such as a percent sign, comma, or dollar sign in your circled answer.

CONTINUE

1

$$y+5=(3y-1)-qy$$

In the equation shown, q is a constant. If the equation has no solution, what is the value of q?

(A) -4

(B) -2

(C) 2

(D) 4

2

A lawn care service charges an initial fee of $30 and an additional $15 fee for every hour of work. The service provider visited a customer's property and charged $150 for the services rendered. At this rate, how many hours did the service provider work on the customer's lawn?

(A) 6 hours

(B) 7 hours

(C) 8 hours

(D) 9 hours

3

$$3x-2y=3$$

$$2x-3y=3$$

How many solutions does the given system of equations have?

(A) Zero

(B) Exactly one

(C) Exactly two

(D) Infinitely many

4

$$h(t)=500,000(1.015)^t$$

The above function $h(t)$ can be used to determine the population of a city since 2010, where t is the number of years since 2010. what is the value of y if the city's population increases by $y\%$ per year compared to the previous year's population?

(A) 0.015%   (B) 0.15%

(C) 1.5%   (D) 15%

5

The population of a certain species of fish in a lake is growing over time. The number of fish, $F(t)$, in the lake at time t (in years) is given in the table below:

t (years)	$F(t)$ (number of fish)
0	1000
2	2000
4	4000
6	8000
8	16000

Based on the data in the table, which of the following best describes the relationship between time and the number of fish?

(A) It is linear because the number of fish is increasing by the same factor every 2 years.

(B) It is linear because the number of fish is increasing by the same number every 2 years.

(C) It is exponential because the number of fish is increasing by the same factor every 2 years.

(D) It is exponential because the number of fish is increasing by the same number every 2 years.

CONTINUE

6

What is the slope of the line that passes through the points $(2, -4)$ and $(-1, 5)$?

7

$$2x^3 + 2x^2 - 24x$$

One of the factors from the expression above is $x+a$, where a is a positive constant. What is the value of a?

8

$$\frac{x^2 - 4x + 1}{x - 3}$$

Which of the following is equivalent to the expression above?

(A) $x + 1 + \dfrac{2}{x - 3}$

(B) $x + 1 - \dfrac{2}{x - 3}$

(C) $x - 1 + \dfrac{2}{x - 3}$

(D) $x - 1 - \dfrac{2}{x - 3}$

9

Consider the function $y = x^2 - 16x + m$, where m is a constant. If the function value has a minimum value at the point (p, q), what is the value of $p - q$ in terms of m?

(A) $56 + m$

(B) $72 + m$

(C) $72 - m$

(D) $56 - m$

10

$$\frac{6}{x+3} + \frac{2}{x-2} = 3$$

What are all possible solutions to the equation above?

(A) $-\dfrac{4}{3}$

(B) 3

(C) $-\dfrac{4}{3}$ and 3

(D) No solution

 CONTINUE

11

The number of smartphone users in a country can be estimated by the function $g(x) = 80x^2 + 250x + 4,500$, where x represents the number of years since 2010. The constant term 4,500 in the function is an estimate for which of the following?

(A) The year the number of smartphone users reached 4,500.

(B) The number of smartphone users in 2010.

(C) The increase in the number of smartphone users each year.

(D) The maximum number of smartphone users in a single year from 2010 through 2020.

12

Which of the following is equal to the expression $4\sqrt[3]{16}$?

(A) $4^{\frac{4}{3}}$

(B) $4^{\frac{5}{2}}$

(C) $2^{\frac{10}{3}}$

(D) $2^{\frac{3}{10}}$

13

In a wildlife reserve, the number of zebras is approximately 240, which is 30% of the total number of animals in the reserve. Based on this information, how many animals are there in the reserve?

(A) 720

(B) 800

(C) 960

(D) 1,200

14

In 2015, the ratio of the number of electric cars to the number of gasoline cars in a certain country was 1:8. If there were a total of 50,000 electric cars in the country in that year, how many gasoline cars were there?

15

$$C = \frac{5}{9}(F - 32)$$

The above equation shows the relationship between Celsius and Fahrenheit. The average human body temperature is approximately 37 degrees Celsius. Which of the following is closest to the average human body temperature in degrees Fahrenheit?

(A) 70°F

(B) 85°F

(C) 99°F

(D) 105°F

CONTINUE

16

What are the coordinates of the center of the circle defined by the equation $(x-4)^2+y^2=25$?

(A) $(4, 0)$

(B) $(-4, 0)$

(C) $(0, 4)$

(D) $(0, -4)$

17

In triangles ABC and DEF, angles A and D are each 12°, and angles B and E are each 68°. Which additional information is needed to determine whether triangle ABC is <u>similar</u> to triangle DEF?

(A) The measure of angle B

(B) The length of side AC

(C) The measure of angle B and angle E

(D) No additional information is needed

18

Data Set I

Data Set II

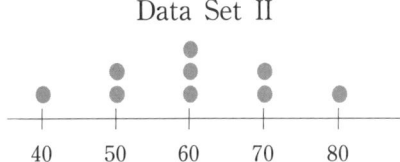

Which of the following statements best compares the standard deviations of the two data sets?

(A) The standard deviation of data set I is equal to the standard deviation of data set II.

(B) The standard deviation of data set I is greater than the standard deviation of data set II.

(C) The standard deviation of data set I is less than the standard deviation of data set II.

(D) There is not enough information to compare the standard deviation.

CONTINUE

19

What is the radian measure of an angle with a measure of 120°?

(A) $\frac{\pi}{3}$

(B) $\frac{2\pi}{3}$

(C) $\frac{5\pi}{6}$

(D) π

21

$$|2x-5|=15$$

What is the sum of the solutions for the equation given above?

20

Which of the following quadratic functions has the vertex $(0, -2)$ and x−intercept 1.

(A) $y=(x+2)^2-2$

(B) $y=2(x+2)^2-2$

(C) $y=x^2-2$

(D) $y=2x^2-2$

22

Points A and B lie on a circle with center O and a radius of 4 centimeters. If the arc length of AB is π, what is the degree measure of angle AOB?

Math
22 Questions

For multiple-choice questions, solve each problem, choose the correct answer from the choices provided, and then circle your answer in this book. Circle only one answer for each question. If you change your mind, completely erase the circle. You will not get credit for questions with more than one answer circled, or for questions with no answers circled.

For student-produced response questions, solve each problem and write your answer next to or under the question in the test book as described below.

- Once you've written your answer, circle it clearly. You will not receive credit for anything written outside the circle, or for any questions with more than one circled answer.

- If you find **more than one correct answer**, write and circle only one answer.

- Your answer can be up to 5 characters for a **positive** answer and up to 6 characters (including the negative sign) for a **negative** answer, but no more.

- If your answer is a **fraction** that is too long (over 5 characters for positive, 6 characters for negative), write the decimal equivalent.

- If your answer is a **decimal** that is too long (over 5 characters for positive, 6 characters for negative), truncate it or round at the fourth digit.

- If your answer is a **mixed number** (such as $3\frac{1}{2}$), write it as an improper fraction (7/2) or its decimal equivalent (3.5).

- Don't include **symbols** such as a percent sign, comma, or dollar sign in your circled answer.

CONTINUE ➤

1

Which of the following describe a decreasing linear relationship between the price of a product and the number of units sold?

(A) For every \$2 increase in product price, units sold decreases by 100.

(B) For every 0.5% decrease in product price, units sold increases by 100.

(C) The price of the product becomes half of the previous price for every 1 unit sold.

(D) The price of the product increases by \$0.002 for every 1 unit sold.

2

$$A = \frac{2B+C}{D-B}$$

In the equation shown, B and C are constants. Which of the following equations gives B in terms of A, C, and D?

(A) $B = \dfrac{AD+C}{2-A}$

(B) $B = \dfrac{AD-C}{2+A}$

(C) $B = \dfrac{2+A}{AD-C}$

(D) $B = \dfrac{2-A}{AD+C}$

3

In the $xy-$plane, line m passes through the point $(2, 3)$ and has a slope of 2. Line n is perpendicular to line m in the $xy-$plane. Which of the following could be an equation of line n?

(A) $2x+y=8$

(B) $2x-y=8$

(C) $x+2y=8$

(D) $x-2y=8$

4

A bakery sells vanilla and chocolate cupcakes. The equation $2x+5y=150$ represents its daily revenue from cupcake sales where x and y are the number of vanilla and chocolate cupcakes sold, respectively. What is the meaning of $2x$ in this context?

(A) The total cost of baking x vanilla cupcakes.

(B) The cost of baking each vanilla cupcake.

(C) The total daily revenue from selling x vanilla cupcakes.

(D) The daily revenue from selling each vanilla cupcake.

5

If the expression $\dfrac{xy^2}{2}\left(\dfrac{4x}{y}-6y^3\right)$ is equal to $2x^a y^b - 3x^c y^d$, where a, b, c, and d are constants, what is the value of $a+b+c+d$?

CONTINUE

6

Consider the quadratic equation $2x^2+7x+6-p=0$. In this equation, p is a constant, and the equation has exactly one real root. What is the value of p?

7

$$P(t)=300,000(0.965)^t$$

The above function $P(t)$ can be used to determine the population of a city since 2010, where t is the number of months since 2010. What is the value of d if the city's population decreases by d% per year compared to the previous year's population?

(A) 0.965%

(B) 0.035%

(C) 0.35%

(D) 3.5%

8

A certain investment grows at a rate of 4.77% per year. If an initial investment of $10,000 was made, what will be the value of the investment after 3 years?

(A) $10,500

(B) $11,000

(C) $11,500

(D) $12,000

9

The function $H(x)$ is defined by $H(x)=4x+3$. If $H(x+b)=ax+b$, where a and b is a constant, what is the value of $a+b$?

(A) 3

(B) 4

(C) 5

(D) 6

10

There is a rectangle whose length is 4 inches less than twice its width. If the width of the rectangle is x inches, which of the following functions $A(x)$ could represent the area, in inches, of the rectangle?

(A) $A(x)=x^2+4x$

(B) $A(x)=\dfrac{x^2}{2}+2x$

(C) $A(x)=2x^2+8x$

(D) $A(x)=2x^2-4x$

11

$$\sqrt{(2x-1)^2}=2x-1$$

Which of the following CAN NOT be the solution to the equation above?

(A) 0

(B) 1

(C) 2

(D) 3

CONTINUE

12

In January, a company produced 800 products. In June, production tripled compared to January. What percent did product production increase from January to June?

(A) 30%

(B) 100%

(C) 200%

(D) 300%

13

John and his father embarked on a hiking trip in a nature reserve, a total distance of 30 kilometers. During the first k kilometers of the hike, they advanced at an average 3 kilometers per hour due to the steep terrain. They hiked at an average pace of 6 kilometers per hour for the remainder of the hike. The total hiking time in the nature reserve was 6.5 hours. How many hours did they hike at 3 kilometers per hour?

(A) 1.5 hours

(B) 3 hours

(C) 4.5 hours

(D) 5.5 hours

14

At a store, the original price of a shirt is x, and it is currently on sale for p% off. After the discount, the shirt costs n. Which expression represents p in terms of x and n?

(A) $p=\dfrac{100(x-n)}{x}$

(B) $p=\dfrac{100(1-n)}{x}$

(C) $p=\dfrac{1-n}{x}$

(D) $p=\dfrac{x-n}{x}$

15

If $4 \cdot 2^{a} - 2^{a+1} = 32$, then what is the value of a?

16

A tile costs $5 per square foot. To the nearest dollar, how much would it cost to buy tiles for a room that measures 20 square meters? (1 meter=3.281 feet)

(A) $13

(B) $328

(C) $820

(D) $1,076

CONTINUE

17

Favorite Food Preferences
for University Students by Major

Food Type	Social Science	Engineering	Language
Pizza	120	80	50
Sushi	90	64	32
Burgers	70	96	45
Total	280	240	127

The table above shows the number of students from each major who prefer each type of food. If a student is selected at random from the surveyed group, which of the following is closest to the difference between the percentage of Social Science students who prefer either Pizza or Sushi as their favorite food and the percentage of Engineering students who prefer either Pizza or Sushi?

(A) 9%

(B) 11%

(C) 13%

(D) 15%

18

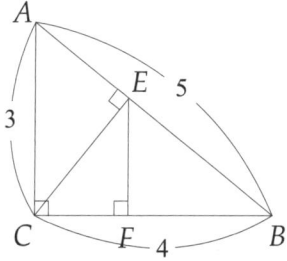

What is the measure of side CF?

19

In the $xy-$plane, the points $(5, -6)$ and $(-3, 4)$ are the endpoints of a diameter of a circle. Which of the following is an equation of the circle?

(A) $(x+1)^2+(y-1)^2=41$

(B) $(x-1)^2+(y+1)^2=41$

(C) $(x+1)^2+(y-1)^2=164$

(D) $(x-1)^2+(y+1)^2=164$

20

Prism A and prism B are similar. The length of each edge of prism A is 1.5 times the edge of the corresponding side of prism B. How many times the volume of prism A is the volume of prism B?

(A) 2.25

(B) 2.5

(C) 3.375

(D) 4.5

CONTINUE

21

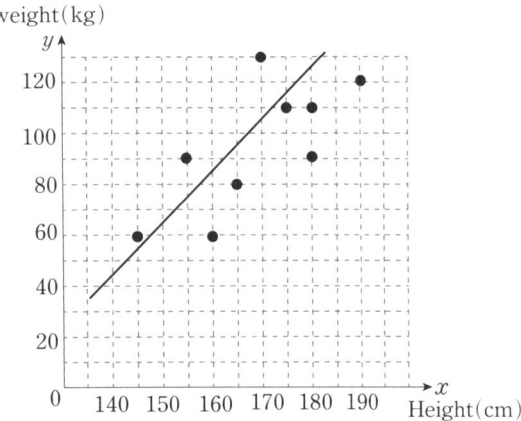

weight(kg)

The scatterplot above displays the weights of various individuals plotted against their respective heights, where $y-$axis represents weight in kilograms and $x-$axis represents height in centimeters. An approximating line is drawn on the graph. Which of the following statements provides the most accurate interpretation for the slope of the line of best fit in this scenario?

(A) The weight of an individual increases by 2 kilograms for every additional centimeter of height.

(B) The weight of an individual increases by 1 kilogram for every additional 2 centimeters of height.

(C) The height of an individual increases by 2 centimeters for every additional 1 kilogram increase in weight.

(D) The height of an individual increases by 1 centimeter for every additional 2 kilograms increase in weight.

22

If the quadratic equation $5x^2+4x+1=0$ can be written in the form $(x+h)^2=k$, what is the value of $\dfrac{h}{k}$?

Math
22 Questions

For multiple-choice questions, solve each problem, choose the correct answer from the choices provided, and then circle your answer in this book. Circle only one answer for each question. If you change your mind, completely erase the circle. You will not get credit for questions with more than one answer circled, or for questions with no answers circled.

For student-produced response questions, solve each problem and write your answer next to or under the question in the test book as described below.

- Once you've written your answer, circle it clearly. You will not receive credit for anything written outside the circle, or for any questions with more than one circled answer.

- If you find **more than one correct answer**, write and circle only one answer.

- Your answer can be up to 5 characters for a **positive** answer and up to 6 characters (including the negative sign) for a **negative** answer, but no more.

- If your answer is a **fraction** that is too long (over 5 characters for positive, 6 characters for negative), write the decimal equivalent.

- If your answer is a **decimal** that is too long (over 5 characters for positive, 6 characters for negative), truncate it or round at the fourth digit.

- If your answer is a **mixed number** (such as $3\frac{1}{2}$), write it as an improper fraction (7/2) or its decimal equivalent (3.5).

- Don't include **symbols** such as a percent sign, comma, or dollar sign in your circled answer.

CONTINUE

1

For what value of a and b does the equation $3(ax+1)-2=9x-b$ have infinitely many solutions for x?

(A) $a=3$ and $b=1$

(B) $a=-3$ and $b=1$

(C) $a=3$ and $b=-1$

(D) $a=-3$ and $b=-1$

2

Given the quadratic equation $f(x)=x^2+kx+12$, where k is a constant. Which of the following could be a value of k if the equation has no real solution?

(A) -8

(B) -7

(C) 6

(D) 7

3

There is a rectangle whose length is 15 meters greater than three times its width. If the width of the rectangle is x meters, which of the following functions $P(x)$ could represent the perimeter, in meters, of the rectangle?

(A) $P(x)=6x+8$

(B) $P(x)=6x+15$

(C) $P(x)=8x+15$

(D) $P(x)=8x+30$

4

$$\sqrt{2x+9}-x=3$$

What are all possible solutions to the equation above?

(A) -4

(B) 0

(C) 0 and -4

(D) No solution

5

If $a\sqrt{a}=\sqrt[3]{b^2}$ and $a^{2x+3}=b^{\frac{3}{2}}$, where both a and b are positive integers greater than 1, what is the value of x?

6

$$4x^2+6x-1=0$$

What is the sum of the solutions to the equation above?

CONTINUE

7

Which expression is equivalent to $3(x+2)^2 + 48(x+2)$?

(A) $3(x+2)(x+18)$

(B) $3(x+2)(x+16)$

(C) $16(x+2)^2 (x+8)$

(D) $16(x+2)(x+8)$

8

Mountain X is the third−highest mountain in the world, with a total height of 7545 meters. The highest mountain in the world, Mountain Y, is approximately 1.12 times the height of Mountain X. The height of Mountain Y is what percent greater than the height of Mountain X?

(A) 11.2%

(B) 12%

(C) 120%

(D) 220%

9

$4x - ky = 1$

$6x + 3y = -2$

If the system of equations given above has exactly one solution, which of the following could be the value of k? (k is a constant)

   I. -2 II. 0   III. 2

(A) I only

(B) II only

(C) I and II only

(D) II and III only

10

In the linear equation $y = 4x - 12.2$, what does the number 4 indicate?

(A) y increases by 4 for every x increases by 1

(B) y decreases by 4 for every x increases by 1

(C) x increases by 4 for every y increases by 1

(D) x decreases by 4 for every y increases by 1

11

The area of a park in a certain city is 2 square kilometers. What is the area, in square meters, of the park?

(1 kilometer=1,000 meters)

(A) 2,000 square meters

(B) 20,000 square meters

(C) 200,000 square meters

(D) 2,000,000 square meters

CONTINUE

12

$$ax^2 - 5x + 4 = 0$$

If the equation above has two real solutions, which of the following must be true?

(A) $16a > 25$

(B) $16a < 25$

(C) $25a < 16$

(D) $25a > 16$

13

$$y = x^2 - 4$$

$$4x + y = b$$

In the given system of equations, b is a positive constant. The system has exactly one distinct real solution. What is the value of b?

14

In a certain city, the number of cars registered is decreasing by 5% every year from 2010 to 2020. There were x cars registered in the city in 2010. Which expression represents the number of cars registered in the city in 2020 in terms of x?

(A) $x - 0.05x$

(B) $x - \dfrac{0.05x}{10}$

(C) $x(1 - 0.05)^{10}$

(D) $x\left(1 - \dfrac{0.05x}{10}\right)^{10}$

15

$$x \geq 4$$

$$5x - y > 12$$

The point $(4, k)$ is a solution to the system of inequalities in the xy-plane. Which of the following could not be the value of k?

(A) 6

(B) 8

(C) -6

(D) -8

16

A store sells a particular item for $50 each and 120 items per day. If the store reduces the price by $a per item, they sell an additional $4a$ items. What price should the store set for the item to maximize revenue?

CONTINUE

17

If b is a positive integer, what is the value of b so that the radius of the circle $x^2+y^2+6x+by-6=0$ has radius $2\sqrt{10}$?

18

A store sells four items with an average price of $20. When a fifth item is added to the list, the average price becomes $40. What is the price of the fifth item?

(A) $100

(B) $120

(C) $140

(D) $160

19

If $f(x)=2x^2+4$, which of the following is equal to $f(x+h)-f(x)$?

(A) $4x+2h$

(B) $4x+2h+4$

(C) $4hx+2h^2-4$

(D) $4hx+2h^2$

20

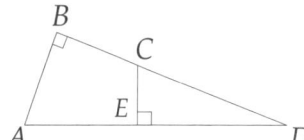

Triangle ABD is a right triangle and side CE is perpendicular to side AD as shown in the figure above. Which of the following must be true?

(A) $\sin\angle A=\sin\angle D$

(B) $\sin\angle D=\cos\angle ECD$

(C) $\tan\angle A=\sin\angle D$

(D) $\tan\angle D=\sin\angle ECD$

CONTINUE

21

Data Set: 12, 15, 18, 21, 24

In the given data set, if each data point is multiplied by 2, which of the following statements are true?

I. The mean will be doubled.

II. The median will be doubled.

III. The range will be doubled.

(A) I only

(B) I and II only

(C) I and III only

(D) I, II, and III

22

Lisa spent a total of $13.2 on apples and bananas. The cost per pound of apples was 1.25 times that of bananas, and Lisa bought 1.5 times as many pounds of apples as pounds of bananas. How much did Lisa spend on bananas?

Math
22 Questions

For multiple-choice questions, solve each problem, choose the correct answer from the choices provided, and then circle your answer in this book. Circle only one answer for each question. If you change your mind, completely erase the circle. You will not get credit for questions with more than one answer circled, or for questions with no answers circled.

For student-produced response questions, solve each problem and write your answer next to or under the question in the test book as described below.

- Once you've written your answer, circle it clearly. You will not receive credit for anything written outside the circle, or for any questions with more than one circled answer.

- If you find **more than one correct answer**, write and circle only one answer.

- Your answer can be up to 5 characters for a **positive** answer and up to 6 characters (including the negative sign) for a **negative** answer, but no more.

- If your answer is a **fraction** that is too long (over 5 characters for positive, 6 characters for negative), write the decimal equivalent.

- If your answer is a **decimal** that is too long (over 5 characters for positive, 6 characters for negative), truncate it or round at the fourth digit.

- If your answer is a **mixed number** (such as $3\frac{1}{2}$), write it as an improper fraction (7/2) or its decimal equivalent (3.5).

- Don't include **symbols** such as a percent sign, comma, or dollar sign in your circled answer.

CONTINUE

1

$$4(x-3)+5=2x+7$$

What is the solution to the given equation above?

(A) 0

(B) 2

(C) 7

(D) 14

2

Voyager 1 is a spacecraft launched by NASA to explore outer space. If Voyager 1 is currently traveling at a rate of 17.5 kilometers per second, how fast is it traveling, in miles per hour?

(1 mile is approximately 1.61 kilometers)

(A) 39,130 miles per hour

(B) 43,470 miles per hour

(C) 44,385 miles per hour

(D) 49,525 miles per hour

3

Which point is NOT on the line defined by $y=4x-3$?

(A) $(0, -3)$

(B) $(-2, -5)$

(C) $(3, 9)$

(D) $(-1, -7)$

4

Last year, Rachel spent $10,000 on groceries. This year, she wants to reduce her grocery expenses by $1,200. By what percent would she save the cost this year?

(A) 10%

(B) 12%

(C) 15%

(D) 20%

5

A real estate agent earns a monthly income of $4000 and a 2% commission on the total value of the properties sold. His target income for this month is at least $7500, including the commission. What must be the minimum total value of the properties sold to achieve his goal?

(A) $175,000

(B) $182,000

(C) $194,000

(D) $210,000

CONTINUE

6

The baker is packaging cookies for sale. Packing 15 cookies in each box leaves 8 cookies. If he chooses to pack 17 cookies in each box, he is left with 5 boxes. How many cookies are there in the bakery?

7

The length of the legs of an isosceles right triangle is 2 inches. If the length of the hypotenuse of this triangle, in inches, can be written as $\sqrt{k}$, where k is a positive integer, what is the value of k?

8

$$(x-2)-(y+3)=7$$
$$(x-2)+(y+3)=-5$$

If the solution to the given system of equation is (x, y), what is the value of $4(x-2)$?

(A) 4

(B) 8

(C) 12

(D) 16

9

$$3x^2+6x+2=0$$

How many distinct real solutions does the above equation have?

(A) Zero

(B) Exactly one

(C) Exactly two

(D) Infinitely many

10

If $a+b=8$ and $a^2-b^2=-24$, what is the value of $a-b$?

(A) -3

(B) 3

(C) -6

(D) 6

11

What is the solution to the equation $9^{x-3}-27=0$?

CONTINUE

12

Cars in Parking Lot by Color and Type

	Sedan	SUV	Truck	Total
Blue	12	18	8	38
Black	20	15	10	45
White	15	10	5	30
Total	47	43	23	113

The table above shows the number of cars in a parking lot categorized by their color and type. If a car is selected at random from the parking lot, which of the following is closest to the probability that the car is blue and is an SUV?

(A) 0.16

(B) 0.28

(C) 0.33

(D) 0.40

13

If $2+\dfrac{1}{x-4}=6+\dfrac{3}{x-4}$ where $x\neq4$, what is the value of $\dfrac{1}{x-4}$?

(A) -2

(B) -1

(C) 1

(D) 2

14

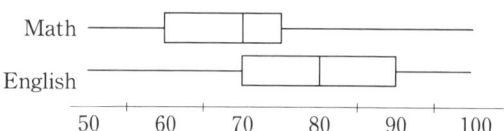

The boxplot provided above summarizes students' test scores in Math and English classes. Based on the box plots, which of the following statements must be true?

(A) The median test score in the Math class is higher than the median test score in the English class.

(B) The mean test score in the Math class is less than the mean test score in the English class.

(C) The range of test scores in the Math class is equal to the range of test scores in the English class.

(D) The standard deviation of test scores in the Math class is less than the standard deviation of test scores in the English class.

15

$4x+y\geq8$

$2x-3y<-2$

Which of the following points does not lies in the solution region of the system of inequalities above?

(A) $(-1,\ 12)$

(B) $(3,\ 4)$

(C) $(2,\ 0)$

(D) $(0,\ 9)$

CONTINUE

16

A tech company conducted a survey among 500 employees to determine their preference for remote work or in−office work. Out of the participants, 350 expressed a preference for remote work. What is the most appropriate population for generalizing the survey findings?

(A) The 350 employees who favored remote work

(B) The 500 employees who took part in the survey

(C) All employees in the tech company

(D) All individuals in the city where the tech company is located

17

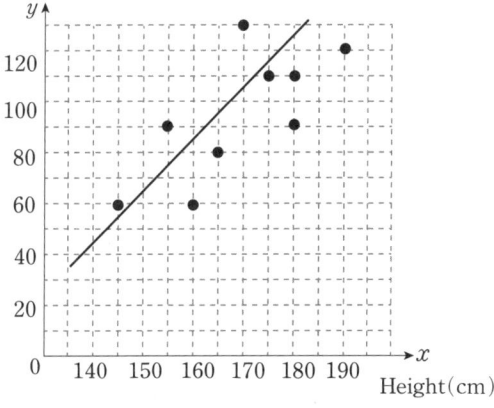

For what fraction of the data points in the scatterplot is the predicted y−value by the line of best fit greater than the actual y−value?

18

If a local cafe sells 3 muffins for $5, what would be the cost of purchasing 9 muffins?

19

The expression $2.4k$ represents the result of increasing a positive number k by what percent?

(A) 24%

(B) 40%

(C) 140%

(D) 240%

20

A substance has a density of $2.5\,\text{g/cm}^3$ and a volume of $80\,\text{cm}^3$. What is the mass of a substance?

(A) $\frac{1}{32}$

(B) 12.8

(C) 32

(D) 200

CONTINUE

21

In a right triangle, if one acute angle measures 20 degrees and the length of the shorter leg is 8 centimeters, what is the area of this triangle?

(A) 88 square centimeters

(B) 106 square centimeters

(C) 124 square centimeters

(D) 148 square centimeters

22

A box of tiles costs $60 and can cover an area of 120 square feet. A bathroom floor is represented by a square with a side length of 10 feet. If the tiles are used to cover the entire bathroom floor, how much does the tiles cost?

Math
22 Questions

For multiple-choice questions, solve each problem, choose the correct answer from the choices provided, and then circle your answer in this book. Circle only one answer for each question. If you change your mind, completely erase the circle. You will not get credit for questions with more than one answer circled, or for questions with no answers circled.

For student-produced response questions, solve each problem and write your answer next to or under the question in the test book as described below.

- Once you've written your answer, circle it clearly. You will not receive credit for anything written outside the circle, or for any questions with more than one circled answer.

- If you find **more than one correct answer**, write and circle only one answer.

- Your answer can be up to 5 characters for a **positive** answer and up to 6 characters (including the negative sign) for a **negative** answer, but no more.

- If your answer is a **fraction** that is too long (over 5 characters for positive, 6 characters for negative), write the decimal equivalent.

- If your answer is a **decimal** that is too long (over 5 characters for positive, 6 characters for negative), truncate it or round at the fourth digit.

- If your answer is a **mixed number** (such as $3\frac{1}{2}$), write it as an improper fraction (7/2) or its decimal equivalent (3.5).

- Don't include **symbols** such as a percent sign, comma, or dollar sign in your circled answer.

CONTINUE

1

Which of the following is an equation of the line that passes through the $(-3, 4)$ and is perpendicular to the line $3x+4y=1$?

(A) $4x+3y=24$

(B) $3x-4y=24$

(C) $3x+4y=-24$

(D) $4x-3y=-24$

2

$$\sqrt{x+3}-3=\sqrt{2-x}$$

How many values of x satisfy the equation above?

(A) None

(B) One

(C) Two

(D) Three

3

A triangular plaza has a base of 40 meters and a height of 24 meters. If the plaza is to be paved with a material costing $12 per square meter, what is the cost of paving the plaza in dollars?

(A) $2,880

(B) $4,320

(C) $5,760

(D) $11,520

4

$$3(x-2)+\frac{5x-4}{4}=\frac{9(1+x)}{2}-\frac{x+46}{4}$$

Which of the following statements is true about the equation given above?

(A) The equation has one solution because only one value of x is true in the equation.

(B) The equation has no solution because the equation is always false for all x.

(C) The equation has infinitely many solutions because the equation is always true for all x.

(D) The number of the solutions to the equation is unknown.

5

A certain motorcycle can hold 12 liters of fuel and travels at a constant speed of 60 kilometers per hour. At this speed, the motorcycle can travel 30 kilometers per liter. How many liters remain when the motorcycle has traveled at this speed for 2 hours and 15 minutes?

(A) 7 liters   (B) 7.5 liters

(C) 8 liters   (D) 8.5 liters

6

$$4^{\frac{1}{3}}\cdot 12^{\frac{2}{3}}=a\cdot\sqrt[3]{b}$$

In the above equation, a and b are positive integers and b is the smallest positive integer. What is the value of $a+b$?

CONTINUE

7

$$3x^2 - 5x + 2m = 0$$

If the equation above has exactly one solution, what is the value of $24m$?

8

In a wildlife sanctuary, there are 300 different species of birds. Among them, 180 species are migratory birds. Of the 180 migratory bird species, 54 species are known to migrate over long distances. If a bird is selected at random from the sanctuary, what is the probability of selecting a non-migratory bird?

(A) 0.3   (B) 0.4

(C) 0.6   (D) 0.7

9

In a school cafeteria, 42.6 kilograms of apples and 28.4 kilograms of oranges were delivered for the students. During lunchtime, 5.2% of the apples and 8.9% of the oranges were left uneaten and had to be discarded. The amount of discarded oranges was approximately what percent greater than that of discarded apples?

(A) 2%   (B) 6%

(C) 9%   (D) 14%

10

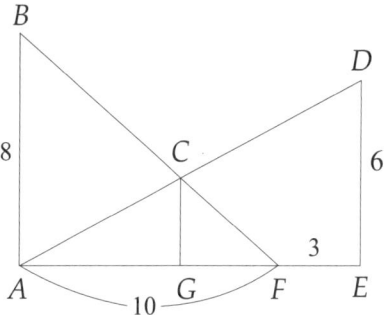

If sides AB, GC, and ED are parallel and sides AB, GC, and ED are all perpendicular to sides AE in the figure above, what is the measure of side CG?

11

If the expression $12x^3 y^2 \left(\dfrac{5}{6x^2 y} - \dfrac{x}{4y^2} \right)$ is equal to $kx^a y - 3x^b$, where k, a, are b are constants, what is the value of $k + a + b$?

(A) 7

(B) 8

(C) 11

(D) 15

CONTINUE

12

Which of the following equations represents a circle that intersects the y-axis at exactly one point?

(A) $(x+4)^2+(y-8)^2=16$

(B) $(x-8)^2+(y+4)^2=16$

(C) $(x+4)^2+(y-8)^2=4$

(D) $(x-8)^2+(y+4)^2=4$

14

$$6x-3y=9$$

$$8x-4y=12$$

Which of the following points in terms of b, where b is a constant, lies on the graph of each equation above in the xy-plane?

(A) $(b+4, 3b-1)$

(B) $\left(\dfrac{b}{2}+1,\ b-3\right)$

(C) $(4b-1,\ 8b-5)$

(D) $\left(\dfrac{b}{3},\ \dfrac{2b-8}{3}\right)$

13

In a recent poll, a sample of 1,000 voters was taken to gauge their preference for a proposed education reform. The results indicated that 55% of the sample supported the reform. With a margin of error of 2.5% and a confidence level of 90%, what is the most accurate estimate for the number of voters in a population of 500,000 who support the education reform?

(A) Between 271,250 to 283,750 voters

(B) Between 262,500 to 287,500 voters

(C) Exactly 275,000 voters

(D) Approximately 450,000 voters

15

Nina traveled to Japan with 2500 euros. The exchange rate during her trip was 130.50 yen per euro. She converted all her euros into yen and spent 75% of the money. Upon returning home, she converted the remaining yen back into euros at a rate of 0.0076 euros per yen. What is the approximate amount she gets in euros?

(A) 619.88 euros

(B) 621.34 euros

(C) 625.00 euros

(D) 628.54 euros

 CONTINUE

16

If the ratio of solutions of the quadratic equation $x^2+10x+n+4=0$ is $2{:}3$, what is the value of n?

17

Suppose that the graph of $y=ax^2+bx+c$ has the axis of symmetry at $x=1$ and passes through two points $(0,\ -2)$ and $(3,\ -4)$. If a, b, and c are all real numbers, what is the value of $a+b+c$?

18

Which expression is equivalent to the expression $(2\sqrt{x}+\sqrt{2y})^{\frac{2}{5}}$, where x and y are positive constants?

(A) $\sqrt[5]{4x+2y}$

(B) $\sqrt[5]{4x+4\sqrt{xy}+2y}$

(C) $\sqrt[5]{4x+8\sqrt{xy}+2y}$

(D) $\sqrt[5]{4x+4\sqrt{2xy}+2y}$

19

A class of 20 students took a math test. The mean score was 75, and the median score was 80. If a student who scored 90 joins the class, which of the following must be true?

(A) The new median score will be greater than 80

(B) The new median score will be less than 80

(C) The new mean score will be greater than 75

(D) The new mean score will be less than 75

20

$$f(x)=2x(x+2)(x-2)$$

The function f is defined above. If the function g is defined as $g(x)=2f(x)-1$, which of the following tables represent the value of g?

(A)

x	y
-2	-4
0	0
2	4

(B)

x	y
-2	-1
0	0
2	1

(C)

x	y
-2	-1
0	-1
2	-1

(D)

x	y
-2	0
0	0
2	0

CONTINUE

21

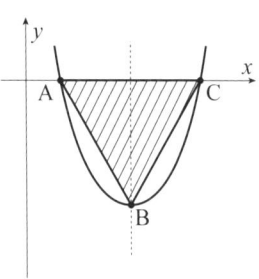

The graph of the quadratic function $y=2x^2-12x+b$ is shown above. If the graph has the vertex at B and $\overline{AC}=2$, what is the area of triangle ABC?

22

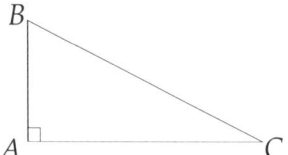

In triangle ABC above, point D(not shown) lies on BC. If $\sin\angle BAD=0.42$, what is the value of $\sin\angle BAD+\cos\angle CAD$?

(A) 0.21

(B) 0.42

(C) 0.84

(D) 1

DSAT MATH

Test Prep. Workbook

JOSEPH PAK

JM EDU

DSAT MATH

TEST PREP. WORKBOOK

SOLUTIONS MANUAL

JM EDU

JOSEPH PAK

Solutions Manual

Solutions Manual

I Algebra

1. Linear Equations

0001

$$10-4(x+1)=2(x+5)$$
$$10-4x-4=2x+10$$
$$6-4x=2x+10$$
$$-6x=4, \ x=-\frac{2}{3}$$

▶ B

0002

$$\frac{x+1}{2}-\frac{2x+5}{3}=\frac{3x-1}{4}$$

$$\left(\frac{x+1}{2}-\frac{2x+5}{3}\right)\cdot 12=\left(\frac{3x-1}{4}\right)\cdot 12$$
$$6(x+1)-4(2x+5)=3(3x-1)$$
$$6x+6-8x-20=9x-3$$
$$-2x-14=9x-3$$
$$-11x=11, \ x=-1$$

▶ C

0003

$$4a-\frac{2}{5}=3$$
$$\left(4a-\frac{2}{5}\right)\cdot 5=3\cdot 5$$
$$20a-2=15$$
$$20a=17$$

▶ D

0004

It is give that $3x-4=-5$. So we have
$$12-9x=-9x+12$$
$$\quad\quad =-3(3x-4)$$
$$\quad\quad =-3(-5)=15$$

▶ D

0005

$$2(x-3k)+1=4k-3(4-x)$$
Substitute -3 for x and solve for k.
$$2((-3)-3k)+1=4k-3(4-(-3))$$
$$-6-6k+1=4k-21$$
$$-6k-5=4k-21$$
$$-10k=-16, \ k=\frac{8}{5}$$

▶ A

0006

$$2(x-2)=3bx-7$$
$$2x-4=3bx-7$$
$$2x-3bx=-7+4$$
$$(2-3b)x=-3$$
For the equation to have no solution, $2-3b$ must be equal to 0.
$$2-3b=0$$
$$-3b=-2, \ b=\frac{2}{3}$$

▶ B

0007

$$4ax-8=3(x+4)+5(x-2)$$
$$4ax-8=3x+12+5x-10$$
$$4ax-8=8x+2$$
$$4ax-8x=2+8$$
$$(4a-8)x=10$$
For the equation to have no solution, $4a-8$ must be equal to 0.
$$4a-8=0$$
$$4a=8, \ a=2$$

▶ B

0008

$$3a=\frac{4}{3}b$$
$$(3a)\cdot 9=\left(\frac{4}{3}b\right)\cdot 9$$
$$27a=12b$$

▶ C

0009

$5x+3=12x-3(2x-2)$

$5x+3=12x-6x+6$

$5x+3=6x+6$

$-x=3,\ x=-3\ \rightarrow\ a=-3$

$\left(\dfrac{x-2}{2}\right)\cdot 6=\left(\dfrac{3x-1}{2}-6\right)\cdot 6$

$2(x-2)=3(3x-1)-36$

$2x-4=9x-3-36$

$2x-4=9x-39$

$-7x=-35,\ x=5\ \rightarrow\ b=5$

Therefore, $ab=(-3)(5)=-15$.

▶ C

0010

$6(3x-2a)+4=-2(bx+5)-8x$

$18x-12a+4=-2bx-10-8x$

$26x+2bx=12a-14$

$(26+2b)x=12a-14$

Since the equation is true for all x,

$26+2b=0 \qquad\qquad 12a-14=0$

$b=-13 \quad\text{and}\qquad a=\dfrac{7}{6}$

Therefore, $6a-b=6\left(\dfrac{7}{6}\right)-(-13)=7+13=20$.

▶ D

0011

$6x-4-3(3+ax)=-13$

$6x-4-9-3ax=-13$

$(6-3a)x-13=-13$

$(6-3a)x=0$

For the equation to have exactly one solution,

$6-3a$ must be NOT equal to 0.

$6-3a\neq 0,\ a\neq 2$

▶ B

0012

$k-ky=4y$

$k=4y+ky$

$k=(4+k)y$

The equation has no solution if

$4+k=0\ \rightarrow\ k=-4$

▶ A

0013

For answer choice D,

$\left(2(x+1)-\dfrac{5}{4}x\right)\cdot 4=\left(\dfrac{3x+8}{4}\right)\cdot 4$

$8(x+1)-5x=3x+8$

$3x+8=3x+8$

$3x-3x=8-8$

$(3-3)x=0$

$0\cdot x=0$

Therefore, the equation has infinitely many solutions.

▶ D

0014

$3-\dfrac{5-3x}{4}=\dfrac{7}{8}+\dfrac{3}{4}x$

$\left(3-\dfrac{5-3x}{4}\right)\cdot 8=\left(\dfrac{7}{8}+\dfrac{3}{4}x\right)\cdot 8$

$24-2(5-3x)=7+6x$

$24-10+6x=7+6x$

$14+6x=7+6x$

$6x-6x=7-14$

$(6-6)x=-7$

$0\cdot x=-7$

The equation has no solution.

▶ B

0015

Let x be the width of the rectangle. Then the length is $2x-4$. Since the perimeter of the field is 300 meters, we have
$$2x+2(2x-4)=64$$
$$2x+4x-8=72$$
$$6x=72, \ x=12$$
The width is 12 inches and the length is $2x-4=2(12)-4=20$ inches. So the area of the rectangle is $12\cdot20=240$ square inches.

▶ D

0016

Let F be the taxi fare. Then we have
$$F=2.5+0.85(n-2)$$
$$=2.5+0.85n-1.7$$
$$=0.85n+0.8$$

▶ A

0017

Assume that John's father is twice as old as John in x years. After x years later, John is $14+x$ years old and his father is $38+x$ years old.
$$38+x=2(14+x)$$
$$38+x=28+2x$$
$$-x=-10, \ x=10$$
John's father is twice as old as John in 10 years.

▶ A

0018

The coefficient 30 in front of $\frac{y}{100}$ indicates that it is associated with the stocks. Since the equation represents the annual income from both investments, the term $30\cdot\frac{y}{100}$ can be interpreted as the annual income from stocks.

▶ B

0019

The coefficient 5 in front of $\left(\frac{4}{3}-x\right)$ represents the speed at which Ben jogs. So $5\left(\frac{4}{3}-x\right)$ represents the total distance Ben jogged. Therefore, the expression $\frac{4}{3}-x$ can be interpreted as the number of hours Ben jogged to work.

▶ D

0020

Let x be the number of dimes. Then, the number of nickels is $x+9$. Since the total value of the coins is 3.60 (360 cents), the equation is
$$10x+5(x+9)=360$$

▶ C

0021

Let x be the length of one side of the larger square. Then, $x-3$ is the length of one side of the smaller square. Since the sum of the perimeters of the two squares is 68 centimeters, we have
$$4x+4(x-3)=68$$
$$4x+4x-12=68$$
$$8x=80, \ x=10$$
Therefore, the length of one side of the larger square is 10 centimeters.

▶ B

0022

The distance car A traveled is 64t and the distance car B traveled is $72(t-1)$. Since two car A and B are 340 miles apart and moving directly towards each other, we have
$$64t+72(t-1)=340$$

▶ C

0023

Let x be the number of students in the laboratory. Since the teacher gave 4 balloons to each of his x students and 1 balloon left, he had a total of $4x+1$ balloons. So we have

$$4x+1=65$$
$$4x=64, \quad x=16$$

Therefore, there are 16 students.

▶ D

0024

Let x and y be the amount in pounds of pork and salmon, respectively. Then we have $x=2y$. Also, let p and s be the price of pork and salmon per pound respectively. Then we have $s=1.5p$. The total price John spend on park is px and on salmon is sy. Since he spend a \$8.4 for pork and salmon, we have

$$px+sy=8.4$$

Now, substitute 1.5p for s and 0.5x for y.

$$px+(1.5p)(0.5x)=8.4$$
$$px+0.75px=8.4$$
$$1.75px=8.4, \quad px=4.8$$

Therefore, John spent \$4.8 on pork.

▶ C

0025

Let x be the speed of the faster plane in miles per hour. Then the speed of the faster plane is $x-80$ miles per hour. Since the total distance is 1860 miles and they pass each other after 4 hours, we have

$$4x+4(x-80)=1860$$
$$4x+4x-320=1860$$
$$8x=2180, \quad x=272.5$$

Therefore, the speed of the faster plane is 272.5 miles per hour.

▶ D

0026

The candle is shortened by 4 cm every 16 minutes, which means that for every 16 minutes that pass, the length of the candle decreases by 4 cm. We can express this relationship using a linear equation:

$$L=20-\frac{4}{16}T \Rightarrow L=20-\frac{1}{4}T$$
$$L \cdot 4=\left(20-\frac{1}{4}T\right) \cdot 4$$
$$4L=80-T \Rightarrow 4L+T=80$$

▶ B

0027

$$5(2x-3)+2=6x-3(2-x)$$
$$10x-15+2=6x-6+3x$$
$$10x-13=9x-6$$
$$x=7$$

▶ 7

0028

$$\frac{3}{4}a+\frac{1}{2}=0$$
$$\left(\frac{3}{4}a+\frac{1}{2}\right) \cdot 4=(0) \cdot 4$$
$$3a+2=0$$

▶ 0

0029

$$\frac{4}{3}a-4=12$$
$$\left(\frac{4}{3}a-4\right) \cdot 3=(12) \cdot 3$$
$$4a-12=36, \quad 4a=48$$

▶ 48

Solutions Manual

0030

$$\frac{ax+5}{2} - \frac{2}{3} = \frac{5}{6}x - \frac{1}{3}b$$

$$\left(\frac{ax+5}{2} - \frac{2}{3}\right) \cdot 6 = \left(\frac{5}{6}x - \frac{1}{3}b\right) \cdot 6$$

$$3(ax+5) - 4 = 5x - 2b$$

$$3ax + 15 - 4 = 5x - 2b$$

$$3ax - 5x = -2b - 11$$

$$(3a - 5)x = -2b - 11$$

Since the equation is true for all x, we must have

$$3a - 5 = 0, \ a = \frac{5}{3} \ \text{ and } \ -2b - 11 = 0, \ b = -\frac{11}{2}$$

▶ $a = \frac{5}{3}, \ b = -\frac{11}{2}$

0031

$$4 - \frac{1}{6}(4x+5) = 2kx + 3$$

$$\left(4 - \frac{1}{6}(4x+5)\right) \cdot 6 = (2kx+3) \cdot 6$$

$$24 - (4x+5) = 12kx + 36$$

$$-4x + 19 = 12kx + 36$$

$$-4x - 12kx = 17$$

$$(-4 - 12k)x = 17$$

For the equation to have no solution, $-4 - 12k$ must be equal to 0.

$$-4 - 12k = 0, \ k = -\frac{1}{3}$$

▶ $-\frac{1}{3}$

0032

Let x be the number. Then we have

$$2x + 4 = 3x - 2$$

$$-x = -6, \ x = 6$$

▶ 6

0033

Let x be the number. Then we have

$$\frac{x}{4} = 2x + 3$$

$$x = 8x + 12$$

$$-7x = 12, \ x = -\frac{12}{7}$$

▶ $-\frac{12}{7}$

0034

Let x be the amount a 18% acid−solution.

	18% acid	12% acid	15% acid
Solution	x	8	$x+8$
Acid	$0.18x$	$0.12(8)$	$0.15(x+8)$

$$0.18x + 0.12(8) = 0.15(x+8)$$

$$0.18x + 0.96 = 0.15x + 1.2$$

$$0.03x = 0.24, \ x = 8$$

There are 8 liters of a 18% acid−solution.

▶ 8

0035

Let x be the rate Linda has been driving for the last two hours. Then, the distance she traveled for the first 3 hours is $55 \times 3 = 165$ and the distance traveled for the next 2 hours is . So we have,

$$165 + 2x = 275$$

$$2x = 110, \ x = 55$$

Therefore, she drove at a rate of 55 miles per hour.

▶ 55

0036

The new length of the rectangle is $8-x$ inches and the new width is $4+3 = 7$ inches. Since the new area is increased by 10 square inches, we have

$$7(8-x) = 4 \cdot 8 + 10$$

$$56 - 7x = 42$$

$$-7x = -14, \ x = 2$$

▶ 2

0037

Let x be the number of adults. Then, $160-x$ is the number of students. Since the total revenue was $4,000, we have

$$27x+19(160-x)=4000$$
$$27x+3040-19x=4000$$
$$8x=960, \ x=120$$

▶ 120

0038

Let x and y be the number of students and balloons, respectively.

1. If each student receives 6 balloons, 3 balloons will remain: $y=6x+3$
2. If each student receives 7 balloons, the teacher will need 4 additional balloons:
   $y+4=7x$

Substituting the value of $6x+3$ from Equation 1 into Equation 2, we have

$$6x+3+4=7x$$
$$-x=-7, \ x=7 \text{ and}$$
$$y=6(7)+3=45$$

Therefore, the teacher has 45 balloons.

▶ 45

0039

Let x be the width of the field. Then the length of the field is $3x+14$. Since the total perimeter of the field 74 feet, we have

$$2x+(3x+14)=74$$
$$2x+3x+14=74$$
$$5x=60, \ x=12$$

Therefore, the length is $3(12)+14=50$ feet.

▶ 50

0040

Let x be the amount of a 45% saline solution. Then, $20-x$ is the amount of a 20% saline solution.

	45% solution	20% solution	30% solution
	x	$20-x$	20
Salt	$0.45x$	$0.2(20-x)$	$0.3(20)$

$$0.45x+0.2(20-x)=0.3(20)$$
$$0.45x+4-0.2x=6$$
$$0.25x=2, \ x=8$$

▶ 8

0041

Let x the time in minutes. Candle A shortens by 3 cm every 10 minutes, so after x minutes, Candle A will be $25-\left(\dfrac{3}{10}\right)x$ cm long. Candle B shortens by 5 cm every 8 minutes, so after x minutes, Candle B will be $30-\left(\dfrac{5}{8}\right)x$ cm long. To find the time when both candles will be the same length, we can set up an equation:

$$25-\frac{3}{10}x=30-\frac{5}{8}x$$
$$\frac{13}{40}x=5, \ x=\frac{200}{13}$$

Therefore, both candles will be the same length after $\dfrac{200}{13}$ minutes.

▶ $\dfrac{200}{13}$

2. Lines in the Coordinate Plane

0042
Given two points $(4, 3)$ and $(2, -1)$, the slope is
$$m = \frac{-1-3}{2-4} = \frac{-4}{-2} = 2.$$

▶ C

0043
Given the slope $m = -\frac{2}{3}$ and the point $(6, 2)$, the equation of the line in point$-$slope form is
$$y - 2 = -\frac{2}{3}(x-6)$$

To determine if a point lies on the graph of a line, we can substitute the coordinates of the point into the equation of the line and check if the resulting statement is true.

(A) $4-2 = -\frac{2}{3}(1-6) \Rightarrow 2 \neq \frac{10}{3}$

(B) $5-2 = -\frac{2}{3}(0-6) \Rightarrow 3 \neq 4$

(C) $-4-2 = -\frac{2}{3}(3-6) \Rightarrow -6 \neq 2$

(D) $8-2 = -\frac{2}{3}(-3-6) \Rightarrow 6 = 6$

The answer is (D).

▶ D

0044
Lines (B) and (C) exhibit a positive slope, indicating an upward trend from left to right. Among the two, line (B) has a steeper inclination, suggesting a larger positive slope value compared to line (C). On the other hand, line (D) is horizontal, indicating a slope of zero. Lastly, line (A) demonstrates a negative slope, indicating a downward trend from left to right. Therefore, line (A) has the smallest slope and line (B)

has the largest slope.

▶ A

0045

▶ B

0046
Since the value of y decreases by 6 units as the value of x increases by 3 units, the slope
$$m = \frac{\Delta y}{\Delta x} = \frac{-6}{3} = -2.$$

▶ A

0047
To find the value of $f(x)$ when $x=2$, we can substitute $x=2$ into the function $f(x) = 5x - 7$ and evaluate it.
$$f(2) = 5(2) - 7 = 10 - 7 = 3$$

▶ C

0048
To find the value of x when $g(x) = -11$, we can substitute $g(x) = -11$ into the function $g(x) = -2x + 5$ and solve for x.
$$-11 = -2x + 5$$
$$-16 = -2x, \quad x = 8$$

▶ B

0049
Given two points $(-2, 5)$ and $(3, 20)$, the slope is
$$m = \frac{20-5}{3-(-2)} = 3$$

The equation of the line in point$-$slope form is
$$y - 5 = 3(x+2)$$

$y=3x+11 \implies f(x)=3x+11$

▶ A

0050

To determine if a point lies on the graph of a line, we can substitute the coordinates of the point into the equation of the line and check if the resulting statement is true.

(A) $4(-2)-5(-1)=-8+5=-3$
(B) $4(-1)-5(-2)=-4+10=6\neq-3$
(C) $4(2)-5(1)=8-5=3\neq-3$
(D) $4(1)-5(2)=4-10=-6\neq-3$

The answer is (A).

▶ A

0051

The equation of the line can be determined using the slope−intercept form of a linear equation, which is $y=mx+b$. Given that the line passes through the point $(-1, 0)$ and has a y−intercept of -2, we can determine the slope (m) and the y−intercept (b).

$$m=\frac{-2-0}{0-(-1)}=-2 \text{ and } b=-2$$

Therefore, the equation of the line is
$$y=-2x-2$$

▶ A

0052

To find the x−intercept of the graph of the function $y=4x-8$, substitute 0 for y.

$0=4x-8$
$8=4x, \ x=2$

Therefore, the x−intercept of the graph is $x=2$.
The correct option is (B) $(2, 0)$.

▶ B

0053

To find the value of ab, we need to determine the x−intercept and y−intercept of the function $f(x)=3x-12$.

x−intercept: $0=3x-12, \ x=4$
y−intercept: $f(0)=3(0)-12=-12$

So the x−intercept is $(4, 0)$, where $a=4$ and the y−intercept is $(0, -12)$, where $b=-12$.
Therefore,
$$ab=4(-12)=-48$$

▶ B

0054

The line passes through two point $(-2, 1)$ and $(2, 0)$. Therefore, the slope is
$$m=\frac{0-1}{2-(-2)}=-\frac{1}{4}.$$

Using the equation of the line in point−slope form, we have
$$y-1=-\frac{1}{4}(x+2)$$
$$y-1=-\frac{1}{4}x-\frac{1}{2}$$
$$y=-\frac{1}{4}x+\frac{1}{2}$$

▶ B

0055

We know that parallel lines have the same slope and the slope of the given line is $-\frac{1}{4}$. So we have to find the equation of the line that passes through $(2, 3)$ with slope $-\frac{1}{4}$.
$$y-3=-\frac{1}{4}(x-2)$$
$$y-3=-\frac{1}{4}x+\frac{1}{2}$$
$$y=-\frac{1}{4}x+\frac{7}{2}$$

▶ D

0056

To find the $y-$intercept of the graph of the equation $8x-12y=72$, we need to determine the value of y when x is equal to 0.

$8(0)-12y=72$

$\quad -12y=72, \; y=-6$

Therefore, the coordinate of $y-$intercept is $(0, \, -6)$.

▶ B

0057

To find the $y-$intercept of a line passing through two points, we can use the slope$-$intercept form of a linear equation, $y=mx+b$.

$$m=\frac{5-(-1)}{6-3}=2$$

Now that we have the slope, we can substitute the point $(3, \, -1)$ into the equation and solve for the $y-$intercept (b).

$-1=2(3)+b$

$-1=6+b, \; b=-7$

Therefore, the $y-$intercept of the line is -7.

▶ B

0058

When the equation is in the form $y=$constant, the slope is always 0. Therefore, the slope of the line with the equation $y=6$ is 0.

▶ A

0059

Given the $x-$intercept of -2 and $y-$intercept of 3, we know that two points on the line are $(-2, 0)$ and $(0, 3)$, respectively. Then, the slope of the line is

$$m=\frac{3-0}{0-(-2)}=\frac{3}{2}$$

Now that we have the slope (m), and the $y-$intercept(b) is given as 3, we can write the equation of the line in slope$-$intercept form:

$$y=\frac{3}{2}x+3$$

$2y=3x+6 \; \Rightarrow \; 3x-2y+6=0$

▶ A

0060

To find the value of k, we can use the slope formula and the given slope of 2.

$$2=\frac{(3k-1)-4}{2-(k+1)}$$

$$2=\frac{3k-5}{-k+1}$$

$2(-k+1)=3k-5$

$-2k+2=3k-5, \; k=\dfrac{7}{5}$

▶ C

0061

The equation $2x+4y-5=0$ can be rewritten in slope$-$intercept form $(y=mx+b)$ by isolating y:

$2x+4y-5=0$

$\quad 4y=-2x+5$

$\quad y=-\dfrac{1}{2}x+\dfrac{5}{4}$

We see that the slope (m) of the given line is $-\dfrac{1}{2}$. To find the slope of a line perpendicular to this line, we take the negative reciprocal of the slope of the given line. The negative reciprocal of $-\dfrac{1}{2}$ is $\dfrac{2}{1}$, or simply 2.

▶ A

0062

The slope of -2.25 means that for every unit increase in x, the corresponding $y-$value decreases by 2.25

units. In other words, y decreases by 2.25 for every x increases by 1

▶ B

0063

Let x be the number of hours Andrea works and y be the total amount she charges. Now, let's find the equation in slope−intercept form

$y=mx+b$. Since Andrea charges a $160 fee plus $30 per hour, the $y-$intercept is $b=160$ and the slope $m=30$. Therefore, the equation is $y=30x+160$. If the project takes 12 hours, she will charge $y=30(12)+160=$520$.

▶ B

0064

Let's calculate the slope(m) using the two points $(1, 1)$ and $(2, -1)$.

$$m=\frac{-1-1}{2-1}=-2$$

Now, we can choose one of the points $(1, 1)$ and use it in the point−slope form:

$$y-1=-2(x-1)$$

When y=5,

$$5-1=-2(x-1)$$
$$-2=x-1, \ x=-1$$

▶ B

0065

The equation of a horizontal line can be written as $y=c$, where c is a constant representing the $y-$coordinate of any point on the line. Since the line "k" passes through the point $(4, -5)$, the equation of the line "k" is $y=-5$.

▶ D

0066

To find the intersection point of two lines, we can set the equations of the two lines equal to each other and solve for the values of x and y.

$$-\frac{1}{2} \ x+6=3x-22$$

$$-\frac{7}{2} \ x=-28, \ x=8$$

Now, substitute the value of y back into one of the original equations to find y.

$$y=3(8)-22=2$$

Therefore, the intersection point of the two lines is $(8, 2)$.

▶ C

0067

Since the line l passes through the two points $(-3, -2)$ and $(1, 3)$, the slope is

$$m=\frac{3-(-2)}{1-(-3)}=\frac{5}{4}$$

The parallel lines have the same slope.

(A) $5x+4y=3 \Rightarrow m=-\frac{5}{4}$

(B) $4x+5y=3 \Rightarrow m=-\frac{4}{5}$

(C) $5x-4y=-3 \Rightarrow m=-\frac{5}{-4}=\frac{5}{4}$

(D) $-5x-4y=-3 \Rightarrow m=-\frac{-5}{-4}=-\frac{5}{4}$

Therefore, the answer is (C).

▶ C

0068

To find the slope of a line perpendicular to line m, we take the negative reciprocal of $\frac{5}{4}$, which is $-\frac{4}{5}$. The answer is (B)

▶ B

0069

First, let's rewrite $x+2y=4$ in slope−intercept form.

$$x+2y=4$$
$$2y=-x+4$$
$$y=-\frac{1}{2}x+2$$

Since the line passes through the point $(0, 2)$ and is parallel to the line above, the equation is

$$y-2=-\frac{1}{2}(x-0)$$
$$2y-4=-x$$
$$x+2y=4$$

▶ B

0070

First, let's rewrite $2y-x+8=0$ in slope−intercept form.

$$2y-x+8=0$$
$$2y=x-8$$
$$y=\frac{1}{2}x-4$$

The line passes through the point $(-3, 2)$ and is perpendicular to the line above. To find the slope of the perpendicular line, we take the negative reciprocal of $\frac{1}{2}$, which gives us -2. So the equation of the line is

$$y-2=-2(x+3)$$
$$y-2=-2x-6$$
$$y=-2x-4$$

▶ C

0071

To find the slope of the perpendicular line, we take the negative reciprocal of -2, which gives us $\frac{1}{2}$. So the equation of the line passing through the point $(2, 5)$ with slope $\frac{1}{2}$ is

$$y-5=\frac{1}{2}(x-2)$$
$$2y-10=x-2$$

$$x-2y=-8$$

▶ A

0072

First, let's rewrite the equation of line m in slope−intercept form.

$$3x-4y+1=0$$
$$-4y=-3x-1$$
$$y=\frac{3}{4}x+\frac{1}{4}$$

To find the slope of a line perpendicular to line m, we take the negative reciprocal of $\frac{3}{4}$, which is $-\frac{4}{3}$. Among answer choices, the equation that has a slope of $-\frac{4}{3}$ is (B).

$$4x+3y-1=0$$
$$3y=-4x+1$$
$$y=-\frac{4}{3}x+\frac{1}{3}$$

▶ B

0073

If two lines f and g are perpendicular to each other at some point, the product of their slopes is -1: $ac=-1$.

▶ C

0074

For line k: $3x+4y=11$ Solving for y in terms of x, we have $y=\left(-\frac{3}{4}\right)x+\left(\frac{11}{4}\right)$

The slope of line k is $-\frac{3}{4}$.

For line p: $4x-3y=9$ Solving for y in terms of x, we have $y=\left(\frac{4}{3}\right)x-3$ The slope of line p is $\frac{4}{3}$.

Since the product of their slopes is

$$\left(-\frac{3}{4}\right)\cdot\frac{4}{3}=-1,$$

lines k and p are perpendicular.

▶ D

0075

Lines l and n both pass through the origin, so the $y-$intercept is zero. Since the equation of line l passes through the point $(a,\ b)$, the slope of the line l is

$$y=mx$$
$$b=m(a),\ m=\frac{b}{a}$$

To find the slope of line n, we take the negative reciprocal of $\left(\frac{b}{a}\right)$, which gives us $-\left(\frac{a}{b}\right)$. So the equation of line passing through the origin with slope $-\left(\frac{a}{b}\right)$ is

$$y=-\frac{a}{b}x$$

▶ C

0076

$$\begin{aligned}f+g&=(ax+1)+(bx-3)\\&=ax+bx-2\\&=(a+b)x-2\end{aligned}$$

The line $f+g$ has a slope of $(a+b)$ and a $y-$intercept of -2. So the correct answer is (B).

▶ B

0077

Since the slope of the line g is 2,
g(the number of games) increases by 2 when q(the number of quarters) increases by 1.
So we need 3 additional quarters to play 6 additional games.

▶ A

0078

The total cost C to rent the equipment for x days consists of the initial cost of \$24 plus the additional fee of \$15 per day multiplied by the number of days. Therefore, the correct representation of the total cost C is

$$C=15x+24$$

▶ D

0079

Jamie has a total budget of \$24. If Jamie buys only oranges, he can buy a total of 4 pounds, and if he buys only apples, he can buy a total of 6 pounds. So, the price of a pound of oranges is $\left(\frac{24}{4}=\$6\right)$, and the price of a pound of apples is $(\frac{24}{6}=\$4)$. The answer is (B).

▶ B

0080

The line passes through the points $(0,\ 4)$ and $(6,\ 0)$. First, let's find the slope (m) using the given points:

$$m=\frac{0-4}{6-0}=-\frac{2}{3}$$

So the equation of the line with point $(0,\ 4)$ is

$$y-4=-\frac{2}{3}(x-0)$$
$$3y-12=-2x$$
$$2x+3y=12\ \Rightarrow\ 4x+6y=24$$

▶ A

Solutions Manual

0081

The best interpretation of the coordinate
$(5, 40)$ is that when Samuel's backyard has an area of
5 square yards, the total cost for mowing the lawn is
$40. So the answer is (B).

▶ B

0082

The slope of the graph in this context is the cost
charged by the company per square yard of mowing.
So the answer is (B) The cost charged by the
company per square yard.

▶ B

0083

The cost, f, that the company charges for mowing m
square yards can be represented by the following
expression:

$f(m)=2m+30$

In this expression, 2m represents the cost for the m
square yards of mowing at a rate of $2 per square
yard, and the $30 represents the one−time fee charged
by the company.

▶ B

0084

The cost, C, that Mr. Jackson charges after x hours
of editing can be represented by the following
expression:

$C=14(x-3)+30$
$=14x-42+30$
$=14x-12$

In this expression, 30 represents the cost for the first
3 pages, and $14(x-3)$ represents the cost for the
additional pages beyond the first 3 pages.

▶ C

0085

In the given equation, the coefficient of x (slope) is
70, which represents the rate of change of the cost (y)
with respect to the number of days (x). This means
that for each additional day the car is rented, the cost
increases by $70. So the answer is (B).

▶ B

0086

In the given linear function, the coefficient of t
(slope), which is -0.045, represents the annual
percentage decrease in the baseball player's average
fastball speed. When we substitute $t=10$ into the
equation, we get
$f(10)=-0.045(10)+1.25=0.8$. This means that 10 years
after 2008, the baseball player's average fastball speed
would be approximately 0.8 times his speed in 2008. So
the answer is (A).

▶ A

0087

We can see that for every 2 additional days, the cost
increases by $60. This means the cost increases by $30
per additional day. Based on this pattern, the
expression that represents the cost y, in dollars, to
rent a lawn mower for x days is:

$y=30x+b$

Now, substitute one of the data points $(3, 70)$ into the
equation.

$70=30(3)+b, \ b=-20$

Therefore, the expression that represents the cost y, in
dollars, to rent a lawn mower for x days is $y=30x-20$.

▶ B

0088

To find the cost if a lawn mower is rented for 10 days, we substitute $x=10$ into the equation:

$$y(10)=30(10)-20=\$280$$

Therefore, the cost of renting a lawn mower for 10 days is $280.

▶ A

0089

From the given data, we can calculate the slope (m) as follows:

$$m=\frac{19-13}{2-1}=6$$

So the equation of the line with point $(1, 13)$ is

$$C-13=6(x-1)$$
$$C-13=6x-6$$
$$C=6x+7$$

From the equation, we can see that when x is 0, the cost C is 7. Therefore, the value of the $y-$intercept is 7

▶ B

0090

The slope represents the rate of change of the cost C with respect to the number of hours x. In this case, the slope is 6. Therefore, the best description of the slope is (A) The cost of renting a bicycle increases by $6 per hour.

▶ A

0091

To find the equation of the perpendicular bisector of the line segment between points A$(-3, 1)$ and B$(2, -4)$, we first need to find the midpoint of the line segment. That is

$$\left(\frac{-3+2}{2}, \frac{1+(-4)}{2}\right)=\left(-\frac{1}{2}, -\frac{3}{2}\right).$$

The slope of the line segment AB is

$$m=\frac{-4-1}{2+3}=-1.$$

Therefore, slope of the perpendicular bisector is 1. Now, the equation of the perpendicular bisector is

$$y+\frac{3}{2}=1\cdot\left(x+\frac{1}{2}\right)$$

$$y+\frac{3}{2}=x+\frac{1}{2}$$

$$x-y-1=0$$

▶ A

0092

In equation K and J, the slopes are -0.004 and -0.0025, respectively. Comparing the two rates of change, we can see that K decreases at a greater rate per year than J. Also, since the $y-$intercept of K is less than the $y-$intercept of J, $K<J$ for all t. So the answer is (B).

▶ B

0093

Given that $f(1)=-2$ and $f(3)=4$, the slope (m) of the line is

$$m=\frac{4+2}{3-1}=3$$

So the equation of the line with point $(1, -2)$ is

$$f(x)+2=3(x-1)$$
$$f(x)+2=3x-3$$
$$f(x)=3x-5$$

Therefore,

$$f(0)=3(0)-5=-5$$

▶ -5

0094

Setting the two equations equal to each other:

$$-4x+a=bx-\frac{1}{2}$$

Now, we can compare the slope and $y-$intercept on both sides:

$$b=-4 \text{ and } a=-\frac{1}{2}$$

Therefore, $ab=\left(-\frac{1}{2}\right)(-4)=2$.

▶ 2

0095

The line in the figure passes through $(0,\ 2)$ and $(4,\ 0)$. So the slope (m) is

$$m=\frac{0-2}{4-0}=-\frac{1}{2}$$

Since the line has the y$-$intercpet 2, we have

$$y=-\frac{1}{2}x+2$$

Therefore, $mb=\left(-\frac{1}{2}\right)(2)=-1$

▶ -1

0096

The slope of the given line is $-\frac{1}{2}$, so the slope of the line $y=ax+c$ must be 2 (the negative reciprocal of $-\frac{1}{2}$). Now, substitute $(-2,\ 0)$ in the equation $y=2x+c$ to find the value of c.

$$0=2(-2)+c,\ c=4$$

Therefore, $a+c=2+4=6$.

▶ 6

0097

$$2ax-5y=b$$

Since the slope is 2, we have

$$m=-\frac{2a}{-5}$$

$$2=\frac{2a}{5},\ a=5$$

Since the $y-$intercept is 6, we also have

$$2a(0)-5(6)=b$$
$$-30=b,\ b=-30$$

▶ -30

0098

Two points A and B are $y-$ and $x-$intercept of the line $7x-5y=21$, respectively.

The $x-$intercept: let $y=0$.

$$7x-5(0)=21$$
$$7x=21$$
$$x=3 \Rightarrow \text{B}=(3,\ 0)$$

The $y-$intercept: let $x=0$.

$$7(0)-5y=21$$
$$-5y=21$$
$$y=-\frac{21}{5} \Rightarrow \text{A}=\left(0,\ -\frac{21}{5}\right)$$

Therefore, the area of $\triangle \text{AOB}$ is

$$\frac{1}{2}(3)\left(\frac{21}{5}\right)=\frac{63}{10}.$$

▶ $\frac{63}{10}$

0099

First, find the intersection of the two lines $y=x+1$ and $y=-x+2$.

$$x+1=-x+2$$

$$2x=1,\ x=\frac{1}{2}$$

$$\Rightarrow y=\frac{1}{2}+1=\frac{3}{2}$$

The $x-$intercept of $y=x+1$ is

$0=x+1, \ x=-1$

The $x-$intercept of $y=-x+2$ is

$0=-x+1, \ x=2$

Therefore, the area bounded by three lines is shown below.

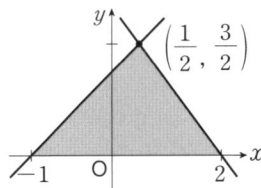

The area of the triangle A is

$A=\frac{1}{2}(3)\left(\frac{3}{2}\right)=\frac{9}{4}$.

▶ $\frac{9}{4}$

0100

Since all three points lie on the same line, the slope from any two given points must be equal. From $(1, 4)$ and $(2, 2a-3)$, we have

$m_1=\frac{2a-3-4}{2-1}=2a-7$

Also, from $(1, 4)$ and $(-2, 3a+1)$, we have

$m_2=\frac{3a+1-4}{-2-1}=\frac{3a-3}{-3}$

Now since $m_1=m_2$, we have the following equation:

$2a-7=\frac{3a-3}{-3}$

$-6a+21=3a-3$

$-9a=-24, \ a=\frac{8}{3}$

▶ $\frac{8}{3}$

0101

Since all three points lie on the same line, the slope from any two given points must be equal to each other. From $(0, 0)$ and $(a-3, 4)$, we have

$m_1=\frac{4-0}{(a-3)-0}=\frac{4}{a-3}$

From $(0, 0)$ and $(3a+2, -2)$, we have

$m_2=\frac{y_3-y_1}{x_3-x_1}=\frac{-2-0}{(3a+2)-0}=\frac{-2}{3a+2}$

Now since $m_1=m_2$, we have the following equation:

$\frac{4}{a-3}=\frac{-2}{3a+2}$

$12a+8=-2a+6$

$14a=-2, \ a=-\frac{1}{7}$

▶ $-\frac{1}{7}$

0102

First, rewrite $4x+3y=24$ in slope$-$intercept form:

$4x+3y=24$

$3y=-4x+24$

$y=-\frac{4}{3}x+8$

The slope of this line is $-\frac{4}{3}$. To find the slope of line $-\frac{4}{3}$, we take the negative reciprocal of $-\frac{4}{3}$, which gives us $\frac{3}{4}$.

▶ $\frac{3}{4}$

3. Linear Inequalities and Absolute Value

0103

First, find the solution of the given inequality.

$3x-5\geq-2(4-x)+1$

$3x-5\geq-8+2x+1$

$3x-5\geq2x-7$

$x\geq-2$

We see that -3 is NOT a solution to the above inequality. Therefore, the answer is (A).

▶ A

0104

$|3x-5|=13$

$3x-5=13$　　or　　$3x-5=-13$

$3x=18$　　　　　$3x=-8$

$x=6$　　　　　$x=-\dfrac{8}{3}$

▶ A

0105

$-8\leq6-x\leq-4$

$-14\leq-x\leq-10$

$14\geq\ x\geq\ 10$　　$\Rightarrow 10\leq x\leq14$

▶ A

0106

Notice that

$\dfrac{4x-2}{3}(-9)=-3(4x-2)$

$=6-12x$

So multiplying each side by -9 gives us

$\left(-4<\dfrac{4x-2}{3}<1\right)\cdot(-9)$

$36>6-12x>-9$　　$\Rightarrow$　$-9<6-12x<36$

▶ A

0107

To determine whether each given point is on the graph of a given inequality, simply substitute each point into the given inequality and see if the equation is true.

(A) $2|-3|+|0|=6\geq5$

$\Rightarrow(-3,\ 0)$ is on the graph

(B) $2|-1|+|3|=5\geq5$

$\Rightarrow(-1,\ -3)$ is on the graph

(C) $2|0|+|-4|=4\ngeq5$

$\Rightarrow(0,\ -4)$ is NOT

(D) $2|3|+|-2|=8\geq5$

$\Rightarrow(3,\ -2)$ is on the graph

▶ C

0108

$|2x+5|<13$

$-13<2x+5<13$

$-18<2x<8$

$-9<x<4$

The positive integer solutions of the inequality are 1, 2, and 3. Therefore, there are 3 positive integers in the solution.

▶ A

0109

$|2x-1|+2=1$

$|2x-1|=-1$

Since $|2x-1|\geq0$, there is no x value such that $|2x-1|=-1$.

▶ D

0110

$$\frac{|x-2|}{2} \leq 8$$

$$\frac{|x-2|}{2} \leq 6$$

$$|x-2| \leq 12$$

$$-12 \leq x-2 \leq 12$$

$$-10 \leq x \leq 14$$

▶ D

0111

If a is a negative integer, then the absolute value of a, denoted as $|a|$, is equal to $-a$. Therefore, $-|a|$ can be written as $-(-a)$ which simplifies to a. The answer is (A).

▶ A

0112

$$|x+1| = 4$$

$$x+1 = 4 \quad \text{or} \quad x+1 = -4$$

$$x = 3 \qquad\qquad x = -5$$

Therefore, the value of $|x-4|$ could be

$$|x-4| = |3-4| = 1 \quad \text{or}$$

$$|x-4| = |-5-4| = 9$$

So the answer is (D).

▶ D

0113

The equation of the line is $y=2$. Since the region of the solution is above the solid line, $y \geq 2$. The answer is (B).

▶ B

0114

The line passes through two points, $(1, 0)$ and $(0, -3)$. So the equation of the line is $y=3x-3$. Since the region of the solution is below the solid line, $y \leq 3x-3$. The answer is (C).

▶ C

0115

$$2x-1 < 7 \qquad\qquad 2-3x < 11$$

$$2x < 8 \qquad\qquad -3x < 9$$

$$x < 4 \quad \text{and} \qquad x > -3$$

The solution to the inequality is $-3 < x < 4$. Therefore, the number of integer values x is 6, from -2 to 3, inclusive.

▶ C

0116

Let x be the number. Then we have

$$x + x^2 \geq 0$$

Now, check if the values in A through D are possible solutions to the inequality.

(A) $\left(-\frac{3}{2}\right) + \left(-\frac{3}{2}\right)^2 = -\frac{3}{2} + \frac{9}{4} = \frac{3}{4} \geq 0$

(B) $(-1) + (-1)^2 = -1 + 1 = 0 \geq 0$

(C) $\left(-\frac{1}{2}\right) + \left(-\frac{1}{2}\right)^2 = -\frac{1}{2} + \frac{1}{4} = -\frac{1}{4} \not\geq 0$

(D) $(0) + (0)^2 = 0 \geq 0$

So the answer is (C).

▶ C

0117

To find which answer choice could be the value of m, we need to determine the number of integers greater than m and less than $(m-1)^2$.

(A) For $m=2$, $(2-1)^2=1$. So, there are no integers greater than 2 and less than 1.

(B) For $m=3$, $(3-1)^2=4$. There is exactly 1 integer(3) greater than 3 and less than 4.

(C) For $m=4$, $(4-1)^2=9$. There are exactly 4 integers(58) greater than 4 and less than 9.

(D) For $m=5$, $(5-1)^2=16$. There are exactly 10 integers(6~15) greater than 5 and less than 16.

Therefore, the answer is (C).

▶ C

0118

Let x be the width of the rectangular field. Then the length of the field is $3x-4$. Since Jack has 121 feet of fences, we have the following inequality:

$2x+(3x-4) \leq 121$

Therefore, the answer is (B).

▶ B

0119

Let x be the number of years after 2016. Then we have the following inequality:

$128+8x > 300$

$8x > 172$, $x > 21.5$

In 22 years, there will be more than 300 million trees in country K. That year is $2016+22=2038$.

▶ B

0120

Let x be the score of the fourth exam. Since Mike needs to get an average of 85 or more, we have the following inequality:

$$\frac{82+90+87+x}{4} \geq 85$$

$82+90+87+x \geq 340$

$259+x \geq 340$, $x \geq 81$

Therefore, the minimum score Mike must receive on the fourth exam is 81.

▶ C

0121

Let x be the speed of the car in miles per hour. Then the absolute value inequality that gives the solution x is

$|x-60| \leq 6$

$-6 \leq x-60 \leq 6$

$54 \leq x \leq 66$

Therefore, the maximum speed is 66 miles per hour

▶ A

0122

If the car averages 26 miles per gallon on the highway and the actual mileage varies from the average by at most 4 miles per gallon, we can represent the possible gas mileage x using the inequality:

$26-4 \leq x \leq 26+4$

$-4 \leq x-26 \leq 4$

$|x-26| \leq 4$

Therefore, the answer is (C).

▶ C

0123

We must have following inequality as shown below.

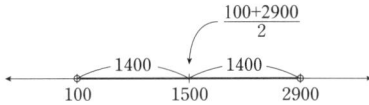

The absolute value inequality that gives the solution above is $|x-1,500|<1,400$. Because

$$|x-1,500|<1,400$$
$$-1,400<x-1,500<1,400$$
$$100<\quad x\quad<2,900$$

Therefore, the answer is (D).

▶ D

0124

Let x be company B's amount of sales in dollars. Then we have the following inequality:

$$39000<25000+0.04x$$
$$14000<0.04x$$
$$350000<x$$

When the amount of sales is over \$350,000, company B's salary is greater than company A's salary. So the answer is (B).

▶ B

0125

Let x be the amount of 15% brine in grams. Create a table as shown below.

	6% brine	15% brine	12% brine
Grams	400	x	$x+400$
Salt	0.06(400)	0.15x	0.12($x+400$)

$$0.06(400)+0.15x>0.12(x+400)$$
$$6(400)+15x>12(x+400)$$
$$2400+15x>12x+4800$$
$$3x>2400$$

$$x>800$$

Therefore, Tom needs to mix more than 800 grams of 15% brine. The answer is D.

▶ D

0126

$$|4x+1|-1\le2$$
$$|4x+1|\le3$$
$$-3\le4x+1\le3$$
$$-4\le4x\le2$$
$$-1\le x\le\frac{1}{2}$$

Any value between -1 and $\frac{1}{2}$, inclusive, is a solution.

▶ $-1\le x\le\frac{1}{2}$

0127

$$|3x-3|=18$$
$$3|x-1|=18$$
$$|x-1|=6$$
$$x-1=6\quad\text{or}\quad x-1=-6$$

The positive value of $x-1$ is 6.

▶ 6

0128

$$|4x-3|=5$$
$$4x-3=5\quad\text{or}\quad4x-3=-5$$
$$4x=8\qquad\qquad4x=-2$$
$$x=2\qquad\qquad x=-\frac{1}{2}$$

Therefore, the sum of the solutions is

$$2+\left(-\frac{1}{2}\right)=\frac{3}{2}$$

▶ $\frac{3}{2}$

Solutions Manual

0129

$$-4 \leq 2(3-x) < 10$$
$$-4 \leq 6-2x < 10$$
$$-10 \leq -2x < 4$$
$$5 \geq x > -2$$

Therefore, the largest value of the solution for the given inequality is 5.

▶ 5

0130

$$4(2-y) \leq 3y - \frac{1}{3}(y+6)$$

$$8-4y \leq 3y - \frac{1}{3}y - 2$$

$$8-4y \leq \frac{8}{3}y - 2$$

$$10 \leq \frac{20}{3}y, \ y \geq \frac{3}{2}$$

The smallest possible value of $2y+1$ is

when $y = \frac{3}{2}$. Therefore, the answer is

$$2y+1 = 2\left(\frac{3}{2}\right) + 1 = 3+1 = 4$$

▶ 4

0131

$$|4x-1| < 5$$
$$-5 < 4x-1 < 5$$
$$-4 < 4x < 6$$
$$-1 < x < \frac{3}{2}$$

Since we are looking for positive integers, we need to find positive integers within this range. The positive integers within this range are 1. Therefore, there is 1 positive integers.

▶ 1

0132

Let David's age be x. According to the given information, Jenny's age would be $x+2$, and Ariel's age would be $x+4$. The sum of their ages is greater than the age of their mother, which is 54:

$$x+(x+2)+(x+4) > 0$$
$$3x+6 > 54$$
$$3x > 48, \ x > 16$$

Since David's age must be a positive integer, the youngest age that David can be is 17.

▶ 17

0133

Let the total amount of furniture in dollars that Nick must sell be x. To earn at least $800 a week, Nick's total earnings (including the base salary and commission) must be greater than or equal to $800. We can set up the following inequality:

$$300+0.02x \geq 800$$
$$0.02x \geq 500$$
$$x \geq 25000$$

Therefore, Nick must sell at least $25,000 worth of furniture to earn at least $800 a week.

▶ 25,000

0134

Let x be the number of movies David downloads. Then we have the following inequality:

$$15.5+2.25x \leq 100$$
$$1550+225x \leq 10000$$
$$225x \leq 8550$$
$$x \leq 38$$

Therefore, the maximum number of movies he can download is 38.

▶ 38

0135

Let the number of hours Jason can play tennis be x. Considering Jason's budget, the total cost (including the registration fee and the hourly charge) must be less than or equal to $200. We can set up the following inequality:

$$20.5+6.5x\leq200$$
$$6.5x\leq179.5$$
$$x\leq27.615$$

Since Jason cannot play a fraction of an hour, the maximum number of hours he can play is 27 hours (rounded down from 27.615).

▶ 27

0136

We need to calculate the maximum number of bottles that can be filled with the available water volume. Since 1 liter is equal to 1000 milliliters, the available water volume is

$2000\times1000=2,000,000$ milliliters.

Now, we divide the available water volume by the volume of one bottle:

$$\frac{2,000,000}{450}=4444.44$$

Since the number of bottles must be a whole number, we round down to the nearest whole number.
Therefore, the largest number of bottles the company can produce in a day is 4444 bottles.

▶ 4444

4. System of Linear Equations and Inequalities

0137

Solve the second equation for y.
$$2x-y=-7$$
$$-y=-2x-7$$
$$y=2x+7$$
Substitute $2x+7$ for y in the other equation.
$$6x-4(2x+7)=-12$$
$$6x-8x-28=-12$$
$$-2x=16,\ x=-8$$

▶ C

0138

Solve the first equation for x.
$$x-12y=4$$
$$x=12y+4$$
Substitute $12y+4$ for x in the other equation.
$$3(12y+4)=20y+28$$
$$36y+12=20y+28$$
$$16y=16,\ y=1$$
Now, substitute 1 for y in the equation
$$x=12(1)+4=16$$
Since the solution of the system is $x=16$

and $y=1$, we have $y=\dfrac{x}{16}$.

So the answer is (A).

▶ A

0139

$$\begin{cases}\left(x-\dfrac{y}{3}=\dfrac{1}{3}\right)\times3\\\left(-\dfrac{x}{2}+\dfrac{2y}{5}=1\right)\times10\end{cases} \Rightarrow \begin{cases}3x-y=1\\-5x+4y=10\end{cases}$$

$$\Rightarrow \begin{cases}3x-1=y\\-5x+4y=10\end{cases}$$

Substitute $3x-1$ for y in the second equation.
$$-5x+4(3x-1)=10$$
$$-5x+12x-4=10$$
$$7x=14, \ x=2 \ \Rightarrow \ a=2$$
Substitute 2 for x in the equation
$$y=3(2)-1=5 \ \Rightarrow \ b=5$$
So the value of a+b=2+5=7.

▶ B

0140

Substitute 4 for x in the equation
$$2x-y=9.$$
$$2(4)-y=9$$
$$-y=1, \ y=-1$$
Now, substitute 4 for x and -1 for y in
the equation $3ax+ay=11$.
$$3a(4)+a(-1)=11$$
$$12a-a=11$$
$$11a=11, \ a=1$$

▶ A

0141

Substitute 2 for x and -1 for y in the system.
$$\begin{cases} a(2)-b(-1)=5 \\ b(2)+a(-1)=-2 \end{cases} \Rightarrow \begin{cases} 2a+b=5 \\ -a+2b=-2 \end{cases}$$
This is a new linear system of equations with two
variables a and b. Now, solve the system.
$$\begin{cases} 2a+b=5 \\ -a+2b=-2 \end{cases} \Rightarrow b=-2a+5$$
Substitute $-2a+5$ for b in the equation

$$-a+2(-2a+5)=-2$$
$$-a-4a+10=-2$$
$$-5a=-12, \ a=\frac{12}{5}$$

▶ B

0142

From $\begin{cases} -x+2y=3 \\ 3x-6y=-8 \end{cases}$, we have $\dfrac{-1}{3}=\dfrac{2}{-6}\neq\dfrac{3}{-8}$.

Therefore, the system has no solution.

▶ A

0143

$$\begin{cases} x-4y=7 \\ 8y=2x-15 \end{cases} \Rightarrow \begin{cases} x-4y=7 \\ -2x+8y=-15 \end{cases}$$
Since we have $\dfrac{1}{-2}=\dfrac{-4}{8}\neq\dfrac{7}{-15}$ from the

system above, it has no solution. Therefore, the
number of solution is zero.

▶ A

0144

$$\begin{cases} 6x-by=-5 \\ (-3x+5y=2)\times-2 \end{cases} \Rightarrow \begin{cases} 6x-by=-5 \\ 6x-10y=-4 \end{cases}$$
If b is 10, this system of equations has no solution.
Otherwise, it always has exactly 1 solution. Therefore,
the answer is (D).

▶ D

0145

If we add two equations,
$$\begin{array}{r} 3x-2y=14 \\ +\underline{\quad 2x+7y=19} \\ 5x+5y=33 \end{array}$$
Therefore, the value of $5x+5y$ is 33.

▶ C

0146

If the system $\begin{cases} x+4y=a \\ 2x=by+10 \end{cases}$ has infinitely many solutions, we must have $\frac{1}{2}=\frac{4}{-b}=\frac{a}{10}$.

$\frac{1}{2}=\frac{4}{-b}$ and $\frac{1}{2}=\frac{a}{10}$

$-b=8 \Rightarrow b=-8$ $\qquad 2a=10 \Rightarrow a=5$

Therefore, $a=5$ and $b=-8$

▶ A

0147

In the system $\begin{cases} a_1x+b_1y=c_1 \\ a_2x+b_2y=c_2 \end{cases}$, if $\frac{a_1}{a_2}=\frac{b_1}{b_2}\neq\frac{c_1}{c_2}$,

there are no solutions to the system. For answer choice (D), we have

$\begin{cases} 4a-3b=131 \\ 12a-9b=-13 \end{cases} \Rightarrow \frac{4}{12}=\frac{-3}{-9}\neq\frac{13}{-13}$

Therefore, the answer is (D).

▶ D

0148

From $\begin{cases} 2x+6y=a \\ 3x-by=6 \end{cases}$, we must have $\frac{2}{3}=\frac{6}{-b}\neq\frac{a}{b}$.

$\frac{2}{3}=\frac{6}{-b}$ and $\frac{2}{3}\neq\frac{a}{6}$

$-2b=18, \ b=-9$ $\qquad 3a\neq12, \ a\neq4$

Therefore, the answer is (A)

▶ A

0149

First, solve $m+n=3$ for m in terms of n.

$m+n=3$

$\quad m=3-n$

Now solve $m-k=4$ for k in terms of n.

$m-k=4$

$3-n-k=4$

$\quad -k=n+1 \Rightarrow k=-n-1$

Substitute $3-n$ and $-n-1$ for m and k in the equation $3m-n+2k=7$.

$3(3-n)-n+2(-n-1)=7$

$9-3n-n-2n-2=7$

$-6n=0, \ n=0$

The answer is (B).

▶ B

0150

to determine which of the options is true, we can substitute the values from the given ordered pair (1, 2) into the system of equations:

$1+a(2)=-3$

$\quad 2a=-4, \ a=-2$ and

$3(1)+b(2)=5$

$\quad 2b=2, \ b=1$

Since $a=-2$ and $b=1$, (D) $a=-2b$ is true.

▶ D

0151

$\begin{cases} 2x-y=3 \\ -6x+3y=-9 \end{cases} \Rightarrow \begin{cases} 2x-y=3 \\ 2x-y=3 \end{cases}$

The two equations in the system of equations are identical. To determine which point lies on the graph of each equation, we can substitute the given coordinates into the equations and check if they satisfy the equations.

(A) $2(k)-(2k-3)=2k-2k+3=3$

(B) $2(2k)-\left(\frac{k+3}{2}\right)=4k-\frac{k+3}{2}\neq3$

(C) $2(2k-3)-(k)=4k-6-2=4k-8\neq3$

(D) $2\left(\frac{k+3}{2}\right)-(2k)=k+3-2k=-k+3\neq3$

From the analysis above, we can conclude that both points $(k, 2k-3)$ lies on the graph of their respective equations. So the answer is (A).

▶ A

0152

Since two systems above have the same solution, we can find the solution (x, y) using the equation $5x+y=13$ and $2x-3y=-5$.

$$\begin{cases} 5x+y=13 & \rightarrow y=-5x+13 \\ 2x-3y=-5 \end{cases}$$

Substitute $-5x+13$ for y in the equation $2x-3y=-5$.

$$2x-3(-5x+13)=-5$$
$$2x+15x-39=-5$$
$$17x=34, \ x=2$$

Substitute 2 for x in the equation $y=-5x+13$.

$$y=-5(2)+13=3$$

Therefore, the solution for both systems is $(2, 3)$ and we can substitute this solution to the equation $4x-ay=7$ and $bx-4y=9$ to find a and b.

$$4(2)-a(3)=7 \qquad b(2)-4(3)=9$$
$$8-3a=7 \qquad 2b-12=9$$
$$-3a=-1 \qquad 2b=21$$
$$a=\frac{1}{3} \qquad b=\frac{21}{2}$$

So the value of $ab=\frac{1}{3} \cdot \frac{21}{2}=3.5$

▶ B

0153

If the point is in the solution region of the system of inequalities, the assigned point satisfies the system.

(A) $\begin{cases} 2(1)-3(2)>-1 \\ -(1)+5(2)\le3 \end{cases} \Rightarrow \begin{cases} -4\not>-1 \\ 9\not\le3 \end{cases}$

(B) $\begin{cases} 2(1)-3(-2)>-1 \\ -(1)+5(-2)\le3 \end{cases} \Rightarrow \begin{cases} 8>-1 \\ -11\le3 \end{cases}$

(C) $\begin{cases} 2(-1)-3(-2)>-1 \\ -(-1)+5(-2)\le3 \end{cases} \Rightarrow \begin{cases} 4>-1 \\ -9\le3 \end{cases}$

(D) $\begin{cases} 2(2)-3(1)>-1 \\ -(2)+5(1)\le3 \end{cases} \Rightarrow \begin{cases} 7>-1 \\ -7\le3 \end{cases}$

Therefore, the answer is (A).

▶ A

0154

The equation of the solid vertical line is $x=-1$. Since the right side of the region is shaded, $x\ge-1$. The other line passes through two points, $(-1, -2)$ and $(0, 0)$. So the equation is $y=2x$. Since the shaded region is above the solid line, $y\ge2x$. Therefore, the

system of inequalities is $\begin{cases} x\ge-1 \\ y\ge2x \end{cases}$.

▶ C

0155

To determine which values of 'a' satisfy the system of inequalities, we need to substitute the given point $(a, 12)$ into the inequalities and check if they are satisfied. For the first inequality, we substitute $(a, 12)$ into $3x-2y>-6$:

$$3(a)-2(12)>-6$$
$$3a-24>-6$$
$$3a>18, \ a>6$$

Since $a>6$, (D) could be the value of 'a' that satisfies the system of inequalities.

▶ D

0156

To determine which values of 'y' satisfy the system of inequalities, we need to substitute the given $x-$coordinate (8) into the inequalities and check for which values of 'y' they are satisfied.

$$5(8)-2y>32$$
$$40-2y>32 \text{ and}$$
$$8>2y, \ 4>y$$
$$2(8)-3y<10$$
$$16-3y<10$$
$$6<3y, \ 2<y$$

Therefore, y must be greater than 2, but less than 4. So (C) could be the value of 'y' that satisfies the system of inequalities.

0157

For the second inequality, $3x+2>8$, we can solve it to find the range of x that satisfies the inequality:

$3x+2>8$

$3x>6$, $x>2$

Combining the information from two inequalities $y>4x+1$ and $x>2$, $y-$coordinates of all points satisfying the system of inequality is

$y>4(2)+1$

$y>9$

So the answer is A.

▶ A

0158

Since the dotted line on the left passes through the points $(-2, 2)$ and $(0, -1)$, the equation is $y=-\dfrac{3}{2}x-1$. Also, since the dotted line on the right passes through the points $(1, 0)$ and $(0, -1)$, the equation is $y=x-1$. To have a solution region shown on the graph, the system of inequalities must be $y<-\dfrac{3}{2}x-1$

$$y<x-1.$$

So the answer is A.

▶ A

0159

Let x and y be the number of packages with 12 buns and 8 buns, respectively. Then we have

$x+y=20$ and $12x+8y=188$.

Now, solve the system $\begin{cases} x+y=20 \\ 12x+8y=188 \end{cases}$ for y.

$\begin{cases} x+y=20 \\ 12x+8y=188 \end{cases} \Rightarrow \begin{cases} x=-y+20 \\ 3x+2y=47 \end{cases}$

Substitute $-y+20$ for x in the second equation.

$3(-y+20)+2y=47$

$-3y+60+2y=47$

$-y=-13$, $y=13$

Therefore, Mike ordered 13 packages of 8 buns

▶ B

0160

Let x and y be the number of dozen pencils and pens, respectively. Then we have

$x+y=8$ and $4.5x+6.5y=42$.

Now, solve the system $\begin{cases} x+y=8 \\ 4.5x+6.5y=42 \end{cases}$ for x.

$\begin{cases} x+y=8 \\ 4.5x+6.5y=42 \end{cases} \Rightarrow \begin{cases} x+y=8 \\ 45x+65y=420 \end{cases}$

$\Rightarrow \begin{cases} y=-x+8 \\ 9x+13y=84 \end{cases}$

Substitute $-x+8$ for y in the second equation.

$9x+13(-x+8)=84$

$9x-13x+104=84$

$-4x=-20$, $x=5$

▶ D

0161

Let x and y be the cost of a butter croissant and a chocolate cream croissant, respectively. According to the given information, we can set up the following system of equations:

$3x+4y=16$

$4x+2y=13$

Let's use the method of elimination to solve the system:

$\begin{cases} 3x+4y=16 \\ (4x+2y=13)\times2 \end{cases} \Rightarrow \begin{cases} 3x+4y=16 \\ 8x+4y=26 \end{cases}$

$\begin{array}{r} 3x+4y=16 \\ -\underline{8x+4y=26} \\ -5x=-10, \ x=2 \end{array}$

Substitute this value of x back into equation

$3x+4y=16$.
$$3(2)+4y=16$$
$$6+4y=16$$
$$4y=10, \ y=2.5$$

So, the cost of a butter croissant is $2, and the cost of a chocolate cream croissant is $2.5. Now, let's calculate the cost of purchasing two butter croissants and three chocolate cream croissants:

$$2(2)+3(2.5)=\$11.5$$

So the answer is (B).

▶ B

0162

Let x and y be the speed of the airplane and wind, respectively.

	Distance (mile)	Time (hour)	Speed (mile/hour)
From N.Y. to L.A.	2550	5	$x+y$
From L.A. to N.Y.	2550	6	$x-y$

Since the distance is equal to speed times time, we have $(x+y)5=2550$ and $(x-y)6=2550$. So we have the system:

$$\begin{cases} (x+y)5=2550 \\ (x-y)6=2550 \end{cases} \Rightarrow \begin{cases} 5x+5y=2550 \\ 6x-6y=2550 \end{cases}$$

Therefore, the answer is A.

▶ A

0163

a and b are the liters of a 16% and 25% saline solution, respectively.

	16% solution	25% solution	20% solution
The amount of solution	a	b	36
The amount of salt	$0.16a$	$0.25b$	$0.2(a+b)$

So we have the system:

$$\begin{cases} a+b=36 \\ 0.16a+0.25b=0.2(a+b) \end{cases}$$
$$\Rightarrow \begin{cases} a+b=36 \\ 16a+25b=20(a+b) \end{cases}$$

Therefore, the answer is (D).

▶ D

0164

Let x and y be the hours worked as a math tutor, and the hours worked in the restaurant, respectively. Emily can work up to 32 hours: This can be represented as $x+y \leq 32$.

Emily must earn at least $600: This can be represented as $18x+15y \geq 600$, where $18x$ represents the amount earned as a math tutor (18 dollars per hour), and $15y$ represents the amount earned in the restaurant (15 dollars per hour). Therefore, the correct system of inequalities is (A).

▶ A

0165

We know that when 4 women get off the bus, the number of women remaining will be $w-4$. Additionally, the number of men will be twice the number of women, which can be represented as $2(w-4)$. Since the total number of men is given as m, we can set up the equation:

$$m=2(w-4)$$
$$m=2w-8$$
$$m+8=2w, \quad w=\frac{m+8}{2}$$

So the answer is (B).

▶ B

0166

Substitute $(1, 3)$ into the system of equations
$\begin{cases} ax+y=2 \\ 3x-by=1 \end{cases}$. Then, we have

$$a(1)+(3)=2$$
$$a+3=2 \quad \text{and}$$
$$a=-1$$

$$3(1)-b(3)=1$$
$$3-3b=1$$
$$-3b=-2$$
$$b=\frac{2}{3}$$

Therefore, $a+b=-1+\dfrac{2}{3}=-\dfrac{1}{3}$.

▶ $-\dfrac{1}{3}$

0167

Solve the first equation for x.
$$3x+y=4$$
$$3x=4-y, \quad x=\frac{4-y}{3}$$

Substitute $\dfrac{4-y}{3}$ for x in the other equation.

$$2\left(\frac{4-y}{3}\right)-5y=14$$
$$\frac{8-2y}{3}-5y=14$$
$$8-2y-15y=42$$
$$-17y=34, \quad y=-2$$

▶ -2

0168

$\begin{cases} x=ay+2 \\ 3x-4y=5 \end{cases} \Rightarrow \begin{cases} x-ay=2 \\ 3x-4y=5 \end{cases}$

If the system has no solution, we must have
$$\frac{1}{3}=\frac{-a}{-4}\neq\frac{2}{5}.$$
$$\frac{1}{3}=\frac{-a}{-4}$$
$$-3a=-4 \Rightarrow a=\frac{4}{3}$$

▶ $\dfrac{4}{3}$

0169

$\begin{cases} 2(x-3)+3y=-9 \\ 2(5-y)-x=11 \end{cases} \Rightarrow \begin{cases} 2x-6+3y=-9 \\ 10-2y-x=11 \end{cases}$

$\Rightarrow \begin{cases} 2x+3y=-3 \\ -2y-x=1 \end{cases}$

$\rightarrow x=-2y-1$

Substitute $-2y-1$ for x in the first equation.
$$2(-2y-1)+3y=-3$$
$$-4y-2+3y=-3$$
$$-y=-1$$
$$y=1$$

Substitute 1 for y in the equation $x=-2y-1$.
$$x=-2(1)-1=-3$$

Therefore, $x+y=-3+1=-2$.

▶ -2

0170

$\begin{cases} x+\dfrac{y-1}{3}=1 \\ \dfrac{2x+6}{5}-\dfrac{y+2}{2}=2 \end{cases}$

$\Rightarrow \begin{cases} \left(x+\dfrac{y-1}{3}=1\right)\times 3 \\ \left(\dfrac{2x+6}{5}-\dfrac{y+2}{2}=2\right)\times 10 \end{cases}$

$\Rightarrow \begin{cases} 3x+(y-1)=3 \\ 2(2x+6)-5(y+2)=20 \end{cases}$

$\Rightarrow \begin{cases} 3x+y=4 \\ 4x+12-5y-10=20 \end{cases} \Rightarrow \begin{cases} y=-3x+4 \\ 4x-5y=18 \end{cases}$

Substitute $-3x+4$ for y in the second equation

$4x-5y=18$.
$$4x-5(-3x+4)=18$$
$$4x+15x-20=18$$
$$19x=38, \ x=2$$

▶ 2

0171

Both expressions are equal to 123, so set them equal to each other.
$$15a-28b=13a-27b$$
$$2a=b$$
Now, substitute $2a$ for b in the equation $15a-28b=123$.
$$15a-28(2a)=123$$
$$15a-56a=123$$
$$-41a=123, \ a=-3$$
$$b=2a=2(-3)=-6$$
Therefore, $a-b=-3-(-6)=3$.

▶ 3

0172

Since two graphs are identical, they have same slope and $y-$intercept. So we have
$4a+b=a$ and $5=-(3b+7)$.
$$4a+(-4)=a \qquad 5=-3b-7$$
$$3a=4 \quad \text{and} \quad 12=-3b$$
$$a=\frac{4}{3} \qquad -4=b$$
Therefore, $b=\left(\frac{4}{3}\right)(-4)=-\frac{16}{3}$

▶ $-\frac{16}{3}$

0173

From the equation $7x+2y=4x+y=2x-y-4$,

let the system be

$$\begin{cases} 7x+2y=4x+y \\ 7x+2y=2x-y-4 \end{cases} \Rightarrow \begin{cases} y=-3x \\ 5x+3y=-4 \end{cases}$$
Substitute $-3x$ for y in the second equation $5x+3y=-4$.
$$5x+3(-3x)=-4$$
$$-4x=-4, \ x=1$$
Substitute 1 for x in the equation $y=-3x$.
$$y=-3(1)=-3$$
Therefore, $x+y=1+(-3)-2$

▶ -2

0174

$$\begin{cases} y\geq-2 \\ x\geq1 \\ 2x+y\leq6 \end{cases} \Rightarrow \begin{cases} y\geq-2 \\ x\geq1 \\ y\leq-2x+6 \end{cases}$$

The intersection of $y=-2$ and $y=-2x+6$ is
$$-2x+6=-2$$
$$-2x=-8, \ x=4$$
$$\Rightarrow (4, \ -2)$$
The intersection of $x=1$ and $y=-2x+6$ is
$$y=-2(1)+6=4$$
$$\Rightarrow (1, \ 4)$$

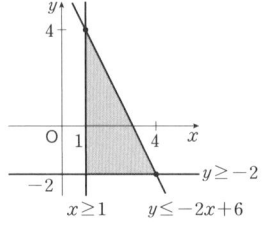

Therefore, the solution region is a right triangle. So the area A is
$$A=\frac{1}{2}(4-1)(4-(-2))$$
$$=\frac{1}{2}(3)(6)=9$$

▶ 9

0175

Let x and y be the width and length of the original rectangle, respectively. Then we have $2x+2y=24$ and $2(3x)+2(2y)=2(24)+10$.

Now, solve the system.

$\begin{cases} 2x+2y=24 \\ 2(3x)+2(2y)=2(24)+10 \end{cases}$

$\Rightarrow \begin{cases} x+y=12 \quad \rightarrow \quad y=-x+12 \\ 6x+4y=58 \end{cases}$

Substitute $-x+12$ for y in the second equation.

$6x+4(-x+12)=58$

$6x-4x+48=58$

$2x=10, \ x=5$

Therefore, the width of the original rectangle is 5 feet.

▶ 5

0176

Let x and y be the age of Kevin and Paul, respectively. Then we have $x=y+22$. Since Kevin is twice as old as Paul in 7 year, we also have $x+7=2(y+7)$.

Now, solve the system $\begin{cases} x=y+22 \\ x+7=2(y+7) \end{cases}$ for y.

$\begin{cases} x=y+22 \\ x+7=2(y+7) \end{cases} \Rightarrow \begin{cases} x=y+22 \\ x+7=2y+14 \end{cases}$

$\Rightarrow \begin{cases} x=y+22 \\ x=2y+7 \end{cases}$

Substitute $y+22$ for x in the second equation.

$y+22=2y+7$

$-y=-15, \ y=15$

Therefore, Paul is 15 years old now.

▶ 15

0177

Let x and y be the price of a burger and a soft drink in dollars, respectively. Then we have

$4x+3y=26$ and $3x+6y=27$.

Now, solve the system $\begin{cases} 4x+3y=26 \\ 3x+6y=27 \end{cases}$.

Multiply first equation by 2 and then subtract.

$\begin{cases} (4x+3y=26)\cdot 2 \\ 3x+6y=27 \end{cases} \Rightarrow \begin{cases} 8x+6y=52 \\ 3x+6y=27 \end{cases}$

$\begin{array}{r} 8x+6y=52 \\ -\underline{3x+6y=27} \\ 5x \quad\quad =25, \ x=5 \end{array}$

Substitute 5 for x in the equation $3x+6y=27$.

$3(5)+6y=27$

$6y=12, \ y=2$

The burger is \$5 and the soft drink is \$2. Therefore, the combined price of a burger and soda is \$7.

▶ \$7

0178

Let x and y be the number of tickets for adults and students, respectively. Then we have

$x+y=170$ and $15x+9y=2250$.

Now, solve the system $\begin{cases} x+y=170 \\ 15x+9y=2250 \end{cases}$ for x.

$\begin{cases} x+y=170 \\ 15x+9y=2250 \end{cases} \Rightarrow \begin{cases} y=-x+170 \\ 15x+9y=2250 \end{cases}$

Substitute $-x+170$ for y in the second equation.

$15x+9(-x+170)=2250$

$15x-9x+1530=2250$

$6x=720, \ x=120$

Therefore, 120 adult tickets were sold.

▶ 120

Solutions Manual

0179

Let x and y be the number of tables for two and the number of tables for four, respectively. Since there are a total of 60 tables, we have

$$x+y=60 \Rightarrow y=60-x$$

Also, since the total number of people attending the seminar is given as 202,

$$2x+4y=202$$

Substitute $60-x$ for y in the second equation.

$$2x+4(60-x)=202$$
$$2x+240-4x=202$$
$$-2x=-38, \ x=19$$

Therefore, there are exactly 19 tables for two people.

▶ 19

 Advanced Math

1. Operations with Polynomials

0180

$$2(3x^2+2)-6(x^2-3x)$$
$$=6x^2+4-6x^2+18x$$
$$=18x+4$$

▶ B

0181

$$(4x^2-2+5x)+2(3x^2+3x-7)$$
$$=4x^2-2+5x+6x^2+6x-14$$
$$=(4x^2+6x^2)+(5x+6x)+(-2-14)$$
$$=10x^2+11x-16$$

▶ B

0182

$$x+3-\frac{3(2-x)}{5}=\frac{x+3}{1} \cdot \frac{5}{5}-\frac{3(2-x)}{5}$$
$$=\frac{5(x+3)-3(2-x)}{5}$$
$$=\frac{5x+15-6+3x}{5}$$
$$=\frac{8x+9}{5}$$

▶ C

0183

$$(x^2-1)(2x+3)$$
$$=(x^2 \times 2x)+(x^2 \times 3)+(-1 \times 2x)+(-1 \times 3)$$
$$=2x^3+3x^2-2x-3$$

▶ D

0184

$(3a+2)(4+a-a^2)$

$=12a+3a^2+-3a^3+8+2a-2a^2$

$=-3a^3+a^2+14a+8$

▶ C

0185

$3x^4-12x^2=3x^2(x^2-4)$

$\qquad =3x^2(x-2)(x+2)$

▶ C

0186

$6xy^3-54xy=6xy(y^2-9)$

$\qquad =6xy(y-3)(y+3)$

▶ D

0187

$(4x-3)(4x+3)-4(2x-1)^2$

$=(4x)^2-3^2-4(4x^2-4x+1)$

$=16x^2-9-16x^2+16x-4$

$=16x-13$

▶ B

0188

$x(3a-2b)+4y(2b-3a)$

$=x(3a-2b)-4y(3a-2b)$

Let $A=3a-2b$. Then we have

$x(3a-2b)-4y(3a-2b)$

$=xA-4yA=A(x-4y)$

$=(3a-2b)(x-4y)$

▶ A

0189

$\dfrac{3(2a^2+a-1)}{2}+\dfrac{3a-a^2+1}{6}$

$=\dfrac{3(2a^2+a-1)}{2}\cdot\dfrac{3}{3}+\dfrac{3a-a^2+1}{6}$

$=\dfrac{9(2a^2+a-1)+(3a-a^2+1)}{6}$

$=\dfrac{18a^2+9a-9+3a-a^2+1}{6}$

$=\dfrac{17a^2+12a-8}{6}$

▶ B

0190

$\dfrac{x-2y}{3}-\dfrac{3x+2y}{4}=\dfrac{x-2y}{3}\cdot\dfrac{4}{4}-\dfrac{3x+2y}{4}\cdot\dfrac{3}{3}$

$\qquad =\dfrac{4(x-2y)-3(3x+2y)}{12}$

$\qquad =\dfrac{4x-8y-9x-6y}{12}$

$\qquad =\dfrac{-5x-14y}{12}=-\dfrac{5}{12}x-\dfrac{14}{12}y$

Since $-\dfrac{5}{12}x-\dfrac{14}{12}y=ax+by$, $a=-\dfrac{5}{12}$ and

$b=-\dfrac{14}{12}$, $a+b=-\dfrac{5}{12}+\left(-\dfrac{14}{12}\right)=-\dfrac{19}{12}$

▶ C

0191

$ax^2-c=(2x+a)(x+b)$

$\qquad =2x^2+2bx+ax+ab$

$\qquad =2x^2+(2b+a)x+ab$

$\Rightarrow a=2$

$0=2b+a$, $0=2b+2$, $b=-1$

$-c=ab=(2)(-1)$, $c=2$

Therefore, $a+b+c=2+(-1)+2=3$

▶ A

0192

$1-2x+x^2=(1-x)^2$

We have $m=x-1 \Rightarrow x=m+1$.

Substitute $m+1$ for x.

$(1-x)^2=(1-x)^2$
$\quad\quad\quad =(1-(m+1))^2$
$\quad\quad\quad =(-m)^2=m^2$

▶ A

0193

$4ab^2\left(\dfrac{a^2}{2}-3b\right)=2a^3b^2-12ab^3$

Since $ma^3b^2-12ab^3=2a^3b^2-12ab^3$, the value of m is 2.

▶ B

0194

Expand only the part of the y terms.

$(3+2y)(ay^2-3y+b)$
$\Rightarrow (3\times(-3y))+(2y\times b)$
$=-9y+2by$
$=(-9+2b)y$

Since the coefficient of y term is 8,

$-9+2b=8$

$2b=17 \Rightarrow b=\dfrac{17}{2}=8.5$

▶ B

0195

$(ax^2+3x-4)(2x-b)=10x^3+11x^2-5x-4$

Expand only x^3 term and constant term on the left side and then compare it with the right side.

For the term with x^3:

$2ax^3=10x^3 \Rightarrow a=5$

For the constant term:

$(-4)(-b)=-4 \Rightarrow b=-1$

Therefore, $a+b=5+(-1)=4$.

▶ D

0196

Expand only the x term in the expression $(x+1)(x^2-2x+3)$ because c is the coefficient of the x term.

x term: $(x\times3)+(1\times-2x)=3x-2x=x$. Therefore, the value of c is 1.

▶ A

0197

$3A-(B+2C)+4C$
$=3A-B-2C+4C=3A-B+2C$
$=3(x^2-2x+3)-(3x^2-2)+2(2x^2+x)$
$=3x^2-6x+9-3x^2+2+4x^2+2x$
$=4x^2-4x+11$

Therefore, $a+b+c=4+(-4)+11=11$.

▶ D

0198

$6x^3y-13x^2y^2+6xy^3=xy(6x^2-13xy+6y^2)$

$\underbrace{6x^2-13xy+6y^2}_{6\times6=36}$

$\rightarrow 36=-9\times-4 \Rightarrow -9+(-4)=-13$

$\begin{array}{lll} 3x & -2y \rightarrow & -4xy \\ 2x & -3y \rightarrow & \underline{(+) \ -9xy} \\ & & -13xy \end{array}$

$x(6x^2-13xy+6y^2)=x(3x-2y)(2x-3y)$

▶ B

0199

The expression on the left can be simplified to:

$\dfrac{a^2-16}{a-4}=\dfrac{(a-4)(a+4)}{a-4}=a+4$

So we have

$a+4=b^2-16$

$\quad a=b^2-20$

The answer is (A).

▶ A

0200

$a(x-y)+b(y-x)$

$=a(x-y)-b(x-y)$ → Let $x-y=A$

$=aA-bA=A(a-b)$

$=(x-y)(a-b)$

▶ A

0201

$x^3-2x^2-9x+18$

$=x^2(x-2)-9(x-2)$ → Let $x-2=A$

$=x^2\,A-9A$

$=A(x^2-9)$

$=A(x-3)(x+3)$

Therefore, in the factor $x+a$, the value of a is 3.

▶ B

0202

$2a^4-32b^4=2(a^4-16b^4)$

$\qquad\qquad =2((a^2)^2-(4b^2)^2)$

$\qquad\qquad =2(a^2-4b^2)(a^2+4b^2)$

$\qquad\qquad =2(a^2-(2b)^2)(a^2+4b^2)$

$\qquad\qquad =2(a-2b)(a+2b)(a^2+4b^2)$

Therefore, the value of m is 4.

▶ D

0203

$9a^2-4b^2=(3a-2b)(3a+2b)=24$

Since $3a-2b=4$, we have

$\quad (3a-2b)(3a+2b)=24$

$\quad 4(3a+2b)=24$

$\quad 3a+2b=6$

Therefore, $6a+4b=2(3a+2b)=2(6)=12$.

▶ D

0204

$2x^3-kx^2-8x+4k$

$\quad =x^2(2x-k)-4(2x-k)$ → Let $2x-k=A$

$\quad =x^2A-4A$

$\quad =A(x^2-4)$

$\quad =(2x-k)(x-2)(x+2)$

Therefore, $x-2k$ is NOT a factor of the polynomial $2x^3-kx^2-8x+4k$.

▶ A

0205

We know that

$\quad a^2-b^2=(a-b)(a+b)=2$.

This can be rewritten as $a+b=\dfrac{2}{a-b}$.

Since $a-b$ is between -2 and 0, the value of $a+b$ must be less than -1. Therefore, the answer is (C).

▶ C

0206

$A-(a^2-3a-2)=4a^2+5a-4$

$A=4a^2+5a-4+(a^2-3a-2)$

$\quad =4a^2+5a-4+a^2-3a-2$

$\quad =5a^2+2a-6$

The answer is (B).

▶ B

0207

The length of the garden is 12 feet longer than the width, which means its length is $a+12$. So the perimeter P of a rectangular garden is

$\quad P=2a+2(a+12)$

$\quad\quad =2a+2a+24$

$\quad\quad =4a+24$

The answer is (B).

▶ B

Solutions Manual

0208

The length of the badminton court is given as 5 feet longer than twice the width, which means its length is

$$2(2k+1)+5=4k+7$$

The area, $A(k)$, of a rectangle is calculated by multiplying the length and width:

$$A(k)=(4k+7)(2k+1)$$
$$=8k^2+14k+4k+7$$
$$=8k^2+18k+7$$

Therefore, the answer is (A).

▶ A

0209

The side of the square base is $10-2x$ and the height is x. So $x(10-2x)$ represents the area of one of the four faces. Therefore,

$4x(10-2x)$ is the surface area of the open box, the sum of the areas of the four sides. The answer is (C).

▶ C

0210

The volume V of a box is the product of the area of its base and its height.

$$V=(10-2x)^2\cdot x$$
$$=x(10-2x)^2$$

The answer is (A).

▶ A

0211

Each side of the new cube is $k+4$. Then the volume V of the cube is

$$V=(a+4)^3$$
$$=(a+4)^2(a+4)$$
$$=(a^2+8a+16)(a+4)$$
$$=a^3+4a^2+8a^2+32a+16a+64$$
$$=a^3+12a^2+48a+64$$

▶ A

0212

$$6(2a^3-a^2+4)-3(4a^3-3a^2-4a+2)$$
$$=12a^3-6a^2+24-12a^3+9a^2+12a-6$$
$$=(12a^3-12a^3)+(-6a^2+9a^2)+12a+(24-6)$$
$$=3a^2+12a+18$$

Since $3a^2+12a+18=ma^2+na+18$, we know that

$$m=3 \text{ and } n=12$$

Therefore, $m+n=3+12=15$.

▶ 15

0213

$$(3a^2-4a+6)-2(a^2-2a+5)=5$$
$$3a^2-4a+6-2a^2+4a-10=5$$
$$a^2-4=5$$
$$a^2=9, \ a=\pm3$$

If $a=3$, then $3a+10=3(3)+10=19$ and
if $a=-3$, then $3a+10=3(-3)+10=1$

▶ 1 or 19

0214

The expression on the left can be simplified to:

$$\frac{3x-1}{2}+\frac{x+2}{3}=\frac{3x-1}{2}\cdot\frac{3}{3}+\frac{x+2}{3}\cdot\frac{2}{2}$$
$$=\frac{3(3x-1)+2(x+2)}{6}$$
$$=\frac{9x-3+2x+4}{6}$$
$$=\frac{11x+1}{6}$$

Since $\frac{3x-1}{2}+\frac{x+2}{3}=\frac{ax+b}{c}$, we know that

$$\frac{ax+b}{c}=\frac{11x+1}{6} \Rightarrow a=11, \ b=1, \ c=6$$

Therefore, $a+b+c=11+1+6=18$.

▶ 18

0215

The expression on the left can be simplified to:
$$(x-a)(2x+3)=2x^2+3x-2ax-3a$$
$$=2x^2+(3-2a)x-3a$$
Since $2x^2+(3-2a)x-3a=2x^2+bx-12$,
$$3a=12 \Rightarrow a=4$$
$$3-2a=b$$
$$3-2(4)=b \Rightarrow b=-5$$
Therefore, $a+b=4+(-5)=-1$.

▶ -1

0216

The expression on the left can be simplified to:
$$(3x+1)(x-2)=3x^2-6x+x-2$$
$$=3x^2-5x-2$$
Since $3x^2-5x-2=ax^2+bx+c$, we know that
$$a=3, \ b=-5, \ \text{and} \ c=-2$$
Therefore, $a+b+c=3+(-5)+(-2)=-4$.

▶ -4

0217

The given expression can be simplified to:
$$(x-3)(x^2-x+1)$$
$$=x^3-x^2+x-3x^2+3x-3$$
$$=x^3-4x^2+4x-3$$
Since $x^3-4x^2+4x-3=ax^3+bx^2+cx+d$, we know that
$$a=1, \ b=-4, \ c=4, \ \text{and} \ d=-3$$
Therefore, $a+b+c+d=1+(-4)+4+(-3)=-2$.

▶ -2

0218

$$(2x^2+ax-b)(4x+3)=8x^3+14x^2+2x-3$$
Expand only x term and constant term on the left side and then compare it with the right side.
For the term with x:
$$3ax-4bx=2x \Rightarrow 3a-4b=2$$

For the constant term:
$$-3b=-3 \Rightarrow b=1$$
Now, substitute 1 for b in equation $3a-4b=2$.
$$3a-4(1)=2$$
$$3a=6, \ a=2$$
Therefore, $a+b=2+1=3$.

▶ 3

0219

The expression on the left can be simplified to:
$$(x-3)(5x+a)=5x^2+ax-15x-3a$$
$$=5x^2+(a-15)x-3a$$
Since $5x^2+(a-15)x-3a=5x^2-11x+b$,
we know that
$$a-15=-11 \Rightarrow a=4$$
$$-3a=b$$
$$-3(4)=b \Rightarrow b=-12$$
Therefore, $b=-12$.

▶ -12

0220

$$5x^2-6x+3+(2x+1)(x-2)$$
$$=5x^2-6x+3+2x^2-4x+x-2$$
$$=7x^2-9x+1$$
Since $7x^2-9x+1=ax^2+bx+c$, we know that
$$a=7, \ b=-9 \ \text{and} \ c=1$$
Therefore, $a+b+c=7+(-9)+1=-1$.

▶ -1

0221

$$\left(\frac{2x}{3}-\frac{y}{5}\right)\left(\frac{2x}{3}+\frac{y}{5}\right)=\left(\frac{2x}{3}\right)^2-\left(\frac{y}{5}\right)^2$$
$$=\frac{4x^2}{9}-\frac{y^2}{25}$$
Since $x^2=3$ and $y^2=5$, we have
$$\left(\frac{2x}{3}-\frac{y}{5}\right)\left(\frac{2x}{3}+\frac{y}{5}\right)=\frac{4x^2}{9}-\frac{y^2}{25}$$

$$=\frac{4(3)}{9}-\frac{5}{25}=\frac{17}{15}$$

▶ $\frac{17}{15}$

Since $3+7\sqrt{3}=a+b\sqrt{c}$, the value of $a=3$.

▶ 3

0222

The expression on the right can be simplified to:

$(x+1)^2+m(x+1)+n$

$=x^2+2x+1+mx+m+n$

$=x^2+(2+m)x+(m+n+1)$

Since $x^2+4x+3=x^2+(2+m)x+(m+n+1)$, we know that

$4=2+m \Rightarrow m=2$

$3=m+n+1$

$3=2+n+1 \Rightarrow n=0$

▶ 0

0226

$9y^2-16x^4=(3y)^2-(4x^2)^2$

$\qquad =(3y-4x^2)(3y+4x^2)$

Since $3y-4x^2=-(4x^2-3y)=-2$,

$9y^2-16x^4=(3y-4x^2)(3y+4x^2)$

$\qquad -8=(-2)(3y+4x^2)$,

$\qquad 4=3y+4x^2$

Therefore, $3y+4x^2=4$.

▶ 4

0223

$x^2(x-y)+y^2(y-x)=x^2(x-y)-y^2(x-y)$

$\qquad =(x-y)(x^2-y^2)$

$\qquad =(x-y)(x-y)(x+y)$

$\qquad =(x-y)^2(x+y)$

$\qquad =(-3)^2(4)=36$

▶ 36

0227

$2x^3-18x=2x(x^2-9)$

$\qquad =2x(x-3)(x+3)$

Since $x+k$ is one of the factors of $2x^3-18x$ and k is a positive integer, the value of k must be 3.

▶ 3

0224

We know that $(a+b)^2=a^2+2ab+b^2$.

Therefore,

$a^2+b^2=(a+b)^2-2ab$

$\qquad =8^2-2(6)=52$

▶ 52

0228

$6x^3+5x^2-6x=x(6x^2+5x-6)$

$\qquad =x(3x-2)(2x+3)$

$\qquad =2x(3x-2)\left(x+\frac{3}{2}\right)$

Since $x+m$ is one of the factors of $6x^3+5x^2-6x$ and m is a positive constant, the value of m must be $\frac{3}{2}$.

▶ $\frac{3}{2}$

0225

$x^2-x-12=(x-4)(x+3)$

$\qquad =(\sqrt{3}+4-4)(\sqrt{3}+4+3)$

$\qquad =\sqrt{3}(\sqrt{3}+7)$

$\qquad =3+7\sqrt{3}$

0229

$x^2-y^2=(x-y)(x+y)$

We know that $x+y=(1-\sqrt{2})+(1+\sqrt{2})=2$ and

$x-y=(1-\sqrt{2})-(1+\sqrt{2})=-2\sqrt{2}$. So we have
$$x^2-y^2=(x-y)(x+y)$$
$$=-2\sqrt{2}\cdot2=-4\sqrt{2}$$
Since $x^2-y^2=a\sqrt{b}$, the value of b is 2.

▶ 2

0230

$$x^2-2xy+y^2=(x-y)^2$$
$$=(-2\sqrt{2})^2=8$$

▶ 8

2. Quadratic Equations

0231

(A) $x^2+4x+4=0$

$(x+2)^2=0$, $x=-2$

(B) $x^2+2x=0$

$x(x+2)=0$, $x=0$ or $x=-2$

(C) $2x^2+5x+2=0$

$(2x+1)(x+2)=0$, $x=-\dfrac{1}{2}$ or $x=-2$

(D) $2x^2-5x+2=0$

$(2x-1)(x-2)=0$, $x=\dfrac{1}{2}$ or $x=2$

Only (D) does NOT have $x=-2$ as the solution.

▶ D

0232

$$x^2-12x+36=0$$
$$(x-6)^2=0$$
$$x-6=0$$
The answer is (C).

▶ C

0233

Use the quadratic formula to find the solution.

$$x^2-3x+1=0 \rightarrow a=1,\ b=-3,\ c=1$$
$$x=\frac{-(-3)\pm\sqrt{(-3)^2-4(1)(1)}}{2(1)}$$
$$=\frac{3\pm\sqrt{9-4}}{2}=\frac{3\pm\sqrt{5}}{2}$$

The solutions are $x=\dfrac{3-\sqrt{5}}{2}$ and $x=\dfrac{3+\sqrt{5}}{2}$.

So the answer is (A).

▶ A

0234

Use the quadratic formula to find the solution.

$$2x^2-4x-1=0 \rightarrow a=2,\ b=-4,\ c=-1$$
$$x=\frac{-(-4)\pm\sqrt{(-4)^2-4(2)(-1)}}{2(2)}$$
$$=\frac{4\pm\sqrt{24}}{4}=\frac{4}{4}\pm\frac{2\sqrt{6}}{4}$$
$$=1\pm\frac{\sqrt{6}}{2}$$

Therefore, $abc=(1)(6)(2)=12$.

▶ B

0235

Given a quadratic equation $ax^2+bx+c=0$, the sum of the solutions is $-\dfrac{b}{a}$.

$$x^2+6x-6=0 \rightarrow a=1,\ b=6,\ c=-6$$

So the sum of the solutions is

$$-\frac{b}{a}=-\frac{6}{1}=-6$$

The answer is (A).

▶ A

Solutions Manual

0236

$$2(x+1)^2+3=15$$
$$2(x+1)^2=12$$
$$(x+1)^2=6$$
$$x+1=\pm\sqrt{6}, \ x=-1\pm\sqrt{6}$$

So the sum of the solutions is
$$(-1+\sqrt{6})+(-1-\sqrt{6})=-2$$
The answer is (B).

▶ B

0237

$$(2a-5)^2-7(2a-5)+10=0$$
Let $2a-5=A$. Then we have
$$A^2-7A+10=0$$
$$(A-2)(A-5)=0$$
$$A=2 \ \text{or} \ A=5$$
$$2a-5=2 \ \text{or} \ 2a-5=5$$
Since $5-2a=-(2a-5)$,
$$5-2a=-2 \ \text{or} \ 5-2a=-5$$
So the answer is (D).

▶ D

0238

Given a quadratic equation $ax^2+bx+c=0$, the sum of the solutions is $-\dfrac{b}{a}$.

(A) $x^2+4x=0 \ \Rightarrow \ -\dfrac{b}{a}=-\dfrac{4}{1}=-4$

(B) $x^2+x+3=0 \ \Rightarrow \ -\dfrac{b}{a}=-\dfrac{1}{1}=-1$

(C) $x^2-x+3=0 \ \Rightarrow \ -\dfrac{b}{a}=-\dfrac{-1}{1}=1$

(D) $(3-4x-x^2=0)\cdot(-1)$

$x^2+4x-3=0 \ \Rightarrow \ -\dfrac{b}{a}=-\dfrac{4}{1}=-4$

So, the equation for which the sum of the solutions is positive is (C).

▶ C

0239

Given a quadratic equation $ax^2+bx+c=0$,

the sum of the solutions is $-\dfrac{b}{a}$.

So the sum of the solutions of $2x^2-6x+9=0$ is
$$-\dfrac{b}{a}=-\dfrac{-6}{2}=3$$
Since this is one of the solutions of equation $5x^2+(a-2)x-3=0$, we substitute 3 for x in this equation.
$$5(3)^2+(a-2)(3)-3=0$$
$$45+3a-6-3=0$$
$$3a=36, \ a=12$$
So the answer is (D).

▶ D

0240

With the given information, we have the following equation.
$$x^2-2x=8$$
$$x^2-2x-8=0$$
$$(x+2)(x-4)=0$$
$$x+2=0 \ \text{or} \ x-4=0$$
$$x=-2 \ \text{or} \ x=4$$
The possible values of x are $x=-2$ and $x=4$.

▶ D

0241

Since $x=4$ is one of the solutions to the equation $x^2+4mx-4=0$, substitute 4 for x in this equation.
$$(4)^2+4m(4)-4=0$$
$$16+16m-4=0$$
$$16m=-12, \ m=-\dfrac{3}{4}$$
So the answer is (A).

▶ A

0242

Since $x=3$ is the solutions of both
$x^2-4x+m=0$ and $2x^2+nx-7=0$,
substitute 3 for x in these equations.

$$(3)^2-4(3)+m=0$$
$$9-12+m=0, \ m=3 \quad \text{and}$$
$$2(3)^2+n(3)-7=0$$
$$18+3n-7=0$$
$$3n=-11, \ n=-\frac{11}{3}$$

Therefore, $m+n=3+\left(-\frac{11}{3}\right)=-\frac{2}{3}$.

So the answer is (C).

▶ C

0243

To determine the number of distinct real solutions for the equation, we have to write the equation in standard form and use the discriminant.

$$(x-3)(x+2)=-2x(x-2)$$
$$x^2+2x-3x-6=-2x^2+4x$$
$$3x^2-5x-6=0$$

The discriminant D is

$$D=b^2-4ac$$
$$=(-5)^2-4(3)(-6)$$
$$=25+72>0$$

Since $D>0$, the equation has exactly two real solutions. So the answer is (C).

▶ C

0244

$$4x-8x+5=0$$

The discriminant D is

$$D=b^2-4ac$$
$$=(-8)^2-4(4)(5)$$
$$=64-80<0$$

Since $D<0$, the equation has no real solution. So the answer is (A).

▶ A

0245

$$4(x+3)(x-4)=\frac{1}{2}(2x+1)(x-2)+\frac{3}{2}x$$
$$4(x^2-x-12)=\frac{1}{2}(2x^2-3x-2)+\frac{3}{2}x$$
$$4x^2-4x-48=x^2-\frac{3}{2}x-1+\frac{3}{2}x$$
$$3x^2-4x-47=0 \ \Rightarrow \ a=3, \ b=-4, \ c=-47$$

Therefore,
$a+b+c=3+(-4)+(-47)=-48$
The answer is (D).

▶ D

0246

Since $f(x)=g(x)$, we have
$$8-2x^2=2x^2-8$$
$$-4x^2=-16$$
$$x^2=4, \ x=\pm2$$
So the answer is (C).

▶ C

0247

$$2x^2-16x=0$$
$$2x(x-8)=0$$
$$x=0 \text{ or } x=8$$

Since x is a positive integer, $x=8$ and the answer must be (C)

$$2\sqrt{2}x=2\sqrt{2(8)}=2\sqrt{16}=8$$

▶ C

Solutions Manual

0248

Solve the equation $2x^2 + mx - 4 = 0$ by using quadratic formula.

$$x = \frac{-m \pm \sqrt{m^2 - 4(2)(-4)}}{2(2)} = \frac{-m \pm \sqrt{m^2 + 32}}{4}$$

Since $x = \frac{1 \pm \sqrt{n}}{2} \cdot \frac{2}{2} = \frac{2 \pm 2\sqrt{n}}{4}$, $-m = 2$, $m = -2$.

So we have

$$2\sqrt{n} = \sqrt{(m)^2 + 32} \Rightarrow 2\sqrt{n} = \sqrt{(-2)^2 + 32}$$
$$2\sqrt{n} = 6$$
$$\sqrt{n} = 3, \ n = 9$$

Therefore, $m + n = -2 + 9 = 7$. The answer is (C).

▶ C

0249

$$\left(\frac{1}{2}x^2 + 4x - 3a = 0\right) \cdot (2)$$
$$x^2 + 8x - 6a = 0$$

Since the equation above has exactly one solution, the discriminant must be $D = 0$.

$$D = b^2 - 4ac$$
$$= 8^2 - 4(1)(-6a)$$
$$= 64 + 24a = 0$$
$$24a = -64$$

Dividing both equations by 8, we get $3a = -8$. So the answer is (C).

▶ C

0250

Equation $2x^2 - kx + 8 = 0$ has more than one real solution (actually exactly two) if the discriminant $D > 0$.

$$D = b^2 - 4ac$$
$$= (-k)^2 - 4(2)(8)$$
$$= k^2 - 64 > 0$$
$$k^2 > 64, \ |k| > 8$$

So the answer is (A).

▶ A

0251

Equation $5x^2 - kx + 4 = 0$ has more no real solution if the discriminant $D < 0$.

$$D = b^2 - 4ac$$
$$= (-k)^2 - 4(5)(4)$$
$$= k^2 - 80 < 0$$
$$k^2 < 80$$

So the answer is (D).

▶ D

0252

Equation $mx^2 - 4x - n = 0$ has exactly one real zero if the discriminant $D = 0$.

$$D = b^2 - 4ac$$
$$= (-4)^2 - 4(m)(-n)$$
$$= 16 + 4mn = 0$$
$$4mn = -16, \ mn = -4$$

So the values of m and n for which the equation has only one real zero are $m = 2$ and $n = -2$ of D.

▶ D

0253

I. $x^2 - x = x(x - 1)$

If the value of x is 0 or 1, then $x^2 - x = 0$, so $x^2 - x$ is NOT greater than 0 for all values of x.

II. $x^2 - 2x + 1 = (x - 1)^2$

If the value of x is 1, then $x^2 - 2x + 1 = 0$, so $x^2 - 2x + 1$ is NOT greater than 0 for all values of x.

III. $x^2 + x + 1 = x^2 + x + \frac{1}{4} - \frac{1}{4} + 1$

$$= \left(x + \frac{1}{2}\right)^2 + \frac{3}{4} > 0$$

The square of a number plus $\frac{3}{4}$ is always greater than zero. Therefore, $x^2 + x + 1 > 0$ for all real values x. So the answer is (C).

▶ C

0254

Equation $2x^2+24x+k=0$ has no real solution if the discriminant $D<0$.

$$D=b^2-4ac$$
$$=24^2-4(2)(k)$$
$$=576-8k<0$$
$$-8k<-576, \ k>72$$

Since $b<k$, the least possible value of b is 72. So the answer is (B).

▶ B

0255

Let x be the negative number. With the given information, we have the following equation.

$$x+x^2=6$$
$$x^2+x-6=0$$
$$(x+3)(x-2)=0, \ x=-3 \ \text{or} \ x=2$$

Since x is negative, the value of x must be -3. So the answer is (B).

▶ B

0256

Let x be the first odd integer. Then next odd integer is $x+2$ and we have the following equation.

$$x(x+2)=3(x+(x+2))+6$$
$$x^2+2x=3(2x+2)+6$$
$$x^2+2x=6x+12$$
$$x^2-4x-12=0$$
$$(x+2)(x-6)=0, \ x=-2 \ \text{or} \ x=6$$

Since we are looking for a positive integer, $x=6$. So the answer is (B).

▶ B

0257

Let x be the number. With the given information, we have the following equation.

$$\left(x+\frac{1}{x}\right)^2=4$$

We can check the solution by trial and error.

$$x=-1-\left(-1+\frac{1}{-1}\right)^2=(-2)^2=4$$
$$x=0-\left(0+\frac{1}{0}\right)^2=(0)^2=0\neq4$$
$$x=1; \ \left(1+\frac{1}{1}\right)^2=(2)^2=4$$

So the answer is (D).

▶ D

0258

Let x be the speed of Nick. Then, the speed of Jeff is $x+1$.

	Nick	Jeff
Speed	x	$x+1$
Time	2	2
Distance	$2x$	$2(x+1)$

By the Pythagorean Theorem, we have

$$(2x)^2+(2(x+1))^2=(2\sqrt{13})^2$$
$$4x^2+4x^2+8x+4=52$$
$$8x^2+8x-48=0$$
$$x^2+x-6=0$$
$$(x+3)(x-2)=0, \ x=-3 \ \text{or} \ x=2$$

Since $x>0$, $x=2$.

Since $x>0$, $x=2$. So Nick and Jeff's speeds are 2 and 3 miles per hour, respectively.

So the correct answer is (B).

▶ B

0259

Let x be the length of one side of the small square. Then, $x+2$ is length of one side of the large square. Since the sum of the areas of the two squares is 100 square inches, we have,

$$x^2+(x+2)^2=100$$
$$x^2+x^2+4x+4=100$$
$$2x^2+4x-96=0$$
$$x^2+2x-48=0$$
$$(x+8)(x-6)=0, \ x=-8 \text{ or } x=6$$

Since $x>0$, $x=6$. The sides of the small square and large square are 6 inches and 8 inches respectively. So the correct answer is (A).

▶ A

0260

When the ball hits the ground, the height of the ball is 0. So we have

$$-16x^2+28x=0$$
$$-4x(4x-7)=0, \ x=0 \text{ or } x=\frac{7}{4}$$

Since $x>0$, $x=\frac{7}{4}$. The ball hits the ground after $\frac{7}{4}$ seconds. So the answer is (B).

▶ B

0261

If the ball reaches 12 feet above the ground, we have

$$-16x^2+28x=12$$
$$16x^2-28x+12=0$$
$$4x^2-7x+3=0$$
$$(4x-3)(x-1)=0, \ x=\frac{3}{4} \text{ or } x=1$$

So the ball reaches 9 feet above the ground at $x=\frac{3}{4}$ (on the way up) and $x=1$ (on the way down). So the answer is (A).

▶ A

0262

Since the area of flower garden is 144 square meters, we have

$$(6+2x)(4+2x)-6\cdot4=144$$
$$24+20x+4x^2-24=144$$
$$4x^2+20x-144=0$$
$$x^2+5x-36=0$$
$$(x+9)(x-4)=0, \ x=-9 \text{ or } x=4$$

Since $x>0$, $x=4$. The width of the flower garden is 4 meters. The answer is (C).

▶ C

0263

Let t be the time it takes for the second bicycle to be 45 miles apart from the first bicycle. After one hour, the first bicycle has already traveled 6 miles south. Therefore, the distance between the two bicycles at time t is given by:

$$(8t)^2+(6(t+1))^2=45^2$$
$$64t^2+36(t^2+2t+1)=2025$$
$$64t^2+36t^2+72t+36=2025$$
$$100t^2+72t-1989=0$$

Using a graphing calculator, we have $t=4.114$ hours, which is approximately equal to 4 hours and 7 minutes. So the answer is (D).

▶ D

0264

Let x be the length of the side of the square.

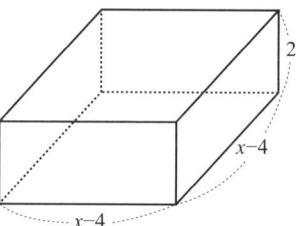

Since the volume of the box is
V=Base×Height, we have

$$(x-4)(x-4) \cdot 2 = 128$$
$$(x-4)^2 = 64$$
$$x-4 = \pm 8, \ x=-4 \text{ or } x=12$$

Since $x>0$, $x=12$. So the length of one side of the square is $x-4=12-4=8$ inches.

The answer is (B).

▶ B

0265

$$x^2+4x=32$$
$$x^2+4x-32=0$$
$$(x+8)(x-4)=0, \ x=-8 \text{ or } x=4$$

The value of the smaller solution subtracted from the larger solution is

$$4-(-8)=12$$

▶ 12

0266

$$(x+1)^2-4(x+1)-5=0$$

Let $x+1=A$. Then we have

$$A^2-4A-5=0$$
$$(A+1)(A-5)=0$$
$$A=-1 \text{ or } A=5$$
$$x+1=-1 \text{ or } x+1=5$$
$$x=-2 \text{ or } x=4$$

So the positive solution to the equation is 4.

▶ 4

0267

$$x^2-3x-10=0$$
$$(x-5)(x+2)=0, \ x=5 \text{ or } x=-2$$

Since k is positive solution of the equation above, the value of k must be 5.

▶ 5

0268

$$x^2-2x+a=0$$

Using the quadratic formula,

$$x=\frac{-(-2)\pm\sqrt{(-2)^2-4(1)(a)}}{2(1)}$$
$$=\frac{2\pm\sqrt{4-4a}}{2}=\frac{2\pm2\sqrt{1-a}}{2}$$
$$=1\pm\sqrt{1-a}$$

Since $x=1\pm\sqrt{7}$, we have

$$1-a=7, \ a=-6$$

▶ −6

0269

$$(x-2)(x+3)=2(x-2)(2x+1)$$
$$x^2+x-6=2(2x^2-3x-2)$$
$$x^2+x-6=4x^2-6x-4$$
$$3x^2-7x+2=0$$
$$(3x-1)(x-2)=0, \ x=\frac{1}{3} \text{ or } x=2$$

The other solution is $x=\frac{1}{3}$.

▶ $\frac{1}{3}$

0270

The equation $3x^2-6x-k=0$ has exactly one real solution if $D=0$.

$$D=b^2-4ac$$
$$=(-6)^2-4(3)(-k)$$
$$=36+12k=0$$
$$12k=-36, \ k=-3$$

▶ −3

0271

Equation $2x^2-14x+a=0$ has 2 real solutions if the discriminant $D>0$.

$$D=b^2-4ac$$

Solutions Manual

$= (-14)^2 - 4(2)(a)$
$= 196 - 8a > 0$
$-8a > -196, \ a < \dfrac{49}{2}$

Since $a < k$, the greatest possible value of k is $\dfrac{49}{2}$.

▶ $\dfrac{49}{2}$

0272

$3x^2 - 20x + 12 = 0$
$(3x-2)(x-6) = 0, \ x = \dfrac{2}{3}$ or $x = 6$

So the greater of the two solutions of the equation is 6.

▶ 6

0273

$x^4 - 9x^2 + 20 = 0$

Let $x^2 = A$. Then we have
$(x^2)^2 - 9(x^2) + 20 = 0$
$A^2 - 9A + 20 = 0$
$(A-5)(A-4) = 0$
$A - 5 = 0$ or $A - 4 = 0$
$x^2 - 5 = 0$ or $x^2 - 4 = 0$
$x = \pm\sqrt{5}$ or $x = \pm 2$

So the value of a must be equal to 5.

▶ 5

0274

If $a^2 = b^2$, then $|a| = |b| (a = \pm b$ or $\pm a = b)$.

So we have
$(x-4)^2 = (2x+3)^2$
$x - 4 = 2x + 3$ or $x - 4 = -(2x+3)$
(1) $x - 4 = 2x + 3, \ x = -7$
(2) $x - 4 = -(2x+3)$
$x - 4 = -2x - 3$
$3x = 1, \ x = \dfrac{1}{3}$

Therefore, the sum of the solutions is

$-7 + \dfrac{1}{3} = -\dfrac{20}{3}$

▶ $-\dfrac{20}{3}$

0275

$x^2 + 5x - 14 = 0$
$(x+7)(x-2) = 0, \ x = -7$ or $x = 2$

Therefore, $x = 2$ is the solution to the equation $5x^2 - 2x - a = 0$. Now, substitute $x = 2$ into the equation $5x^2 - 2x - a = 0$.
$5(2)^2 - 2(2) - a = 0$
$20 - 4 - a = 0$
$16 - a = 0, \ a = 16$

▶ 16

0276

Equation $2x^2 + 3ax + a + \dfrac{1}{8} = 0$ has only one real solution if the discriminant $D = 0$.
$D = b^2 - 4ac$
$= (3a)^2 - 4(2)\left(a + \dfrac{1}{8}\right)$
$= 9a^2 - 8a - 1 = 0$
$(a-1)(9a+1) = 0, \ a = 1$ or $a = -\dfrac{1}{9}$

Since $a > 0$, the value of a is 1.

▶ 1

0277

Let x the width of the rectangle. Since the length of the rectangle is twice its width, the formula for the area of a rectangle is given by:
$x \cdot 2x = 450$
$x^2 = 225, \ x = \pm 15$

Because the width cannot be negative, the width of the rectangle must be $x = 15$. Also, since the length is twice the width, the length would be 30. Therefore, the length of the rectangle is 30 meters.

▶ 30

0278

Let x and y be the length and width of the rectangle. We are given two pieces of information:

1. The area is $xy=36$

2. The perimeter is $2x+2y=30 \rightarrow y=15-x$

Now substitute $15-x$ for y. Then we have

$$x(15-x)=36$$
$$15x-x^2=36$$
$$x^2-15x+36=0$$
$$(x-12)(x-3)=0, \ x=12 \text{ or } x=3$$

Since the length is longer side of the rectangle while width is the shorter side, $x=3$ and $xy=(3)y=36$, $y=12$. So the width and length of the rectangle are 3 and 12 respectively. Therefore, the difference between the length and width of the rectangle is 9 centimeters.

▶ 9

0279

The equation given is:

$$3x^2-13x-10=0$$
$$(x-5)(3x+2)=0, \ x=5 \text{ or } x=-\frac{2}{3}$$

Since it is mentioned that $x>0$, the number of tickets David's family needs is $x=5$. Multiplying this by the cost per ticket (340), we get the total cost:

$$5\cdot340=1700$$

So the total cost of the tickets for David's family is $1700.

▶ 1700

0280

Let x be the number of students. Then, $x-5$ is the number of marbles each student receives. Since there are 300 marbles in total,

$$x(x-5)=300$$
$$x^2-5x-300=0$$
$$(x+15)(x-20)=0, \ x=-15 \text{ or } x=20$$

Since $x>0$, $x=20$. Therefore, the number of students in Christina's Algebra class is 20.

▶ 20

0281

When I opened the algebra book, the number of pages are two consecutive positive integers. So let x and $x+1$ be the number of two pages. Then, we have

$$x(x+1)=210$$
$$x^2+x-210=0$$
$$(x+15)(x-14)=0, \ x=-15 \text{ or } x=14$$

Since $x>0$, $x=14$. The number of pages on each page are 14 and 15. Therefore, we can conclude that the sum of the two pages is 29.

▶ 29

0282

Let x be the length of one side of the original square. Since the area of the resulting rectangle is 70 square inches, we have

$$(x+1)(x-2)=70$$
$$x^2-x-2=70$$
$$x^2-x-72=0$$
$$(x+8)(x-9)=0, \ x=-8 \text{ or } x=9$$

Since $x>0$, $x=9$. So the length of one side of the original square is 9 inches.

▶ 9

0283

Let x be the distance traveled by the bicycle heading east. Then the distance between the bicycles is $2x+3$.

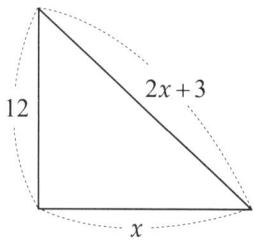

By the Pythagorean Theorem, we have
$$12^2+x^2=(2x+3)^2$$
$$144+x^2=4x^2+12x+9$$
$$3x^2+12x-135=0$$
$$x^2+4x-45=0$$
$$(x+9)(x-5)=0,\ x=-9\ \text{or}\ x=5$$

Since $x>0$, $x=5$. So the distance between two bicycles is $2x+3=2\cdot5+3=13$ miles.

▶ 13

3. Quadratic Functions

0284

To determine which point is not on the graph of the quadratic function $y=2x^2-3$, we can substitute the x and y values of each point into the equation and see if it holds true.

(A) $-3=2(0)^2-3,\ -3=-3$
(B) $-1=2(1)^2-3,\ -1=-1$
(C) $5=2(2)^2-3,\ 5=5$
(D) $1=2(-1)^2-3,\ 1\neq-1$

So the correct answer is (D).

▶ D

0285

To find the value of a in the quadratic

function $y=\left(\dfrac{9}{2}\right)x^2$, we need to substitute the

given point $(a,\ 72)$ into the equation and solve for "a"
$$72=\frac{9}{2}x^2$$
$$a^2=16,\ a^2=\pm4$$

Since a is a positive constant, the value of a is 4. So the answer is (C).

▶ C

0286

First, we need to substitute $x=-1$ and $f(x)=8$ into the equation $f(x)=a(x+3)^2-4$.
$$8=a(-1+3)^2-4$$
$$12=4a,\ a=3$$
So the equation of the function is
$$f(x)=3(x+3)^2-4$$
Now substitute $x=-4$ to find the value of $f(-4)$.
$$f(-4)=3(-4+3)^2-4=-1$$
So the answer is (B).

▶ B

0287

Substitute 3 for x and -6 for y to find a.

$y = ax^2$

$-6 = a(3)^2$, $-6 = 9a$, $a = -\dfrac{2}{3}$

So the function is $y = -\dfrac{2}{3}x^2$.

Now substitute the x and y values of each point into the equation and see if it holds true.

(A) $y(1) = -\dfrac{2}{3}(1)^2 = -\dfrac{2}{3}$

$\to \left(1, -\dfrac{2}{3}\right)$ is on the graph

(B) $y(2) = -\dfrac{2}{3}(2)^2 = -\dfrac{8}{3}$

$\to \left(2, \dfrac{8}{3}\right)$ is NOT on the graph

(C) $y(-3) = -\dfrac{2}{3}(-3)^2 = -6$

$\to (-3, -8)$ is NOT on the graph

(D) $y(-4) = -\dfrac{2}{3}(-4)^2 = -\dfrac{32}{3}$

$\to (-4, 10)$ is NOT on the graph

So the answer is (A)

▶ A

0288

Since the graph of $y = ax^2 + 5x - 2$ passes through $(-1, -3)$, we have

$-3 = a(-1)^2 + 5(-1) - 2$

$-3 = a - 5 - 2$, $a = 4$

So the value of a is 4. The answer is (D).

▶ D

0289

Since the quadratic function that has vertex$(-3, -2)$, the function is $y = a(x+3) - 2$. Now, we can substitute the $y-$intercept

$16(0, 16)$ into the equation and solve for a.

$16 = a(0+3)^2 - 2$

$18 = 9a$, $a = 2$

So the equation of the function is

$y = 2(x+3) - 2$

The answer is (C).

▶ C

0290

when the graph is shifted k units up, the shifted equation is $y = -\dfrac{1}{2}(x-1)^2 + k$. Since the graph passes through the point $(3, 4)$, we can substitute the x and y values of the given point into the equation

$y = -\dfrac{1}{2}(x-1)^2 + k$

$4 = -\dfrac{1}{2}(3-1)^2 + k$, $4 = -\dfrac{1}{2} \cdot 4 + k$

$4 = -2 + k$, $k = 6$

So the answer is (D).

▶ D

0291

The translation to the left by 1 unit corresponds to replacing x with $(x+1)$ in the equation, while the translation up by 2 units corresponds to adding 2 to the equation. So we have

$f(x) = -4x^2 \Rightarrow y = -4(x+1)^2 + 2$

The answer is (B)

▶ B

Solutions Manual

0292

In the graph of $y=a(x-h)^2+k$,

(1) The graph opens upward: $a>0$

(2) The vertex is in quadrant III: $h<0$, $k<0$

So the answer is (C).

▶ C

0293

In the graph of $f(x)=a(x-m)(x-n)$,

(1) The graph opens downward: $a<0$

(2) Since both h and k are positive, the axis of symmetry $\dfrac{m+n}{2}$ must be positive.

Therefore, it can be inferred that either m or n is positive or both are positive. Only the answer choice (C) satisfies (1) and (2) above. Therefore, the answer must be (C).

▶ C

0294

$a>0$: The graph opens upward.

$h>0$, $k<0$: The vertex is in quadrant IV.

So the correct answer is (B).

▶ B

0295

Subtracting 3 from the function shifts the graph downward by 3 units, maintaining the same shape and characteristics of the original graph. So the correct answer is (D).

▶ D

0296

The vertex of the function $y=3x^2-2$ is $(0, -2)$. So, if the graph is shifted 4 unit to the right and 2 units up, the coordinate of the vertex of the new function is

$$(0+4, -2+2) \Rightarrow (4, 0).$$

The answer is (C).

▶ C

0297

To find the value of "a" in the quadratic function with a vertex at $(2, 3)$ and x-intercepts at $(-1, 0)$ and $(a, 0)$, we can use the fact that the x-coordinate of the vertex is the average of the x-intercepts. So we have

$$\frac{-1+a}{2}=2$$

$$-1+a=4, \quad a=5$$

The answer is (C).

▶ C

0298

Given quadratic function has $(2, 3)$ as vertex. So we have $y=a(x-2)^2+3$. Now, since the graph passes through the point $(0, 2)$, we have

$$2=a(0-2)^2+3$$

$$-1=4a, \quad a=-\frac{1}{4}$$

Therefore, the equation of the function is

$$y=-\frac{1}{4}(x-2)^2+3$$

$$=-\frac{1}{4}(x^2-4x+4)+3$$

$$=-\frac{x^2}{4}+x+2$$

So the answer is (C).

▶ C

0299

The translation to the left by 3 units corresponds to replacing x with $(x+3)$ in the equation, while the translation up by 1 unit corresponds to adding 1 to the equation. So we have

$$y = -\frac{1}{4}(x-2)^2 + 3$$

$$\Rightarrow y = -\frac{1}{4}(x+3-2)^2 + 3 + 1$$

$$= -\frac{1}{4}(x+1)^2 + 4$$

So the answer is (C).

▶ C

0300

From the graph of $y = -2x^2 + 8x - 3$, the x-coordinate of the vertex of a quadratic function is

$$x = -\frac{b}{2a} = -\frac{8}{2}(-2) = 2$$

Now, to find the maximum value of the function, we substitute this x-coordinate back into the function:

$$y = -2(2)^2 + 8(2) - 3 = 5$$

So the answer is (B).

▶ B

0301

To find the distance between the two x-intercepts of the quadratic function $y = x^2 - x - 6$, we need to find the values of x where the function intersects the x-axis.

$$x^2 - x - 6 = 0$$

$$(x+2)(x-3) = 0, \ x = -2 \text{ or } x = 3$$

To find the distance between these two points, we subtract the smaller value from the larger value:

$$\text{Distance} = 3 - (-2) = 5$$

So the answer is (A).

▶ A

0302

(A) True because $a = 2 > 0$

(B) True

(C) True

(D) False because the graph is shifted 2 units to the right, NOT to the left.

So the answer is (D).

▶ D

0303

Since the vertex of the graph is $(-2, 1)$, we have $y = a(x+2)^2 + 1$. The graph passes through the point $(0, -3)$. By substituting the point, we have

$$y = a(x+2)^2 + 1$$

$$-3 = a(0+2)^2 + 1,$$

$$-3 = 4a + 1, \ a = -1$$

Therefore, the equation of the function is $y = -(x+2)^2 + 1$. The answer is (A).

▶ A

0304

(A) True

(B) True

(C) False. The range is the set of real numbers less than or equal to 1

(D) True

So the answer is (C).

▶ C

0305

The graph of a quadratic function has two zeros at $x=-1$ and $x=3$. So the equation is:

$y=a(x+1)(x-3)$

Since the graph passes through the point $(0, -3)$, we have

$-3=a(0+1)(0-3)$

$-3=-3a, \ a=1$

So the equation of the function is $y=(x+1)(x-3)$.

Now the $x=5$, the value of y is

$y=(5+1)(5-3)=12$

So the answer is (D).

▶ D

0306

If the discriminant D is negative, it means that the quadratic equation has no real roots, and the graph of the quadratic function does not intersect the x-axis.

$D=b^2-4ac=(-4)^2-4a(-5)$

$=16+20a<0$

$20a<-16, \ a<-\dfrac{4}{5}$

So the answer is (B).

▶ B

0307

Two zeros of the function $y=4x-x^2$ are

$0=4x-x^2$

$0=x(4-x), \ x=0$ and $x=4$

$\Rightarrow A(0, 0)$ and $C(4, 0)$

The axis of symmetry of function is at the midpoint of two zeros: $x=\dfrac{0+4}{2}=2$. So the maximum is

$y(2)=4(2)-(2)^2=4$

$\Rightarrow B(2, 4)$

Therefore, the area of triangle ABC is

$\dfrac{1}{2}\times 4\times 4=8$

The answer is (B).

▶ B

0308

The graph goes through the point $(0, 2)$.

So the value of k is 2. The answer is (A).

▶ A

0309

The graph above has one x-intercept at $x=3$. So the equation of the graph must be

$y=\dfrac{2}{9}(x-3)(x-3)$

$=\dfrac{2}{9}(x-3)^2$

Therefore, the value of a is 3. The answer is (B).

▶ B

0310

The graph opens downward: $a<0$

The vertex is in quadrant II: $h<0, \ k>0$

So the answer is (D).

▶ D

0311

If the graph intersects the x-axis at one point, the function has one zero and then the discriminant of the quadratic equation must be equal to zero.

$D=b^2-4ac$

$=(-6)^2-4(4)(b)=0$

$36-16b=0, \ -16b=-36, \ b=\dfrac{9}{4}$

So the answer is (D).

▶ D

0312

Since the graph of the quadratic function opens downward, $a<0$. Also, If the quadratic function has 1 real zero, it means that the discriminant

$D=b^2-4ac=0$. So the answer is (D).

▶ D

0313

Since the coefficient of x^2 is negative ($a=-1$), the graph of the quadratic function opens downward. To find the range, we need to determine the maximum point of this quadratic function. The x−coordinate of the vertex is

$$x=-\frac{b}{2a}=-\frac{5}{2(-1)}=\frac{5}{2}$$

Then the corresponding y−coordinate is

$$y=-\left(\frac{5}{2}\right)^2+5\left(\frac{5}{2}\right)+2=\frac{33}{4}$$

Therefore, the vertex of the quadratic function is $\left(\frac{5}{2}, \frac{33}{4}\right)$. Since the graph of the quadratic function opens downward, the range of the function is $y\leq\frac{33}{4}$. The answer is (C).

▶ C

0314

Since the parabola is symmetric about the line $x=-4$, the vertex of the parabola must lie on this line. Since the parabola passes through the origin $(0, 0)$, another x−intercept of this graph must be at $(-8, 0)$. Therefore, the correct answer is (A).

▶ A

0315

Since the parabola is symmetric about $x=2$ and passes through the point $(4, 2)$, it also passes through the point $(0, 2)$. So the answer is (B).

▶ B

0316

The graph of a quadratic function must open downward ($a<0$) to avoid points in either the first or second quadrant. Also, the graph must NOT have an x−intercept. That means the discriminant D is negative. Therefore, the correct answer is (C).

▶ C

0317

Since the graph of a quadratic function opens upward and has 2 real zeros, we know that $a>0$ and $D=b^2-4ac>0$. So the correct answer is (A).

▶ A

0318

Since x is the width of the rectangular garden, the length of the garden will be $28-2x$. To find the area A of the rectangular garden, we multiply the width by the length:

$$A(x)=x(28-2x)$$

So the answer is (A).

▶ A

0319

The vertex of the given equation

$g(t)=-16(t-2)^2+76$ is $(2, 76)$. Since $a=-16<0$, the graph of the parabola opens downwards. So, the best interpretation of the vertices in the graph is that the soccer ball's maximum value is 76 feet after 2 seconds. The correct answer is (C).

▶ C

Solutions Manual

0320

The graph of the quadratic function has its maximum at its vertex. The x−coordinate of the vertex is:

$$x = -\frac{b}{2a} = -\frac{12}{2\left(-\frac{1}{2}\right)} = 12$$

Now we can find the maximum daily profit by substituting x=12 into the profit function:

$$-\frac{(12)^2}{2} + 12(12) - 40 = 32$$

So the maximum daily profit is 32 hundred dollars ($3,200) when the factory produces 12 products. The correct answer is (A).

▶ A

0321

The x−coordinate of the vertex is:

$$t = -\frac{b}{2a} = -\frac{19.6}{2(-4.9)} = 2$$

Now, the maximum height of the ball is

$$h(2) = -4.9(2)^2 + 19.6(2) = 19.6$$

So the ball reaches its maximum height of 19.6 meters. The answer is (D).

▶ D

0322

To find the height from which the ball was thrown, we need to find the initial height when the time, t, is equal to zero.

$$h(0) = -16(0)^2 + 80(0) + 96 = 96$$

Therefore, the number that represents the height, in feet, from which the ball was thrown is 96 feet. Thus, the correct answer is (C)

▶ C

0323

To find the time when the ball hits the ground, we need to determine the value of t when the height, h, is equal to 0.

$$0 = -16t^2 + 80t + 96$$
$$0 = -16(t^2 - 5t - 6)$$
$$0 = -16(t+1)(t-6), \ t=-1 \text{ or } t=6$$

Since the time cannot be negative, the ball hits the ground after 6 seconds. So the answer is (A).

▶ A

0324

To find the time when the ball passes the top of the building on its way down, we need to determine the value of t when the height, h, is equal to 96 feet (the height of the building).

$$96 = -16t^2 + 80t + 96$$
$$0 = -16t^2 + 80t$$
$$0 = -16t(t-5), \ t=0 \text{ or } t=5$$

Therefore, the ball passes the top of the building on its way down after 5 seconds. The answer is (C).

▶ C

0325

The equation for the height of the object is

$$h(t) = -\frac{1}{2}(9.8)t^2 + (68.6)t + (6)$$
$$= -4.9t^2 + 68.6t + 6$$

To find the maximum height of the object, we need to determine the vertex of the parabola. The x−coordinate of the vertex is:

$$t = -\frac{b}{2a} = -\frac{68.6}{2(-4.9)} = 7$$

Now, the maximum height of the ball is

$$h(7) = -4.9(7)^2 + 68.6(7) + 6 = 246.1$$

Therefore, the maximum height of the object is approximately 246.1 meters. The correct answer is (A).

▶ A

0326

The number 8 represents the height of the baseball at $t=0$, which is the initial height at which the baseball was first thrown. So the correct answer is (A).

▶ A

0327

If the price is increased by $x per piece, the number of pieces sold per day decreases by $2x$. Therefore, the new revenue can be calculated as:

$$y=(5+x)(30-2x)$$

So the correct answer is (D).

▶ D

0328

Let's assume the rectangle has a width of $2x$ (twice the value of x) and a height of y (corresponding to the $y-$value on the curve). The area A of the rectangle is given by:

$A=2x\cdot y$, where $y=4-x^2$

Now, substitute $4-x^2$ for y in the equation $A=2x\cdot y$. Then we have

$$A=2x\cdot(4-x^2)$$
$$=8x-2x^3$$

Using the graphing calculator, the area is largest when $x=\dfrac{\sqrt{3}}{3}$. Substituting this value into x gives:

$$y=4-\left(\dfrac{\sqrt{3}}{3}\right)^2=\dfrac{8}{3}$$

So the dimensions $2x$ and y are $\dfrac{2\sqrt{3}}{3}$ and $\dfrac{8}{3}$.

The answer is (C).

▶ C

0329

Let x and h be the side length of the square base and the height of the box, respectively. Since the volume of the box is given as 6 cubic inches:

$$V=x^2h$$

$$6=x^2h \implies h=\dfrac{6}{x^2}$$

The cost of the base is $4 per square inch, and the area of the base is x^2:

Cost of the base $=4\cdot x^2=4x^2$

The cost of the sides is $2 per square inch, and there are four sides. The total area of the four sides is

Cost of the sides $=2\cdot 4xh=8xh$

The total cost C for the materials needed to make the box is:

$$C=4x^2+8xh$$

Now, substitute $\dfrac{6}{x^2}$ for h. Then we have

$$C=4x^2+8x\left(\dfrac{6}{x^2}\right)=4x^2+\dfrac{48}{x}$$

Using the graphing calculator, the minimum cost for the materials needed to make the box is approximately $40. So the answer is (B).

▶ B

0330

The vertex is given as $(2, 5)$, so the equation becomes

$$f(x)=a(x-2)^2+5$$

To find the value of 'a', we can substitute the given point $(3, 3)$ into the equation.

$$3=a(3-2)^2+5$$
$$3=a+5, \ a=-2$$

Therefore, the equation is

$$f(x)=-2(x-2)^2+5$$

The answer is (B).

▶ B

0331

Substitute -2 for x and 32 for y to find at.

$$y=ax^2$$
$$32=a(-2)^2, \ 32=4a, \ a=8$$

Now, substitute $\dfrac{1}{2}$ for x and b for y to

find b.
$$y=8x^2$$
$$b=8\cdot\left(\frac{1}{2}\right)^2,\ b=2$$
Therefore, $a+b=8+2=10$.

▶ 10

0332

The shifted equation is $y=2(x-3)^2$.
By substituting $(a,\ 8)$, we have
$$y=2(x-3)^2$$
$$8=2(a-3)^2,\ 4=(a-3)^2$$
$$a-3=\pm2,\ a=5 \text{ or } a=1$$

▶ 1 or 5

0333

The function $y=-3x^2-6x+m+1$ has the axis of symmetry at
$$x=-\frac{b}{2a}=-\frac{-6}{2(-3)}=-1$$
Since the graph opens downward, the maximum value is $y(-1)$. So we have
$$y(-1)=-3(-1)^2-6(-1)+m+1$$
$$12=-3+6+m+1,\ m=8$$
Therefore, the value of m is 8.

▶ 8

0334

Since the graph passes through $(-2,\ 6)$, substitute -2 for x and 6 for y to find a.
$$y=ax^2$$
$$6=a(-2)^2,\ 6=4a,\ a=\frac{3}{2}$$
Now, substitute 4 for x and m for y to find m.
$$y=\frac{3}{2}x^2,\ m=\frac{3}{2}\cdot(4)^2=24$$
Therefore, the value of m is 24.

▶ 24

0335

We are given that the quadratic function intersects the $x-$axis at $(-6,\ 0)$ and $(2,\ 0)$. So the $x-$coordinate value of this graph's symmetry line is the midpoint of these two $x-$intercepts:
$$x=\frac{-6+2}{2}=-2$$
Therefore, the value of the $x-$coordinate is -2.

▶ -2

0336

Two zeros of the function $y=6x-x^2$ are
$$0=6x-x^2$$
$$0=x(6-x),\ x=0 \text{ and } x=6$$
$$\Rightarrow A(0,\ 0) \text{ and } C(6,\ 0)$$
The axis of symmetry of function is at the midpoint of two zeros: $x=\frac{0+6}{2}=3$. So the maximum is
$$y(3)=4(3)-(3)^2=9$$
$$\Rightarrow B(3,\ 9)$$
Therefore, the area of triangle ABC is
$$\frac{1}{2}\times6\times9=27$$

▶ 27

0337

Substitute $x-h$ into x and add k to the equation.
$$y=5(x+2)^2-1$$
$$\Rightarrow y=5(x-h+2)^2-1+k$$
The shifted function is the same as the function $y=5(x-1)^2-4$. So we have
$$x-h+2=x-1,\ h=3$$
$$-1+k=-4,\ k=-3$$
Therefore, $h+k=3+(-3)=0$.

▶ 0

0338

The axis of symmetry of $y=-\frac{1}{2}x^2-6x+k$ is

$$x=-\frac{b}{2a}=-\frac{-6}{2\left(-\frac{1}{2}\right)}=-6$$

Since the axis of symmetry is the midpoint of two zeros, the graph passes through $(-2,\,0)$ and $(-10,\,0)$ as shown below.

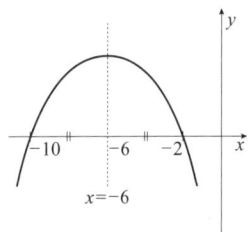

Now, by substituting $(-2,\,0)$ into the function, we have

$$0=-\frac{1}{2}(-2)^2-6(-2)+k$$

$$0=-2+12+k,\ \ k=-10$$

Therefore, the value of the $k=-10$.

▶ -10

0339

Let x be the smaller of two numbers. Then, the larger number is $x+6$. Also, let y be the product of these two numbers. Then we have

$$y=x(x+6)$$

Since $y=x(x+6)$ has two zeros $x=0$ and $x=-6$, the axis of symmetry is

$$x=\frac{0+(-6)}{2}=-3 \text{ and}$$

$$y(-3)=-3(-3+6)=-9.$$

Therefore, the product of two numbers, the value of y, is the minimum when the smaller number x is -3.

▶ -3

0340

Let x be the width of the henhouse. Then, the length is $50-2x$, as shown in Figure below.

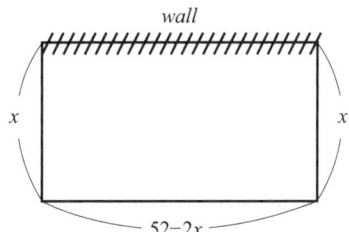

If we let y be the area of the henhouse, then we have

$$y=x(52-2x)$$

$$=-2x^2+52x$$

The axis of symmetry is

$$x=-\frac{b}{2a}=-\frac{52}{2(-2)}=13$$

The area of the henhouse is maximum when $x=13$, which is equal to:

$$y(13)=-2(13)^2+52(13)=338$$

Therefore, the maximum area of the henhouse is 338 square inches.

▶ 338

0341

In addition to using the axis of symmetry, you can use perfect squares to find the minimum or maximum. Let $h=xy$. Since $x+2y=12$, we have

$$2y=12-x,\ \ y=6-\frac{x}{2}$$

By substituting $y=6-\frac{x}{2}$ into $h=xy$, we have

$$h=xy=x\left(6-\frac{x}{2}\right)$$

$$=-\frac{1}{2}x^2+6x$$

$$=-\frac{1}{2}\left(x^2-12x+6^2-6^2\right)$$

$$=-\frac{1}{2}(x-6)^2+18$$

So the maximum value of xy is 18.

▶ 18

Solutions Manual

0342

Let $h=2xy$. Since $2x-y=4$,
we have $y=2x-4$.
By substituting $y=2x-4$ into $h=2xy$,
we have
$$h=2xy=2x(2x-4)$$
$$=4(x^2-2x)$$
$$=4(x^2-2x+1^2-1^2)$$
$$=4(x-1)^2-4$$
So the minimum value of $2xy$ is -4.

▶ -4

0343

To find the maximum height of the object, we need to determine the vertex of the parabola.
The $t-$coordinate of the vertex is:
$$t=-\frac{b}{2a}=-\frac{80}{2(-16)}=\frac{5}{2}$$
So the ball reaches its maximum height after $\frac{5}{2}$ seconds.

▶ $\frac{5}{2}$

0344

The length and width of the new rectangle is $10-x$ and $6+x$, respectively. If we let y be the area of the new rectangle, then we have
$$y=(10-x)(6+x)$$
$$=-x^2+4x+60$$
$$=-(x^2-4x+2^2-2^2)+60$$
$$=-(x-2)^2+64$$
So the maximum area of the new rectangle is 64.

▶ 64

0345

Let x and h be the base and height of the triangle, respectively. Also, let y be the area of the triangle
Then, we have
$x+h=16$, $h=16-x$ and
$$y=\frac{1}{2}xh=\frac{1}{2}x(16-x)$$
$$=-\frac{1}{2}x^2+8x$$
$$=-\frac{1}{2}(x^2-16x+8^2-8^2)$$
$$=-\frac{1}{2}(x-8)^2+32$$

▶ 32

0346

Let x be the larger of the two numbers Then, the other number is $x-6$. If y is the product of these two numbers, we have
$$y=x(x-6)=x^2-6x+3^2-3^2$$
$$=(x-3)^2-9$$
y is minimum when $x=3$.

▶ 3

0347

If Jason drops the price by \$$x$ per product, the price of the product is $8-x$ and the number of products sold each day is $12+2x$.
If y is profit, then we have
$$y=(8-x)(12+2x)$$
$$=-2x^2+4x+96$$
$$=-2(x^2-2x+1^2-1^2)+96$$
$$=-2(x-1)^2+2+96$$
$$=-2(x-1)^2+98$$
The value of y is maximum when x is 1. So the profit is maximized when the price of the product is $8-x=8-1=\$7$.

▶ 7

Since $y > x$, $x = 1$ and $y = 4$. So the value of $x + y = 1 + 4 = 5$. So the answer is D.

▶ D

4. Exponentials and Radicals

0348

A given radical expression can be expressed in base 2 or base 4.

Base 4: $16\sqrt[3]{4} = 4^2 \cdot 4^{\frac{1}{3}} = 4^{2+\frac{1}{3}} = 4^{\frac{7}{3}}$

Base 2: $4^{\frac{7}{3}} = (2^2)^{\frac{7}{3}} = 2^{\frac{14}{3}}$

So the correct answer is (D).

▶ D

0349

$$4^{\frac{1}{5}}\sqrt[3]{2} = (2^2)^{\frac{1}{5}} \cdot 2^{\frac{1}{3}} = 2^{\frac{2}{5}} \cdot 2^{\frac{1}{3}}$$
$$= 2^{\frac{2}{5}+\frac{1}{3}} = 2^{\frac{11}{15}}$$

The answer is (B).

▶ B

0350

$$8^{\frac{4}{3}} = (2^3)^{\frac{4}{3}} = 2^4 = 16$$

The answer is (B).

▶ B

0351

$$k^{\frac{5}{4}} = k^{\frac{5}{4} \cdot \frac{5}{5}} = k^{\frac{25}{20}} = \sqrt[20]{k^{25}}$$

The answer is (C).

▶ C

0352

We can have two possible expressions for $a^{\frac{7}{3}}$.

(1) $a^{\frac{7}{3}} = a^{1+\frac{4}{3}} = a^1 \cdot a^{\frac{4}{3}} = a \cdot \sqrt[3]{a^4} \Rightarrow x = 1, \ y = 4$

(2) $a^{\frac{7}{3}} = a^{2+\frac{1}{3}} = a^2 \cdot a^{\frac{1}{3}} = a^2 \cdot \sqrt[3]{a} \Rightarrow x = 2, \ y = 1$

0353

$$3^{-\frac{3}{4}} = \frac{1}{3^{\frac{3}{4}}} = \frac{1}{\sqrt[4]{3^3}} = \frac{1}{\sqrt[4]{27}}$$

The answer is (C).

▶ C

0354

$$3^{\frac{2}{n}}\sqrt[n]{5} = 3^{\frac{2}{n}} \cdot 5^{\frac{1}{n}} = (3^2 \cdot 5)^{\frac{1}{n}} = 45^{\frac{1}{n}}$$

or $45^{\frac{1}{n}} = \sqrt[n]{45}$

The answer is (B).

▶ B

0355

$$\left(\frac{1}{\sqrt[3]{b}}\right)^m = \left(\frac{1}{b^{\frac{1}{3}}}\right)^m = \left(b^{-\frac{1}{3}}\right)^m = b^{-\frac{m}{3}}$$

The answer is (B).

▶ B

0356

$$\frac{(a^{3-b})^2}{a^6} = \frac{a^{6-2b}}{a^6} = a^{6-2b-6} = a^{-2b} = \frac{1}{a^2b}$$

The answer is (D).

▶ D

0357

$$a^{\frac{3}{4}}b^{\frac{1}{2}} = a^{\frac{3}{4}}b^{\frac{2}{4}} = (a^3 b^2)^{\frac{1}{4}} = \sqrt[4]{a^3 b^2}$$

The answer is (B).

▶ B

Solutions Manual

0358

We can have two different equations from

$3^x = 9^y = \dfrac{1}{81}$.

$$3^x = \dfrac{1}{81} \qquad\qquad 9^y = \dfrac{1}{81}$$

$$3^x = \dfrac{1}{3^4} \quad \text{and} \quad 9^y = \dfrac{1}{9^2}$$

$$3^x = 3^{-4},\ x = -4 \qquad 9^y = 9^{-2},\ y = -2$$

Therefore, the value of
$x - y = (-4) - (-2) = -2$.
So the answer is (B).

▶ B

0359

$$\sqrt[3]{0.024} = \sqrt[3]{\dfrac{24}{1000}} = \sqrt[3]{\dfrac{3}{125}} = \sqrt[3]{\dfrac{3}{5^3}} = \dfrac{1}{5}\sqrt[3]{3}$$

Since $\sqrt[3]{0.024} = a\sqrt[3]{b}$, $a = \dfrac{1}{5}$ and $b = 3$.

So the value of $\dfrac{b}{a} = \dfrac{3}{\dfrac{1}{5}} = 15$.

So the answer is (A).

▶ A

0360

$$\sqrt{360} = \sqrt{2^3 \times 3^2 \times 5} = \sqrt{2^3} \times \sqrt{3^2} \times \sqrt{5}$$
$$= (\sqrt{2})^3 \times (\sqrt{3})^2 \times \sqrt{5}$$
$$= a^3 \times b^2 \times c = a^3 b^2 c$$

▶ D

0361

$$2^n + 2^{n+1} = 2^n + 2^n \cdot 2$$
$$= 2^n(1+2) = 3 \cdot 2^n$$

Since $2^n + 2^{n+1} = k$, we have

$$2^n + 2^{n+1} = k$$
$$3 \cdot 2^n = k,\ 2^n = \dfrac{k}{3}$$

So the value of 2^{n+2} in terms of k is

$$2^{n+2} = 2^n \cdot 2^2 = \left(\dfrac{k}{3}\right) \cdot 4 = \dfrac{4k}{3}$$

Therefore, the answer is (D).

▶ D

0362

Use the FOIL method to multiply binomials.
$$(1 + 2\sqrt{2})(1 - \sqrt{2}) = 1 - \sqrt{2} + 2\sqrt{2} - 4$$
$$= -3 + \sqrt{2}$$
The answer is (B).

▶ B

0363

Remember $(x-y)^2 = x^2 - 2xy + y^2$.
$$(\sqrt{3} - 2\sqrt{7})^2 = 3 - 4\sqrt{21} + 28$$
$$= 31 - 4\sqrt{21}$$
Since $(\sqrt{3} - 2\sqrt{7})^2 = a + b\sqrt{c}$, $a = 31$, $b = -4$, and $c = 21$.
Therefore, the value of
$a + b + c = 31 + (-4) + 21 = 48$.
So the answer is (D).

▶ D

0364

Use the FOIL method to multiply binomials.
$$(\sqrt{x} - 1)(2 - \sqrt{x}) = 2\sqrt{x} - x - 2 + \sqrt{x}$$
$$= 3\sqrt{x} - x - 2$$
The answer is (D).

▶ D

0365

$$\dfrac{\sqrt{2}}{\sqrt{3} - 2} = \dfrac{\sqrt{2}}{\sqrt{3} - 2} \cdot \dfrac{\sqrt{3} - 2}{\sqrt{3} + 2}$$
$$= \dfrac{\sqrt{6} - 2\sqrt{2}}{3 - 4} = -\sqrt{6} - 2\sqrt{2}$$

The answer is (D).

▶ D

0366

$$(\sqrt{2}a+\sqrt{2}b)^2=2a+2(\sqrt{2a}\cdot\sqrt{2b})+2b$$
$$=2a+4\sqrt{ab}+2b$$

The answer is (C).

▶ C

0367

$$(\sqrt{a}-\sqrt{2}y)^{\frac{2}{3}}=\left((\sqrt{a}-\sqrt{2}y)^2\right)^{\frac{1}{3}}$$
$$=\left(a-2\sqrt{a}\sqrt{2}y+2y\right)^{\frac{1}{3}}$$
$$=\sqrt[3]{a-2\sqrt{2ay}+2y}$$

The answer is (D).

▶ D

0368

Let x be a positive real number. Then, the product of the square root of x and its reciprocal can be written as:

$$\sqrt{x}\cdot\frac{1}{\sqrt{x}}=1$$

Therefore, the product of the square root of a positive real number and its reciprocal is always equal to 1. The answer is (B).

▶ B

0369

Let's substitute the given x and $f(x)$ values into the equation and create a system of equations.
When $x=0$: $f(0)=ab^0=a=3$.
When $x=1$: $f(1)=ab^1=3b=6$, $b=2$
So the value of $a+b=3+2=5$.

The answer is (B).

▶ B

0370

The graph passes through $(0, 4)$. Let's substitute this point into the equation $y=3^{a-x}+1$.
$(0, 4)$: $4=3^{a-0}+1$, $3=3^a$, $a=1$
So the answer is (B).

▶ B

0371

The equation of the graph is $y=3^{1-x}+1$. Now substitute y=0 to find the x-intercept.
$0=3^{1-x}+1$, $-1=3^{1-x}$
Since $3^{1-x}>0$ for all x, there is no x value such that $3^{1-x}=-1$. Therefore, the graph has no x-intercept.

▶ D

0372

In the graph above, the graph passes through $(0, 3)$, so the y-intercept is 3. So the correct answer is (C).

▶ C

0373

Since the graph passes through $(0, 3)$ and $\left(1, \frac{7}{4}\right)$, the equation must be true when the value of the point is substituted. For (D)

$$y=\left(\frac{3}{2}\right)^x+2,$$

$(0, 3)$: $y(0)=\left(\frac{3}{2}\right)^0+2=1+2=3$

$(0, 3)$: $y(1)=\left(\frac{3}{2}\right)^1+2=\frac{3}{2}+\frac{4}{2}=\frac{7}{2}$

Therefore, the correct answer is (D).

▶ D

Solutions Manual

0374

Let's substitute the $(2, 4)$ into the equation $y=a^x$.

$4=a^2$, $a=2$

Now substitute $\left(k, \dfrac{1}{8}\right)$ into the equation $y=2^x$.

$\dfrac{1}{8}=2^k$, $2^{-3}=2^k$, $k=-3$

So the value of k is -3. The answer is (C).

▶ C

0375

Since $f(4)=\dfrac{16}{81}$, we have

$\dfrac{16}{81}=a^4$, $\dfrac{2^4}{3^4}=a^4$, $\left(\dfrac{2}{3}\right)^4=a^4$, $a=\dfrac{2}{3}$

So $f(x)=\left(\dfrac{2}{3}\right)^x$ and the value of

$f(6)=\left(\dfrac{2}{3}\right)^6\approx0.088$

So the answer is (B).

▶ B

0376

$g(2)=4(1.5)^{2+1}=4(1.5)^3=13.5$

The answer is (C).

▶ C

0377

$2^{2x-3}-32=0$

$2^{2x-3}=32$

$2^{2x-3}=2^5 \Rightarrow 2x-3=5$, $x=4$

The answer is (A).

▶ A

0378

$64^{2x+1}=\dfrac{1}{256}$

$(4^3)^{2x+1}=\dfrac{1}{4^4}$

$4^{6x+3}=4^{-4} \Rightarrow 6x+3=-4$, $x=-\dfrac{7}{6}$

The answer is (B).

▶ B

0379

$a^b=c^d$

$(a^b)^{\frac{1}{d}}=(c^d)^{\frac{1}{d}}$, $a^{\frac{b}{d}}=c$

The answer is (A).

▶ A

0380

$\sqrt{(2x+1)^2}=5$

$|2x+1|=5$

$2x+1=5$ or $2x+1=-5$

$x=2$ or $x=-3$

Check the solutions.

$x=2$: $\sqrt{(2(2)+1)^2}=\sqrt{25}=5$

$x=-3$: $\sqrt{(2(-3)+1)^2}=\sqrt{25}=5$

Therefore, both $x=2$ and $x=-3$ are solutions to the equation. The answer is (D).

▶ D

0381

$\sqrt{x-3}-x=-5$

$\sqrt{x-3}=x-5$

$(\sqrt{x-3})^2=(x-5)^2$

$x-3=x^2-10x+25$

$x^2-11x+28=0$

$(x-4)(x-7)=0$, $x=4$ or $x=7$

Check the solutions.

$x=4$: $\sqrt{4-3}-4=1-4=-3\neq-5$
$x=7$: $\sqrt{7-3}-7=2-7=-5$
Therefore, only $x=7$ is a solution to the equation. The answer is (B).

▶ B

0382

This can be checked by substituting each x value in the given answer choices.
(A) $\sqrt{(3-4)^2}=3-4$, $\sqrt{1}=-1$ $\Rightarrow$ $1\neq-1$
(B) $\sqrt{(4-4)^2}=4-4$, $\sqrt{0}=0$ $\Rightarrow$ $0=0$
(C) $\sqrt{(5-4)^2}=5-4$, $\sqrt{1}=1$ $\Rightarrow$ $1=1$
(D) $\sqrt{(6-4)^2}=6-4$, $\sqrt{4}=2$ $\Rightarrow$ $2=2$
So the correct answer is (A).

▶ A

0383

Notice that the expression $\sqrt{2x-k}\geq0$, but $k<0$. Therefore, there is no solution for $\sqrt{2x-k}=k$. The correct answer is (A).

▶ A

0384

The given information states that the value of $f(x)$ increases by 0.2% for every increase in x by 1. This exponential growth is given by
$$f(x)=50(1+0.002)^x=50(1.002)^x$$
where $f(0)=50$ represents the initial value of the function. Therefore, the answer is (D).

▶ D

0385

The equation that models the number of bacteria y in a culture after x hours can be obtained by considering the initial number of bacteria (100) and the growth

rate of 9% per hour. This exponential growth is given by
$$y=100(1+0.09)^x=100(1.09)^x$$
Therefore, the answer is (C).

▶ C

0386

Exponential growth implies that the value of the antique is increasing at an increasing rate over time. The answer choice (C) states that the value of the antique increases by 6% each year compared to the previous year. This represents exponential growth, where the value is multiplied by a constant factor (1.06 in this case) each year. Therefore, the answer is (C).

▶ C

0387

To determine the growth factor over a century, we need to consider the growth factor for each decade. Since the population grows by 5% each decade, the growth factor for a decade is $1+0.05=1.05$. To find the growth factor for a century, we need to multiply the growth factor for a decade by itself 10 times:
Growth factor for a century$=(1.05)^{10}\approx1.63$
Therefore, the answer is (C).

▶ C

0388

In the given function $S(t)=2,000(1.02)^{\frac{t}{2}}$, the best interpretation of the number 1.02 in this context is that the model predicts that the number of squirrels grows by approximately 2% every two years. Therefore, the answer is (D).

▶ (D)

0389

To find the equation that best models the number of squirrels m months after 2022, we need to convert the given function from years to months. Therefore, we need to divide t by 12 to represent the time in months.

$$S(m) = 2{,}000(1.02)^{\frac{m-12}{2}}$$

$$= 2{,}000(1.02)^{\frac{m}{24}}$$

So the correct answer is (C).

▶ C

0390

Let x be the annual percentage decrease in truck value. Then, the equation that models the value of truck y after t years is given by:

$$y = 28{,}000\left(1 - \frac{x}{100}\right)^t$$

If the value of a new truck was $28,000
5 years ago and it has been halved by now, we have

$$14000 = 28000\left(1 - \frac{x}{100}\right)^5$$

$$0.5 = \left(1 - \frac{x}{100}\right)^5, \ 0.5^{\frac{1}{5}} = 1 - \frac{x}{100}$$

$$\frac{x}{100} = 1 - 0.5^{\frac{1}{5}}, \ x = 100\left(1 - 0.5^{\frac{1}{5}}\right) \approx 12.9$$

Therefore, the annual percent decrease over the last 5 years is about 13%. The answer is (D).

▶ D

0391

Comparing the values of the two functions, we see that they are equal for both $x=0$ and $x=2$. On this interval $0 < x < 2$, the exponential function is less than the linear function. Therefore, the correct statement is (D).

▶ D

0392

$$2^{\frac{3}{2}} \cdot 3 = \sqrt{x}$$

$$\left(2^{\frac{3}{2}} \cdot 3\right)^2 = (\sqrt{x})^2$$

$$2^3 \cdot 3^2 = x, \ x = 72$$

▶ 72

0393

$$\left(\sqrt[3]{a^2}\right)^n = a^{12}, \ \left(a^{\frac{2}{3}}\right)^n = a^{12}$$

$$a^{\frac{2n}{3}} = a^{12} \quad \Rightarrow \quad \frac{2n}{3} = 12, \ n = 18$$

▶ 18

0394

$$\sqrt[3]{2 \cdot 5^2} = \left(2 \cdot 5^2\right)^{\frac{1}{3}} = 2^{\frac{1}{3}} \cdot 5^{\frac{2}{3}}$$

$$\Rightarrow a = \frac{1}{3}, \ b = \frac{2}{3}$$

Therefore, $a + b = \frac{1}{3} + \frac{2}{3} = 1$.

▶ 1

0395

$$(\sqrt{2} - \sqrt{3})(\sqrt{2} + \sqrt{3}) = (\sqrt{2})^2 - (\sqrt{3})^2$$

$$= 2 - 3 = -1$$

▶ −1

0396

$$\frac{1}{1 + \sqrt{2}} \cdot \frac{1 - \sqrt{2}}{1 + \sqrt{2}} = \frac{1 - \sqrt{2}}{1 - 2}$$

$$= -1 + \sqrt{2} \Rightarrow a = -1, \ b = 2$$

Therefore, $a + b = -1 + 2 = 1$.

▶ 1

0397

$$\sqrt{4-2xy}=x-y$$
$$(\sqrt{4-2xy})^2=(x-y)^2$$
$$4-2xy=x^2-2xy+y^2$$
$$4=x^2+y^2$$

Therefore, $x^2+y^2=4$.

▶ 4

0398

$$9\sqrt{27}=3^2\sqrt{3^3}=3^2\cdot3^{\frac{3}{2}}=3^{2+\frac{3}{2}}=3^{\frac{7}{2}}$$

Since $3^{x+1}=3^{\frac{7}{2}}$, we have

$$x+1=\frac{7}{2},\ x=\frac{5}{2}$$

▶ $\frac{5}{2}$

0399

$$2^{1-2x}=4^{1+2x},\ 2^{1-2x}=(2^2)^{1+2x}$$
$$2^{1-2x}=2^{2+4x}\ \Rightarrow\ 1-2x=2+4x,\ x=-\frac{1}{6}$$

▶ $-\frac{1}{6}$

0400

$$2^{x^2-4x}=\left(\frac{1}{2}\right)^{x+2},\ 2^{x^2-4x}=(2^{-1})^{x+2}$$
$$2^{x^2-4x}=2^{-x-2}$$
$$\Rightarrow\ x^2-4x=-x-2$$
$$x^2-3x+2=0$$
$$(x-1)(x-2)=0,\ x=1\ \text{or}\ x=2$$

▶ 1 or 2

0401

$$(x^2)^3\times(xy^2)^4\times x^3y=x^6\times x^4\ y^8\times x^3y$$
$$=x^{6+4+3}y^{8+1}$$
$$=x^{13}\ y^9\ \Rightarrow a=13,\ b=9$$

Therefore, $a-b=13-9=4$.

▶ 4

0402

$$3^x+3^x+3^x=3^{2x-1}$$
$$3\cdot3^x=3^{2x-1}$$
$$3^{1+x}=3^{2x-1}\ \Rightarrow\ 1+x=2x-1,\ x=2$$

▶ 2

0403

Substitute $x=0$ to find the $y-$intercept.

$$f(0)=4(5)^{2(0)}-3$$
$$=4-3=1$$

▶ 1

0404

Let's simplify the given function f.

$$f(x)=4\left(\frac{1}{2}\right)^{x-h}+k$$
$$=2^2(2^{-1})^{x-h}+k=2^2\cdot2^{-x+h}+k$$

Solve each equation for k by substituting the two points $(0,\ 18)$ and $(1,\ 1)$ into the given equation.

$$(0,\ 18):\ f(0)=2^2\cdot2^{-0+h}+k=18$$
$$k=18-2^2\cdot2^h$$
$$(1,\ 10):\ f(1)=2^2\cdot2^{-1+h}+k=10$$
$$k=10-2^2\cdot2^h$$

Now, by equating the two expressions for k and solving, we can find the value of h.

$$18-2^2\cdot2^h=10-2\cdot2^h$$
$$18-4\cdot2^h=10-2\cdot2^h$$
$$8=2\cdot2^h,\ 2^h=4,\ h=2$$

Finally, substitute $h=2$ into $k=10-2\cdot2^h$ to find the value of k.

$$k=10-2\cdot2^2=2$$

Therefore, the value of $hk=2\cdot2=4$.

▶ 4

0405

Substitute $(2, 4)$ into $y=a^{x-1}+2$.

$4=a^{2-1}+2$, $a=2$

Substitute $\left(m, \dfrac{9}{4}\right)$ into $y=2^{x-1}+2$.

$\dfrac{9}{4}=2^{m-1}+2$, $\dfrac{1}{4}=2^{m-1}$

$2^{-2}=2^{m-1}$ $\Rightarrow$ $-2=m-1$, $m=-1$

Therefore, the value of m is -1.

▶ -1

0406

The number of bacteria B doubles when $\dfrac{2t}{150}=1$. Solving this equation, we have

$\dfrac{2t}{150}=1$, $2t=150$, $t=75$ seconds.

Therefore, 75 sec$\times\dfrac{1 \text{ min}}{60 \text{ sec}}=\dfrac{5}{4}$ min.

▶ $\dfrac{5}{4}$

---

5. More about Polynomials
and Equations

0407

If the divisor is not linear, divide polynomials using long division.

$$
\begin{array}{r}
x^2-2 \\
x^2+2\overline{)x^4-5} \\
\underline{x^4+2x^2} \\
-2x^2-5 \\
\underline{-2x^2-4} \\
-1
\end{array}
$$

$\dfrac{x^4-5}{x^2+2}=x^2-2-\dfrac{1}{x^2+2}$

The answer is (C).

▶ C

0408

If the divisor is linear, divide polynomials using synthetic division.

$$\dfrac{x^3+4x^2-9x+2}{x+3} \rightarrow \begin{array}{r|rrrr} & 1 & 4 & -9 & 2 \\ -3 & & -3 & -3 & 36 \\ \hline & 1 & 1 & -12 & \boxed{38} \end{array}$$

$\dfrac{x^3+4x^2-9x+2}{x+3}=x^2+x-12+\dfrac{38}{x+3}$

The answer is (A).

▶ A

0409

$\dfrac{4x(x+2)-3(x+2)}{5x+10}=\dfrac{4x(x\!\!\!\!\diagup+2)-3(x\!\!\!\!\diagup+2)}{5(x\!\!\!\!\diagup+2)}$

$=\dfrac{4x-3}{5}$

The answer is (B).

▶ B

0410

$$\frac{f(x)}{g(x)} = \frac{2x^2+11x+12}{3x^2+11x-4}$$

$$= \frac{(2x+3)(x+4)}{(3x-1)(x+4)} = \frac{2x+3}{3x-1}$$

The answer is (C).

▶ C

0411

Let x be a number. Then, we have

$x=9k+4$, where k is an integer.

Now, let's consider three times that number:

$3(9k+4)=27k+12$

When we divide $27k+12$ by 9, the remainder will be the same as the remainder when 12 is divided by 9. 12 divided by 9 leaves a remainder of 3. Therefore, the correct answer is (C).

▶ C

0412

If the polynomial $P(x)$ evaluates to 0 when $x=3$, it means that $(x-3)$ is a factor of $P(x)$. At the same time, it means that the remainder when $P(x)$ is divided by $(x-3)$ equal to 0. Therefore, the correct answer is (B)

▶ B

0413

$$\frac{x-1}{x+1} + \frac{3}{2x+3}$$

$$= \frac{(x-1)(2x+3)}{(x+1)(2x+3)} + \frac{3(x+1)}{(2x+3)(x+1)}$$

$$= \frac{2x^2+x-3+3x+3}{(x+1)(2x+3)}$$

$$= \frac{2x^2+4x}{(x+1)(2x+3)}$$

$\Rightarrow a=2$, $b=4$, and $c=0$

Therefore, $a+b+c=2+4+0=6$.

The answer is (B).

▶ B

0414

$$\frac{2x-4}{x+3} - \frac{x+1}{3x-1}$$

$$= \frac{(2x-4)(3x-1)}{(x+3)(3x-1)} - \frac{(x+1)(x+3)}{(3x-1)(x+3)}$$

$$= \frac{6x^2-14x+4-(x^2+4x+3)}{(x+3)(3x-1)}$$

$$= \frac{6x^2-14x+4-x^2-4x-3}{(x+3)(3x-1)}$$

$$= \frac{5x^2-18x+1}{(x+3)(3x-1)}$$

$\Rightarrow a=5$, $b=-18$, and $c=1$

Therefore, the value of $b=-18$. The answer is (B).

▶ B

0415

$$2 - \frac{x-4}{x-1} = \frac{2(x-1)}{x-1} - \frac{x-4}{x-1}$$

$$= \frac{2x-2-(x-4)}{x-1}$$

$$= \frac{x+2}{x-1}$$

Therefore, the answer is (A).

▶ A

0416

$$\frac{2}{x-2} - \frac{x-1}{x} = \frac{2x}{(x-2)x} - \frac{(x-1)(x-2)}{x(x-2)}$$

$$= \frac{2x-(x^2-3x+2)}{x(x-2)}$$

$$= \frac{2x-x^2+3x-2}{x(x-2)}$$

Solutions Manual

$$= \frac{-x^2+5x-2}{x(x-2)} = -\frac{x^2-5x+2}{x(x-2)}$$

Therefore, the answer is (D).

▶ D

0417

$$\frac{1}{a} \cdot \frac{b}{b} - \frac{1}{b} \cdot \frac{a}{a} = \frac{b-a}{ab}$$

The reciprocal of $\dfrac{b-a}{ab}$ is $\dfrac{1}{\dfrac{b-a}{ab}} = \dfrac{ab}{b-a}$.

Therefore, the answer is (D).

▶ D

0418

First, let's simplify the original expression.

$$\frac{m-n-l}{\dfrac{r}{s}} \cdot \frac{ns}{ns} = \frac{ms-nsl}{rn} = \frac{s(m-nl)}{rn}$$

I. Dividing n by 4: $\dfrac{s(m-nl)}{r \cdot \dfrac{r}{4}} = 4 \cdot \dfrac{s(m-nl)}{rn}$

II. Multiplying r by 4: $\dfrac{s(m-nl)}{4r} = \dfrac{1}{4} \cdot \dfrac{s(m-nl)}{rn}$

III. Dividing s by 4: $\dfrac{\dfrac{s}{4}(m-nl)}{rm} = \dfrac{1}{4} \cdot \dfrac{s(m-nl)}{rn}$

Therefore, the answer is (D).

▶ D

0419

$$\frac{2}{x+4} = 8(x+4)$$

$$\frac{1}{4} = (x+4)^2$$

$$x+4 = 0.5 \text{ or } x+4 = -0.5$$

So the correct answer is (C).

▶ C

0420

$$1 + \frac{2}{x} = 2 + \frac{4}{x}$$

$$1 + \frac{2}{x} = 2\left(1 + \frac{2}{x}\right) \Rightarrow \text{Let } 1 + \frac{2}{x} = A$$

$$A = 2A$$

$$0 = A \Rightarrow 1 + \frac{2}{x} = 0$$

Therefore, the answer is (B).

▶ B

0421

The expression $\dfrac{x^2-x-6}{x+2}$ equal to 0 when the numerator $x^2-x-6=0$, but $x+2 \neq 0$.

$$x^2-x-6=0$$

$$(x-3)(x+2)=0, \ x=3 \text{ or } x=-2$$

Since $x+2 \neq 0$, $x \neq -2$. So the solution to the equation must be $x=3$. The answer is (D).

▶ D

0422

$$\frac{5}{x-3} - 2 = \frac{30}{x^2-9}$$

$$\left(\frac{5}{x-3} - 2 = \frac{30}{(x-3)(x+3)}\right) \cdot (x-3)(x+3)$$

$$5(x+3) - 2(x-3)(x+3) = 30$$

$$2x^2 - 5x - 3 = 0$$

$$(2x+1)(x-3) = 0,$$

$$x = -\frac{1}{2} \text{ or } x=3$$

However, since $x=3$ is the value that makes the denominator zero, it is an extraneous solution.
So the only solution for this equation is

$x = -\dfrac{1}{2}$. The answer is (A).

▶ A

0423

$$\frac{5}{x^2-2x}+\frac{2}{x}=\frac{5}{x^2-2x}$$

$$\left(\frac{5}{x(x-2)}+\frac{2}{x}=\frac{5}{x(x-2)}\right)\cdot x(x-2)$$

$$5+2(x-2)=5$$

$$5+2x-4=5, \ 2x=4, \ x=2$$

However, since $x=2$ is the value that makes the denominator zero, it is an extraneous solution. Therefore, the equation has $\underline{\text{NO}}$ solution. The answer is (D).

▶ D

0424

$$\left(\frac{1}{k}=\frac{1}{a}+\frac{1}{b}+\frac{1}{c}\right)\cdot kabc$$

$$abc=kbc+kac+kab$$

$$abc=k(bc+ac+ab), \ k=\frac{abc}{bc+ac+ab}$$

The answer is (D).

▶ D

0425

The expression $\dfrac{2x}{x^3+x^2-6x}$ is undefined when the denominator x^3+x^2-6x is equal to 0.

$$x^3+x^2-6x=0$$

$$x(x^2+x-6)=0$$

$$x(x+3)(x-2)=0-x=0, \ x=-3, \text{ or } x=2$$

So the correct answer is (B).

▶ B

0426

The expression $\dfrac{3x^2-27}{m^2-16}$ is undefined when the denominator m^2-16 is equal to 0.

$$m^{2-16}=0$$

$$m^2=16, \ m=\pm4$$

So the correct answer is (D).

▶ D

0427

First, substitute one equation into the other to eliminate the variable y. Then we have

$$x^2-1=x+1$$

$$x^2-x-2=0$$

$$(x-2)(x+1)=0, \ x=2 \text{ or } x=-1$$

Now, substitute these values of x back into one of the original equations to find the corresponding $y-$values.

$$y=2+1=3 \text{ and } y=-1+1=0$$

Therefore, the set of ordered pairs that satisfy the system of equations is $\{(2, 3), (-1, 0)\}$. The answer is (D).

▶ D

0428

$$x+y=-1 \Rightarrow x=-y-1$$

Substitute $-y-1$ for x in the second equation. Then we have

$$y=(-y-1)^2-4(-y-1)+1$$

$$y=y^2+2y+1+4y+4+1$$

$$0=y^2+5y+6$$

$$0=(y+2)(y+3), \ y=-2 \text{ or } y=-3$$

Therefore, the correct answer is (D).

▶ D

0429

First, substitute x^2+8 for y in the second equation. Then we have

$$x^2+8=2(4-3x)$$
$$x^2+8=8-6x$$
$$x^2+6x=0$$
$$x(x+6)=0, \ x=0 \text{ or } x=-6$$

Now, substitute these values of x back into one of the original equations to find the corresponding $y-$values.

$$y=0^2+8=8 \text{ and } y=(-6)^2+8=44$$

Therefore, the correct answer is (C).

▶ C

0430

To find the point of intersection of the given equations, we need to set the two equations equal to each other and solve for x.

$$3x^2-2x=2x^2+24$$
$$x^2-2x-24=0$$
$$(x-6)(x+4)=0, \ x=6 \text{ or } x=-4$$

Since $x<0$, the correct answer is (A).

▶ A

0431

$$a^2-2ab+b^2=16$$
$$(a-b)^2=16, \ a-b=\pm 4$$

For $a-b=-4$ and $2b-a=6$, we have $a=-2$ and $b=2$.
For $a-b=4$ and $2b-a=6$, we have $a=14$ and $b=10$.
Therefore, the correct answer is (D).

▶ D

0432

$$2x-y=-1 \Rightarrow y=2x+1$$

substitute $2x+1$ for y in the first equation. Then we have

$$2x+1=x^2-2x+5$$

$$0=x^2-4x+4$$
$$0=(x-2)^2, \ x=2$$

The system has exactly one solution $x=2$. The answer is (B).

▶ B

0433

substitute $3x^2$ for y in the second equation. Then we have

$$8x-3x^2=k$$
$$3x^2-8x+k=0$$

To have exactly one distinct real solution for this quadratic equation, the discriminant D should be equal to zero.

$$D=b^2-4ac=(-8)^2-4(3)(k)$$
$$=64-12k=0$$

$$12k=64, \ k=\frac{16}{3}$$

Therefore, the answer is (D).

▶ D

0434

Set the two equations equal to each other.

$$x^2+1=2x+4$$
$$x^2-2x-3=0$$
$$(x-3)(x+1)=0, \ x=3 \text{ or } x=-1$$

Now, substitute these values of x back into one of the original equations to find the corresponding $y-$values.

$$f(3)=2(3)+4=10 \text{ and }$$
$$f(-1)=2(-1)+4=2$$

So points M and N have coordinates of $(3, \ 10)$ and $(-1, \ 2)$ respectively or vice versa. Therefore, the slope of MN is

$$\frac{2-10}{-1-3}=\frac{-8}{-4}=2$$

The answer is (C).

▶ C

0435

To determine which of the given lines has two intersections with the graph of $y=x^2+2x+3$, substitute x^2-1 for y into the equations of the lines and use discriminant.

(A) $x^2+2x+3=2x-1 \Rightarrow x^2+4=0$

$D=0^2-4(1)(4)<0 \Rightarrow$ No intersection

(B) $x^2+2x+3=2x \Rightarrow x^2+3=0$

$D=0^2-4(1)(3)<0 \Rightarrow$ No intersection

(C) $x^2+2x+3=4x+3 \Rightarrow x^2-2x=0$

$D=(-2)^2-4(1)(0)>0 \Rightarrow$ 2 intersections

(D) $x^2+2x+3=4x-5 \Rightarrow x^2-2x+8=0$

$D=(-2)^2-4(1)(8)<0 \Rightarrow$ No intersection

So the answer is (C).

▶ C

0436

Since James can paint the house in 14 hours less time than John, we can represent John's time as $x+14$ hours. Then we have

James' work rate: $\dfrac{1 \text{ house}}{x \text{ hours}}$

John's work rate: $\dfrac{1 \text{ house}}{(x+14) \text{ hours}}$

When they work together, their combined

work rate is: $\dfrac{1 \text{ house}}{24 \text{ hours}}$

Now, we can set up the equation:

$$\frac{1}{x}+\frac{1}{x+14}=\frac{1}{24}$$

So the correct answer is (C).

▶ C

0437

Let x be the speed of motorcycle.

	With Winds	Against winds
Speed	$x+3$	$x-3$
Distance	60	30
Time	$\dfrac{60}{x+3}$	$\dfrac{30}{x-3}$

Since it took same amount of time for Min against the wind and with the wind, we have

$$\frac{60}{x+3}=\frac{30}{x-3}$$

So the correct answer is (D).

▶ D

0438

Let be x and t be the speed and time of roller skate, respectively.

	Roller Skate	Bicycle
Speed	x	$2x$
Distance	24	24
Time	t	$t-2$

Since $r=\dfrac{d}{t}$, we have $x=\dfrac{24}{t}$ and $2x=\dfrac{24}{t-2}$

Now, substitute $\dfrac{24}{t}$ for x into the second equation. Then we have

$$2\left(\frac{24}{t}\right)=\frac{24}{t-2}, \quad \frac{48}{t}=\frac{24}{t-2}$$

$$\left(\frac{48}{t}=\frac{24}{t-2}\right)\cdot t(t-2)$$

$$48(t-2)=24t$$

$$24t=96, \quad t=4$$

The average speed (total distance÷total time) is

$$\frac{24+24}{t+(t-2)}=\frac{48}{4+(4-2)}=\frac{48}{6}=8$$

So the answer is (C).

▶ C

Solutions Manual

0439

Simplify the left side of the given equation.

$$\frac{2}{2x-3} \cdot \frac{2x-3}{2x-3} = \frac{2-2(2x-3)}{2x-3}$$

$$= \frac{-4x+8}{2x-3}$$

$$\Rightarrow a=-4, \ b=8, \ c=2, \ d=-3$$

Therefore, $a+b+c+d=-4+8+2-3=3$.

▶ 3

0440

Simplify the right side of the given equation.

$$\frac{a}{2x-1} + \frac{b}{x+2} = \frac{a(x+2)+b(2x-1)}{(2x-1)(x+2)}$$

$$= \frac{(a+2b)x+2a-b}{(2x-1)(x+2)}$$

Therefore, the equation is

$$\frac{10}{(2x-1)(x+2)} = \frac{(a+2b)x+2a-b}{(2x-1)(x+2)}$$

$$10 = (a+2b)x+2a-b$$

$$\Rightarrow a+2b=0, \ 2a-b=10$$

Solving the system of equations, we have

$$a=4 \text{ and } b=-2.$$

Therefore, $a+b=4+(-2)=2$.

▶ 2

0441

Simplify the right side of the given equation.

$$\frac{a}{x-2} + \frac{b}{x-2} = \frac{a(x+2)+b(x-2)}{(x-2)(x+2)}$$

$$= \frac{ax+2a+bx-2b}{(x-2)(x+2)}$$

$$= \frac{(a+b)x+(2a-2b)}{x^2-4}$$

Therefore, the equation is

$$\frac{12}{x^2-4} = \frac{(a+b)x+(2a-2b)}{x^2-4}$$

$$12 = (a+b)x+(2a-2b)$$

$$\Rightarrow a+b=0 \text{ and } 2a-2b=12$$

Solving the system of equations, we have

$$a=3 \text{ and } b=-3.$$

Therefore, $a+b=3+(-3)=0$.

▶ 0

0442

Let $P(x)=x^4-4x^3+x^2+2x-3$ Using remainder theorem, We can use the remainder theorem to find the remainder of dividing some polynomial expression by a linear expression. Let $P(x)$ be $x^4-4x^3+x^2+2x-3$. Then the remainder when $P(x)$ is divided by $x-2$ is $P(2)$:

$$P(2)=(2)^4-4(2)^3+(2)^2+2(2)-3$$

$$=16-32+4+4-3=-11$$

▶ −11

0443

$f(k)=3k^2-7k+2$ and $g(k)=3k+10$.

If $f(k)=g(k)$, then we have

$$3k^2-7k+2=3k+10$$

$$3k^2-10k-8=0$$

$$(3k+2)(k-4)=0, \ k=-2 \text{ or } k=4$$

Since $k>0$, the value of k is 4.

▶ 4

0444

$$3y-2x=8 \ \Rightarrow \ -2x=8-3y$$

Substitute $8-3y$ for $-2x$ in the first equation. Then we have

$$2y^2-y+8-3y=8$$

$$2y^2-4y=0$$

$$2y(y-2)=0, \ y=0 \text{ or } y=2$$

Since $y>0$, the value of y is 2.

▶ 2

0445

substitute $8x^2+32$ for y in the second equation. Then we have
$$8x^2+32=40x-a$$
$$8x^2-40x+32+a=0$$
To have exactly two distinct real solutions for this quadratic equation, the discriminant D should be greater than zero.
$$D=b^2-4ac=(-40)^2-4(8)(32+a)$$
$$=1600-1024-32a$$
$$=576-32a>0$$
$$-32a>-576,\ a<18$$
Since $b>a$, the least value of b is 18.

▶ 18

0446

Let two positive integers be x and y, and $x>y$. Then we have $\begin{cases} x=y+2 \\ \dfrac{1}{y}-\dfrac{1}{x}=\dfrac{1}{4} \end{cases}$. Solving

by substituting the first expression into the second expression, we have
$$\frac{1}{y}-\frac{1}{y+2}=\frac{1}{4}$$
$$\left(\frac{1}{y}-\frac{1}{y+2}=\frac{1}{4}\right)\cdot 4y(y+2)$$
$$4(y+2)-4y=y(y+2)$$
$$4y+8-4y=y^2+2y$$
$$y^2+2y-8=0$$
$$(y+4)(y-2)=0,\ y=-4\ \text{or}\ y=2$$
Therefore, the value of the smaller integer is -4.

▶ -4

0447

Let x be the son's work rate.

Eric's work rate: $\dfrac{1\ \text{backyard}}{3\ \text{hours}}$

Son's work rate: $\dfrac{1\ \text{backyard}}{x\ \text{hours}}$

When they work together, their combined work rate is: $\dfrac{1\ \text{backyard}}{2\ \text{hours}}$

Now, we can set up the equation:
$$\frac{1}{3}+\frac{1}{x}=\frac{1}{2}$$
$$\frac{1}{x}=\frac{1}{6},\ x=6$$
If Eric's son works alone, it will take 6 hours to complete the backyard.

▶ 6

0448

Let x be the speed of the car from home to work. Since 10 minutes is equal to $\dfrac{1}{6}$ hour, we have

	Going	Returning
Speed	x	$x+10$
Distance	50	50
Time	$\dfrac{50}{x}$	$\dfrac{50}{x+10}$

$$\frac{50}{x}-\frac{50}{x+10}=\frac{1}{6}$$
$$\left(\frac{50}{x}-\frac{50}{x+10}=\frac{1}{6}\right)\cdot 6x(x+10)$$
$$300(x+10)-300x=x^2+10x$$
$$3000=x^2+10x$$
$$x^2+10x-3000=0$$
$$(x-50)(x+60)=0$$
$$x=50\ \text{or}\ x=-60$$
Since the speed of the car is positive, $x=50$
Andy drove at 50 miles per hour from home to work.

▶ 50

Solutions Manual

6. Representation of Functions

0449

$$f(1)+2f(2)=2(1)-1+2(2(2)-1)$$
$$=2-1+6=7$$

The answer is (D).

▶ D

0450

Substitute 0 for $f(x)$ and solve the equation $3-2x^2=0$.

$$3-2x^2=0$$
$$2x^2=3, \ x^2=\frac{3}{2},$$
$$x=\pm\frac{\sqrt{3}}{\sqrt{2}}=\pm\frac{\sqrt{6}}{2}$$

So the answer must be (C).

▶ C

0451

$$g(0)=\frac{0}{0-2}=0$$
$$f(g(0))=f(0)=2^0-1=0$$

The answer is (C).

▶ C

0452

$$g(1)=1^2-5=-4$$
$$f(g(1))=f(-4)=\sqrt{1-2(-4)}=\sqrt{9}=3$$

The answer is (A).

▶ A

0453

$$f(f(1))=f(2)=4$$

The answer is (C).

▶ C

0454

$$f(2)=2f(-1)$$
$$\frac{a}{2-1}+2-1=2\left(\frac{a}{-1-1}+(-1)-1\right)$$
$$a+1=2\left(\frac{a}{-2}-2\right)$$
$$a+1=-a-4, \ 2a=-5, \ a=-\frac{5}{2}$$

The answer is (A)

▶ A

0455

$$f(x+h)-f(x)$$
$$=(x+h)^2-(x+h)-1-(x^2-x-1)$$
$$=x^2+2hx+h^2-x-h-1-x^2+x+1$$
$$=2xh+h^2-h$$

The answer is (B).

▶ B

0456

$$f\left(\frac{x}{2}\right)=2\left(\frac{x}{2}\right)+1=x+1$$
$$g\left(f\left(\frac{x}{2}\right)\right)=g(x+1)=(x+1)^2-2$$
$$=x^2+2x+1-2$$
$$=x^2+2x-1$$

The answer is (A).

▶ A

0457

$g(x)=2(x-2)=2x-4$

(A) $f(x-2)=(x-2)-4=x-6$

(B) $f(x+2)=(x+2)-4=x-2$

(C) $2f(x)-4=2(x-4)-4=2x-12$

(D) $2f(x)+4=2(x-4)+4=2x-4$

Therefore, the correct answer is (D).

▶ D

0458

$g(2)=2\cdot2-3=1$ and $f(a)=a^2-1$

$$f(g(2))=g(f(a))$$

$$f(1)=2(a^2-1)-3$$

$$1^2-1=2a^2-5$$

$5=2a^2,\ a^2=\dfrac{5}{2},\ a=\pm\dfrac{\sqrt{5}}{\sqrt{2}}=\pm\dfrac{\sqrt{10}}{2}$

Therefore, the correct answer is (D).

▶ D

0459

Since the leading coefficient is negative (-1) and the highest degree is even, the graph eventually decreases as x increases and also decreases as x decreases. Therefore, the answer is (D).

▶ D

0460

In the graph, as x increases, y increases and as x decreases, y decreases. So the equation of the graph has a positive leading coefficient. Also, the graph has three $x-$intercepts at $x=-1$, $x=1$, and $x=2$. So the equation must have three factors $x+1$, $x-1$, and $x-2$. Therefore, the correct answer is (B).

▶ B

0461

In the graph, as x increases, y decreases and as x decreases, y increases. So the equation of the graph has a negative leading coefficient. Also, the graph has three $x-$intercepts at $x=-a$ (graph touches the $x-$axis) and $x=c$ (the graph passes through the x axis). So the equation must have three factors $(x+a)^2$ and $x-c$. Therefore, the correct answer is (D).

▶ D

0462

In the graph, as x increases, y decreases and as x decreases, y increases. So the equation of the graph has a negative leading coefficient: $a<0$.

Also, the graph has the $y-$intercept at $x=0$: $e=0$.

Therefore, the correct answer is (D).

▶ D

0463

To have 3 solutions such that $f(x)=h(x)$,

f and h must have 3 intersections. Since the horizontal line $h(x)=1$ intersects the graph f at three different points, so the value of b can be 1. The answer is (C).

▶ C

0464

Given that $f(x)$ is a polynomial function, the graph of the function will be continuous.

Looking at the given points:

$(0, 3)$: The $y-$coordinate is positive.

$(1, -2)$: The $y-$coordinate is negative.

From this information, we can conclude that the function $f(x)$ must cross the $x-$axis at least once between $x=-2$ and $x=0$ because it changes from positive (at $(0, 3)$) to positive (at $(1, -2)$). The answer is (D).

▶ D

Solutions Manual

0465

For a function to have a real zero, the value of $f(x)$ must be equal to zero. Therefore, we set $f(x)=0$ and solve the equation:

$$0=(x^2+2.5)(x-4)(x+1)$$

Since $x^2+2.5>0$ for all x, we only have two distinct real zeros: $x=4$ and $x=-1$. Therefore, the correct answer is (B).

▶ B

0466

Setting $f(x)=0$, we can solve for x:

$$0=(x-5)(x-3)(x-2)$$

So the $x-$intercepts are $x=5$, $x=3$, and $x=2$. Among the given options, the point $(3, 0)$ represents an $x-$intercept of the graph. The answer is (B).

▶ B

0467

Setting $f(x)=0$, we can solve for x:

(A) $0=(x^2-16)(x+3)=(x-4)(x+4)(x+3)$
　　$\Rightarrow x=\pm 4$, -3. There are 3 $x-$intercepts.
(B) $0=(x^2+16)(x-4)$
　　$\Rightarrow x=4$. There is 1 $x-$intercept.
(C) $0=(x^2-16)(x-4)^2=(x+4)\ (x-4)^3$
　　$\Rightarrow x=\pm 4$. There are 2 $x-$intercepts.
(D) $0=(x^2+x-12)(x-1)^2=(x+4)(x-3)(x-1)^2$
　　$\Rightarrow x=-4$, -3, 1.
　　There are 3 $x-$intercepts.

Therefore, the answer is (C).

▶ C

0468

The factors of function $h(x)=(x-2)(x-1)$ are $x-2$ and $x-1$. So the answer is (C).

▶ C

0469

$$y=h(x)+4$$
$$=(x-2)(x-1)-4$$
$$y(0)=(0-2)(0-1)+4=6$$
$$y(1)=(1-2)(1-1)+4=4$$
$$y(2)=(2-2)(2-1)+4=4$$

So the answer is (D).

▶ D

0470

$$y=(x-2)h(x)=(x-2)(x-2)(x-1)$$
$$=(x-2)^2(x-1)$$

Setting $y=0$, we can solve for x:

$$0=(x-2)^2(x-1)$$

So there are 2 zeros, which are $x=2$ and $x=1$. The answer is (B).

▶ B

0471

A rational function has zeros when its numerator is equal to zero.

I. $0=\dfrac{x^2+x-2}{x-2}=\dfrac{(x+2)(x-1)}{x-2}$
　　$\Rightarrow x=-2$ or $x=1$

II. $0=\dfrac{x^3+x^2-2x}{x+2}=\dfrac{x(x+2)(x-1)}{x+2}$
　　$\Rightarrow x=0$ or $x=1$

III. $0=\dfrac{x+1}{x^2+x-2} \Rightarrow x=-1$

Therefore, only (I) have zeros at $x=-2$ and $x=1$. The answer is (A).

▶ A

0472

The graph of f in the table has two zeros at $x=-2$ and $x=1$. This tells us that the function f must have two arguments $(x+2)$ and $(x-1)$. So the answer must be (B) or (C). Now we need to check if the value of $f(x)$ for a given value of x matches the corresponding value in the table.

Substitute $(0, 4)$ into (B) and (C).

(B) $(0-1)\left(0-\dfrac{1}{2}\right)(0+2)=1$

(C) $(0-2)(0-1)(0+2)=4$

Since $(0, 4)$ is on the graph of(C),
the function f must be (C).

▶ C

0473

Since $f(k)=2$, we have
$$f(k)=k^2-3k+7=2$$
$$k^2-3k+5=0$$
Now, using the discriminant D,
$$D=b^2-4ac=(-3)^2-4(1)(5)$$
$$=9-20<0$$
So there is no solution of k to the equation. The answer is (C).

▶ C

0474

To shift a function $y=f(x)$ 2 units to the left and 3 units up, we must have $y=f(x+2)+3$. So the answer is (A).

▶ A

0475

If the graph of $y=f(x)$ is shifted 2 units to the right and 1 unit down, we can add 2 to the $x-$coordinate and 4 to the $y-$coordinates of $(-2, 4)$.
$$(-2+2, 4-1) \Rightarrow (0, 3)$$
So the answer is (C).

▶ C

0476

The vertex of the graph of f is $(-2, 1)$. Since the graph of h is shifted 4 units down the graph of f, the vertex of the graph of h is
$$(-2, 1-4) \Rightarrow (-2, -3)$$
Therefore, the maximum value of the h is -3 when $x=-2$. The answer is (D).

▶ D

0477

The graph of f passes through the point $(-3, 0)$. If the graph of g is shifted 3 units to the right and 1 unit up from the graph of f, $(-3, 0)$ will be located at the $y-$intercept of the graph of g. That is
$$(-3+3, 0+1) \Rightarrow (0, 1)$$
So the $y-$intercept of the graph of g is 1. The answer is (D).

▶ D

0478

The vertex of the graph of $y=-(x+3)^2+2$ is $(-3, 2)$. If this graph is shifted 1 unit to the left and 2 units down, the new vertex will be
$$(-3-1, 2-2) \Rightarrow (-4, 0)$$
Then the equation of the resulting graph is $y=-(x+4)^2$. The answer is (B). ▶ B

Solutions Manual

0479

To determine the translation that results in the graph of g, convert the graph of g to standard form.

$$g(x) = -x^2 + 2x + k$$
$$= -(x^2 - 2x) + k$$
$$= -(x^2 - 2x + 1 - 1) + k$$
$$= -(x-1)^2 + k + 1$$

Since $k > 0$, the graph of f is translated 1 unit to the right and $k+1$ units up. So the answer is (A).

▶ A

0480

To find the equivalent value of k in the expression $g(x) = f(x)(2x-1) + k$, we need to substitute value of x so that $2x-1=0$.

$$2x-1=0, \ x = \frac{1}{2}$$

Therefore,

$$g\left(\frac{1}{2}\right) = f\left(\frac{1}{2}\right)\left(2\left(\frac{1}{2}\right) - 1\right) + k$$
$$= f\left(\frac{1}{2}\right)(0) + k = k$$

The answer is (D).

▶ D

0481

To find the temperature at which the Celsius temperature equals twice that of the Fahrenheit temperature, substitute $C = 2F$ into the equation and solve for F:

$$F = \frac{9}{5}(2F) + 32$$
$$F = \frac{18F}{5} + 32$$
$$-\frac{13}{5}F = 32, \ F = -12.31$$

So the answer is (A).

▶ A

0482

$$f(0) = a(0)^3 + b(0)^2 + c(0) + d = 2$$
$$d = 2$$
$$f(1) = a(1)^3 + b(1)^2 + c(1) + 2 = 2$$
$$a + b + c = 0 \Rightarrow (1)$$
$$f(-1) = a(-1)^3 + b(-1)^2 + c(-1) + 2 = -2$$
$$-a + b - c = -4 \Rightarrow (2)$$

If we subtract the equation (2) from (1), we have

$$2a + 2c = 4, \ a + c = 2$$

So the value of $a + c = 2$.

▶ 2

0483

$$f(g(x)) = f(3x+2)$$
$$= \sqrt{(3x+2) - 1} = \sqrt{3x+1}$$

Since $f(g(x)) = 1$, we have

$$\sqrt{3x+1} = 1$$
$$3x+1 = 1, \ x = 0$$

So the value of $x = 0$.

▶ 0

0484

To shift the function $y = 4x - 1$ four units to the right, replace x with $(x-4)$. Then we have

$$y = 4(x-4) - 1$$
$$= 4x - 17$$

So the y-intercept of the shifted function is -17.

▶ -17

0485

The graph of g has two zeros at $x = m$ and $x = n$. The graph of g is a parabola and since $g(-4) > 0$, and $g(2) < 0$, m is between -4 and 2 and n is greater than 2. Therefore, the possible values of m are -3, -2, -1, 0, or 1.

▶ -3, -2, -1, 0, or 1

0486

given that one zero is -4, we can use synthetic division to divide $f(x)$ by $(x+4)$ and find the remaining factors.

$$
\begin{array}{r|rrrr}
-4 & 1 & 2 & -7 & 4 \\
   &   & -4 & 8 & -4 \\
\hline
   & 1 & -2 & 1 & \boxed{0}
\end{array}
$$

Therefore,

$$
\begin{aligned}
f(x) &= x^3 + 2x^2 - 7x + 4 \\
&= (x+4)(x^2 - 2x + 1) \\
&= (x+4)(x-1)^2
\end{aligned}
$$

$f(x) = 0$ when $x = -4$ or $x = 1$.

So the other zero is 1.

▶ 1

0487

$$
f(f(-1)) = f(2) = -2
$$

The value of $f(f(-1))$ is -2.

▶ -2

0488

If the function f is symmetric about the line $x=1$, it means that when the value of $f(0)$ is -2, the value of $f(2)$ is also -2. Therefore, $f(2) = -2$.

▶ -2

III Problem Solving and Data Analysis

1. Ratio and Proportion

0489

$$
\frac{2}{3x+1} = \frac{3}{x-4}
$$

$$
2(x-4) = 3(3x+1)
$$

$$
2x - 8 = 9x + 3, \quad x - \frac{11}{7}
$$

The answer is (A).

▶ A

0490

$$
\frac{4x}{3y} = \frac{2}{3}
$$

$$
12x = 6y, \quad 2 = \frac{y}{x}
$$

The answer is (D).

▶ D

0491

Since y varies inversely as x, we have

$$
xy = k
$$

$$
(10)(4) = k, \quad k = 40
$$

Therefore, we have $xy = 40$ and when $y = 12$,

$$
x(12) = 40, \quad x = \frac{10}{3}
$$

So the answer is (B).

▶ B

Solutions Manual

0492

The ratio of a to b is equal to the value of $\frac{a}{b}$.

$$\frac{4a+9b}{7b-6a}=\frac{3}{2}$$

$$2(4a+9b)=3(7b-6a)$$
$$8a+18b=21b-18a$$
$$26a=3b,\ \frac{a}{b}=\frac{3}{26}$$

The answer is (D).

▶ D

0493

$A:\ \dfrac{x-4a}{3a}=4-x$

$$x-4a=12-3x$$
$$4x=4a+12,\ x=a+3$$

$B:\ \dfrac{x+5a}{4}=\dfrac{2x}{3}$

$$3x+15a=8x$$
$$15a=5x,\ x=3a$$

Since the ratio of the solutions of equation A to equation B is $2:3$, we have

$$\frac{a+3}{3a}=\frac{2}{3},\ 3a+9=6a$$

$$9=3a,\ a=3$$

The answer is (B).

▶ B

0494

$$\frac{3}{8a}=\frac{5b}{4c}$$

$$12c=40ab,\ c=\frac{10ab}{3}$$

The answer is (B).

▶ B

0495

$$\frac{5c}{4a-1}=\frac{b}{a}$$

$$5ac=4ab-b$$
$$b=4ab-5ac$$

$$b=a(4b-5c),\ a=\frac{b}{4b-5c}$$

The answer is (D).

▶ D

0496

Let x be the price of 5 half−gallons of milk. Using the given information, we have

$$\frac{2\text{ half}-\text{gallons}}{\$7}=\frac{5\text{ half}-\text{gallons}}{\$x}$$

$$2x=35,\ x=\frac{35}{2}=17.5$$

Therefore, the answer is (D).

▶ D

0497

The ratio of boys to girls in the school is 4 to 3. Then we can assume the number of boys is $4x$ and the number of girls is $3x$. Since the total number of students in the school is given as 105:

$$4x+3x=105$$
$$7x=105,\ x=15$$

So the number of boys is $4x=4(15)=60$.

The answer is (C).

▶ C

0498

Let x be the price of k kilograms of apples. Using the given information, we have

$$\frac{3\text{ kg}}{\$4}=\frac{k\text{ kg}}{\$x}$$

$$3x = 4k, \quad x = \frac{4k}{3}$$

The answer is (D).

▶ D

0499

Let x be the number of people in $4m$ square miles. Using the given information, we have

$$\frac{384 \text{ people}}{48 \text{ mi}^2} = \frac{x \text{ people}}{4m \text{ mi}^2}$$

$$8 = \frac{x}{4m}, \quad 32m = x$$

The answer is (C).

▶ C

0500

Let x be the number of days it takes her to hit 1,040 balls. Using the given information, we have

$$\frac{80 \text{ balls}}{3 \text{ days}} = \frac{1040 \text{ balls}}{x \text{ days}},$$

$$80x = 3120, \quad x = 39$$

The answer is (B).

▶ B

0501

We are given that one pack of vitamin C powder is enough for 4 children under the age of 10 to consume for d days.

1 Pack=d days for 4 children

Since adults consume twice as much vitamin C as children under the age of 10,

1 Pack=d days for 2 adults

If we have 8 adults,

1 Pack=$\frac{d}{4}$ days for 8 adults

Therefore, the total number of days, A, if 8 adults consume 1 packet of vitamin C powder is $\frac{d}{4}$ days for 8

adults. The answer is (B).

▶ B

0502

The ratio of girls to boys in the 9th grade is 4 to 5. Then we can assume the number of girls is $4x$ and the number of boys is $5x$. Since the total number of students in the school is given as 162:

$$4x + 5x = 162$$

$$9x = 162, \quad x = 18$$

Since we have x more boys than girls ($5x - 4x = x$), there are 18 more boys. The answer is (A).

▶ A

0503

Let x be the number of 3−pointers the basketball player made to reach the $1.2 million donation. Using the given information, we have

$$\frac{5 \ 3-\text{pointers}}{\$2000} = \frac{x \ 3-\text{pointers}}{\$1200000}$$

$$2000x = 6000000, \quad x = 3000$$

The answer is (C).

▶ C

0504

Let x and y be the number of students and the time taken to complete the project, respectively. Since y varies inversely as x,
we have

$$xy = k$$

$$(4)(8) = k, \quad k = 32$$

Therefore, we have $xy = 32$ and when $x = 5$,

$$(5)y = 32, \quad y = \frac{32}{5}$$

So the answer is (D).

▶ D

Solutions Manual

0505

Let x, y, and z be the weights of Jennifer, Jeff, and Chris, respectively. Using the given information, we have

$$\frac{x}{y}=\frac{y}{z} \quad \Rightarrow \quad \frac{120}{130}=\frac{130}{z}$$

$120z=16900$, $z=140.83$

The answer is (A).

▶ A

0506

The ratio of black balls to white balls to blue balls is 2:1:3. Then we can assume the number of black to white to blue balls is $2x$, x, and $3x$, respectively. Since the total number of balls is 42:

$$2x+x+3x=42$$
$$6x=42, \ x=7$$

Therefore, the number of blue balls is $3x=3(7)=21$. The answer is (C).

▶ C

0507

If there are 48 black balls in the bag, we know that

$$2x=48, \ x=24$$

Since there are a total of $6x$ balls, the total number of balls in the bag is $6x=6(24)=144$. The answer is (D).

▶ D

0508

To find the actual area of the ranch in square miles, we need to convert these dimensions to miles.

$$2.5\,\text{in}\times\frac{0.5\,\text{mi}}{1\,\text{in}}=1.25\,\text{mi and}$$

$$4\,\text{in}\times\frac{0.5\,\text{mi}}{1\,\text{in}}=2\,\text{mi}$$

Therefore, the actual area of the ranch is

$$1.25\times2=2.5\,\text{mi}^2$$

The answer is (A).

▶ A

0509

The ratio of what David spends and deposits out of his paycheck is 250 to 70. Then we can assume the amount he spends is $250x$ and the amount he saves is $70x$. If his paycheck is \$960:

$$250x+70x=960$$
$$320x=960, \ x=3$$

Therefore, he will spend $250(3)=\$750$.

The answer is (B).

▶ B

0510

Let y be the width of the actual parking lot. We can set up a proportion between the dimensions of the scale drawing and the actual parking lot:

$$\frac{5}{120}=\frac{x}{y}$$

$$5y=120x, \ y=24x$$

So, the function that represents the area (in square feet) of the actual parking lot is:

$$A(x)=120\cdot24x=2880x$$

The answer is (B).

▶ B

0511

Since the radius of sphere A to the radius of sphere B is 2:1, the ratio of the volume of sphere A to the volume of sphere B is

$$2^3:1^3=8:1 \ \Rightarrow \ \frac{8}{1}=8$$

The answer is (D).

▶ D

0512

Triangle A and Triangle B are similar. Since the length of each side of triangle A is 4 times the length of the corresponding side of triangle B, the ratio of the area of triangle A to the area of triangle B is

$$4^2 : 1^2 = 16 : 1 \implies \frac{16}{1} = 16$$

The answer is (B).

▶ B

0513

The two cones are similar and the volume of the larger cone is 81 cubic inches. Then we have

$$3^2 : 1^2 = 27 : 1 \implies \frac{27}{1} = 27$$

Volum $e \implies 81 : x = 27 : 1$

$x = 3$

The answer is (A).

▶ A

0514

If two cones are similar with a length ratio of $1 : 2$, then the ratio of area and volume of the larger cone to the smaller cone is as follows

Area $2^2 : 1^2 = 4 : 1$

Volume $2^3 : 1^3 = 8 : 1$

Therefore, the correct answer is (B).

▶ B

0515

The ratio of the radius to height of the cylinder is $3 : 5$.

$$r : h = 3 : 5, \quad \frac{r}{h} = \frac{3}{5}, \quad r = \frac{3}{5} h$$

To maintain this ratio when the height of the tank increases by 10 units, we have

$$\frac{r+x}{h+10} = \frac{3}{5}$$

$$5r + 5x = 3h + 30$$

$$5\left(\frac{3}{5} h\right) + 5x = 3h + 30$$

$$3h + 5x = 3h + 30, \quad 5x = 30, \quad x = 6$$

Therefore, the radius must increase by 6 units to maintain the $3 : 5$ ratio. The answer is (B).

▶ B

0516

$$\frac{4a - 4b}{3x + 3y} = \frac{4(a-b)}{3(x+y)} = \frac{4}{3} \cdot \frac{a-b}{x+y}$$

$$= \frac{4}{3} \cdot \frac{3}{4} = 1$$

▶ 1

0517

$$\frac{12k}{9m} = \frac{8n}{6} \implies \frac{4k}{3m} = \frac{4n}{3}$$

$$12nm = 12k, \quad m = \frac{k}{n}$$

Since $m = \frac{ak}{n}$, the value of a is 1.

▶ 1

Solutions Manual

0518

Let x be the minimum number of black pens to be removed. To find the minimum number of black pens to be removed, we need to set up the following equation:

$$\frac{20-x}{20}=\frac{4}{5},\ 100-5x=80$$
$$-5x=-20,\ x=4$$

So the answer is 4.

▶ 4

0519

Let x and y be the number of people and the number of hours, respectively. Since y varies inversely as x, we have

$$xy=k$$
$$(6)(36)=k,\ k=216$$

Therefore, we have $xy=216$ and when $x=8$,

$$(8)y=216,\ y=27$$

Thus, it would take 27 hours for 8 people to paint the same house.

▶ 27

0520

The ratio of the number of adults to children is 13 to 7. Then we can assume the number of adults is $13x$ and the number of children is $7x$. Since the total number of people at the movie theater is 680:

$$7x+13x=680$$
$$20x=680,\ x=34$$

Therefore, the number of adults is $13x=13(34)=442$.

▶ 442

0521

We can set up a proportion using the heights of the actual buildings and their corresponding replicas. Let x be the height of the Trump Tower replica:

$$\frac{381}{202}=\frac{2.5}{x}$$
$$381x=505,\ x=1.33$$

So, the height of the small-scale replica of the Trump Tower would be about 1.33 meters.

▶ 1.33

0522

Let x be the number of hours it would take for 24 pumps to empty the same tank:

$$16 \cdot 12=24 \cdot x$$
$$x=\frac{192}{24}=8$$

So, 24 pumps could empty the same tank in 8 hours.

▶ 8

0523

Let x be the amount of rice when 3 tablespoons of sugar is used. Then we have the following proportion:

$$\frac{3}{\frac{2}{3}}=\frac{x}{3}$$
$$\frac{2}{3}x=9,\ x=\frac{27}{2}=13.5$$

The cook should use 13.5 scoops of rice if he used 3 tablespoons of sugar according to the given recipe.

▶ 13.5

0524

Pencils produced by one machine in 16 minutes:

$$\frac{5 \text{ pencils}}{2 \text{ min}} = \frac{x \text{ pencils}}{16 \text{ min}}$$

$$2x = 80, \quad x = 40$$

Since you have 4 machines, total number of pencils that can be produced in 16 minutes is $40 \times 4 = 160$ pencils.

▶ 160

0525

Since the radius of sphere A to the radius of sphere B is $2 : 1$, the ratio of the volume of sphere A to the volume of sphere B is

$$2^3 : 1^3 = 8 : 1 \quad \Rightarrow \quad \frac{8}{1} = 8$$

▶ 8

0526

When the $x-$ and $y-$coordinates of each vertex of a triangle are doubled, each side of the triangle is also doubled. So the ratio of the area of new triangle to the area of the original triangle is

$$2^2 : 1^2 = 4 : 1 \quad \Rightarrow \quad \frac{4}{1} = 4$$

▶ 4

---

2. Unit Conversion and Percentage

0527

Conversion Factors:

1 mi=1.609 km, 1 km=1000 m, 1 hr=3600 sec

$$\frac{60 \text{ mi}}{\text{hr}} \times \frac{1.609 \text{ km}}{1 \text{ mi}} \times \frac{1000 \text{ m}}{1 \text{ km}} \times \frac{1 \text{ hr}}{3600 \text{ sec}}$$

$$= \frac{26.82 \text{ m}}{\text{sec}}$$

Therefore, the car's speed is approximately 26.82 meters per second. The answer is (A)

▶ A

0528

Conversion Factors:

1 recipe=2 cups, 1 cup=120 g, 1 kg=1000 g

$$\frac{2 \text{ cups}}{1 \text{ recipe}} \times \frac{120 \text{ g}}{1 \text{ cup}} \times \frac{1 \text{ kg}}{1000 \text{ g}} = \frac{0.24 \text{ kg}}{1 \text{ recipe}}$$

Therefore, the weight of the flour needed for the recipe is 0.24 kilograms. The answer is (A).

▶ A

Solutions Manual

0529

The volume of water in cubic feet is
$$V = \pi r^2 h = (3.14)(5)^2(15) = 1177.5 \text{ ft}^3$$
Conversion Factors: 1 gal=0.134 ft³

$$1177.5 \text{ ft}^3 \times \frac{1 \text{ gal}}{0.134 \text{ ft}^3} = 8787.31 \text{ gal}$$

Therefore, the volume of water in the cylindrical tank is approximately 8787 gallons. The answer is (B).

▶ B

0530

For a package weighing 7 pounds, we first calculate the cost for the first 5 pounds:

$$5 \text{ lb} \times \frac{\$2.5}{1 \text{ lb}} = \$12.5$$

Then we calculate the additional cost for the remaining 2 pounds:

$$2 \text{ lb} \times \frac{\$3}{1 \text{ lb}} = \$6$$

Finally, we sum up the two costs:
$$\$12.50 + \$6.00 = \$18.50$$
Therefore, the cost of shipping a 7−pound package is $18.50. The answer is (B)

▶ B

0531

The area of the rectangular garden is
$$20 \text{ ft} \times 30 \text{ ft} = 600 \text{ ft}$$
Now, we multiply the area by the cost per square foot:

$$\text{Cost} = 600 \text{ ft}^2 \times \frac{\$0.5}{\text{ft}^2} = \$300$$

Therefore, the cost of covering the garden with grass is $300. The answer is (A).

▶ A

0532

Conversion Factors: 1 yd=3 ft

$$270 \text{ ft}^2 \times \frac{(1 \text{ yd})^2}{(3 \text{ ft})^2} \Rightarrow 270 \text{ ft}^2 \times \frac{1 \text{ yd}^2}{9 \text{ ft}^2} = 30 \text{ yd}^2$$

Therefore, the size of the parking lot is 30 square yards. The answer is (A).

▶ A

0533

Conversion Factors:
1 mi=5280 ft, 1 hr=3600 sec

$$\frac{60 \text{ mi}}{\text{hr}} \times \frac{5280 \text{ ft}}{1 \text{ mi}} \times \frac{1 \text{ hr}}{3600 \text{ sec}} = \frac{88 \text{ ft}}{\text{sec}}$$

Therefore, Jason's speed is 88 feet per second. The answer is (D)

▶ D

0534

Conversion Factors:
16 mi=1 hr, 1 day=4 hr

$$320 \text{ mi} \times \frac{1 \text{ hr}}{16 \text{ mi}} \times \frac{1 \text{ day}}{4 \text{ hr}} = 5 \text{ days}$$

Therefore, it will take Rick 5 days to run 320 miles at a constant speed of 16 miles per hour, running 4 hours each day. The answer is (D)

▶ D

0535

Conversion Factors:
$\frac{3}{4}$ mi=1 min, 1 hr=60 min

$$90 \text{ mi} \times \frac{1 \text{ min}}{\frac{3}{4} \text{ mi}} \times \frac{1 \text{ hr}}{60 \text{ min}} = 2 \text{ hour}$$

Therefore, Nick drove for 2 hours. The answer is (B)

▶ B

0536

Conversion Factors: $1=130$ Yen

$$5200 \text{ Yen} \times \frac{\$1}{130 \text{ Yen}} = \$40$$

Therefore, with 5200 Japanese yen, you can buy 40 US dollars. The answer is (B)

▶ B

0537

The amount of baht Kevin initially exchanged:

$$\$4000 \times \frac{36.04 \text{ baht}}{\$1} = 144,160 \text{ baht}$$

The amount of baht Kevin has left:

$$144,160 \times 0.2 = 28,832 \text{ baht}$$

The amount of dollars Kevin gets after exchanging the remaining baht:

$$28,832 \text{ baht} \times \frac{\$1}{35.95 \text{ baht}} = \$802$$

Therefore, Kevin gets approximately $802 in dollars after exchanging the remaining baht. The answer is (C)

▶ C

0538

Jenny paid $89(1.08)=\$96.12$ in total. Andrew paid 1300 pesos$+250$ pesos$=1550$ pesos.

Since $1=19.32$ pesos, Andrew paid, in US dollars:

$$1550 \text{ pesos} \times \frac{\$1}{19.32 \text{ pesos}} = \$80.23$$

Therefore, Jenny paid about $16 ($96.12$-$80.23$) more than Andrew.

The answer is (B).

▶ B

0539

Conversion Factors:

40 mi$=1$ hr, 1 mi$=5280$ ft, 1 rev $=2\pi(2)$ ft

$$\frac{40 \text{ mi}}{\text{hr}} \times \frac{5280 \text{ ft}}{1 \text{ mi}} \times \frac{1 \text{ rev}}{2\pi(2) \text{ ft}} \times \frac{1 \text{ hr}}{60 \text{ min}}$$
$$= \frac{280 \text{ rev}}{\text{min}}$$

Therefore, the approximate revolutions per minute (RPM) of the tire is approximately 280. The answer is (A)

▶ A

0540

To find the percentage, we can set up the equation:

$$x \times 240 = 60$$
$$x = \frac{60}{240}, \ x = 0.25 \Rightarrow 25\%$$

Therefore, 60 is 25% of 240. The answer is (B)

▶ B

0541

To find the number that is 150% of 27, we can set up the equation:

$$27 = 1.5 \times x, \ x = 18$$

Therefore, 27 is 150% of 18.

The answer is (C)

▶ C

0542

To find the value of p percent, we can set up the equation:

$$p \times 240 = 108$$
$$p = \frac{108}{240}, \ p = 0.45 \Rightarrow 45\%$$

So 45% of 340 is

$$340(.45) = 153$$

Therefore, p percent of 340 is 153.

The answer is (A)

▶ A

0543

To determine the percentage decrease x represented by the expression $0.4m$, we can set up the equation:

$$0.4\,m=\left(1-\frac{x}{100}\right)m,\ 0.4=1-\frac{x}{100}$$

$$\frac{x}{100}=0.6,\ x=60$$

Therefore, the expression $0.4m$ represents a decrease of 60%. The answer is (D).

▶ D

0544

If k is 150% greater than m, it means that k is equal to m plus 150% of m. So we have the following equation:

$$k=m+1.5m=2.5m,\ m=\frac{k}{2.5}$$

Therefore, the value of m is $m=\frac{k}{2.5}$.
The answer is (D).

▶ D

0545

To represent Nick's current weight after a decrease of 3.5% from the original weight m, we can express this as:

$$m-0.035m=0.965m$$

Therefore, the expression that represents Nick's current weight is $0.965m$. The answer is (D).

▶ D

0546

Discount amount=20% of \$86.50. Therefore, the sale price of the dress is

$$\$86.50-\$86.50(0.2)=\$69.2$$

Therefore, the sale price of the dress is \$69.2. The answer is (B).

▶ B

0547

Number of people who completed the marathon race is $400-(36+24)=340$.

Therefore, the percentage of people who completed the marathon race is

$$\frac{340}{400}\times100\%=85\%$$

The answer is (C).

▶ C

0548

Given that the number of people who gave up from injuries (36) is b times the number of people who gave up from physical exhaustion (24), we have

$$36=b(24),\ b=1.5$$

Therefore, the value of b is 1.5. The answer is (A).

▶ A

0549

To calculate the selling price of each bottle of shampoo, we need to add the markup to the cost price.

$$\$6.00+\$6.00(0.45)=\$8.7$$

Therefore, the beauty shop sells each bottle of shampoo for \$8.70. The answer is (A).

▶ A

0550

For Bank M, the total amount after 1 year is $\$3,800+\$3,800(0.025)=\$3,800(1.025)$.

For Bank N, the total amount after 1 year is $\$5,000+\$5,000(0.03)=\$5,000(1.03)$.

Therefore, he sum of the amounts in both bank accounts after 1 year is:

$$\$3,800(1.025)+\$5,000(1.03)$$

The answer is (C).

▶ C

0551

Let x and y be the price of the shirt and a pair of pants, respectively. We have the following system:

$$\begin{cases} x+y=76 \Rightarrow x=-y+76 \\ 1.08x+1.05y=81 \end{cases}$$

Substitute $-y+76$ for x in the second equation.

$$1.08(-y+76)+1.05y=81$$
$$-1.08y+82.08+1.05y=81$$
$$-0.03y=-1.08, \ y=36$$

Now, Substitute 36 for y in the first equation.

$$x+36=76, \ x=40.$$

Therefore, the shirt is $40 and the pair of pants is $36. The answer is (B).

▶ B

0552

Let x be the rate of increase from 2022 to 2023. Then we have the following equation.

$$120x=132, \ x=1.1$$

The number of employees in the year 2023 will be:

$$132(1.1)=145.2$$

Therefore, if the rate of increase remains constant, we can assume that the company will hire $13(145-132)$ more employees in 2023. So the answer is (D).

▶ D

0553

The increase in profits from 2022 to 2023 is $3 million. So the profit growth percentage is equal to

$$\frac{3}{27}\times100\%=11.11\%$$

The answer is (A).

▶ A

0554

To calculate the total amount Mrs. Kaup has to pay for the car,

1. Calculate the price after the discount:
   $$\$24,000-\$24,000(0.2)=\$19,200$$

2. Add the sales tax to the price after discount to get the total amount
   $$\$19,200+\$19,200(0.06)=\$20,352$$

So the answer is (B).

▶ B

0555

Let x and y be the liters of a 20% and 35% saline solution, respectively.

	20%	35%	25%
Solution	x	y	8
Salt	$0.2x$	$0.35y$	$0.25(x+y)$

We have the following system:

$$\begin{cases} x+y=8 \\ 0.2x+0.35y=0.25(x+y) \end{cases}$$
$$\Rightarrow \begin{cases} x+y=8 \\ 0.2x+0.35y=0.25x+0.25y \end{cases}$$
$$\Rightarrow \begin{cases} x+y=8 \\ 0.1y=0.05x \rightarrow y=0.5x \end{cases}$$

Substitute $0.5x$ for y in the first equation.

$$x+0.5x=8, \ 1.5x=8, \ x=5.33$$

So there are about 5.3 liters of a 20%−saline solution. The answer is (C).

▶ C

Solutions Manual

0556

To determine how many times the number of bacteria today is the number of bacteria yesterday, we need to calculate the growth factor. The growth factor is given by:

$$1 + \frac{20.6}{100} = 1 + 0.206 = 1.206$$

Therefore, the number of bacteria today is 1.206 times the number of bacteria yesterday. The answer is (C).

▶ C

0557

Salary per week: $300

Commission rate: 0.5% of total sales (x)

Since the car dealer's weekly income is the sum of the salary and the commission amount, their weekly income is

$$300 + \frac{0.5}{100}x$$

The answer is (B).

▶ B

0558

Let x be the original price. The item was marked down by $13, so the price after the markdown is $(x - \$13)$. Then, there is an additional discount of 20% of the marked−down price, which means a discount of $0.2(x - \$13)$. Therefore, the final price of the item is:

$$(x - 13) - 0.2(x - 13) = 28$$
$$0.8(x - 13) = 28$$
$$x - 13 = 35, \quad x = 48$$

The answer is (C).

▶ C

0559

Let b and c be the price of a butter croissant and a chocolate cream croissant, respectively. Then we have

$$\begin{cases} 3b + 4c = 16 \\ 4b + 2c = 13 \end{cases} \Rightarrow \begin{cases} 3b + 4c = 16 \\ (4b + 2c = 13) \cdot 2 \end{cases}$$

$$\Rightarrow \begin{cases} 3b + 4c = 16 \quad (1) \\ 8b + 4c = 26 \quad (2) \end{cases}$$

If we subtract (1) from (2), we have

$$5b = 10, \quad b = 2$$

Now substitute $b = 2$ into (1).

$$3(2) + 4c = 16, \quad 4c = 10, \quad c = 2.5$$

If a customer buys a dozen butter croissants with 10% discount,

$$(12 \times \$2)0.9 = \$21.6$$

and half a dozen chocolate cream croissants

$$6 \times \$2.5 = \$15,$$

the total price before the discount is

$$\$21.6 + \$15 = \$36.6.$$

The answer is (B).

▶ B

0560

Let b and g be the number of boys and girls last year, respectively. Then we have

$$\begin{cases} b + g = 820 \\ 1.1b + 0.92g = 820 + 19 \end{cases}$$

$$\Rightarrow \begin{cases} g = 820 - b \\ 1.1b + 0.92g = 839 \end{cases}$$

Substitute $820 - b$ for g in the second equation.

$$1.1b + 0.92(820 - b) = 839$$
$$1.1b + 754.4 - 0.92b = 839$$
$$0.18b = 84.6, \quad b = 470$$

So the number of boys this year is

$$470 + 0.1(470) = 517$$

The answer is (D).

▶ D

0561

Number of 10 in tablets: $0.55(24000)=13200$

Number of 8 in tablets: $0.45(24000)=10800$

Let's create a table with the given information.

	10 in	8 in	
Black	9,500	8,500	18,000
White	2,300		
	13,200	10,800	24,000

The number of black tablet PCs that are 8 inches is $18,000-9,500=8,500$.

Therefore, the number of white tablet PCs that are 8 inches is $10,800-8,500=2,300$.

The answer is (A).

▶ A

0562

Conversion Factors:

1 mile=1.6 km, 1 km=1000 m, 1 hr=3600 sec

$$\frac{65 \ \cancel{mi}}{\cancel{hr}} \times \frac{1.6 \ \cancel{km}}{1 \ \cancel{mi}} \times \frac{1000 \ m}{1 \ \cancel{km}} \times \frac{1 \ \cancel{hr}}{3600 \ sec}$$

$$=\frac{28.89 \ m}{sec}$$

Therefore, the speed of the car is approximately 28.89 meters per second.

▶ 28.89

0563

Conversion Factors: 1000 won=$0.75

$$\cancel{\$}45 \times \frac{1000 \ won}{\cancel{\$} \ 0.75}=60,000 \ won$$

Therefore, 45 US dollars is equal to 60,000 Korean won.

▶ 60,000

0564

Conversion Factors:

1 mile=5280 feet, 1 hr=3600 sec

$$\frac{67 \ \cancel{mi}}{\cancel{hr}} \times \frac{5280 \ ft}{1 \ \cancel{mi}} \times \frac{1 \ \cancel{hr}}{3600 \ sec}=\frac{98.27 \ ft}{sec}$$

Therefore, the equivalent speed of the car in feet per second is approximately 98.27 feet per second.

▶ 98.27

0565

Conversion Factors:

1 c=8 oz, 1 pt=2 c, 1 qt=2 pt, 1 gal=4 qt

$$\frac{2 \ \cancel{oz}}{\cancel{hr}} \times \frac{1 \ \cancel{c}}{8 \ \cancel{oz}} \times \frac{1 \ \cancel{pt}}{2 \ \cancel{c}} \times \frac{1 \ \cancel{qt}}{2 \ \cancel{pt}} \times \frac{1 \ gal}{4 \ \cancel{qt}} \times \frac{24 \ \cancel{hr}}{1 \ \cancel{day}} \times 3 \ day$$

$$=1.125 \ gal$$

Therefore, the faucet wastes approximately 1.125 gallons of water in three days.

▶ 1.125

0566

Conversion Factors: 1 mile=5,280 feet

$$2,500,000 \ ft^2 \times \frac{(1 \ mi)^2}{(5280 \ ft)^2}$$

$$2,500,000 \ \cancel{ft^2} \times \frac{1 \ mi^2}{5280 \ \cancel{ft^2}}=0.09 \ mi^2$$

Therefore, the area of the cornfield is approximately 0.09 square miles.

▶ 0.09

0567

Conversion Factors:

180 km=1 hr, 1 hr=3600 sec

$$2 \ \cancel{km} \times \frac{1 \ \cancel{hr}}{180 \ \cancel{km}} \times \frac{3600 \ sec}{1 \ \cancel{hr}}=40sec$$

Therefore, it takes approximately 40 seconds for the red−tailed hawk to fly to the snake at its maximum speed.

▶ 40

0568

Conversion Factors: 1 cubic feet=7.48 gal
The volume of water V in the rectangular swimming pool is

$V=50\ ft\times25\ ft\times10\ ft=12{,}500\ ft^3$

Therefore, the number of gallons of water in the pool is

$12{,}500\ ft^3\times\dfrac{7.48\ \text{gal}}{1\ ft^3}=93{,}500\ \text{gal}$

So, there are approximately 93.5 thousands of gallons of water in the pool.

▶ 93.5

0569

To calculate p, we can add 60% of 60 to 60:

$p=60+(0.6)60=96$

To calculate c, we can subtract 60% of p from p:

$c=96-(0.6)96=38.4$

Therefore, the value of c is 38.4.

▶ 38.4

0570

Percent decrease is

$\dfrac{\$30{,}000-\$32{,}000}{\$32{,}000}\times100\%=-6.25\%$

The percent decrease in value of the car is 6.25%.

▶ 6.25

0571

Let x be the price of the suit. Then the sale price of the suit is

$x-0.2x=0.8x$

Next, the store offers an additional 12% off the sale price. Then the final price of the suit is

$0.8x-0.12(0.8x)=0.704x$

We are given that Christian paid $280.8 for the suit, so we can set up the equation:

$0.704x=\$281.8,\ \ x=\$400$

Therefore, the original price of the suit was $400.

▶ 400

0572

Let x be the original price of the item. The list price of the item is obtained by adding a 20% profit to the original price:

$x+0.2x=1.2x$

Selling the item at a discount of $2 from the list price resulted in a 10% profit from the original price:

$1.2x-2=x+0.1x$
$1.2x-2=1.1x$
$\quad\ \ 0.1x=2,\ \ x=20$

Therefore, the original price of the item is $20.

▶ 20

0573

1.5−liter is equal to 1500 milliliters. Let x and y be the liters of a 20% and 60% orange juice, respectively.

	20%	60%	35%
Juice	x	y	1500
Orange	$0.2x$	$0.6y$	$0.35(x+y)$

We have the system

$\begin{cases} x+y=1500 \\ 0.2x+0.6y=0.35(x+y) \end{cases}$

$$\Rightarrow \begin{cases} x=-y+1500 \\ 0.2x+0.6y=0.35x+0.35y \end{cases}$$

$$\Rightarrow \begin{cases} x=-y+1500 \\ 0.25y=0.15x \Rightarrow y=0.6x \end{cases}$$

Substitute $-y+1500$ for x in the second equation.

$$y=0.6(-y+1500)$$

$$y=-0.6y+900$$

$$1.6y=900, \ y=562.5$$

Therefore, Mr. Henderson needs to add 562.5 milliliters of the 60% orange juice.

▶ 562.5

0574

Let m and s be the weekend rental price for a mountain bike and a standard bike, respectively. Based on the given information, we can set up the following equations:

$$\begin{cases} 2m+s=80 \\ m=1.5s \Rightarrow s=\dfrac{2}{3}m \end{cases}$$

Substitute $\dfrac{2}{3}m$ for s in the first equation.

$$2m+\frac{2}{3}m=80, \ \frac{8m}{3}=80, \ m=30$$

Now, let x be the weekday rental price for a mountain bike. On weekends, rental prices are 20% higher than on weekdays. So we have

$$30=x+0.2x, \ 30=1.2x, \ x=25$$

Therefore, it would cost $25 to rent a mountain bike for a weekday.

▶ 25

3. Data Analysis

0575

Since there are 20 data points, which is an even number, the median is the average of the two middle values. In this case, the two middle values are 74 and 75. So the median is

$$\text{median}=\frac{74+75}{2}=74.5$$

Therefore, the median number of the heart rates is 74.5. The answer is (C).

▶ C

0576

Since there are 18 data points, which is an even number, the median is the average of the two middle values. In this case, the two middle values are 76 and 80. So the median is

$$\text{median}=\frac{76+80}{2}=78$$

Therefore, the median score for this group of students is 78. The answer is (B).

▶ B

0577

Since there are 14 data points, which is an even number, the median is the average of the two middle values. In this case, the two middle values are 76 and 80. So the median is

$$\text{median}=\frac{86+88}{2}=87$$

Therefore, the median score for this class of students is 87. The answer is (C).

▶ C

Solutions Manual

0578

To find the mean, we add up all the scores and divide by 14 (the total number of students):

$$\text{mean} = \frac{72 + 78 + \cdots + 98 + 99}{14} = 86.5$$

Therefore, the mean score for this class of students is 86.5. The answer is (B).

▶ B

0579

From the given data, we can see that the maximum data value is 3. So the answer is (B).

▶ B

0580

The total number of data values is 14. Since the total is even, the median is the average of the two middle values. In this case, the two middle values are the 7th and 8th values: 1 and 2.

$$\text{median} = \frac{1 + 2}{2} = 1.5$$

Therefore, the median data value in the data set is 1.5. The answer is (B).

▶ B

0581

To find the mean, we multiply each data value by its frequency, sum up these products, and divide by the total frequency:

$$\text{mean} = \frac{0(4) + 1(3) + 2(5) + 3(2)}{14} = 1.357$$

Therefore, the mean data value in the data set is approximately 1.357. The answer is (A).

▶ A

0582

To find the mean, we multiply each data value by its frequency, sum up these products, and divide by the total frequency:

$$\text{mean} = \frac{0(2) + 1(4) + 2(3) + 3(6) + 4(3) + 5(2)}{2 + 4 + 3 + 6 + 3 + 2}$$
$$= 2.5$$

Therefore, the mean of the number of films released per day is 2.5. The answer is (B).

▶ B

0583

The total number of males is given as 24. Fraction of males whose favorite color is blue is (Number of males whose favorite color is blue) / (Total number of males):

$$\frac{6}{24} = \frac{1}{4}$$

Therefore, the answer is (A).

▶ A

0584

From the given table: Number of customers who ordered both soda and fries = 54.

Total number of customers = Sum of all values in the table = 54 + 18 + 25 + 7 = 104.

Probability $= \frac{54}{104} = \frac{27}{52}$.

Therefore, the answer is (A).

▶ A

0585

From the given table: Number of customers who did not order fries=25+7=32.

Number of customers who did not order fries but ordered soda=25.

Probability=$\frac{25}{32}$.

Therefore, the answer is (D).

▶ D

0586

(A) Probability=Number of males who are independent / Total number of males

$=\frac{45}{81}=0.556$

(B) Probability=Number of females who are independent / Total number of females

$=\frac{30}{59}=0.508$

(C) Probability=Number of males who are independent / Total number of people

who are independent$=\frac{45}{(45+30)}=0.6$

(D) Probability=Number of females who are independent / Total number of people

who are independent$=\frac{30}{(45+30)}=0.4$

Comparing the values, we can see that option (C) has the greatest value. Therefore, the answer is (C).

▶ C

0587

Sum of the ages of the 5 people=$37\times5=185$.

Sum of the ages of all 6 people

$=185+$Age of the 6th person$=185+43=228$.

Therefore, the mean age of the 6 people in

the group is $\frac{228}{6}=38$. The answer is (A).

▶ A

0588

The mean of x, y, and z in terms of k is

$\frac{x+y+z}{3}$.

Then the mean of x, y, and z in terms of k is

$\frac{x+y+z}{3}\cdot\frac{3}{3}=\frac{3x+3y+3z}{9}=k$.

So the answer is (C).

▶ C

0589

Total average=Total sum of ages / Total number of people (men and women)

$=\frac{12x+16y}{12+16}=\frac{12x+16y}{28}$

Therefore, the answer is (B).

▶ B

0590

Let x the score Eric needs on his 5th quiz. The sum of his scores on the first four quizzes is

$88\times4=352$

To increase his average to 90, we can set up the equation:

$\frac{352+x}{5}=90$

$352+x=450$, $x=98$

Therefore, Eric will need to score 98 on his 5th quiz to

Solutions Manual

increase his average to 90. The answer is (D).

▶ D

0591

Since the mean and median of the data set above is 3, adding the number 3 to the data set will keep the mean and median unchanged. Therefore, the answer is (B).

▶ B

0592

Since the new salary ($38,000) is greater than the current mean salary ($35,624), the new mean salary will be greater than the current mean salary. We do not know how the newly added data affects the existing median. Therefore, the answer must be (C).

▶ C

0593

Total Sum of Visitors in the Last 50 Days=
$$3,800 \times 50 = 190,000$$
Total Number of Visitors needed for the entire 90 days to achieve the goal=
$$4,000 \times 90 = 360,000$$
Remaining Number of Visitors needed=
$$360,000 - 190,000 = 170,000$$
Average Number of Visitors per Day for the Remaining 40 Days=

$$\frac{170,000}{40} = 4,250$$

Therefore, the average number of visitors per day for the remaining 40 days to achieve the company's goals is 4250. The answer is (C).

▶ C

0594

Mode: the mode is 12 because it appears 7 times, which is the highest frequency.

Median: the median is the value in the middle position, which is the 11th data point. In this case, the median is 12.

$$\text{Mean} = \frac{10(2) + 11(4) + \cdots + 14(2) + 15(1)}{2 + 4 + 7 + 5 + 2 + 1} = 12.19$$

Therefore, the correct answer is (C)
median=mode<mean.

▶ C

0595

For Data Set I: Mean=

$$\frac{20(3) + 30(3) + 40(3) + 50(3) + 60(3)}{3 + 3 + 3 + 3 + 3} = 40$$

Median=40

For Data Set II: Mean=

$$\frac{20(2) + 30(3) + 40(5) + 50(3) + 60(2)}{2 + 3 + 5 + 3 + 2} = 40$$

Median=40

Therefore, the correct answer is (A) Both data sets have the same mean and median.

▶ A

0596

Data set I has a mean of 40, the data values are evenly distributed, and many data values do not come close to the mean value. In Data set II, the mean is also 40, and the data values are more closely clustered around the mean. Therefore, the standard deviation of the data values in Data set I is greater than the standard deviation of the data values in Data set II. The answer is (B).

▶ B

0597

Since the corrected score is still greater than any other scores, it will remain the highest value in the data set. Therefore, the position of the median within the data set will not change. Therefore, the answer is (B).

▶ B

0598

If each data point is increased by 5, the mean and median will also increase by 5. However, the standard deviation measures the spread or dispersion of the data. It is not affected by a uniform increase in each data point. So it does not affect the standard deviation. Therefore, the answer is (D).

▶ D

0599

(A) The range of $Y(10-1=9)$ is equal to the range of $X(11-2=9)$.

(B) At least 50% of the data in Y(data from 6 to 10) are greater than 50% of the data in X(data from 2 to 4).

(C) The median of $Y(6)$ is greater than the median of $X(4)$.

(D) The mean of Y is less than the mean of X.

(E) The mean cannot be directly evaluated from a box plot.

Therefore, the correct answer is (B).

▶ B

0600

The standard deviation cannot be directly evaluated from a box plot. To calculate the standard deviation, we need the actual values of the data set. So the correct answer is (D).

▶ D

0601

There are a total of 27 data points. Since there is an odd number of data points,

the median will be the value at the $\frac{n+1}{2}$

position, where n is the total number of data points.

$$\frac{27+1}{2}=14$$

So, the 14th value in the ordered list is the median. Therefore, the median number of sit−ups is 31.

▶ 31

0602

We can identify the following data points that satisfy the condition: 20, 21, 22, 24, 26, 26, 27

There are a total of 7 data points that fall within the range of 20 or more sit−ups but less than 30.

▶ 7

0603

We can identify the following data points that are below the passing threshold: 12, 12, 13, 15, 17

There are a total of 5 data points that are below the passing threshold. Therefore, the number of students who did not pass is 5.

▶ 5

Solutions Manual

0604

Range=Maximum value−Minimum value

$\quad$ =183−168=15

Q1=median of lower half=$\dfrac{170+172}{2}$=171

Q3=median of upper half=$\dfrac{180+1822}{2}$=181

IQR=Q3−Q1=181−171=10

Therefore, the range of the data set is 15−10=5 greater than the interquartile range.

▶ 5

0605

Let x be the fifth number. Then we can set up an equation to solve for the fifth number:

$$\dfrac{4(16)+x}{5}=32$$

$$64+x=160, \ x=96$$

▶ 96

0606

Given that there are twenty numbers with a mean of 16, the sum of those twenty numbers would be 20(16)=320. If we remove the numbers 36 and 50 from the twenty numbers, we have

$\quad$ New sum=320−36−50=234.

Therefore, the mean of the remaining numbers is

$\dfrac{234}{18}$=13

▶ 13

0607

To find the average waiting time, we need to calculate the weighted mean of the waiting time values using their corresponding frequencies.

$$\dfrac{5(6)+10(7)+15(4)+20(2)+25(1)}{6+7+4+2+1}=11.25$$

Therefore, the average time students waited is 11.25 minutes.

▶ 11.25

0608

The total number of students in both grades is 170+190+65+25=450.

The total number of students who own a car is 170+190=360.

Therefore, the probability that a randomly chosen student owned a car is $\dfrac{360}{450}$=0.8.

▶ 0.8

0609

The total number of students who own a car is 170+190=360.

The number of students who own a car in 12th grade is 190.

Therefore, the probability that a randomly chosen student who owns a car is in 12th grade is $\dfrac{190}{360}=\dfrac{19}{36}$

▶ $\dfrac{19}{36}$

0610

To determine the largest possible mean of the data set, we need to consider each interval with the highest integers. Therefore, the largest possible means is

$$\frac{24(6)+29(8)+34(18)+39(14)}{6+8+18+14} = \frac{767}{23}$$

▶ $\frac{767}{23}$

0611

To determine the largest possible mean of the data set, we need to consider each interval with the smallest integers. Since the median is in the interval from 30 to 35, the smallest possible median of the data set is 30.

▶ 30

4. Designing Studies and Scatterplots

0612

The survey was conducted among a random sample of 200 residents in the city. Therefore, the survey results can be generalized to all residents in the city. The answer is (D).

▶ D

0613

The survey was conducted among a random sample of 1,000 students from universities in the state. Therefore, the largest population to which the results of the survey can be generalized is all students who attend universities in the state. The answer is (D).

▶ D

0614

To estimate the total number of senior students who will be enrolled in a program of study, we can use the percentage of students who expressed interest in the SAT program from the random sample. Estimated number of senior students interested is

$$0.42(250)=105$$

The answer is (A).

▶ A

0615

If 300 out of 500 randomly selected employees used the company's wellness program, we can use the proportion to estimate the number of employees who would have used the program in the past year among the total employee population.

$$\frac{300}{500} = \frac{x}{28},000 \Rightarrow \frac{3}{5} = \frac{x}{28,000}$$

Solutions Manual

$5x = 84,000$, $x = 16,800$

Therefore, the approximate number of employees who would have used the wellness program in the past year is 16,800 employees.

The answer is (C).

▶ C

0616

If 408 out of 1,200 randomly selected adults traveled abroad in the past year, we can use the proportion to estimate the number of adults who would have traveled abroad among the total adult population.

$$\frac{480}{1,200} = \frac{x}{4.5} \quad \Rightarrow \quad \frac{2}{5} = \frac{x}{4.5}$$

$$5x = 9, \quad x = 1.8$$

Therefore, the approximate number of adults who would have traveled abroad in the past year is 1.8 million adults. The answer is (D).

▶ D

0617

To estimate the plausible range for the true mean weight, we can subtract and add the margin of error to the sample mean:

4.3 ± 0.2

This gives us a range of 4.1 pounds to 4.5 pounds. Therefore, the most plausible value for the true mean weight of the laptops is (C) 4.2 pounds.

▶ C

0618

To estimate the range for the number of residents who support the new tax policy,

we first need to find 69% of the population:

$0.69(200,000) = 138,000$

The margin of error is 3%.

$0.03(200,000) = 6,000$

Therefore, the best estimate for the number of residents who support the new tax policy is

$138,000 \pm 6,000$

It is between 132,000 to 144,000 residents. The answer is (A).

▶ A

0619

According to the survey, the estimated annual average PM2.5 concentration is $12.5\ \mu g/m^3$ with a margin of error of $1.2\ \mu g/m^3$. Therefore, the most reasonable claim for the city's average annual PM2.5 concentration is

12.5 ± 1.2

It is between $11.3\ \mu g/m^3$ and $13.7\ \mu g/m^3$.

The answer is (A).

▶ A

0620

The survey of 2,000 randomly selected households found that the average monthly spending on electricity bills is $180 with a margin of error of $5. This means that the true average monthly spending is likely to fall within a range that is $5 above or below the reported average. Therefore, it is reasonable to claim that the average monthly spending of households in the city is between $175 and $185. The answer is (C).

▶ C

0621

To estimate the number of residents who support the new tax policy, we first need to find 60% of the population:

$0.60(250,000) = 150,000$

The margin of error is 5%.

$0.05(250,000) = 12,500$

Therefore, the best estimate for the number of

residents who support the new tax policy is

150,000±12,500

It is between 162,500 to 137,500 residents.

The answer is (B).

▶ B

0622

Based on the random sample of 600 employees, 84 of them reported that they were planning to leave their job within the next six months.

To estimate the number of employees planning to leave their job in the entire company, we can use this estimate as a proportion of the total number of employees.

$$\frac{84}{600} \times 13,000 = 1,820$$

Since the margin of error is 130, the best estimate for the number of employees planning to leave their job within the next six months is

1,820±130

It is between 1,690 and 1,950 employees.

The answer is (B).

▶ B

0623

The line of best fit seems to go through the two points (2, 4) and (12, 9). The slope of the line is

$$m = \frac{9-4}{12-2} = \frac{1}{2}$$

Now we can use the point (2, 4) to find the y−intercept.

$$y = mx + b$$

$$4 = \frac{1}{2}(2) + b, \ b = 3$$

So, the equation of the line of best fit is

$$y = \frac{1}{2}x + 3$$

The answer is (B).

▶ B

0624

There are 2 data points(when $x=5$ and $x=12$) whose actual y−values are at least 2 greater than the y−values predicted by the best−fit line. So the answer is (B).

▶ B

0625

The equation of the line of best fit is

$y = \frac{1}{2}x + 3$. So when the value of x is 2,

the predicted value of y is

$$y = \frac{1}{2}(2) + 3 = 4$$

▶ 4

0626

There are 4 data points where the predicted y−value by the line of best fit are less than the actual y−value. Since there are 11 data points in total, the fraction is $\frac{4}{11}$.

▶ $\frac{4}{11}$

0627

When the value of x is 11, the predicted value of y is

$$y = \frac{1}{2}(11) + 3 = 8.5$$

The actual y−value when $x=11$ is approximately 6.5. So the difference is 2. The answer is (B).

▶ B

0628

If the store has 225 customers, the amount the store expects to make per customer is:

$$y = 0.04(225) + 2.5 = 11.5$$

Solutions Manual

So the answer is (C).

▶ C

$5(11)+6(20)=175$
Therefore, the answer is (C).

▶ C

0629

In this equation, the slope is 0.04. The best interpretation of the slope in this situation is the average amount of money spent per customer increases by \$0.04 for every additional customer in the store. So the answer is (A).

▶ A

0630

The line of best fit seems to go through the two points $(0, 80)$ and $(7, 430)$. The slope represents the yearly increase in subscribers from 2015 to 2022, that is:

$$m=\frac{430-80}{7-0}=50$$

So the answer is (B).

▶ B

0631

The line of best fit seems to go through the two points $(1, 28)$ and $(11, 20)$. The slope of the line is

$$m=\frac{20-28}{11-1}=-0.8$$

This slope represents the gas mileage of a car decreases by 0.8 mpg for each additional year of age. So the answer is (A).

▶ A

0632

The line of best fit seems to go through the two points $(1, 28)$ and $(11, 20)$. When these two points are substituted, equation $5a+6m=174$ is the best fit:

$$5(1)+6(28)=173$$

0633

$$5a+6m=174$$

$$6m=-5a+174, \quad m=-\frac{5}{6}a+29$$

When the value of a is 7, the predicted value of m is

$$m=-\frac{5}{6}(7)+29=23.2 \text{ mpg}$$

The actual $m-$value when $a=11$ is approximately 20 mpg. So the difference is approximately 3 mpg. The answer is (C).

▶ C

Geometry and Trigonometry

1. Basic Geometry

0634

Since line m is parallel to line n,

$x+42=180$ (supplementary angles)

$x=138$

The answer is (D).

▶ D

0635

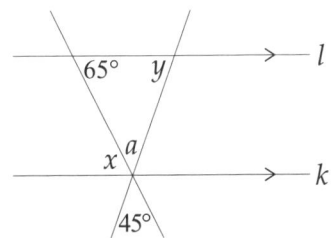

Since line l is parallel to line k,

$x=65$ (alternate interior angles)

$a=45$ (vertical angles). So we have

$a+65+y=180$

$45+65+y=180$, $y=70$

Therefore, $x+y=65+70=135$.

The answer is (C).

▶ C

0636

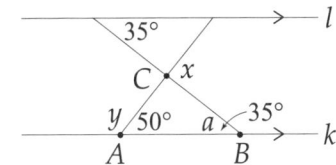

$y+50=180$ (straight angles)

$y=130$

Since line l is parallel to line k,

$a=35$ (alternate interior angles)

Also, x is the exterior angle of triangle ABC:

$x=a+50=35+50=85$

Therefore, $x+y=85+130=215$.

The answer is (B).

▶ B

0637

$(2x+16)+x=4x-8$ (vertical angles)

$3x+16=4x-8$, $x=24$

Therefore, $2x+16=2(24)+16=64$.

The answer is (D).

▶ D

0638

Since BCD is an equilateral triangle,

$\angle BDC=\angle DBC=\angle C=60$.

$\angle DBA=180-60=120$.

Since BAD is an isosceles triangle, $\angle BAD=x$.

$\angle BAD+x+\angle DBA=180$

$2x+120=180$, $x=30$

So the answer is (B).

▶ B

Solutions Manual

0639

Since CBD is an isosceles triangle, $\angle DBC=70$.

Also, $\angle DBA=180-70=110$.

Since BAD is an isosceles triangle, $\angle BDA=x$.

$\angle BDA+x+\angle DBA=180$

$2x+110=180°$, $x=35$

So the answer is (C).

▶ C

0640

Since BE=CE,

$\angle EBC=\angle ECB=\dfrac{180-100}{2}=40$.

Also, $\angle ECD=180-40=140$.

Since CE=CD, $\angle CED=\angle D=\dfrac{180-140}{2}=20$.

$\angle AEB=180-100-20=60$.

Since AB=BE, $\angle AEB=\angle A=60$.

Finally, $\angle ABE=180-60-60=60$.

So the answer is (D).

▶ D

0641

Since BO=DO, AO=CO, and $\angle AOB\cong\angle COD$, triangles AOB and COD are congruent by SAS congruence.

So, $x=2y-70$ and $y=x+10$.

Now substitute $x+10$ for y in the first equation and solve for x and y.

$x=2(x+10)-70$

$x=2x-50$, $x=50$

$y=x+10=60$

Therefore, the value of $x+y=50+60=110$.

The answer is (A).

▶ A

0642

Since two sides AB and ED are parallel,

$\angle B=\angle E$. Also, $\angle ACE=\angle DCE$ (vertical angles).

Therefore, triangle ABC is similar to triangle DEC by AA similarity. Using the ratio, we have

$\dfrac{AC}{DC}=\dfrac{AB}{x}$, $\dfrac{1}{2}=\dfrac{\frac{5}{2}}{x}$, $x=5$

So the answer is (C).

▶ C

0643

First, $\angle B=\angle D=60$ and $\angle CED=90$.

In triangle CDE, $\angle CDE=180-90-40=50$.

Since $\angle D=\angle CDE+x$, $x=60-50=10$

So the answer is (B).

▶ B

0644

Using the Pythagorean theorem,

$3^2+x^2=5^2$

$x^2=16$, $x=4$

So the answer is (B).

▶ B

0645

Since AB and DC are parallel,

$\angle ABD=\angle CDB=30$. Also, since side AB is equal to side AD, $\angle ABD=\angle ADB=30$.

So, in triangle ABD, $\angle A=180-30-30=120$ and

$\angle A=\angle B=\angle ABD+x$

$120=30+x$, $x=90$

So the answer is (D).

▶ D

0646

Let x be the length of the rectangle The length is three times the width,

so the width is $\frac{x}{3}$.

Given that the area is 48 square centimeters, we have

$$x \cdot \frac{x}{3} = 48$$

$x^2 = 144$, $x = 12$

The answer is (C).

▶ C

0647

Shaded region = Parallelogram − Triangle

$$(8)(7) - \frac{1}{2}(8)(7) = 28$$

So the answer is (A).

▶ A

0648

In the given figure, angle A is equal to angle CBD and angle ABD is equal to angle C. Therefore, triangles ABC, ABD, and CBD are all similar to each other by AA similarity. From triangles ABD and CBD, we have

$$\frac{8}{6} = \frac{10}{b}, \ 8b = 60, \ b = 7.5 \text{ and}$$

$$\frac{8}{6} = \frac{6}{a}, \ 8a = 36, \ a = 4.5$$

Therefore, $a + b = 7.5 + 4.5 = 12$. So the answer is (B).

▶ B

0649

Given that the vertices of the equilateral triangle are $(0, 0)$ and $(12, 0)$, the side length of the triangle is 12. Using the formula of an equilateral triangle,

$$A = \frac{\sqrt{3}}{4}(12)^2 = 36\sqrt{3}$$

So the answer is (C).

▶ C

0650

Since the width is represented by x, we can express the length as $1.5x$. So the area of a rectangle is:

$$A = (1.5x)(x) = 1.5x^2$$

The answer is (C).

▶ C

0651

the perimeter in terms of x would be:

$$P = 2(1.5x + x) = 5x$$

So the answer is (B).

▶ B

0652

In the given figure,

$\angle C = \angle C$ and $\angle CDB = \angle CAE$.

So triangle CDB is similar to triangle CAE by AA similarity. Using the ratio,

$$\frac{x}{CE} = \frac{BD}{EA}, \quad \frac{x}{5} = \frac{2}{4}, \ x = 2.5$$

So the answer is (C).

▶ C

Solutions Manual

0653

Since triangle ABD is similar to triangle CED, we have
$$\angle DEC = \angle B = 180 - \angle A - \angle D$$
$$= 180 - 45 - 75 = 60$$
So the answer is (B).

▶ B

0654

Triangle ABC shown above is similar to triangle DEF. since angle C and side AC corresponds to angle F and side DF respectively,
$$\angle F = 40 \text{ and } DF = \frac{1}{2}(8) = 4$$
So the correct answer is (D).

▶ D

0655

Since the two corresponding angles are congruent, sufficient information is provided to prove that the two triangles ABC and DEF are similar by AA similarity. Therefore, the correct answer is (D).

▶ D

0656

From the given information, we have information about the angles but not the sides. In order to determine congruence, we would need the information about the side lengths. Specifically, we would need the lengths of at least one pair of corresponding sides to establish congruence. That will be the sides AC and DF for SAS congruence. So the answer is (C).

▶ C

0657

A: If the measure of angle B and angle E are equal, then triangle ABC is congruent to triangle DEF by SAS congruence.

C: If the length of side AC and DF, then triangle ABC is congruent to triangle DEF by SSS congruence.

B is not necessary information for the two triangles ABC and DEF to be congruent.

Therefore, the answer is (B).

▶ B

0658

$$AC = \sqrt{AB^2 + BC^2} = \sqrt{x^2 + x^2} = \sqrt{2}\,x$$
$$AD = \sqrt{AC^2 + CD^2} = \sqrt{(\sqrt{2}x)^2 + x^2} = \sqrt{3}\,x$$
$$AE = \sqrt{AD^2 + DE^2} = \sqrt{(\sqrt{3}x)^2 + x^2} = 2x$$
$$AF = \sqrt{AE^2 + EF^2} = \sqrt{(2x)^2 + x^2} = \sqrt{5}\,x$$
$$AG = \sqrt{AF^2 + FG^2} = \sqrt{(\sqrt{5}x)^2 + x^2} = \sqrt{6}\,x$$

Since AG is $2\sqrt{6}$, the value of x must be equal to 2. So the answer is (A).

▶ A

0659

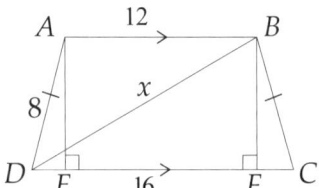

Draw AE and BF perpendicular to DC so that DE=CF and AE=BF.
$$DE + EF + CF = 2DE + 12 = 16, \ DE = 2$$
In a right triangle ADE,
$$2^2 + AE^2 = 8^2, \ AE = 2\sqrt{15}$$
Also, in a right triangle BDF,
$$x^2 = (16 - CF)^2 + BF^2$$
$$= (16 - 2)^2 + (2\sqrt{15})^2 = 256$$
$$x = 16$$
So the answer is (C).

▶ C

0660

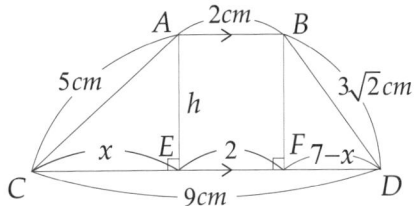

Using the Pythagorean theorem in triangle ADE and BCF,

$$h^2+x^2=5^2, \quad h^2=25-x^2 \quad (1)$$
$$h^2+(7-x)^2=(3\sqrt{2})^2 \quad (2)$$

By substituting (1) into (2), we have

$$(25-x^2)+(7-x)^2=18$$
$$25-x^2+49-14x+x^2=18$$
$$-14x=-56, \quad x=4$$
$$h=\sqrt{25-4^2}=3$$

So the area of parallelogram ABCD is

$$\frac{1}{2}(2+9)(3)=\frac{33}{2}$$

The answer is (D).

▶ D

0661

Since the ratio of the angles is $2:3:4:5:6$, we can assume the angles are $2a$, $3a$, $4a$, $5a$, and $6a$. Also, since the sum of interior angles of a pentagon is 540,

$$2a+3a+4a+5a+6a=540$$
$$20a=540, \quad a=27$$

So the smallest angle is

$$2a=2(27)=54$$

The answer is (B).

▶ B

0662

The zeros of the parabola $y=x^2-8$ are

$$0=x^2-8, \quad x^2=8, \quad x=\pm2\sqrt{2}$$

Then the length of RU is $2\sqrt{2}-(-2\sqrt{2})=4\sqrt{2}$.

Since the length of ST is 4, the x−coordinate of T is 2. Then, the y−coordinate of T is

$$y=2^2-8=-4$$

This tells us that the height of the trapezoid RSTU is 4. So the area of the trapezoid RSTU is

$$A=\frac{1}{2}(4\sqrt{2}+4)(4)=19.31$$

The answer is (A).

▶ A

0663

The volume of the greenhouse is

$$V=\frac{1}{2}\pi\left(\frac{5}{2}\right)^2(16)=50\pi$$

The answer is (A).

▶ A

0664

The volume of the empty cone is

$$V=\frac{1}{3}\pi(2)^2(6)=8\pi$$

Since water is being poured into the empty cone at a constant rate of 1.6π, it would take

$$\frac{8\pi}{1.6\pi}=5 \text{ seconds}$$

to fill the cone with water. So the answer is (C).

▶ C

0665

Pyramid BCDG has the base triangle BCG and height CD. So the volume of the pyramid BCDG is

$$V=\frac{1}{3}\left(\frac{1}{2}\cdot2\cdot3\right)(5)=5 \text{ cubic meters.}$$

The answer is (A).

▶ A

0666

Volume of a sphere: $V=\dfrac{4}{3}\pi r^3$

Surface area of a sphere: $A=4\pi r^2$

Given that the volume is the same numerical value as the surface area,

$$\dfrac{4}{3}\pi r^3=4\pi r^2,\quad \dfrac{r}{3}=1,\ r=3$$

So the answer is (A).

▶ A

0667

The volume of cylinder: $V=\pi r^2 h=86$

For a smaller cylinder, $r\to 0.7r$ and

$h\to 0.8h$

Therefore, the volume of smaller cylinder is

$$V_{small}=\pi(0.7r)^2(0.8h)$$
$$=0.392\pi r^2 h=0.392(86)=33.71$$

So the answer is (A).

▶ A

0668

To find the total surface area that needs to be painted, we need to calculate the areas of all 5 sides of the rectangular room (four walls and a ceiling).

Walls: $(2)(16)(9)+(2)(14)(9)=540$

Ceiling: $(16)(14)=224$

So, John must paint $540+224=764$ square feet. The answer is (B).

▶ B

0669

Let s be each side of the cube.

Surface Area: $A=6s^2=x^2$

$$s^2=\dfrac{x^2}{6},\ s=\dfrac{x}{\sqrt{6}}$$

Volume: $V=s^3=\left(\dfrac{x}{\sqrt{6}}\right)^3=\dfrac{x^3}{6\sqrt{6}}=\dfrac{6x^3}{36}$

Therefore, the answer is (D).

▶ D

0670

Given that the original volume is 216 and the height is 8,

$$\pi r^2(8)=216,\ \pi r^2=27$$

Now, the new volume is 189 and the base area remains the same. Let h be the height of the new can. Then we have

$$\pi r^2 h=189$$
$$27h=189,\ h=7$$

So the height of the reduced can is 7 centimeters. The answer is (A).

▶ A

0671

$\angle BAD=180-110=70$. Since

$$\angle BAC=\angle CAD,\ \angle CAD=\dfrac{70}{2}=35.$$

In triangle ACD, $b=180-35-70=75$.

Also, $\angle ACB=180-75=105$.

In triangle ABD, $a=\angle BAD+70=140$.

Therefore, the value of $a+b=75+140=215$.

▶ 215

0672

Using the Pythagorean theorem,

$$x^2+12^2=(2x+3)^2$$
$$x^2+144=4x^2+12x+9$$
$$3x^2+12x-135=0$$
$$3(x-5)(x+9)=0,\ x=5\text{ or }x=-9$$

Since $x>0$, $x=5$.

▶ 5

0673

Since $\angle D = \angle D$ and $\angle B = \angle E$, triangle BDA is similar to triangle EDC by AA similarity. Using the ratio,

$$\frac{BD}{ED} = \frac{x+ED}{CD}, \quad \frac{1+2}{1.5} = \frac{x+1.5}{2}$$
$$x+1.5 = 4, \quad x = 2.5$$

Therefore, the value of x is 2.5.

▶ 2.5

0674

First, $\angle ADE = \angle CDE$. Since AD is parallel to EC, $\angle ADE = \angle CED$ (alternate interior angles). As a result, $\angle ADE = \angle CDE = \angle CED$ and this tells us that triangle CDE is an isosceles triangle.
Therefore,
$$\overline{CD} = \overline{CE}$$
$$8 = 6+x, \quad x = 2$$

The value of x is 2.

▶ 2

0675

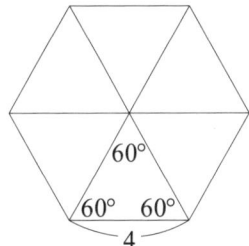

Each of the little six triangles formed by drawing three long diagonals is equilateral as shown above. So the area of the hexagon is 6 times the area of an equilateral triangle with side length 4:

$$A = 6 \times \frac{\sqrt{3}}{4}(4)^2 = 24\sqrt{3}$$

▶ $24\sqrt{3}$

0676

In triangle ABC, the side length of AC is
$$3^2 + AC^2 = 5^2, \quad AC = 4$$

Since AB=3 and DE=9, the ratio of the lengths of corresponding sides of triangle ABC to triangle DEF is 1 to 3. Therefore, the ratio of the area of triangle ABC to the area of triangle DEF is
$$1^2 : 3^2 = 1 : 9$$

The area of triangle ABC is
$$A = \frac{1}{2}(3)(4) = 6$$

So the area of triangle DEF is $(6)(9) = 54$.

▶ 54

0677

The ratio of the perimeters of DEF to ABC is 3 to 1. So the ratio of the areas of DEF to ABC is
$$3^2 : 1^2 = 9 : 1 \quad \Rightarrow \quad \frac{9}{1} = 9$$

The area of equilateral triangle DEF is 9 times the area of equilateral triangle ABC.

▶ 9

0678

The area of an equilateral triangle ABC is
$$A = \frac{\sqrt{3}}{4}(8)^2 = 16\sqrt{3}$$

Since the area of triangle DEF is 9 times the area of triangle ABC, the area of triangle DEF is
$$A = (9)16\sqrt{3} = 144\sqrt{3}$$

▶ $144\sqrt{3}$

0679

Since triangles ABC and DEF are similar and angle A is 15 degrees and angle A corresponds to angle D, the measure of angle D is 15 degrees.

▶ 15

Solutions Manual

0680

It is given that $\angle A = \angle A$ and $\angle AEC = \angle ABD$. So triangle AEC is similar to triangle ABD by AA similarity. Now, using the ratio,

$$\frac{AC}{AD} = \frac{x}{AB}, \quad \frac{3+8}{10} = \frac{x}{3}, \quad x = 3.3$$

▶ 3.3

0681

It is given that $\angle A = \angle A$ and $\frac{AB}{AD} = \frac{AE}{AC} = \frac{2}{3}$.

So triangle ABE is similar to triangle ADC by SAS similarity. Now, using the ratio,

$$\frac{AB}{AD} = \frac{BE}{x}, \quad \frac{6}{8+1} = \frac{4}{x}, \quad x = 6$$

▶ 6

0682

It is given that $\angle C = \angle C$ and $\frac{CD}{CB} = \frac{BC}{AC} = \frac{1}{2}$.

So triangle CBD is similar to triangle CAB by SAS similarity. Now, using the ratio,

$$\frac{CD}{CB} = \frac{x}{AB}, \quad \frac{1}{2} = \frac{x}{3}, \quad x = 1.5$$

▶ 1.5

0683

In the given figure, angle A is equal to angle CBD and angle ABD is equal to angle C. Therefore, triangles ABC, ABD, and CBD are all similar to each other by AA similarity. In triangle ABC,

$$AB^2 + 8^2 = 12^2, \quad AB = 4\sqrt{5}$$

The area of triangle ABC can be written in two different ways:

$$\frac{1}{2} \cdot AB \cdot BC = \frac{1}{2} \cdot AC \cdot BD$$

$$\frac{1}{2}(4\sqrt{5})(8) = \frac{1}{2}(12)BD$$

$$16\sqrt{5} = 6BD, \quad BD = \frac{8\sqrt{5}}{3}$$

▶ $\frac{8\sqrt{5}}{3}$

0684

In the given figure, angle AEF is equal to angle BFC and angle AFE is equal to angle BCF. Therefore, triangle AEF is similar to triangle BFC by AA similarity. Also,

$DE = 16 - 6 = 10$ and $DE = FE = 10$.

Now, using the ratio,

$$\frac{AF}{BC} = \frac{EF}{FC}, \quad \frac{8}{16} = \frac{10}{FC}, \quad FC = 20$$

▶ 20

0685

Let x be the length of the longer base. Then the length of the shorter base is $x - 4$. Using the area of the trapezoid, we have

$$\frac{1}{2}(x + x - 4)(8) = 64$$

$$2x - 4 = 16, \quad x = 10$$

So the longer side of the trapezoid is 10 inches.

▶ 10

0686

The lengths of AB and CD are the values of y when $x = 1$ and $x = 4$, respectively. They are

$$2^{-1} = \frac{1}{2} \text{ and } 2^{-4} = \frac{1}{2^4} = \frac{1}{16}$$

So the area of the trapezoid ABCD is

$$A = \frac{1}{2}\left(\frac{1}{2} + \frac{1}{16}\right)(4 - 1) = \frac{27}{32}$$

▶ $\frac{27}{32}$

0687

Since the diagonals of the rhombus intersect at the origin, and all four vertices lie on the coordinate axes, the diagonals will be along the coordinate axes. The vertices of the rhombus lie on the coordinate axes and because the rhombus is symmetric about the x–axis, the sum of the y–coordinate is zero.

▶ 0

0688

The volume of the sphere with radius 3 is

$$V = \frac{4}{3}\pi(3)^3 = 36\pi$$

▶ 36π

0689

The volume can be calculated by subtracting the volume of the smaller sphere from the volume of the larger sphere.

$$V = \frac{4}{3}\pi(4)^3 - \frac{4}{3}\pi(2)^3 = \frac{224\pi}{3}$$

▶ $V = \frac{224\pi}{3}$

0690

The volume of the entire cone is:

$$V = \frac{1}{3}\pi(4)^2(16) = \frac{256\pi}{3}$$

Since Sam drank half the full height of the cup and Eugene drank the remaining juice, the amount of juice Eugene drank is

$$V = \frac{1}{3}\pi(2)^2(8) = \frac{32\pi}{3}$$

So the amount of juice Sam drank is

$$V = \frac{256\pi}{3} - \frac{32\pi}{3} = \frac{224\pi}{3}$$

Therefore, Sam drank $\dfrac{\frac{224\pi}{3}}{\frac{32\pi}{3}} = 7$ times as much juice as Eugene drank.

▶ 7

0691

Let r be the radius of the cylinder. Then the height of the cylinder is $6r$. Since the volume of the cylinder is 48π, we have

$$\pi r^2(6r) = 48\pi$$
$$r^3 = 8, \quad r = 2$$

This means that the radius of a tennis ball inside a cylinder is 2 centimeters. Therefore, the volume of a tennis ball is:

$$V = \frac{4}{3}\pi(2)^3 = \frac{32\pi}{3}$$

▶ $\frac{32\pi}{3}$

0692

The volume of the empty space around 3 tennis balls is the difference between the volume of the cylinder and the volume of 3 tennis balls.

$$V = 48\pi - 3 \cdot \frac{32\pi}{3} = 16\pi$$

▶ 16π

0693

The volume of water in the cone is:

$$V = \frac{1}{3}\pi(3)^2(12) = 36\pi$$

Now, when the water is poured into the cylinder, the volume of the water in the cylinder is the same as the volume of water in the cone. If we let h be the height of the water in the cylinder, we have

$$\pi(6)^2 h = 36\pi, \quad h = 1$$

The height of the water in the cylinder is 1 inches.

▶ 1

Solutions Manual

0694

The surface area of a given figure must be the sum of the areas of all the figures below.

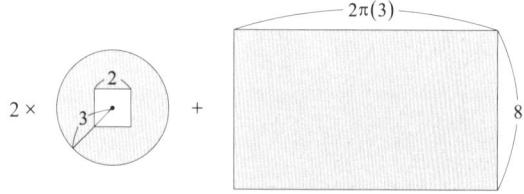

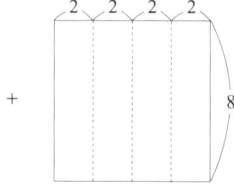

So the surface area is
$$A=2\times(\pi(3)^2-(2)(2))+2\pi(3)(8)+(8)(8)$$
$$=66\pi+56$$
$$b-a=56-66\pi$$

▶ $56-66\pi$

0695

Using the Pythagorean theorem,
$$a\sqrt{b}=\sqrt{12^2+18^2}=6\sqrt{13}$$
The values of a and b are 6 and 13. Therefore,
$$a+b=6+13=19$$

▶ 19

---

2. Circle Theorem

0696

In triangle CDO, since CD=CO, $\angle$COD=30.

Because the length of arc CE is $\frac{\pi}{2}$, we have
$$2\pi r\times\frac{30}{360}=\frac{\pi}{2}, \quad \frac{\pi r}{6}=\frac{\pi}{2}, \quad r=3$$
So the radius of the circle is 3. The answer is (A).

▶ A

0697

Since $\angle$D=30 and $\angle$COD=30,
$\angle$BCO=30+30=60. Also in triangle COB,
since CO=BO, $\angle$CBO=60 and
$\angle$COB=180−60−60=60.
Therefore, triangle COB is an equilateral triangle. So the area of the COB is:
$$A=\frac{\sqrt{3}}{4}(3)^2=\frac{9\sqrt{3}}{4}$$
So the answer is (A).

▶ A

0698

$\angle$AOB=180−30−60=90. Using the ratio,
$$\frac{x}{\frac{\pi}{2}}=\frac{90}{30}, \quad 30x=45\pi, \quad x=\frac{3\pi}{2}$$

So the answer is (D).

▶ D

0699

Since $\dfrac{\widehat{AB}}{\widehat{BC}}=\dfrac{2}{1}$, $\angle AOB=180\times\dfrac{2}{2+1}=120$

In triangle AOB, AO=BO so that

$\angle ABO=\dfrac{180-120}{2}=30$. So the answer is (C).

▶ C

0700

Given that the ratio of angles AOB to BOC to COA is 2 to 3 to 4, let's denote these angles $2x$, $3x$, and $4x$, respectively. Since the sum of the central angles in a circle is 360, we have

$$3x+2x+4x=360$$
$$9x=360, \ x=40$$

So the measure of angle BOC is $2x=2(40)=80$. The area of sector BOC is

$$A=\pi(6)^2\cdot\dfrac{80}{360}=8\pi$$

Therefore, the answer is (D).

▶ D

0701

Let θ be the central angle for sector AOB in degree measure. Given that the area of sector AOB is 24π and the radius r is 6 inches, we have

$$\pi(6)^2\times\dfrac{\theta}{360}=24\pi$$

$$\dfrac{\pi\theta}{10}=24\pi, \ \theta=240$$

Now convert 240 degrees into radians.

$$240°\times\dfrac{\pi}{180°}=\dfrac{4\pi}{3}$$

So the answer is (D).

▶ D

0702

Let r be the length of the pendulum. First, convert $2\dfrac{\pi}{3}$ radians into degrees.

$$\dfrac{2\pi}{3}\times\dfrac{180°}{\pi}=120°$$

Given that the tip of the pendulum sweeps out an arc of 8π inches, we have

$$2\pi r\times\dfrac{120}{360}=8\pi$$

$$\dfrac{2\pi r}{3}=8\pi, \ r=12$$

So the length of the pendulum is 12 inches. The answer is (C).

▶ C

0703

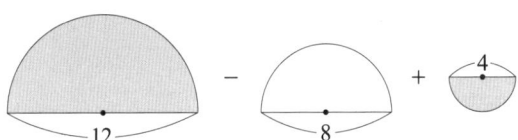

The area of the shaded region is

$$A=\dfrac{\pi(6)^2}{2}-\dfrac{\pi(4)^2}{2}+\dfrac{\pi(2)^2}{2}=12\pi.$$

So the answer is (C).

▶ C

0704

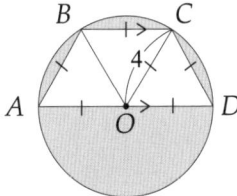

AO, BO, CO, and DO are radii of the circle, so $AO=BO=CO=DO=4$. So triangles ABO, BCO, and CDO are all equilateral triangles with sides 4. The area of the shaded area is the difference between the area of the circle and the area of the three equilateral triangles. That is:

$$A=\pi(4)^2-3\times\frac{\sqrt{3}}{4}(4)^2=16\pi-12\sqrt{3}$$

So the answer is (A).

▶ A

0705

Given that angle ACB is a right angle, we have

$$\theta+2\theta=90,\ 3\theta=90,\ \theta=30$$

So triangle ABC is special triangle with $30°-60°-90°$. Since AB=8, using the ratio, we have:

$$\frac{1}{2}=\frac{BC}{8},\ BC=4\ \text{and}$$

$$\frac{\sqrt{3}}{2}=\frac{AC}{8},\ AC=4\sqrt{3}$$

Therefore, the area of the triangle ABC is

$$A=\frac{1}{2}(4)(4\sqrt{3})=8\sqrt{3}$$

So the answer is (C).

▶ C

0706

Let θ be the angle of the sector in degree measure. Given that the area of the sector is 6π square inches and the arc length is 2π inches, we have

$$\pi r^2\times\frac{\theta}{360}=6\pi,\ r^2\theta=2160 \qquad (1)$$

$$2\pi r\times\frac{\theta}{360}=2\pi,\ r\theta=360,\ r=\frac{360}{\theta} \qquad (2)$$

Now substitute $\frac{360}{\theta}$ for r in equation (1). Then we have

$$\left(\frac{360}{\theta}\right)^2(\theta)=2160$$

$$\frac{60}{\theta}=1,\ \theta=60$$

So the answer is (C).

▶ C

0707

Since AC⊥OB, AM=CM=8.

Also, in triangle AOM,

$$OM=\sqrt{10^2-8^2}\ \text{and}$$

$$BM=OB-OM=10-6=4$$

Now, in triangle CBM,

$$x=\sqrt{BM^2+CM^2}=\sqrt{4^2+8^2}=4\sqrt{5}$$

So the answer is (B).

▶ B

0708

First, OC=OD=OB=13 because they are radii of the same circle. Since AC⊥BD, we know that CM=AM=12. In triangle OCM,

$$OM=\sqrt{OC^2-CM^2}=\sqrt{13^2-12^2}=5$$

So $DM=OD-OM=13-5=8$.

Now, in triangle CMD,

$$x=\sqrt{DM^2+CM^2}=\sqrt{8^2+12^2}=4\sqrt{13}$$

So the answer is (B).

▶ B

0709

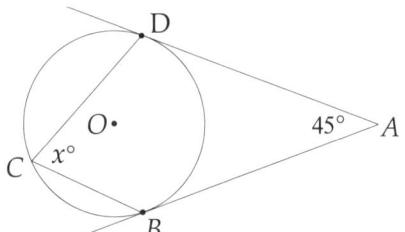

If we draw two radii BO and DO in a circle O, then AD and AB are perpendicular to OD and OB, respectively. Since angle C is an inscribed angle formed by arc BD, we have

$$x=\frac{\angle BOD}{2},\ \angle BOD=2x$$

Now, in a quadrilateral ABOD,

$$45+90+2x+90=360$$

$$2x=130,\ x=67.5$$

So the answer is (D).

▶ D

0710

Since AB and AC are tangent to the circle O, AB=AC and angle B is a right angle. Using the Pythagorean theorem,
$$x=\sqrt{12^2+5^2}=13$$
So the answer is (A).

▶ A

0711

The equation of a circle in the standard form is $(x-h)^2+(y-k)^2=r^2$, where (h, k) are the coordinates of the center of the circle and r is the radius. Comparing this with the given equation, we can see that the coordinates of the center is $(h, k)=(-3, 2)$. The answer is (C).

▶ C

0712

Let's test each point from the options to see if it lies on the circle:
(A) $(-4+1)^2+(-1-3)^2=25$: On the circle
(B) $(0+1)^2+(2-3)^2=26$: Not on the circle
(C) $(2+1)^2+(-1-3)^2=25$: On the circle
(D) $(3+1)^2+(6-3)^2=25$: On the circle
So the answer is (B).

▶ B

0713

To determine the radius of a circle, we need to rewrite the equation in the standard form.
$$x^2+y^2-6x+8y=0$$
$$x^2-6x+\underline{9}+y^2+8y+\underline{16}=\underline{9}+\underline{16}$$
$$(x-3)^2+(y+4)^2=25$$
Thus, the radius r is 5. The answer is (B).

▶ B

0714

First, rewrite the equation in the standard form.
$$2x^2+2y^2+8x-16y=0$$
$$2+y^2+4x-8y=0$$
$$x^2+4x+\underline{4}+y^2-8y+\underline{16}=\underline{4}+\underline{16}$$
$$(x+2)^2+(y-4)^2=20$$
Since $r^2=20$, the area of a circle is
$$A=\pi r^2=\pi(20)=20\pi$$
So the answer is (A).

▶ A

0715

Let's test each point from the options to see if it lies inside the circle:
(A) $(0-2)^2+4^2=20>16$: Outside the circle
(B) $(-2-2)^2+0^2=16=16$: On the circle
(C) $(-2-2)^2+(-4)^2=32>16$
     : Outside the circle
(D) $(2-2)^2+(-3)^2=9<16$
     : Inside the circle
So the answer is (D).

▶ D

0716

To determine the center of a circle, we need to rewrite the equation in the standard form.

$$2x^2 + 2y^2 + 12x - 6y + 1 = 0$$

$$x^2 + y^2 + 6x - 3y + \frac{1}{2} = 0$$

$$x^2 + 6x + \underline{9} + y^2 - 3y + \frac{9}{4} = -\frac{1}{2} + \underline{9} + \frac{9}{4}$$

$$(x+3)^2 + \left(y - \frac{3}{2}\right)^2 = \frac{43}{4}$$

So the coordinates of the center is $\left(-3, \frac{3}{2}\right)$. The answer is (D).

▶ D

0717

Given the equation of the original circle $(x+2)^2 + (y-4)^2 = 16$, its center is $(-2, 4)$.

If the circle is translated 3 units to the left and 4 units down, the new center becomes

$$(-2-3, \ 4-4) = (-5, \ 0)$$

Now, using the new center coordinates, we can write the equation of the translated circle:

$$(x+5)^2 + y^2 = 16$$

So the answer is (B).

▶ B

0718

A circle is tangent to the line $y = -2$ and y-axis when the distance from the center to these two lines is the radius r. Given the answer choices, the center $(1, \ -3)$ satisfy the condition. So the answer is (B).

▶ B

0719

For a circle to intersect the x-axis at exactly one point, the distance from the center to the x-axis must equal the radius r. Since the center of equation (D) is $(-18, \ 6)$, the distance from the center to the x-axis is equal to the radius 6, so the condition is satisfied. So the answer is (D).

▶ D

0720

The center $(h, \ k)$ in the second quadrant is tangent to the x-axis and the line $x = 1$ when the distances from the center to these two lines are equal to the radius of the circle.

The distances from the center $(h, \ k)$ to the x-axis and line $x = 1$ are k and $1 - h$, respectively. Therefore,

$$k = 1 - h$$

So the answer is (D).

▶ D

0721

Since AB is parallel to CO,

∠COD = ∠BAO = 40.

Also, since OA = OB, ∠BAO = ∠ABO = 40.

In triangle ABO, ∠AOB = 180 − 2(40) = 100.

Using the ratio, the length of arc AB is

$$\frac{\overset{\frown}{AB}}{\overset{\frown}{CD}} = \frac{100}{40}, \quad \frac{\overset{\frown}{AB}}{4} = \frac{5}{2}, \quad \overset{\frown}{AB} = 10$$

▶ 10

0722

Since angle B is an inscribed angle formed by arc AC,

$$\angle B=\frac{\angle AOC}{2}, \quad 40=\frac{\angle AOC}{2}$$
$$\angle AOC=80$$

Also, since OA=OC, $\angle OAC=\angle OCA=x$.

Therefore, in triangle OAC,

$$x+x+80=180$$
$$2x=100, \quad x=50$$

▶ 50

0723

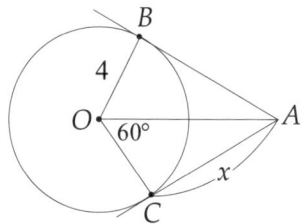

First, OB=OC=4 because they are radii of the same circle. Since AC is perpendicular to OC, $\angle ACO=90$ and $\angle CAO=180-60-90=30$.

Now, we know that triangle ACO is a $30°-60°-90°$ triangle. Using the ratio,

$$\frac{OC}{AC}=\frac{1}{\sqrt{3}}=\frac{4}{x}, \quad x=4\sqrt{3}$$

▶ $4\sqrt{3}$

0724

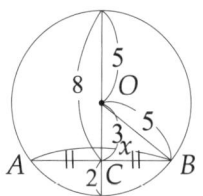

$BC=\sqrt{5^2-3^2}=4$ and $x=2BC=(2)(4)=8$.

▶ 8

0725

Area of shaded region=2(Area of square)
2(Area of two semicircles of radius 4)

$$2\left(8^2-\frac{1}{2}\pi(4)^2(2)\right)=2(64-16\pi)$$
$$=128-32\pi$$

Since $a+b\pi=128-32\pi$, $a=128$ and $b=-32$. So the value of $a+b=128+(-32)=96$.

▶ 96

0726

The fraction of the circumference that the arc length AB represents is

$$\frac{\frac{3\pi}{4}}{2\pi(6)}=\frac{3\pi}{48\pi}=\frac{1}{16}$$

▶ $\frac{1}{16}$

0727

Since the point $(-1, 4)$ is on the circle $(x-h)^2+(y-3)^2=5$, we can substitute this point into the circle's equation.

$$(-1-h)^2+(4-3)^2=5$$
$$(1+h)^2+1=5$$
$$(1+h)^2=4$$
$$1+h=\pm2, \quad h=-3 \text{ or } h=1$$

Since $h>0$, $h=1$.

▶ 1

0728

Let's complete the square for both x and y first.

$$x^2+y^2+4x-6y=3$$
$$x^2+4x+\underline{4}+y^2-6y+\underline{9}=3+\underline{4}+\underline{9}$$
$$(x+2)^2+(y-3)^2=16$$

The radius r of the circle above is 4. So the circumference is

$$C=2\pi(4)=8\pi$$

Since the circumference is $c\pi$, the value c is 8.

▶ 8

Solutions Manual

0729

Let's complete the square for both x and y first.

$$x^2+y^2+2x-ky=4$$

$$x^2+2x+\underline{1}+y^2-ky+\frac{k^2}{4}=4+\underline{1}+\frac{k^2}{4}$$

$$(x+1)^2+\left(y-\frac{k}{2}\right)^2=5+\frac{k^2}{4}$$

Since the radius of the circle is 3, we must have

$$5+\frac{k^2}{4}=3^2,\ \frac{k^2}{4}=4$$

$$k^2=16,\ k=4$$

So the value of k is 4.

▶ 4

0730

The equation of a circle with a radius 3 and a center $(6, 2)$ is $(x-6)^2+(y-2)^2=9$. To find the points of intersection between the line and the circle, we can substitute $x=4$ into the equation of the circle and solve for y.

$$(4-6)^2+(y-2)^2=9$$

$$4+(y-2)^2=9$$

$$(y-2)^2=5$$

$$y-2=\pm\sqrt{5},\ y=2\pm\sqrt{5}$$

So the values of a and b are 2 and 5, respectively. Therefore, $a+b=2+5=7$.

▶ 7

3. Trigonometry

0731

$$\frac{2\pi}{3}\ \text{rad}\times\frac{180°}{\pi\ \text{rad}}=120°$$

So, an angle with a measure of $\frac{2\pi}{3}$ radians is equivalent to $120°$ in degrees. The answer is (C).

▶ C

0732

$$225°\times\frac{\pi\ \text{rad}}{180°}=\frac{5\pi}{4}\ \text{rad}$$

So, an angle with a measure of $225°$ in degree is equivalent to in $\frac{5\pi}{4}$ radians. The answer is (B).

▶ B

0733

Measure of angle A$-$Measure of angle B$=$

$$\frac{5\pi}{4}-\frac{11\pi}{12}=\frac{4\pi}{12}=\frac{\pi}{3}\ \text{and}$$

$$\frac{\pi}{3}\ \text{rad}\times\frac{180°}{\pi\ \text{rad}}=60°$$

So, the measure of angle A is 60 degrees greater than the measure of angle B. The answer is (A).

▶ A

0734

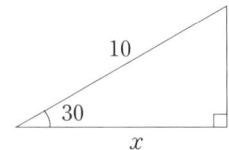

Let x be the length of the longer leg as shown above. Using the cosine function,

$$\cos 30°=\frac{\text{adj}}{\text{hyp}}$$

$$\frac{\sqrt{3}}{2}=\frac{x}{10}, \ x=5\sqrt{3}$$

So, the length of the longer leg is $5\sqrt{3}$. The answer is (C).

▶ C

0735

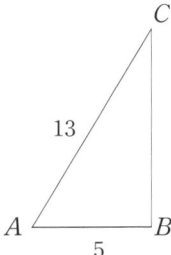

In triangle ABC with right angle B,

if $\cos A=\frac{5}{13}$, the figure above is obtained.

Since the since function is $\frac{\text{opp}}{\text{hyp}}$, $\sin C=\frac{5}{13}$.

So the answer is (A).

▶ A

0736

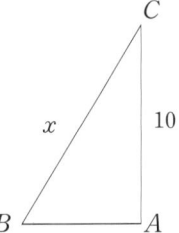

Let x be the length of the hypotenuse. Then the triangle above satisfies the conditions given in the problem. Using the sine function,

$$\sin B=\frac{10}{x}$$

$$0.8=\frac{10}{x}, \ x=12.5$$

So the answer is (A).

▶ A

0737

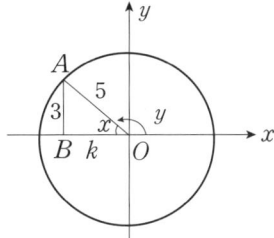

Let x be the length BO as show above.

If $\sin x=\frac{3}{5}$, we know that AB=3.

Also in triangle ABO, using the Pythagorean theorem,
$$3^2+k^2=5^2, \ k=4$$

So the value of cos y is

$$\cos y=\frac{-k}{5}=-\frac{4}{5}$$

The answer is (D).

▶ D

0738

Using the cofunction identity of a right triangle,
$$\cos(\theta)=\sin(90°-\theta).$$

Therefore, the value of $\sin(90°-\theta)$ is 0.8.

The answer is (D).

▶ D

0739

Using the cofunction identity of a right triangle,
$$\sin(\theta)=\cos(90°-\theta).$$

So, $\sin(44°)=\cos(90°-44°)=\cos(46°)$.

The answer is (B).

▶ B

Solutions Manual

0740

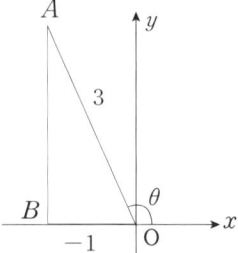

If $\cos\theta=-\dfrac{1}{3}$ and θ is in quadrant II, we have the following figure as shown above. Using the Pythagorean theorem, we have

$$AB^2+(-1)^2=3^2,\ AB^2=8,\ AB=2\sqrt{2}$$

So, the value of $\sin\theta$ is

$$\sin\theta=\frac{AB}{3}=\frac{2\sqrt{2}}{3}$$

The answer is (C).

▶ C

0741

If $\tan\theta=2$ and $\sin\theta<0$, the angel θ must be in quadrant III. Then we have following figure as shown below.

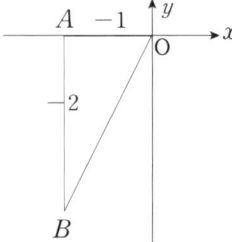

Using the Pythagorean theorem, we have

$$(-2)^2+(-1)^2=BO^2,\ BO=\sqrt{5}$$

So, the value of $\cos\theta$ is

$$\cos\theta=\frac{-1}{\sqrt{5}}=-\frac{\sqrt{5}}{5}$$

The answer is (B).

▶ B

0742

Let x be angle BAD. The angle CAD is $90-x$. From the cofunction identity of a right triangle, we know that $\sin(x)=\cos(90°-x)$. Therefore,

$$\sin(x)-\cos(90°-x)=0.$$

The answer is (B).

▶ B

0743

Since C is the midpoint of side BD, BC=CD=2. Using the Pythagorean theorem in triangle ABD,

$$AD^2+4^2=5^2,\ AD=3$$

Again using the Pythagorean theorem in triangle ACD,

$$2^2+3^2=AC^2,\ AC=\sqrt{13}$$

Therefore, the value of $\sin\theta$ is

$$\sin\theta=\frac{3}{\sqrt{13}}=\frac{3\sqrt{13}}{13}$$

The answer is (D).

▶ D

0744

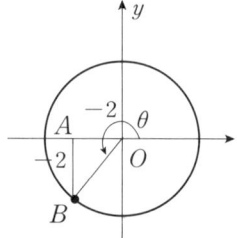

As shown in the figure above, since AB=AO, triangle ABO is an isosceles triangle and angle AOB is $45°=\dfrac{\pi}{4}$. So the measure of angle θ is

$$\theta=180°+45°$$
$$=\pi+\frac{\pi}{4}=\frac{5\pi}{4}$$

The answer is (B).

▶ B

0745

Using the Pythagorean theorem in triangle BCD,

$3^2 + BC^2 = 5^2$, $BC = 4$

Again using the Pythagorean theorem in triangle ABC,

$AC^2 + BC^2 = 7^2$

$AC^2 + 4^2 = 7^2$, $AC = \sqrt{33}$

Therefore, the tangent of angle A is

$\tan A = \dfrac{BC}{AC} = \dfrac{4}{\sqrt{33}}$

The answer is (D).

▶ D

0746

In triangle ABD,

$\tan 40° = \dfrac{BD}{4}$, $BD = 4 \tan 40°$

So the answer is (A).

▶ A

0747

Using the cofunction identity of right triangle BCD, $\cos \angle C = \sin \angle DBC$. So the answer is (D).

▶ D

0748

In triangle ABC,

$\sin x = \dfrac{1}{b}$, $b = \dfrac{1}{\sin x}$ and

$\tan x = \dfrac{1}{a}$, $a = \dfrac{1}{\tan x}$.

Therefore,

$a + b = \dfrac{1}{\tan x} + \dfrac{1}{\sin x}$

$= \dfrac{\cos x}{\sin x} + \dfrac{1}{\sin x} = \dfrac{1 + \cos x}{\sin x}$

The answer is (D).

▶ D

0749

If the measure of angle x is 30 degrees, then

$\sin 30° = \dfrac{1}{b}$

$\dfrac{1}{2} = \dfrac{1}{b}$, $b = 2$

So the answer is (D).

▶ D

0750

Using the Pythagorean theorem in triangle ABD,

$5^2 + BD^2 = 13^2$, $BD = 12$

So the answer is (D).

▶ D

0751

From the figure, we know that the angle DCE is equal to the angle DAB. Therefore,

$\sin \angle DCE = \sin \angle DAB$

$= \dfrac{BD}{13} = \dfrac{12}{13}$

The answer is (C).

▶ C

0752

Triangle ABD is similar to triangle CED by AA similarity. Using the ratio,

$\dfrac{BD}{AD} = \dfrac{ED}{CD}$

$\dfrac{12}{13} = \dfrac{ED}{6.5}$, $ED = 6$

So the answer is (A).

▶ A

Solutions Manual

0753

The ratio of the corresponding sides of BD to ED is 2 to 1. So the ratio of the area of triangle ABD to the area of triangle CED is

$$2^2:1^2=4:1 \Rightarrow \frac{4}{1}=4$$

The answer is (B).

▶ B

0754

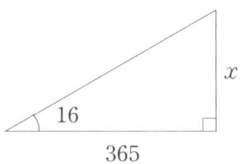

Let x be the height of the building as shown above. We have a right triangle where the horizontal distance from Rick to the building's base is 365. Using the tangent function,

$$\tan 16°=\frac{x}{365}, \quad x=365\tan 16°$$

Therefore, the height of the building is $365\tan 16°$. The answer is (C).

▶ C

0755

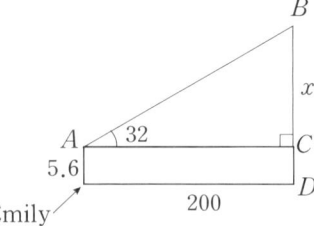

Let BD$=x$ be the height of the building as shown above. Using the tangent function in triangle ABC,

$$\tan 32°=\frac{x-5.6}{200}$$
$$x-5.6=200\ \tan 32°$$

$$x=130.57$$

Therefore, the height of the building is 130.57 feet. The answer is (C).

▶ C

0756

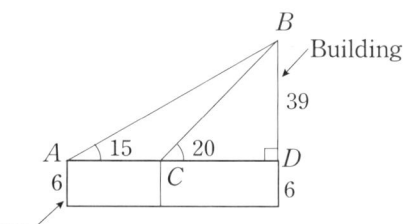

Let AC$=x$ be the distance the person traveled as shown above. Using the tangent function in triangle BCD,

$$\tan 20°=\frac{39}{\text{CD}}$$

$$\text{CD}=\frac{39}{\tan 20°}=107.15$$

Now, using the tangent function in triangle ABD,

$$\tan 15°=\frac{39}{x+107.15}$$

$$x+107.15=\frac{39}{\tan 15°}$$

$$x=\frac{39}{\tan 15°}-107.15=38.4$$

So the distance the person traveled is 38.4 feet. The answer is (D).

▶ D

0757

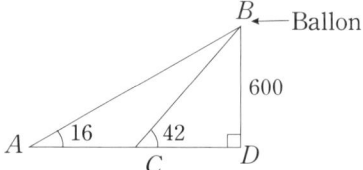

Let AC$=x$ be the motorcycle traveled as

shown above. Using the tangent function in triangle BCD,

$$\tan 42° = \frac{600}{CD}$$

$$CD = \frac{600}{\tan 42°} = 666.37$$

Now, using the tangent function in triangle ABD,

$$\tan 16° = \frac{600}{x + 666.37}$$

$$x + 666.37 = \frac{600}{\tan 16°}$$

$$x = \frac{600}{\tan 16°} - 666.37 = 1426.08$$

Therefore, the speed of the motorcycle is

$$Speed = \frac{Distance}{Time}$$

$$= \frac{1426.08}{30} = 47.54 \text{ ft/sec}$$

So the answer is (B).

▶ B

0758

Let $BD = x$ be the height of the mountain as shown above. Using the tangent function in triangle BCD,

$$\tan 12° = \frac{x}{CD}, \quad CD = \frac{x}{\tan 12°}$$

Using the tangent function in triangle ABD,

$$\tan 9° = \frac{x}{1000 + CD}$$

$$1000 + CD = \frac{x}{\tan 9°}$$

Now substitute $\frac{x}{\tan 12°}$ for CD and solve for x.

$$1000 + \frac{x}{\tan 12°} = \frac{x}{\tan 9°}$$

$$\frac{x}{\tan 9°} - \frac{x}{\tan 12°} = 1000$$

$$x\left(\frac{1}{\tan 9°} - \frac{1}{\tan 12°}\right) = 1000$$

$$x = \frac{1000}{t\left(\frac{1}{\tan 9°} - \frac{1}{\tan 12°}\right)} = 621.46$$

So the height of the mountain 621.46 feet. The answer is (D).

▶ D

0759

$$90° \times \frac{\pi \text{ rad}}{180°} = \frac{\pi}{2} \text{ rad}$$

So the value of a is 2.

▶ 2

0760

$$\frac{2\pi}{15} \text{ rad} \times \frac{180°}{\pi \text{ rad}} = 24°$$

So, an angle with a measure of $\frac{2\pi}{15}$ radians is equivalent to 24° in degrees.

▶ 24

0761

Let x be the length of side AB. Then

$$\sin A = \frac{6}{x} = \frac{3}{5}$$

$$3x = 30, \quad x = 10$$

Now, using the Pythagorean theorem,

$$6^2 + AC^2 = 10^2, \quad AC = 8$$

So the value of AC is 8.

▶ 8

Solutions Manual

0762

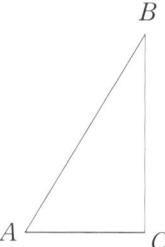

Using the cofunction identity of right triangle ABC, we know that $\sin B = \cos A$. So

$$\sin B = \cos A = \frac{3}{5}$$

▶ $\frac{3}{5}$

0763

Since $\cos A = \frac{3}{5}$, we can assume that $AC = 3a$ and $AB = 5a$, where a is positive real number. Using the Pythagorean theorem,

$$(3a)^2 + BC^2 = (5a)^2$$
$$BC^2 = 16a^2, \quad BC = 4a$$

So the value of $\tan A$ is

$$\tan A = \frac{4a}{3a} = \frac{4}{3}$$

▶ $\frac{4}{3}$

0764

In triangle ADE,

$$\tan A = \frac{6}{AE}$$

$$\frac{3}{4} = \frac{6}{AE}, \quad AE = \frac{24}{3}$$

In triangle ABC,

$$\tan A = \frac{4}{AC}$$

$$\frac{3}{4} = \frac{4}{AC}, \quad AC = \frac{16}{3}$$

So the value of side CE is

$$CE = AE - AC = \frac{24}{3} - \frac{16}{3} = \frac{8}{3}$$

▶ $\frac{8}{3}$

0765

In the given figure, angle A is equal to angle CBD. So $\sin \angle CBD = \sin A$. In triangle ABC,

$$\sin A = \frac{BC}{AC} = \frac{8}{10} = \frac{4}{5}$$

Therefore, the value of $\sin \angle CBD$ is $\frac{4}{5}$.

▶ $\frac{4}{5}$

0766

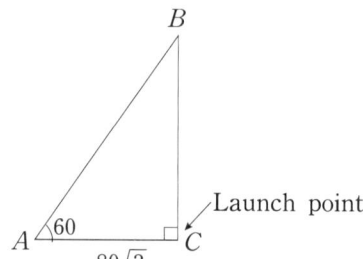

Let $AC = x$ be the height of the rocket as shown above. Using the tangent function in triangle ABC,

$$\tan 60° = \frac{x}{80\sqrt{3}}$$

$$x = 80\sqrt{3}\,\tan 60° = 240$$

So the height of the rocket is 240 meters.

▶ 240

0767

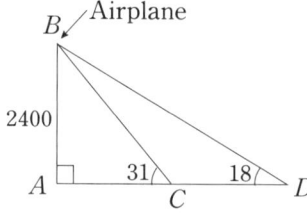

Let $AC = x$ be the distance between two the mountains.

Using the tangent function in triangle ABC,

$$\tan 31° = \frac{2400}{AC}$$

$$AC = \frac{2400}{\tan 31°} = 3994.27$$

Using the tangent function in triangle ABD,

$$\tan 18° = \frac{2400}{3994.27 + x}$$

$$3994.27 + x = \frac{2400}{\tan 18°}$$

$$x = \frac{2400}{\tan 18°} - 3994.27 = 3392.17$$

Therefore, the two mountains are 3392 feet

▶ 3392

Memo

01

$$\begin{cases} 2x+3y=10 \\ 4x-6y=15 \end{cases} \Rightarrow \begin{cases} 4x+6y=20 \\ 4x-6y=15 \end{cases}$$

Since we have $\dfrac{4}{4} \neq \dfrac{6}{-6}$ from the system above,

it has one solution. Therefore, the answer is (A).

→ **A**

02

Since the slope is 5,000, m increases by 5,000 for every c increases by 1. So, the increase in carat weight required to increase the value by $25,000 is 5 carats. The answer is (D).

→ **D**

03

The total cost $C(p)$ of shipping p packages is composed of two parts: the flat rate of $20 for the first package and an additional cost of $12 for each additional package beyond the first. Therefore, the function for the total cost $C(p)$ can be expressed as:

$$C(p) = 20 + 12(p-1)$$
$$= 12p + 8$$

The answer is (B).

→ **B**

04

In the function $A(t)$, 0.6 represents the proportion of the substance that remains after each 20 minutes. So the answer is (D).

→ **D**

05

$$g(0) = 5(0.8)^0 + 5$$
$$= 5 \cdot 1 + 5 = 10$$

The answer is 10

→ **10**

06

Since the function f passes through the vertex point $(1, -15)$, we have

$$\Rightarrow \begin{cases} -15 = a(1+3)(1-5) \\ -15 = -16a, \ a = \dfrac{15}{16} \end{cases}$$

So the answer is $\dfrac{15}{16}$.

→ $\dfrac{15}{16}$

07

The initial amount is 1,200 colonies and the rate of decrease is 35% per hour. So, the function $g(t)$ that models this situation is:

$$g(t) = 1,200(1 - 0.35)^t$$
$$= 1,200(0.65)^t$$

So the answer is (B).

→ **B**

08

Since $3x^2 + 8x - 16 = (3x-4)(x+4)$, factors of the expression $3x^2 + 8x - 16$ are

1, $3x-4$, $x+4$, and $3x^2 + 8x - 16$

So the answer is (A).

→ **A**

09

Substitute $3x+5$ for y in the equation $y=2x^2$.

$$3x+5=2x^2$$
$$2x^2-3x-5=0$$

The sum of the $x-$coordinates is

$$-\frac{b}{a}=-\frac{-3}{2}=1.5$$

So the answer is (B).

$$\rightarrow \mathbf{B}$$

10

$$(2\sqrt{a}+\sqrt{2b})^2$$
$$=(2\sqrt{a})^2+2(2\sqrt{a})(\sqrt{2b})+(\sqrt{2b})^2$$
$$=4a+4\sqrt{2ab}+2b$$

The answer is (D).

$$\rightarrow \mathbf{D}$$

11

The $x-$coordinate of the vertex is:

$$t=-\frac{b}{2a}=-\frac{29.4}{2(-9.8)}=1.5$$

So the ball reaches its maximum height after 1.5 seconds.

$$\rightarrow 1.5$$

12

The percent change is

$$\frac{900-1200}{1200}\times100\%=-25\%$$

So, bicycle rentals in August were 25% less than bicycle rentals in July. Therefore, the answer is (B).

$$\rightarrow \mathbf{B}$$

13

$$\sqrt{(4x-3)^2}=x$$
$$16x^2-24x+9=x^2$$
$$15x^2-24x+9=0$$
$$3(x-1)(5x-3)=0,\ x=1 \text{ or } x=\frac{3}{5}$$

So the sum of all solutions to the equation is

$$1+\frac{3}{5}=\frac{8}{5}$$

$$\rightarrow \frac{8}{5}$$

14

Using unit conversion, we have

$$\frac{1 \text{ rev}}{90 \text{ sec}}\times\frac{2\pi(12) \text{ m}}{1 \text{ rev}}\times\frac{1 \text{ km}}{1000 \text{ m}}\times\frac{3600 \text{ sec}}{1 \text{ hr}}$$
$$=3.016 \text{ km/hr}$$

So the answer is (B).

$$\rightarrow \mathbf{B}$$

15

8 dozen$=8\times12=96$ servings.

We can set up a proportion to find out how many cups of milk are needed for 96 servings:

$$\frac{4 \text{ servings}}{2 \text{ cups}}=\frac{96 \text{ servings}}{x \text{ cups}}$$
$$4x=192,\ x=48$$

So, the restaurant should use 48 cups of milk to make eight dozen servings of the fruit smoothie.

$$\rightarrow 48$$

16

Let x be the total price of the items before the discount. Then we have

$$x(1-0.3)(1+0.08)=245$$
$$x=324$$

So, the total price of the items, before the discount, was approximately \$324.

→ 324

17

P(Undergraduate | Economics) is

$$\frac{120}{120+85}=0.585$$

The answer is (C).

→ C

18

Because sides AE and AB are perpendicular to sides ED and BD, respectively, it follows that angles AED and ABD are both right angles. Furthermore, as AE=AB and AD=AD, we can establish that triangles AED and ABD are congruent due to HL congruence criterion. Consequently, angle ADE must be equal to angle ADB. Now, in triangle BCD, we can deduce that angle BCD equals:

$$180°-30°-90°=60°$$

If we denote angle ADE as x,

$$2x+60=180, \quad x=60°$$

Therefore, angle ADE is indeed 60°. The answer is (C).

→ C

19

$$x^2+y^2-x+3y=\frac{15}{4}$$
$$x^2-x+\frac{1}{4}+y^2+3y+\frac{9}{4}=\frac{15}{4}+\frac{1}{4}+\frac{9}{4}$$
$$\left(x-\frac{1}{2}\right)^2+\left(y+\frac{3}{2}\right)^2=\left(\frac{5}{2}\right)^2$$

The radius of the circle is $\frac{5}{2}$. So the diameter is 5.

→ 5

20

The standard deviation measures the spread or dispersion of the data points from the mean. When you subtract 3 points from each score, you are effectively shifting the entire dataset downward by 3 units. So it won't change the relative distances between the data points. Therefore, the standard deviation will remain unchanged. The answer is (D).

→ D

21

Let x be the number of residents who would be expected to have visited the museum in the last month in a city with a population of 60,000. Using the concept of proportion:

$$\frac{480}{800}=\frac{x}{60000}$$
$$800x=480 \cdot 60000, \quad x=36000$$

So, approximately 36,000 residents would be expected to have visited the museum in the last month. The answer is (D).

→ D

22

In right triangles ABD and BCD, $\angle A = \angle DBC$. Therefore, $\sin \angle A = \sin \angle DBC$. The answer is (D).

→ D

01

$$y+5=(3y-1)-qy$$
$$y+5=3y-qy-1$$
$$y+5=(3-q)y-1$$

For the equation to have no solution, $3-q$ must be equal to 1.

$$3-q=1, \quad q=2$$

So the answer is (C).

$$\rightarrow \text{C}$$

02

Let x be the number of hours the service provider worked. Then we have

$$30+15x=150$$
$$15x=120, \quad x=8$$

So, the service provider worked for 8 hours on the customer's lawn. The answer is (C).

$$\rightarrow \text{C}$$

03

From $\begin{cases} 3x-2y=3 \\ 2x-3y=3 \end{cases}$, we have $\dfrac{3}{2} \neq \dfrac{-2}{-3}$.

Therefore, the system has exactly one solution. The answer is (B).

$$\rightarrow \text{B}$$

04

$$h(t)=500,000(1.015)^t$$
$$=500,000(1+0.015)^t$$

So, the value of y, which represents the percentage by which the city's population increases per year compared to the previous year's population, is 1.5%. The answer is (C).

$$\rightarrow \text{C}$$

05

The number of fish is doubling (by factor of 2) every 2 years, which is characteristic of exponential growth, not linear growth. So the answer is (C).

$$\rightarrow \text{C}$$

06

The slope of the line is

$$m=\frac{5-(-4)}{-1-2}=-3$$

$$\rightarrow -3$$

07

$$2x^3+2x^2-24x=2x(x^2+x-12)$$
$$=2x(x+4)(x-3)$$

Therefore, the value of a is 4.

$$\rightarrow 4$$

08

Using synthetic division,

$$\frac{x^2-4x+1}{x-3} \rightarrow 3\begin{array}{|rrr} 1 & -4 & 1 \\ & 3 & -3 \\ \hline 1 & -1 & \boxed{-2} \end{array}$$

$$\frac{x^2-4x+1}{x-3}=x-1-\frac{2}{x-3}$$

Therefore, the answer is (D).

$$\rightarrow \text{D}$$

09

To find the minimum value of the function, we can complete the square to express it in vertex form.

$$y = x^2 - 16x + m$$
$$= x^2 - 16x + 8^2 - 8^2 + m$$
$$= (x-8)^2 + m - 64$$

$\Rightarrow p = 8$ and $q = m - 64$

Therefore, the value of $p - q$ in terms of m is

$$8 - (m - 64) = 72 - m$$

The answer is (C).

$\rightarrow$ C

10

$$\left(\frac{6}{x+3} + \frac{2}{x-2}\right)(x+3)(x-2) = 3(x+3)(x-2)$$
$$6(x-2) + 2(x+3) = 3(x^2 + x - 6)$$
$$8x - 6 = 3x^2 + 3x - 18$$
$$3x^2 - 5x - 12 = 0$$
$$(x-3)(3x+4) = 0$$
$$x = 3 \text{ and } x = -\frac{4}{3}$$

Both of these x values are valid solutions to the equation because when we substitute them into the equation, neither of them makes the denominator equal to zero. So the answer is (C).

$\rightarrow$ C

11

The answer is (B) because x is 0 (which corresponds to the year 2010), the function evaluates to:

$$g(0) = 80(0)^2 + 250(0) + 4{,}500$$
$$= 4{,}500$$

So, the constant term 4,500 represents the estimated number of smartphone users in the year 2010.

$\rightarrow$ B

12

$$\Rightarrow \begin{cases} 4\sqrt[3]{16} = 4 \cdot (4^2)^{\frac{1}{3}} = 4 \cdot 4^{\frac{2}{3}} = 4^{1+\frac{2}{3}} = 4^{\frac{5}{3}} \text{ or} \\ 4\sqrt[3]{16} = 4^{\frac{5}{3}} = (2^2)^{\frac{5}{3}} = 2^{\frac{10}{3}} \end{cases}$$

Therefore, the answer is (C).

$\rightarrow$ C

13

Let x be the total number of animals. Then we have

$$0.3x = 240, \quad x = 800$$

So, there are 800 animals in the wildlife reserve. The answer is (B).

$\rightarrow$ B

14

Using ratios,

$$\frac{\text{Electric}}{\text{Gasoline}} = \frac{50{,}000}{x} = \frac{1}{8}$$
$$x = 400{,}000$$

So, there were 400,000 gasoline cars in the country in 2015.

$\rightarrow$ 400,000

15

Substituting 37 for C in the formula and solving for F:

$$37 = \frac{5}{9}(F - 32)$$
$$66.6 = F - 32, \quad F = 98.6$$

So, the closest temperature in degrees Fahrenheit to the average human body temperature of 37 degrees Celsius is 99°F. The answer is (C).

$\rightarrow$ C

16

The gencral equation for a circle with center coordinates (h, k) and radius r is given as:

$$(x-h)^2+(y-k)^2=r^2$$

So, in this case, the center of the circle has coordinates $(h, k)=(4, 0)$. The answer is (A).

$$\to \text{A}$$

17

Because we have two corresponding angles that are congruent, it is enough to conclude that triangles ABC and DEF are similar through the AA similarity. Hence, no further information is required. The answer is (D).

$$\to \text{D}$$

18

Both data sets exhibit the same level of dispersion from their respective means. Therefore, the standard deviation of data set I is equal to the standard deviation of data set II. The answer is (A).

$$\to \text{A}$$

19

Using unit conversion,

$$120° \times \frac{\pi \text{ rad}}{180°} = \frac{2\pi}{3} \text{ rad}$$

So the answer is (B).

$$\to \text{B}$$

20

Use the vertex form of a quadratic equation:

$$y=a(x+0)^2-2$$

Since the quadratic passes through the point $(1, 0)$,

$$0=a(1+0)^2-2$$
$$0=a-2, \ a=2$$

So we can write the quadratic function:

$$y=2x^2-2$$

The answer is (D).

$$\to \text{D}$$

21

$$|2x-5|=15$$
$$\Rightarrow 2x-5=15 \text{ or } 2x-5=-15$$
$$2x=20 \text{ or } \quad 2x=-10$$
$$x=10 \text{ or } \quad x=-5$$

So the sum of the solutions is

$$10+(-5)=5$$

$$\to 5$$

22

The arc length(s) is given as π, and the radius (r) is 4 centimeters:

$$s=2\pi r \times \frac{\theta}{360}$$
$$\pi=2\pi(4) \times \frac{\theta}{360}, \ 1=\frac{\theta}{45}, \ \theta=45$$

So, the degree measure of angle AOB is 45 degrees.

$$\to 45$$

01

(A) describes a decreasing linear relationship because as the price increases by \$2, the units sold decrease by 100. This is consistent with the idea of a negative linear relationship. So the answer is (A).

$\rightarrow$ **A**

02

$$A=\frac{2B+C}{D-B}$$
$$A(D-B)=2B+C$$
$$AD-AB=2B+C$$
$$AD-C=2B+AB$$
$$AD-C=B(2+A), \quad B=\frac{AD-C}{2+A}$$

The answer is (B).

$\rightarrow$ **B**

03

Since line n is perpendicular to line m, the slope of m is $-\frac{1}{2}$. Among the answer choices, the equation in (C) has a slope of $-\frac{1}{2}$.

$$x+2y=8$$
$$2y=-x+8, \quad y=-\frac{1}{2}x+4$$

The answer is (C).

$\rightarrow$ **C**

04

$2x$ represents the total daily revenue generated by selling x vanilla cupcakes. So the answer is (C).

$\rightarrow$ **C**

05

$$\frac{xy^2}{2}\left(\frac{4x}{y}-6y^3\right)=2x^2y-3xy^5$$

Therefore,

$$a+b+c+d=2+1+1+5=9$$

$\rightarrow$ **9**

06

Using the discriminant,

$$D=7^2-4(2)(6-p)=0$$
$$49-48+8p=0$$
$$1=-8p, \quad p=-\frac{1}{8}$$

$\rightarrow -\frac{1}{8}$

07

$$P(t)=300{,}000(0.965)^t$$
$$=300{,}000(1-0.035)^t$$

So, the value of d, which represents the percentage by which the city's population decreases per year compared to the previous year's population, is 3.5%. The answer is (D).

$\rightarrow$ **D**

08

To find the value of the investment after 3 years, you can use the formula for compound interest:

$$A(t)=10{,}000(1+0.0477)^3=11{,}500$$

So, the answer is (C) \$11,500.

→ C

09

Let's calculate $H(x+b)$ using the definition of $H(x)$:

$$H(x+b)=4(x+b)+3$$
$$ax+b=4x+(4b+3)$$
$$\Rightarrow a=4 \text{ and } b=4b+3$$
$$-3=3b,\ b=-1$$

Therefore,

$$a+b=4+(-1)=3$$

The answer is (A).

→ A

10

Let x be the width of the rectangle. Then the length is $2x-4$. So the area $A(x)$ of the rectangle is

$$A(x)=(2x-4)\cdot x$$
$$=2x^2-4x$$

The answer is (D).

→ D

11

Let's check each answer choice:

(A) 0: $\sqrt{(2\cdot0-1)^2}=2\cdot0-1 \rightarrow 1\neq-1$
(B) 1: $\sqrt{(2\cdot1-1)^2}=2\cdot1-1 \rightarrow 1=1$
(C) 2: $\sqrt{(2\cdot2-1)^2}=2\cdot2-1 \rightarrow 3=3$
(D) 3: $\sqrt{(2\cdot3-1)^2}=2\cdot3-1 \rightarrow 5=5$

So the answer is (A).

→ A

12

The percent increase is

$$\frac{3(800)-800}{800}\times100\%=200\%$$

So, the product production increased by 200% from January to June. The answer is (C).

→ C

13

Let x be the time John and his father spent hiking at 3 kilometers per hour. Then they spent $6.6-x$ hours hiking at 6 kilometers per hour. Since the total hiking time is 6.5 hours:

$$3x+6(6.5-x)=30$$
$$3x+39-6x=30$$
$$-3x=-9,\ x=3$$

So, they hiked at 3 kilometers per hour for 3 hours. The answer is (B).

→ B

14

$$x-\frac{p}{100}\cdot x=n$$
$$\frac{p}{100}\cdot x=x-n$$
$$px=100(x-n),\ p=\frac{100(x-n)}{x}$$

So the answer is (A).

→ A

15

$$4\cdot2^a-2^{a+1}=32$$
$$4\cdot2^a-2\cdot2^a=2^5$$
$$2\cdot2^a=2^5$$
$$2^{1+a}=2^5 \Rightarrow 1+a=5,\ a=4$$

So the value of a is 4.

→ 4

16

Using unit conversion,

$$20 \cancel{m^2} \times \frac{3.281 \cancel{ft}}{1 \cancel{m}} \times \frac{3.281 \cancel{ft}}{1 \cancel{m}} \times \frac{\$5}{\cancel{ft^2}} = \$1,076.5$$

So the answer is (D).

→ **D**

17

Percentage of Social Science students who prefer either Pizza or Sushi is

$$\frac{120+90}{280} \times 100\% = 75\%$$

Percentage of Engineering students who prefer either Pizza or Sushi is

$$\frac{80+64}{240} \times 100\% = 60\%$$

So the difference in percentages is

$$75-60 = 15\%$$

The answer is (D).

→ **D**

18

In triangles ABC and ACE, we notice that angles A and BCE are congruent. This observation allows us to establish that these two triangles are similar by AA similarity criterion. Applying this similarity, we can set up the proportion:

$$\frac{AB}{CB} = \frac{AC}{CE} \implies \frac{5}{4} = \frac{3}{CE}$$

$$CE = \frac{12}{5}$$

Moving on to triangles ABC and CEF, we again observe that angles A and ECF are congruent, leading to the conclusion that these two triangles are also similar by AA similarity. Using this similarity, we set up the proportion:

$$\frac{AB}{CE} = \frac{AC}{CF} \implies \frac{5}{\frac{12}{5}} = \frac{3}{CF}$$

$$CF = \frac{36}{25}$$

Hence, we determine that CF is equal to $\frac{36}{25}$.

→ $\frac{36}{25}$

19

The center of the circle is the midpoint of the line segment connecting the two endpoints $(5, -6)$ and $(-3, 4)$:

$$\left(\frac{5+(-3)}{2}, \frac{-6+4}{2} \right) = (1, -1)$$

Now, use the distance formula to find the radius between one of the endpoints and the center:

$$\sqrt{(5-1)^2+(-6-(-1))^2} = \sqrt{16+25}$$
$$= \sqrt{41}$$

So, the equation of the circle is:

$$(x-1)^2+(y+1)^2 = (\sqrt{41})^2$$
$$(x-1)^2+(y+1)^2 = 41$$

The answer is (B).

→ **B**

20

The two prisms are similar. Since the length of each edge of prism A is 1.5 times the edge of the corresponding side of prism B, the ratio of volume of prism A to the volume of prism B is

$$\frac{1.5^3}{1^3} = 3.375$$

So, the volume of prism A is 3.375 times the volume of prism B. The answer is (C).

→ **C**

21

The slope of the line of best fit is about

$$\frac{125-45}{180-140}=2$$

Since the slope represents the rate of change in weight for each unit change in height, (A) is the correct interpretation of the slope of the line of best fit.

$$\rightarrow \textbf{A}$$

22

$$5x^2+4x+1=0$$

$$x^2+\frac{4}{5}x=-\frac{1}{5}$$

$$x^2+\frac{4}{5}x+\left(\frac{2}{5}\right)^2=-\frac{1}{5}+\left(\frac{2}{5}\right)^2$$

$$\left(x+\frac{2}{5}\right)^2=-\frac{1}{25} \Rightarrow h=\frac{2}{5} \text{ and } k=-\frac{1}{25}$$

So the value of $\frac{h}{k}$ is

$$\frac{h}{k}=\frac{\frac{2}{5}}{-\frac{1}{25}}=\frac{2}{5}\cdot-25=-10$$

$$\rightarrow \textbf{-10}$$

01

$$3(ax+1)-2=9x-b$$

$$3ax+1=9x-b$$

For the equation to have exactly one solution,

$$3a=9, \ a=3 \text{ and}$$

$$1=-b, \ b=-1$$

So the answer is (C).

$$\rightarrow \textbf{C}$$

02

Equation $x^2+kx+12=0$ has more no real solution if the discriminant D<0.

$$D=k^2-4(1)(12)$$

$$=k^2-48<0$$

$$k^2<48$$

$$|k|<\sqrt{48} \Rightarrow -6.93<k<6.93$$

So the answer is (C).

$$\rightarrow \textbf{C}$$

03

Since x is the width of the rectangle, the expression for length is $3x+15$. So, the function that represents the perimeter (P) of the rectangle in terms of its width (x) is:

$$P(x)=2(3x+15+x)$$

$$=8x+30$$

The answer is (D).

$$\rightarrow \textbf{D}$$

04

$$\sqrt{2x+9}-x=3$$
$$(\sqrt{2x+9})^2=(x+3)^2$$
$$2x+9=x^2+6x+9$$
$$x^2+4x=0$$
$$x(x+4)=0 \Rightarrow x=0 \text{ and } x=-4$$

Now, let's check the solution:
$$\sqrt{2(0)+9}-0=3, \ 3=3$$
$$\sqrt{2(-4)+9}-(-4)=3, \ 5\neq 3$$

So, the only solution to the equation is $x=0$. The answer is (B).

$$\rightarrow \textbf{B}$$

05

$$a\sqrt{a}=\sqrt[3]{b^2}, \ a\cdot a^{\frac{1}{2}}=b^{\frac{2}{3}}, \ a^{\frac{3}{2}}=b^{\frac{2}{3}}$$

$$\left(a^{\frac{3}{2}}\right)^{\frac{3}{2}}=\left(b^{\frac{2}{3}}\right)^{\frac{3}{2}}, \ a^{\frac{9}{4}}=b$$

Now, substitute $a^{\frac{9}{4}}$ for b in $a^{2x+3}=b^{\frac{3}{2}}$.

$$a^{2x+3}=\left(a^{\frac{9}{4}}\right)^{\frac{3}{2}}, \ a^{2x+3}=a^{\frac{27}{8}}$$

$$\Rightarrow 2x+3=\frac{27}{8}$$

$$2x=\frac{3}{8}, \ x=\frac{3}{16}$$

Therefore, the value of x is $\frac{3}{16}$.

$$\rightarrow \frac{3}{16}$$

06

The sum of the solutions is
$$-\frac{b}{a}=-\frac{6}{4}=-\frac{3}{2}$$

$$\rightarrow -\frac{3}{2}$$

07

Let $x+2=A$. Then we have
$$3A^2+48A=3A(A+16)$$
$$=3(x+2)(x+2+16)$$
$$=3(x+2)(x+18)$$

So the answer is (A).

$$\rightarrow \textbf{A}$$

08

The height of Mountain Y is 1.12 times the height of Mountain X, which is
$$Y=7545(1.12)$$
$$=7545(1+0.12)$$

So, the height of Mountain Y is 12% greater than the height of Mountain X. The answer is (B).

$$\rightarrow \textbf{B}$$

09

I. $k=-2$:
$$\frac{4}{6}=\frac{-(-2)}{3} \Rightarrow \text{The system has no solution.}$$
II. $k=0$:
$$\frac{4}{6}\neq\frac{0}{3} \Rightarrow \text{The system has one solution.}$$
III. $k=2$:
$$\frac{4}{6}\neq\frac{-2}{3} \Rightarrow \text{The system has one solution.}$$

So the answer is (D).

$$\rightarrow \textbf{D}$$

10

The number 4 in the equation represents the slope of the line. Therefore, the correct interpretation is "y increases by 4 for every x increases by 1". The answer is (A).

→ A

11

Using unit conversion,

$$2 \text{ km}^2 \times \frac{1000 \text{ m}}{1 \text{ km}} \times \frac{1000 \text{ m}}{1 \text{ km}} = 2{,}000{,}000 \text{ m}^2$$

So the answer is (D).

→ D

12

Since the equation has two real solutions, the discriminant of quadratic equation must be greater than zero.

$$D = (-5)^2 - 4a(4) > 0$$
$$25 > 16a$$

So the answer is (B).

→ B

13

substitute the expression $x^2 - 4$ for y into the second equation:

$$4x + x^2 - 4 = b$$
$$x^2 + 4x - 4 - b = 0$$

To have exactly one distinct real solution, the discriminant of this quadratic equation must be equal to zero.

$$D = 4^2 - 4(1)(-4-b) = 0$$
$$16 + 16 + 4b = 0$$

$$32 = -4b, \quad b = -8$$

Therefore, the value of b is -8.

→ −8

14

Let $N(t)$ represent the number of cars at a given time t, measured in years from the year 2010:

$$N(t) = x(1-0.05)^t$$

So, the expression that represents the number of cars registered in the city in 2020 in terms of x is:

$$N(10) = x(1-0.05)^{10}$$

So the answer is (C).

→ C

15

Substitute the point $(4, k)$ into the inequality $5x - y > 12$:

$$5(4) - k > 12$$
$$-k > -8, \quad k < 8$$

So the only value that could not be the value of k is 8. The answer is (B).

→ B

16

When the store reduces the price of the item by \$$a$, the new price becomes \$$(50-a)$ per item. As a result of this price reduction, they sell an additional $4a$ items. Therefore, the new number of items sold per day is $120 + 4a$, and the new revenue $R(a)$ is

$$R(a) = (50-a)(120+4a)$$

The function $R(a)$ has zeros at $a=50$ and $a=-30$. This means that $R(a)$ equals zero when a is either 50 or -30. The midpoint between these two zeros is $a=10$, which corresponds to the axis of symmetry.

139

Consequently, the revenue is maximized when $a=10$ and the new price per item is $\$50-\$10=\$40$. This price results in maximum revenue.

$$\rightarrow \textbf{40}$$

17

$$x^2+y^2+6x+by-6=0$$

$$x^2+6x+3^2+y^2+by+\left(\frac{b}{2}\right)^2=6+3^2+\left(\frac{b}{2}\right)^2$$

$$(x+3)^2+\left(y+\frac{b}{2}\right)^2=15+\frac{b^2}{4}$$

Since the radius of the circle is $2\sqrt{10}$:

$$15+\frac{b^2}{4}=(2\sqrt{10})^2$$

$$15+\frac{b^2}{4}=40$$

$$b^2=100,\ b=10$$

So the value of b is 10.

$$\rightarrow \textbf{10}$$

18

Let x be the price of the fifth item. Then we have

$$20\cdot4+x=40\cdot5$$

$$80+x=200,\ x=120$$

So, the price of the fifth item is $120. The answer is (B).

$$\rightarrow \textbf{B}$$

19

$$f(x+h)=2(x+h)^2+4$$
$$=2(x^2+2xh+h^2)+4$$
$$=2x^2+4xh+2h^2+4$$

Therefore,

$$f(x+h)-f(x)$$
$$=2x^2+4xh+2h^2+4-(2x^2+4)$$
$$=4xh+2h^2$$

So the answer is (D).

$$\rightarrow \textbf{D}$$

20

By using the cofunction identity, we can express that in right triangle CDE, the sine of angle D is equal to the sine of angle ECD. So the answer is (B).

$$\rightarrow \textbf{B}$$

21

If each data point is multiplied by 2, the sum of the data points will also be doubled, but the number of data points remains the same. So, the mean will indeed be doubled. Also, multiplying each data point by 2 does not change their relative order, so the median will also be doubled. Finally, if each data point is multiplied by 2, both the maximum and minimum values will be doubled. Therefore, the range will also be doubled. So the answer is (D).

$$\rightarrow \textbf{D}$$

22

Let x and y be the cost per pound of apples and bananas, respectively. Also, let a and b be the number of pounds of apples and bananas Lisa bought, respectively.

The cost per pound of apples was 1.25 times that of bananas:

$$x=1.25y$$

Lisa bought 1.5 times as many pounds of apples as pounds of bananas:

$$a=1.5b$$

Now, we can set up an equation for the total cost:

$$ax+by=13.2$$

$$(1.5b)(1.25y)+by=13.2$$

$$1.875by+by=13.2$$

$$2.875by=13.2,\ by=4.59$$

So, Lisa spent approximately $4.59 on bananas.

$$\rightarrow \textbf{4.59}$$

01

$$4(x-3)+5=2x+7$$
$$4x-7=2x+7$$
$$2x=14, \ x=7$$

The answer is (C).

→ C

02

Using unit conversion,

$$\frac{17.5 \ \cancel{km}}{1 \ \cancel{sec}} \times \frac{1 \ mi}{1.61 \ \cancel{km}} \times \frac{3600 \ \cancel{sec}}{1 \ hr} = \frac{39,130 \ mi}{hr}$$

So the answer is (A)

→ A

03

To determine which point is NOT on the line defined by the equation, you can plug each of the given points into the equation of the line and see if they satisfy it.

For (B): $y=4(-2)-3=-8-3=-11$

This point does not satisfy the equation, so it is NOT on the line. The answer is (B).

→ B

04

To calculate the percentage by which Rachel would save on her grocery expenses this year, we have

$$\frac{1,200}{10,000} \times 100\% = 12\%$$

So, Rachel would save 12% on her grocery expenses this year. The answer is (B).

→ B

05

Let x be the total value of the properties sold. Then we have

$$4,000+0.02x \geq 7,500$$
$$0.02x \geq 3,500, \ x \geq 175,500$$

So, the minimum total value of the properties sold to achieve the agent's goal of at least $7,500 in income is $175,000. The answer is (A).

→ A

06

Let x and y be the total number of cookies and boxes, respectively. Given that packing 15 cookies in each box leaves 7 cookies, we have

$$x=15y+7$$

When he chooses to pack 17 cookies in each box, he is left with 5 boxes:

$$x=17(y-5)$$

Now, substitute 15y+8 for x into second equation.

$$15y+7=17(y-5)$$
$$15y+7=17y-85$$
$$92=2y, \ y=46$$

So the number of cookies in the bakery is

$$x=15(46)+7=697 \text{cookies}$$

→ 697

07

In an isosceles right triangle, the ratio of the leg to the hypotenuse is 1 to $\sqrt{2}$. So using ratios,

$$\frac{\text{leg}}{\text{hyp}} = \frac{1}{\sqrt{2}} = \frac{2}{\sqrt{k}}$$
$$\sqrt{k}=2\sqrt{2}, \ k=8$$

So the value of k is 8.

→ 8

141

08

$$\begin{array}{l} (x-2)-(y+3)=7 \\ +\ (x-2)+(y+3)=-5 \\ \hline \qquad 2(x-2)=2 \\ \qquad 4(x-2)=4 \end{array}$$

The answer is (A).

$\rightarrow$ A

09

Using the discriminant D,

$$D=6^2-4(3)(2)=12>0$$

Therefore, the equation has two distinct real solutions.
The answer is (C).

$\rightarrow$ C

10

$a^2-b^2=-24$

$(a+b)(a-b)=-24$

$8(a-b)=-24,\ a-b=-3$

The answer is (A).

$\rightarrow$ A

11

$9^{x-3}-27=0$

$(3^2)^{x-3}=27$

$3^{2x-6}=3^3,\ 2x-6=3,\ x=\dfrac{9}{2}$

$\rightarrow \dfrac{9}{2}$

12

From the table, you can see that there are 18 blue SUVs. So, the probability of selecting a blue SUV is:

$$\frac{18}{113}=0.16$$

The answer is (A).

$\rightarrow$ A

13

$$2+\frac{1}{x-4}=6+\frac{3}{x-4}$$

$$2+\frac{1}{x-4}=6+3\cdot\frac{1}{x-4}$$

Let $A=\dfrac{1}{x-4}$. Then we have

$$2+A=6+3A$$

$$-4=2A,\ A=-2$$

Therefore, $\dfrac{1}{x-4}=-2$. The answer is (A).

$\rightarrow$ A

14

The median and range of the test scores in the Math class are 70 and 50 (100−50), respectively.
Also, the median and range of the test scores in the English class are 80 and 50 (100−50), respectively. So the correct answer is (C). For (B) and (D), the mean and standard deviation cannot be directly evaluated from a box plot.

$\rightarrow$ C

15

To determine which point does not lie in the solution region of the system of inequalities, you can plug each point's coordinates into the inequalities and check if they satisfy both inequalities.

For (C): $4(2)+0\geq8$, $8\geq8$, but
$$2(2)-3(0)<-2, \ 4\not<-2$$

Therefore, the answer is (C).

$$\rightarrow \text{C}$$

16

Generalizing the findings to the entire population of employees within the tech company makes the most sense because the survey was conducted among employees of that specific company. So the answer is (C).

$$\rightarrow \text{C}$$

17

In the graph, 6 out of the 9 actual data points fall below the line of best fit. Therefore, the fraction of data points where the predicted $y-$value by the line of best fit is greater than the actual $y-$value is:
$$\frac{6}{9}=\frac{2}{3}$$

$$\rightarrow \frac{2}{3}$$

18

Using ratios,
$$\frac{3 \text{ muffins}}{\$5}=\frac{9 \text{ muffins}}{\$x}$$
$$3x=45, \ x=15$$

So, the cost of purchasing 9 muffins is $15.

$$\rightarrow 15$$

19

The percent increases is
$$\frac{2.4k-k}{k}\times100\%=140\%$$

So, the expression $2.4k$ represents an increase of 140%. The answer is (C).

$$\rightarrow \text{C}$$

20

To calculate the mass of a substance, we can use the formula:
$$\text{Density D}=\frac{\text{mass } m}{\text{volume } V}$$
$$2.5=\frac{m}{80}, \ m=200$$

So, the mass of the substance is 200 grams. The answer is (D).

$$\rightarrow \text{D}$$

21

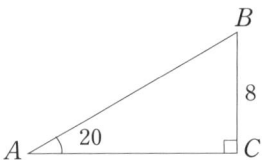

As shown in the figure above,
$$\tan20°=\frac{8}{\text{AC}}$$
$$\text{AC}=\frac{8}{\tan20°}=22$$

Now, we can find the area of the triangle:
$$\text{A}=\frac{1}{2}\cdot22\cdot8=88$$

So, the area of the triangle is closest to 88 square centimeters. The answer is (A).

$$\rightarrow \text{A}$$

22

Using ratios

$$\frac{\$60}{120\ ft^2} = \frac{\$x}{10 \cdot 10\ ft^2}$$

$$120x = 6000,\ x = 50$$

So, the tiles to cover the entire bathroom floor cost $50.

→ 50

01

The slope of the line $3x + 4y = 1$ is $-\frac{3}{4}$.

So the slope of a line perpendicular to this line is $\frac{4}{3}$.

Now, the equation of the line with slope $\frac{4}{3}$ and passing through the point $(-3,\ 4)$ is:

$$y - 4 = \frac{4}{3}(x - (-3))$$

$$3(y - 4) = 4(x + 3)$$

$$3y - 12 = 4x + 12$$

$$4x - 3y = -24$$

So the answer is (D).

→ D

02

$$\sqrt{x+3} - 3 = \sqrt{2-x}$$

$$(\sqrt{x+3} - 3)^2 = (\sqrt{2-x})^2$$

$$(x+3) - 6\sqrt{x+3} + 9 = 2 - x$$

$$6\sqrt{x+3} = 2x + 10,\ 3\sqrt{x+3} = x + 5$$

$$(3\sqrt{x+3})^2 = (x+5)^2$$

$$9(x+3) = x^2 + 10x + 25$$

$$x^2 + x - 2 = 0$$

$$(x+2)(x-1) = 0,\ x = -2\ \text{or}\ x = 1$$

Now, check the solution:

$$x = -2:\ \sqrt{-2+3} - 3 = \sqrt{2-(-2)},\ -2 \neq 2$$

$$x = 1:\ \sqrt{1+3} - 3 = \sqrt{2-1}),\ -1 \neq 1$$

There is no solution to the equation. So the answer is (A).

→ A

03

The area of a triangular plaza is

$$A = \frac{1}{2} \cdot 40 \cdot 24 = 480 \text{ m}^2$$

Now, the cost of paving the plaza is

$$480 \text{ m}^2 \times \frac{\$12}{1 \text{ m}^2} = \$5,760$$

So the answer is (C).

→ C

04

$$\left(3(x-2) + \frac{5x-4}{4}\right) \cdot 4 = \left(\frac{9(1+x)}{2} - \frac{x+46}{4}\right) \cdot 4$$
$$12(x-2) + (5x-4) = 18(1+x) - (x+46)$$
$$17x - 26 = 17x - 28$$
$$-26 \neq -28$$

The equation has no solution because the equation is always false for all x. The answer is (B).

→ B

05

15 minutes is 0.25 hour. So 2 hours and 15 minutes is 2.25 hours. Now, using unit conversion,

$$12 \text{ liters} - \frac{1 \text{ liter}}{30 \text{ km}} \cdot \frac{60 \text{ km}}{1 \text{ hr}} \cdot 2.25 \text{ hr}$$
$$= 7.5 \text{ liters}$$

Therefore, the motorcycle will have 7.5 liters of fuel remaining. The answer is (B)

→ B

06

$$4^{\frac{1}{3}} \cdot 12^{\frac{2}{3}} = (2^2)^{\frac{1}{3}} \cdot (2^2 \cdot 3)^{\frac{2}{3}}$$
$$= (2^2 \cdot 2^4 \cdot 3^2)^{\frac{1}{3}}$$
$$= (2^6 \cdot 3^2)^{\frac{1}{3}} = 4 \cdot \sqrt[3]{9}$$

$\Rightarrow a = 4$ and $b = 9$

So the value of $a + b$ is $4 + 9 = 13$.

→ 13

07

For a quadratic equation to have exactly one solution, the discriminant D must equal zero.

$$D = (-5)^2 - 4(3)(2m) = 0$$
$$25 - 24m = 0, \quad m = \frac{25}{24}$$

So the value of $24m$ is

$$24 \cdot \frac{25}{24} = 25.$$

→ 25

08

There are 300 species of birds in total, and 180 of them are migratory. So the number of non−migratory bird is 120. The probability of selecting a non−migratory bird is then

$$\frac{120}{300} = 0.4$$

So the answer is (B).

→ B

09

First, let's calculate the amount of apples and oranges that were discarded.

For apples: $0.052 \cdot 42.6 = 2.2152$

For oranges: $0.089 \cdot 28.4 = 2.5276$

So the difference in percent between the amount of discarded oranges and apples is:

$$\frac{2.5276-2.2152}{2.2152}\times 100\%=14.1\%$$

So, the amount of discarded oranges was approximately 14% greater than that of discarded apples. The answer is (D).

$$\rightarrow \text{D}$$

10

Let's define the lengths of segments CG and AB as x and y, respectively. Since AB is parallel to GC, it follows that angle ABF is equal to angle GCF. Consequently, triangles FCG and FBA are similar due to AA similarity criterion:

$$\frac{CG}{BA}=\frac{FG}{FA}, \ \frac{x}{8}=\frac{10-y}{10}, \ 10x=8(10-y)$$

Next, considering that GC is parallel to DE, we can establish that angle GCA is equal to angle EDA. This similarity leads to triangles ACG and ADE also being similar by AA similarity:

$$\frac{CG}{DE}=\frac{AG}{AE}, \ \frac{x}{6}=\frac{y}{10+3}$$

$$13x=6y, \ y=\frac{13x}{6}$$

By substituting this expression for y into the first equation, we obtain:

$$10x=8\left(10-\frac{13x}{6}\right)$$

$$10x=80-\frac{52x}{3}, \ \frac{82x}{3}=80, \ x=\frac{120}{41}$$

Therefore, the measure of side CG is $\frac{120}{41}$.

$$\rightarrow \frac{120}{41}$$

11

$$12x^3y^2\left(\frac{5}{6x^2y}-\frac{x}{4y^2}\right)=10xy-3x^4$$

So $k=10$, $a=1$, are $b=4$. The value of $k+a+b$ is

$$10+1+4=15$$

The answer is (D).

$$\rightarrow \text{D}$$

12

For a circle to intersect the $y-$axis at exactly one point, the distance from the center to the $y-$axis must equal the radius r. Since the center of equation (A) is $(-4, 8)$, the distance from the center to the $y-$axis is equal to the radius 4, so the condition is satisfied. Therefore, the answer is (A).

$$\rightarrow \text{A}$$

13

The range for the estimated percentage of voters who support the reform is

$$55\%\pm 2.5\%=(52.5\%, \ 57.5\%)$$

Lower bound: $0.525(500,000)=262,500$

Upper bound: $0.575(500,000)=287,500$

So, the most accurate estimate for the number of voters in a population of 500,000 who support the education reform is between 262,500 to 287,500 voters. The answer is (B).

$$\rightarrow \text{B}$$

14

Since $\frac{6}{8}=\frac{-3}{-4}=\frac{9}{12}$, there are infinitely many solutions to the system. To show that the point lies on the graph of the equation, we need to substitute these values into the equation and check if it satisfies the equation.

For (C):

$$6(4b-1)-3(8b-5)=9$$
$$24b-6-24b+15=9$$
$$9=9$$

Therefore, the answer is (C).

→ C

15

Convert the initial amount from euros to yen:

$$2{,}500 \text{ euro} \times \frac{130.5 \text{ yen}}{1 \text{ euro}} = 326{,}250 \text{ yen}$$

After spending 75% of the yen, remaining amount is:

$$326{,}250(0.25)=81{,}562.5 \text{ yen}$$

Now, Convert the remaining yen back into euros:

$$81{,}562.5 \text{ yen} \times \frac{0.0076 \text{ euro}}{1 \text{ yen}} = 619.88 \text{ euro}$$

So the answer is (A).

→ A

16

Let two solutions of $x^2+10x+n+4=0$ be $2a$ and $3a$.

Use the sum and product of the solutions.

The sum of solutions:

$$2a+3a=-\frac{10}{1}, \quad 5a=-10, \quad a=-2$$

The product of solutions:

$$2a\times 3a=\frac{n+4}{1}$$
$$6a^2=n+4$$
$$6(-2)^2=n+4, \quad n=20$$

So the value of n is 20.

→ 20

17

If the function has the axis of symmetry at $x=1$, we have

$$y=a(x-1)^2+k$$

Since the graph passes through two points $(0, -2)$ and $(3, -4)$, we have

$$-2=a(0-1)^2+k, \quad a+k=-2 \to (1)$$
$$-4=a(3-1)^2+k, \quad 4a+k=-4 \to (2)$$

Solving the system of equations (1) and (2),

$$a=-\frac{2}{3} \text{ and } k=-\frac{4}{3}$$

and then

$$y=-\frac{2}{3}(x-1)^2-\frac{4}{3}$$
$$=-\frac{2}{3}(x^2-2x+1)-\frac{4}{3}$$
$$=-\frac{2}{3}x^2+\frac{4}{3}x-2$$

Therefore, $a+b+c=-\frac{2}{3}+\frac{4}{3}+(-2)=-\frac{4}{3}$

→ $-\frac{4}{3}$

18

$$(2\sqrt{x}+\sqrt{2y})^{\frac{2}{5}}$$
$$=\sqrt[5]{(2\sqrt{x})^2+2\cdot 2\sqrt{x}\cdot\sqrt{2y}+(\sqrt{2y})^2}$$
$$=\sqrt[5]{4x+4\sqrt{2xy}+2y}$$

The answer is (D).

→ D

19

When students with scores higher than the class average are added to the class, the class average increases. So the answer is (C).

→ C

147

20

$$g(x)=2f(x)-1$$
$$=2\cdot 2x(x+2)(x-2)-1$$
$$=4x(x+2)(x-2)-1$$
$$g(-2)=4(-2)(-2+2)(-2-2)-1$$
$$=0-1=-1$$
$$g(0)=4(0)(0+2)(0-2)-1$$
$$=0-1=-1$$
$$g(2)=4(2)(2+2)(2-2)-1$$
$$=0-1=-1$$

Therefore, the answer is (C).

$$\rightarrow \text{C}$$

21

The axis of symmetry of $y=2x^2-12x+b$ is

$$x=-\frac{b}{2a}=-\frac{-12}{2(2)}=3$$

Since the axis of symmetry is the midpoint of two zeros A and C, we have A(2, 0) and C(4, 0).

Now, by substituting (2, 0) into the function, we have

$$0=2(2)^2-12(2)+b$$
$$b=16$$

So, $y=2x^2-12x+16$ and

$$y(3)=2(3)^2-12(3)+16=-2$$
$$\Rightarrow \text{B}(3,-2)$$

Therefore, the area of triangle ABC is

$$A=\frac{1}{2}\times 2\times 2=2$$

$$\rightarrow 2$$

22

By observing that the sum of angle BAD and angle CAD equals 90 degrees, we can apply the cofunction identity, which tells us that the sine of angle BAD is equivalent to the cosine of angle CAD. Therefore,

$$\sin \angle \text{BAD}+\cos \angle \text{CAD}=2\cdot \sin \angle \text{BAD}$$
$$=2\cdot 0.42=0.84$$

So the answer is (C).

$$\rightarrow \text{C}$$

Memo

Memo

1 Suitable for students of all levels, from beginner to advanced

2 Complete coverage of Digital SAT Math topics included

3 Hundreds of problems with detailed explanations and solutions

4 Complements YouTube lectures for interactive learning

JM EDU Workbook Series

REVIEW AND WORKBOOK	TEST PREP. WORKBOOK
☑ PRE-ALGEBRA	☑ DIGITAL SAT MATH
☑ ALGEBRA 1	☑ AP CALCULUS AB&BC
☑ GEOMETRY	MCQ&FRQ
☑ ALGEBRA 2	☑ AP CALCULUS AB
☑ AP PRECALCULUS	MCQ PRACTICE EXAMS
☑ AP CALCULUS AB&BC	☑ AP CALCULUS BC
	MCQ PRACTICE EXAMS

9791197067051   53410

ISBN 979-11-970670-5-1

Online Math Courses and Books
www.jmeducation.net

 YouTube Channel: "Math-Up PLUS"
https://youtube.com/@math-upplus

JM EDU